Industrial Clusters and Regional Business Networks in England, 1750–1970

Industrial Clusters and Regional Business Networks in England, 1750–1970

Edited by

JOHN F. WILSON
University of Nottingham, UK

ANDREW POPP
Royal Holloway, University of London, UK

ASHGATE

Published by
Ashgate Publishing Limited
Gower House
Croft Road
Aldershot
Hampshire GU11 3HR
England

Ashgate Publishing Company
Suite 420
101 Cherry Street
Burlington, VT 05401-4405
USA

Ashgate website: http://www.ashgate.com

British Library Cataloguing in Publication Data
Industrial clusters and regional business networks in England, 1750-1970. -
(Modern economic and social history)
1. Industrial location - England - History - 18th century
2. Industrial location - England - History - 19th century
3. Industrial location - England - History - 20th century
4. Industrial districts - England - History - 18th century
5. Industrial districts - England - History - 19th century
6. Industrial districts - England - History - 20th century
7. Business networks - England - History - 18th century
8. Business networks - England - History - 19th century
9. Business networks - England - History - 20th century
I. Wilson, J. F. (John Franics), 1955- II. Popp, Andrew
338.6'042'0942'09034

Library of Congress Cataloging-in-Publication Data
Industrial clusters and regional business networks in England, 1750-1970 / edited by John Wilson and Andrew Popp.
    p. cm. -- (Modern economic and social history)
  Includes bibliographical references and index.
  ISBN 0-7546-0761-5
    1. Industrial location--Great Britain--Congresses. 2. Industrial districts--Great Britain--Congresses. 3. Industrial policy--Great Britain --Congresses. I. Wilson, J. F. II. Popp, Andrew. III. Modern economic and social history series

HC260.G7 D565 2003
338.0942--dc21

2002032686

ISBN 0 7546 0761 5

Printed and bound by Athenaeum Press, Ltd., Gateshead, Tyne & Wear.

Contents

List of tables and figures

Tables

Figures

List of contributors

Sue Bowden is a Reader in Economics at Sheffield University. She has published widely in the field of business, industrial and economic history, contributing original work on the automobile and electrical industry, as well as in the fields of corporate governance and finance.

Francesca Carnevali is a Lecturer in Economic History at the University of Birmingham. The focus of her research is on regional economies in Europe in the 20th century. Her publications include articles in *Business History, Financial History Review, Enterprise and Society*, and the *Journal of Industrial History*.

M.C. Casson is Professor of Economics at the University of Reading. He has published widely in economics and business history. His most recent books include *Entrepreneurship and Leadership* (2000) and *Economics of International Business* (2000). He is currently researching the economic history of the British railway network prior to 1914.

Steven Caunce is a Senior Lecturer in Economic History at the University of Central Lancashire. His main research interests are industrial districts, especially West Yorkshire. He is currently working on a project looking at the links between Yorkshire and Lancashire.

Gillian Cookson is County Editor, Victoria County History of Durham, based in the History Department of the University of Durham. Her main research interests include industrial history, especially mechanical and electrical engineering in the nineteenth century, as well as local and regional history. Apart from articles in *Business History*, she has also published studies of Fleming Jenkin and Henry Maudsley.

Richard Coopey is a Lecturer in History at the University of Wales, Aberystwyth. He has written on the history of venture capital, civil-military technology history and the history of retailing in Britain. His current research interests include post-war technology policy, the history of water resources, and industrialisation and the landscape in eighteenth-century Britain.

Igor Filatotchev is Professor of Strategic Management at Bradford University School of Management. His research interests include comparative corporate governance, strategic restructuring and business history. He has published extensively on the subjects of empirical corporate governance and business strategy areas in many of the leading management journals, including the *Academy of Management Journal* and the *Journal of International Business Studies.*

Till Geiger is an Honorary Research Fellow in the Department of History at the University of Manchester. His main research interests are British, Irish and western European international and economic history since 1945. He is about to publish two books (with Ashgate and with the Presses de l'Université de Paris-Sarbonne) on these subjects.

David Higgins is a Lecturer in Economics at Sheffield University. His main research interests are modern economic history, especially industrial performance and the protection of intellectual property rights. He has written extensively on the decline of the Lancashire cotton textile industry, publishing in *Business History*, the *Journal of Industrial History*, and *Accounting, Business and Financial History.*

M.J. Lewis is a Senior Lecturer in Economic History at Sheffield Hallam University. He has, with Roger Lloyd-Jones, recently published a history of Raleigh and the British bicycle industry. Together they are currently writing a business history of the British machine tool industry.

Roger Lloyd-Jones is Professor of Business History at Sheffield Hallam University. He has published widely in the fields of economic and business history. His most recent book, with M.J. Lewis, is a history of Raleigh and the British bicycle industry, and he is currently writing a business history of the British machine tool industry.

Lucy Newton is a Lecturer in the Department of Management and a member of the Centre for International Business History at the University of Reading. She has published extensively on the subject of industrial organisation and finance, with particular interest in bank/industry interactions and the role of reputation and trust in bank/customer credit relations. She is also a former Council member and Newsletter editor of the Association of Business Historians and a former editor of the Business Archives Council journal.

Andrew Popp is a Lecturer in the School of Management at Royal Holloway, University of London. A business historian, his principal research interests lie in English industrial districts, especially the North Staffordshire Potteries. He has also conducted research on international supply chains. He is a Council member of the Association of Business Historians.

John Singleton is a Senior Lecturer in Economic History at Victoria University of Wellington, New Zealand. He is currently working on a commissioned history of the Reserve Bank of New Zealand. Dr Singleton has published extensively on British and New Zealand economic history. His most recent book (co-authored with Paul Robertson) is *Economic Relations Between Britain and Australasia 1945-1970*.

Steve Toms is Professor of Accounting and Business History at Nottingham University Business History and Director of the University of Nottingham International Business History Institute. His main research interests are accounting history and business history, including the history of the Lancashire cotton textile industry. Recent publications include articles in *Business History*, *Accounting Organizations and Society*, and *Accounting and Business Research*.

John F. Wilson is Research Director at the University of Nottingham International Business History Institute. His main research interests are business and industrial history, management education and training, and the finance of business. He has published several books, including the only long-term study of British business, as well as articles in several leading journals. He also edits the *Journal of Industrial History*.

Modern Economic and Social History Series
General Editor's Preface

Economic and social history has been a flourishing subject of scholarly study during recent decades. Not only has the volume of literature increased enormously but the range of interest in time, space and subject matter has broadened considerably so that today there are many sub-branches of the subject which have developed considerable status in their own right.

One of the aims of this new series is to encourage the publication of scholarly monographs on any aspect of modern economic and social history. The geographical coverage is world-wide and contributions on non-British themes will be especially welcome. While emphasis will be placed on works embodying original research, it is also intended that the series should provide the opportunity to publish studies of a more general and thematic nature which offer a reappraisal or critical analysis of major issues of debate.

Derek H. Aldcroft

University of Leicester

Preface

This collection emerged out of a single session at the highly successful 1999 conference on 'Theory and History', organised by Tony Slaven and his Glasgow University team. This session involved papers from Mark Casson, Roger Lloyd-Jones and Merv Lewis, Andrew Popp, and John Wilson, as well as a sparky discussant's comment from Phil Scranton. Such was the interest in our discussions that we were encouraged to bring together a significant group of scholars capable of throwing more light on a fascinating subject. A workshop was then organised, at which the authors were able to present an impressive array of original material, laying solid foundations for the chapters that are presented here. We would like to thank the Economic History Society for funding this workshop, and Joe Pope and his team for kindly agreeing to host the event at the University of Central Lancashire. Thanks must also go to Barbara Wilson, who performed an admirable organising role, ensuring that the authors were both fed and ferried around at appropriate times. Above all, though, the editors would like to express their wholehearted appreciation of the authors' efforts in writing chapters that provide fresh and vibrant insights into several of England's industrial districts. We hope that in fulfilling our aim that 'we stand on great men's shoulders', most notably those of Alfred Marshall, we have contributed significantly to the debate.

The cover illustration was taken from the *Illustrated News*, 1857, and every effort has been made to trace the original copyright holder.

Finally, this book is dedicated to our wives, Barbara and Diane.

John F. Wilson and Andrew Popp

Chapter 1

Districts, networks and clusters in England: An introduction

John F. Wilson and Andrew Popp

Introduction

Industrialisation in England, far from erasing regional differences and heralding the creation of a homogenous national economy, emerged from and reinforced patterns of economic activity and linkages that showed marked spatial variegation. Throughout the nineteenth and twentieth centuries, the industrial economy of England remained a patchwork of industrial districts, clusters and regional systems. While there are those who diminish the importance of this feature of English industrialisation, we would argue that it was central to the broad sweep of the path towards forging an industrialised society. Understanding why these patterns emerged and how they affected the nature and course of industrial and business history in England prompts a search for approaches that take this spatial patterning as a central concern. It also opens up perspectives that have been relatively neglected in the historiography of English business.

A path breaking study in this respect was the collection *Regions and Industries*, edited by Pat Hudson and published in 1989.[1] In its introduction, Hudson played an indispensable role in mounting a powerful critique of the then prevailing aggregate level analyses of industrialisation, in so doing she also argued for serious consideration of the part played by regions in the Industrial Revolution in Britain. However, the book did not, indeed, was not intended to, provide a sustained exploration of the business structures and practices of territorially bounded industrial systems. More recently a number of studies have appeared that do address these issues directly, however, for the most part they have focused either on a single industry or on a single region.[2]

This study, bringing together a series of original essays examining a wide range of sectors and regions from the eighteenth century to the twentieth

---

[1] P. Hudson, *Regions and Industries: Perspectives on the Industrial Revolution* (Cambridge University Press, 1989).
[2] See for example, M. Rose, *Firms, Networks and Business Values: The British and American Cotton Industries Since 1750* (Cambridge University Press, 2000); A. Popp, *Business Structure, Business Culture and the Industrial District: The Potteries, c. 1850–1914* (Ashgate, 2001).

century, attempts to lay the foundation for a more comparative perspective on districts, networks and clusters in England. At the same time, this study also stresses the importance of dynamic, long-run perspectives on districts. Framed in these terms, the study aims to improve our understanding of not only the specific phenomena of districts and clusters, but also wider debates in business history. There is an array of important questions. How did clusters and districts emerge and how did they evolve over the long-term? How did they adapt in the face of foreign competition and fresh market-cum-technological challenges? A third, equally important component of the study is an explicit engagement with theoretical developments across a range of disciplines. To that end, a challenging essay by economist Mark Casson is included alongside the historical studies. Much of the theoretical material raises questions about the formal and informal organisational institutions of districts and clusters, what we may term their governance systems. In particular, it is important to assess the range and balance of co-ordination and signalling systems that existed in industrial districts to assist entrepreneurial decision-making. How did these balances change over time and to what extent is there evidence of 'social embeddedness' and 'co-operative competition'? How did these factors influence entrepreneurial responses to new challenges?

The three-fold purpose of this chapter is to introduce the scope and structure of the volume, to review a voluminous literature and to set out an analytical framework within which the empirical chapters can be situated. The third task can only begin with an appraisal of the work of economist Alfred Marshall, who laid the foundations of the industrial district model.[3] In the final section, we shall then go on to address broader issues, in particular the forces making for change over time. This will link the work of Marshall, economic geography, network analysis, embeddedness perspectives, path-dependency and contingency, outlining the importance and impact of the context within which change occurs. While these issues can only be fully addressed in the concluding chapter, by highlighting them at this stage readers will be in a better position to assess how change was expressed over time and the mechanisms involved. The case-studies will naturally present the empirical evidence to support these insights, providing considerable cohesion across the collection.

Definitions and taxonomies

Before introducing the key themes of the volume, it would be useful to lay down some clear definitions of a terminology that has in the past lacked clarity. Indeed, a serious limitation on research into clustering has been the lack of clear definitions of terms that have often been used with different, though frequently unstated, intent. The three key initial terms are district, cluster and

---

[3] A. Marshall, *Industry and Trade* (Macmillan, 1919); ibid., *Principles of Economics* (Macmillan, 1952).

region. As far as this collection of essays is concerned, we would like to offer the following set of definitions:

District: a concentration of firms in an industry either in a single town or in a zone of a city.

Cluster: a wider agglomeration of industries that may be connected by common products, technologies, markets (either of supply or demand) or institutional frameworks.

Region: a geographical system of differently-sized urban conurbations with inter-linking and interdependent industrial and commercial profiles.

A further key concept that is central to many studies of clustered industries is that of the network. As Storper points out, the seminal work of Piore and Sabel stressed how 'appropriately institutionalized networks are essential to successful ongoing adaptation of a regional economy in the face of uncertainty'.[4] Above all, this characterisation of Piore and Sabel's contribution to the debate about regional business networks suggests that there has been a strong tendency to idealize both the form and function of networks. Consequently, definitions of regional business networks frequently stress aspects such as their role in transmitting information or in reducing transaction costs, or highlight attributes such as a basis in trust. This reveals how not only is the concept of a network crucial, but also highly contentious, persuading us to refrain from offering a definition until a fuller discussion of the variety of approaches taken to this issue has been conducted.

It is important to stress that the definitions offered earlier are presented simply as working definitions of terms central to this study. As we shall see from the case studies, the empirical record reveals considerable diversity with regard to these definitions, and especially with regard to the network concept. This diversity further highlights the value of presenting these original studies, contributing positively to the debate surrounding districts, networks and regional economic development.

A final introductory point worth making is to explain why a spatial limit has been placed on the case-study material. In the first place, a single book would have provided inadequate space to cover the entire British Isles, or even Britain (namely, England, Scotland and Wales). More importantly, to provide detailed answers to the questions posed earlier it is necessary to study a relatively homogenous spatial unit, in order to develop a range of comparators that are not affected by contrasting legal, socio-cultural and even economic traditions, mores and institutions. To have included Scotland, for example, would have seriously compromised our stated aim of providing decisive insights into the

---

[4] M. Storper, *The Regional World: Territorial Development in a Global Economy* (The Guilford Press, 1997), p. 6.

causes of change across a number of industrial districts operating within a single legal entity. While Wales and Ireland (up until 1921) were more effectively integrated into a London-dominated legal system, difficulties would still have arisen when it came to economic structure and socio-cultural issues. Finally, as the heartland of the world's first modern industrial economy, England offers a micro-study in the difficulties of sustaining an industrial district model over time. These reasons help to explain why we are pursuing this pioneering approach, filling a significant gap in the literature covering key issues in long-term industrial and business change.

Marshall and the industrial district

Working from sustained and detailed observation of industrial development in both Britain and elsewhere, Marshall developed in the late nineteenth century powerful insights into what he termed the 'localization' of industry. As an economist, Marshall was particularly concerned to uncover the forces that lay behind the apparent frequency with which similar firms, very often of relatively modest size, cluster geographically. He was also intrigued by the continued vitality of these clusters, or industrial districts, in the face of market and technological forces that tended to promote the growth of the individual firm. In particular, he stressed the interdependencies of business structure, business strategy, technology and markets. For Marshall, these interdependencies played themselves out through a nexus that determined the balance of economies of scale and scope available to an industry. In this respect, his key insight was that economies of scale and scope may be realized not only by very large individual firms, that is through internal economies, but also by groups of small firms 'welded almost automatically into an organic whole', that is through external economies.[5]

Having made this most important distinction, Marshall proceeded to lay the foundation stone of the industrial district concept by proposing to examine 'those very important external economies which can often be secured by the concentration of many small businesses of a similar character in particular industries: or, as is commonly said by the localization of industry'.[6] He consequently proposed that a defined geographical space provides the location for that nexus of interdependencies. In addition, he continued, this proximity of firms in geographical space is far from incidental to a range of economic outcomes. External economies of scale and of scope in marketing, in labour, in the supply of inputs and in many other transaction costs, were all largely dependent on and specific to clustering. Such economies are explored in a number of the chapters in this volume.

---

[5]   Marshall, *Trade and Industry*, p. 599.
[6]   Ibid., *Principles*, p. 221

At the same time, most famously through appeal to the notion of an 'industrial atmosphere', Marshall also recognized, however incompletely, that geographical space was overlain by constructions of place, or *'genius loci'*. In other words, localized industries, or industrial districts, must be understood as being 'located' not only in the physical sense, but also with regard to specific social spaces, each such space having its own structure and history. As he concluded, these industrial atmospheres 'cannot be quickly acquired ... [but] yield *gratis* to the manufacturers ... great advantages that are not easily to be had elsewhere: and an industrial atmosphere cannot be moved'.[7]

Clearly, Marshall viewed the structures, resources and capabilities of industrial districts as both historically and socially specific. Furthermore, he recognized that personal relationships tended to reinforce these specificities, arguing that 'personal contact is most needed in trade between allied branches'.[8] In this schema, then, the economic and the social may be seen to act over time as co-determinate forces in the growth and development of clustered industries.

However, care is required if we are not to overstate the extent to which Marshall explored in detail the social aspects of districts and clusters. Indeed, his principal concern was with the conditions under which external economies of scale and scope were to be realized. In this respect, it is important to stress that Marshall expressed a clear preference for co-ordination 'effected without conscious effort' via market-based mechanisms.[9] As Langlois and Robertson note, the 'Marshallian industrial district' is 'highly competitive in the neo-classical sense'.[10] Marshall's discussion of industrial districts consequently has little room for many of the themes prominent in recent re-formulations of the concept, including, for example, business networks and trust. Indeed, alongside his ground-breaking insights into external economies and their relationship to the structure of industries, Marshall left subsequent scholars with tantalizing, but barely half-formed, glimpses of the importance of the social aspects of districts.

Since Marshall, the interest in clusters, districts and regions has grown steadily in a number of disciplines, experiencing in the process many points of bifurcation and evolution. In order to capture key elements of district and cluster models, we will now follow core routes through that process, beginning in the field of economic geography.

---

[7]   Ibid., *Trade and Industry*, pp. 284–7.
[8]   Ibid., p. 284.
[9]   Ibid., pp. 601–3.
[10]   R.N. Langlois and P.L. Robertson, *Firms, Markets and Economic Change: A Dynamic Theory of Business Institutions* (Routledge, 1995), p. 125.

The industrial district in economic geography

Given the range and scope of insights into clustering made by Marshall, it is hardly surprising that scholars have subsequently pursued some increasingly divergent lines of enquiry. For example, some in economics and economic geography have concentrated on elaborating the concept of 'agglomeration economies', that is the economies derived from co-location or clustering. Typical of this approach is the work of Paul Krugman, who, though building explicitly on Marshall, explores industrial districts in a manner that totally excludes social phenomena.[11] Instead, according to Krugman, the factors that promote clustering, such as labour market pooling, are modelled mathematically. For example, labour and capital (note, not workers and entrepreneurs) are assumed to make rational optimising choices over location in order to realise external economies. Factors such as skill and knowledge, and how their generation and distribution through physical and social space relate to clustering and history, are absent from this analysis.

However, other economic geographers such as Scott, Enright and Swann have proved themselves effective successors to Marshall, via work on the emergence and evolution of districts and clusters.[12] Scott, in particular, has provided clear conceptual insights into the evolution of what he calls 'regional economic systems'. According to Scott's schema, this evolutionary pattern begins with disruption of the established order, creating an impetus that leads to the generation of significant agglomeration effects, in the form of both complementarities and competitors and adequate and appropriate pools of labour and capital. In turn, these synergies gather momentum over time, resulting in the emergence of business communities that take on 'identifiable cultural attributes marked by distinctive conventions and routines'.[13] Further, these regional economic systems simultaneously 'evolve forward on the basis of a deepening stock of external economies of scale and scope'. Whilst establishing a new socio-economic order, Scott goes on to claim that the 'regional economy will [also] ensure that this trajectory acquires a marked dependence on its own past'. This implies that the evolutionary process contains both dangers and advantages, with significant 'agglomeration diseconomies' arising from, for example, an introverted business culture or the emergence of strong interest groups such as trade unions and trade associations.[14]

---

[11] P. Krugman, *Geography and Trade* (MIT Press, 1991).
[12] A.J. Scott, *Regions and the World Economy: The Coming Shape of Global Production, Competition and Political Order* (Oxford University Press, 1998); M.J. Enright, 'Regional Clusters and Firm Strategy' in A.D. Chandler, P. Hagstrom and O. Solvell (eds), *The Dynamic Firm: The Role of Technology, Strategy, Organisation and Regions* (Oxford University Press, 1998); G.M. Peter Swann, 'Introduction' in G.M. Peter Swann, M. Prevezer and D. Stout (eds), *The Dynamics of Industrial Clustering: International Comparisons in Computing and Biotechnology* (Oxford University Press, 1998).
[13] Scott, *Regions and the World Economy*, p. 107.
[14] Ibid, pp. 107–9.

In illuminating the dynamic nature of industrial districts, Scott has indicated how much economic geography has to offer the historian. His work is bolstered by that of Enright, who has demonstrated how in charting the origins of clusters the analyst must look for 'specific local factor conditions, [and] local demand or related industries'. Together, Enright claims that this leads to the 'creation of industry-specific knowledge, development of supplier and buyer networks, and local competitive pressures' that stimulate innovation and upgrade cluster competitiveness.[15] Similarly intriguing is Swann's proposed life-cycle model of industrial districts, in which clusters pass through four principal stages: critical mass, take-off, peak entry and saturation. These stages form the core of a life-cycle model of district development that brings into play concepts such as agglomeration economies, congestion effects and technological and organizational convergence. Of course, Marshall himself noted these effects, observing how:

> even a little obstinacy or inertia may ruin an old home of an industry whose conditions are changing; and ... the opening out of new sources of supply or new markets for sale may quickly overbear the strength which old districts have inherited from past conditions.[16]

As we shall see in several later chapters, the life-cycle concept possesses real-time historical significance when applied to English industrial districts, aiding our understanding of how both vibrant local economic systems emerged originally and the manner in which that dynamism was eventually eroded. However, whilst providing some support for a generic model of life-cycles in districts and clusters the detailed studies presented in this collection also point to the fact that the course of development followed by each and any cluster is temporally, as well as spatially, specific. For example, the eighteenth and the twentieth centuries presented districts and the actors they contained with very different institutional environments. This is most obvious with regard to legal systems, and in particular to laws relating to economic activity. The impact of differing institutional environments, which have both national and local dimensions, is to be seen in many different aspects of district formation and evolution, not least in the form and extent of networking behaviour displayed. As Staber notes, and as the historian is all too aware, it is clear that no single model can capture the diversity apparent from an empirical study of industrial districts.[17] The life-cycle models, then, provide overarching theories that necessarily gloss over some of the 'messiness' and complexity of the empirical record. Countering this tendency may require a call on the narrative skills of the historian.

---

[15]   Enright, 'Regional clusters', pp. 316–7.

[16]   Marshall, *Trade and Industry*, p. 287.

[17]   U. Staber, 'The Social Embeddedness of Industrial District Networks' in U. Staber, N. Schaeffer and B. Sharma (eds), *Regional Business Networks: Prospects for Prosperity* (de Gruyter, 1996).

The work of Scott, Swann and Enright also reveals that there is no decisive relationship between clustering and long-term economic success. While districts and firms may be capable of generating and extracting significant agglomeration economies, whether of scale or scope, from the clustering of supplies of labour, capital and knowledge, technical and commercial, this does not necessarily equip an industry or region with the ability to cope with major market or technological challenges. It is consequently important to assess and take account of not only the changing institutional environment, but also the economic context within which the evolution of the district or cluster is set, including the macro-economic context at both the national and international levels. Over the last two decades, a number of scholars have investigated the links between clustering and competitive success. Perhaps most important in highlighting the near universal significance of clustering has been Michael Porter, especially in *The Competitive Advantage of Nations*. Indeed, so struck was Porter by the frequency of clustering that he doubted whether 'the nation is a relevant unit of analysis' for most discussions of the roots of competitiveness. Building on what he termed the 'diamond' model of the forces determining of competitiveness, Porter argued that:

> geographic concentration of firms in internationally successful industries often occurs because the influence of the individual determinants in the 'diamond' and their mutual reinforcement are heightened by close geographical proximity within a nation. A concentration of rivals, customers and suppliers will promote efficiencies and specialisation.[18]

As ever, we may detect in these words the long shadow of Alfred Marshall.

Most recently, economic geographer Michael Storper has focused on the region as a 'locus of what economists are beginning to call "untraded interdependencies", which take the form of conventions, informal rules and habits'. Crucially, Storper characterizes these interdependencies as '*relations* [that] constitute region-specific assets in production'.[19] This directs our attention towards the vital concept of the network, given its prominence in both the studies of districts and clusters and in the theories of how they function.

Networks and network analysis

Powell and Smith-Doerr identify two broad strands of research focused on 'networks and economic life'.[20] The first, derived from sociology and

---

[18] M.E. Porter, *The Competitive Advantage of Nations* (Macmillan, 1990), pp. 156–7.
[19] Storper, *The Regional World*, p. 5.
[20] W.W. Powell and L. Smith-Doerr, 'Networks and Economic Life' in N.J. Smelser and R. Swedberg (eds), *The Handbook of Economic Sociology* (Princeton University Press, 1994), pp. 368–402.

organizational theory, 'employs networks as an analytical device for illuminating social relations, whether inside a firm, in the interorganizational ties that link firms, or in the environments of organizations'. The second views networks more metaphorically, as 'a kind of organizing logic, a way of governing relations among economic actors'.[21] Interestingly, this view of the network, as a 'form of governance, a social glue that binds individuals together into a coherent system', is immediately illustrated by reference to the 'web of interdependence found in industrial districts'.[22] Explicit theorisation of the use of the network concept has been rare in business history, but it is probably true to note that within the discipline it has been typically conceived of and applied in this second way; namely, as a metaphor.[23] The elaboration of this approach in the specific context of districts and clusters is explored in a subsequent section. Here we lay out some key features of the network as an analytical tool. Does it offer anything to the business historian studying clustered industries?

Firstly, noting Powell and Smith-Doerr's claim that networks both allow for human agency whilst also emphasising structure and constraint, we would highlight the key contention that the 'actions (attitudes and behaviours) of actors ... can be best explained in terms of their position in networks'. The central unit of analysis is then an actor's position in a structure of relationships, rather than the attributes that they bring to that structure. In Nohria's words, 'variations in the actions of actors (and the success or failure of these actions) can be better explained by knowing the position of actors relative to others in various networks of relationships, than by knowing how their attributes differ from one another'.[24] It is important to stress how this understanding differs from that of the network as a governance form, associated specifically with industrial districts, where, as we shall see in the following section, membership of the network (and the network itself) is defined by the possession of particular attributes and the ability of the network to constrain or facilitate the actions of actors by the extent to which these attributes are shared. In turn, network analysts have isolated five principles that help to capture an actor's position in a network: cohesion, equivalence, prominence, range and brokerage. Rather more concretely, Powell and Smith-Doerr stress the structural 'autonomy' of actors whose 'immediate networks are dense and

---

[21] Powell and Smith-Doerr, 'Networks and Economic Life', p. 368.

[22] Ibid., p. 369. Indeed, they later identify 'trust-based governance' with 'industrial districts [where] the bonds of community are forged out of ties of place and kinship. Here trust builds on norms of reciprocity and civic engagement, hence it is "thick"', p. 385.

[23] See though, G. Soda, 'The Convergence of History, Organisation and Networks: An Introductory Research Note' in W. Feldenkirchen and T. Gourvish (eds), *The European Yearbook of Business History*, No. 2 (Ashgate, 1999).

[24] N. Nohria, 'Introduction: Is a Network Perspective a Useful Way of Studying Organizations', in N. Nohria and R.G. Eccles (eds), *Networks and Organizations: Structure, Form, and Action* (Harvard University Press, 1992), p. 5. This emphasis on the overall structure of a set of relationships seems promising in the context of Marshall's interest in the structure of industries and in the determinants of those structures.

overlapping, and who are linked to more distant networks rich in non-redundant contacts'.[25]

Secondly, it is worth noting Nohria's emphasis on how networks 'are as much process as they are structure, being continually shaped and reshaped by the action of actors'.[26] This perspective has immediate appeal to the historian, reflecting the constant process of change that features prominently in any study of business and industry. Moreover, this is an area where the historian may be well positioned to make a real contribution, for, as Powell and Smith-Doerr observe, it is a 'curious irony of network research that despite its focus on the causal importance of structures of relations among actors rather than properties of actors, the research treats network positions as properties themselves'. In other words, there has been a tendency to treat network positions as given, rather than as made.[27] The historian studying networks in a variety of contexts may then be able to illuminate how network positions are constructed over time. This kind of dynamic perspective is undoubtedly harder to forge in the context of an attributes-based understanding of networks, but it is one worth pursuing.

Thirdly, network analysis, whilst recognizing the 'slipperiness' of the concept, has very interesting things to say about power.[28] Again, this is a challenge to the historian schooled in the governance perspective on networks, where the issue of power and its distribution across a field of actors is generally secondary to an emphasis on cohesion and consensus and on shared attributes that build identity and trust. Power in networks, defined as the 'ability to produce intended effects on the attitudes and behaviours of other actors', again lies in what Powell and Smith-Doerr claim to be a 'structural position' and can be derived from three 'resources': legitimacy, information and force. Particularly important may be the centrality of positions in networks, 'where valued information and scarce resources are transferred from one actor to another'.[29]

An alternative reading of power is that derived from McGovern and Mottiar's extension of the discussion on traditions and structures of relationships into a Foucauldian analysis of local power relations. For Foucault, power was the network itself, legitimised by decades of tradition. In trying to explain why firms collaborate in industrial districts, McGovern and Mottiar use this notion to observe how, in balancing competition and co-operation, local actors accept a kind of collective power that binds the district together. In other words, 'Foulcauldian power is synonymous with co-operative competition',

[25] Powell and Smith-Doerr, 'Networks and Economic Life', p. 369.

[26] Nohria, 'Introduction', p. 7.

[27] Powell and Smith-Doerr, 'Networks and Economic Life', p. 379.

[28] Powell and Smith-Doerr claim that a 'persistent concern with power marks one of the key points of divergence between sociologists and economists who study organizations'. Ibid., p. 376.

[29] Ibid., p. 377, quoting D. Knoke, *Political Networks: The Structural Perspective* (Cambridge University Press, 1990), p. 9.

where all firms accept that commercial relationships are based on established norms fashioned over time. This results in the evolution of a 'web of relations' capable of cementing local actors together cohesively, thereby strengthening the district economically and socially. This interpretation of power has clear affinities with the social embeddedness perspective on industrial districts.

Networks and social embeddedness in districts and clusters

Does an acknowledgement of the region as a 'fundamental unit of social life in ... capitalism [and] a fundamental motor process in social life' inevitably force us to recast our approach to the analysis of networks in clusters and districts?[30] Certainly, in contrast to the agglomeration economies approach charted by Krugman and others, what may be termed the social embeddedness perspective has increasingly privileged the social and the cultural in explanations of the growth and development of clustered industries. An explicit contrast is drawn with more economistic approaches. Staber, for example, argues that 'from a social embeddedness perspective, co-location implies an additional quality' to standard agglomeration theory, not to mention standard network analysis. In his analysis, 'communities, clans, families, professions' are the key actors, as opposed to the firms and entrepreneurs of the Marshallian industrial district. This indicates how the 'embeddedness of firms in a distinctive local social fabric is a key feature of the industrial district model'.[31] The contemporary industrial district model consequently posits a form of socio-spatial organization supportive of *particular* patterns of industrial development. Piore and Sabel go on to emphasize the economic consequences of this developmental pattern, describing how North Italian districts rely for their effectiveness upon institutions that, in balancing co-operation and competition, stimulate technical innovation. This leads to a form of flexible specialization from which districts derive significant competitive advantages.[32]

Here, then, the stress is placed firmly on the *localism* of the socio-cultural frameworks, including both their normative and more discursive dimensions, within which economic activity and business behaviour occurs. In turn, these arguments highlight consideration of issues such as 'territory' and identity:

> sense-making takes place at the collective level, in that actors may ... arrive at *shared* assumptions about the identity of their partners and the rules for coordinating individual decisions. Inter-firm networks in industrial districts are *socially* constructed, reflecting *collective* beliefs about economic exchange ... In the ideal-typical industrial district actors

---

[30] Storper, *The Regional World*, p. 3.
[31] Staber, 'Social Embeddedness', p. 152 and p. 148.
[32] M. Piore and C. Sabel, *The Second Industrial Divide: Possibilities for Prosperity* (Basic Books, 1984).

seek a sense of belonging to the community and are interested in building
a distinctive collective identity.[33]

Taken together, these arguments prompt consideration of the links between
clustering, business networks and issues such as entrepreneurship and co-
ordination, given that business networks are the principal mechanism through
which, it is claimed, entrepreneurship is expressed and co-ordination achieved
in industrial districts. Clustering is assumed to promote through frequent face-
to-face contact the formation of cohesive, 'appropriately institutionalized'
networks characterised by their high-trust properties. Similarly, networks are
assumed to promote particular embedded forms of entrepreneurship and co-
ordination, founded, in the words of Sabel and Zeitlin, on an 'ethos that
reconciled and gave immediate human content to the claims of competition and
ambition on the one hand and community and co-operation on the other'. The
particular form of embedded networking that occurs in districts and clusters
consequently has a real effect on how business is done.[34]

It is useful at this point to try and identify the range of business networks
that might be found in the 'ideal-typical' industrial district, differentiated
according to membership, mechanisms and role. This exercise will allow us to
understand the scope of the claims made from what Mark Granovetter has
termed the 'strong embeddedness position'.[35] We will than be able to sketch
briefly some of the ways in which it has been applied and tease out its core
assumptions. Firstly, two network types based in specific inter-firm relations
may be identified. Vertical networks of firms engaged in the exchange of
goods and services, though drawing on socially constructed reserves of trust
and tacit knowledge and understandings, are essentially economic, with the
benefits members derive from belonging to these systems taking the form of
reduced uncertainty and lower transaction costs. Horizontal networks of firms
and entrepreneurs engaged in the same stage of the decomposed production
process, which are assumed to set the terms of competition, tend to be looser
and their benefits less obvious. At the same time, one must remember that
horizontal networks tend to work to deflect local competition away from price
and towards differentiation and quality. Both vertical and horizontal networks
are relatively tractable, using the conventional tools of transaction cost
analysis. At times, both vertical and horizontal may coalesce into or be
expressed through a third network type, the association or club, institutions into
which Mark Casson provides many striking insights in his chapter.

Finally, however, and most problematically, many writers on industrial
districts appear to propose a fourth highly diffuse form of network comprising

---

[33]   Ibid., pp. 148 and 157–8 (emphasis in the original).
[34]   C. Sabel and J. Zeitlin, 'Historical Alternatives to Mass Production: Politics,
Markets and Technology in Nineteenth Century Industrialization', *Past and Present*, 108
(1985), p. 152.
[35]   M. Granovetter, 'Problems of Explanation in Economic Sociology', in Nohria
and Eccles, *Networks and Organization*, p. 28.

all the actors in a localized industry and the wider community from which those actors are drawn. It is this diffuse network that gives shape to the 'ethos' identified by Sabel and Zeitlin.

To give some sense of the scope accorded to this fourth network type, we suggest that proponents of the embeddedness perspective on regional business networks posit that industrial districts generate a *moral economy* of district development. We make this claim on the basis of the stress typically placed on the existence of a generalized disposition towards the economic – its role, position and conduct within the local social context – that is community-based, consensual, customary and operationalized through moral suasion and normative rules.[36] This localized moral economy of district development establishes the frameworks within which entrepreneurship is legitimized and delimited and co-ordination achieved.

These precepts have set much of the agenda for empirical studies of industrial districts, most obviously those in Northern Italy, and the embeddedness perspective has become the default mode of analysis in studies of regional development. Rinaldi, for example, claims that in Emilia-Romagna 'economic tissue' was embedded in a 'network of social relations', ensuring that:

> People in the districts shared a cultural homogeneity which lubricated social relations among economic actors, reinforced consensus and group loyalty among both entrepreneurs, ensured the social ostracism of rule-violators, provided a common language to speed innovation and information exchange and established the basis for trustful behaviour.[37]

For Colli, in a study of Lecco, an important function of networks was to act as transmitters of 'rules and norms ... culture and ideology'. From an embeddedness perspective, then, networks are most effectively promoted amongst communities of producers (workers and entrepreneurs) deeply rooted in both space and time. Indeed, Colli argues that '[n]etworks of producers develop *primarily* thanks to the fact of being in the same "place"'.[38]

Further support for the positive impact of networking is also derived from Fruin's work on the Japanese enterprise system, where co-operation between groups of firms, often clustered around a hub firm, results in the creation of

---

[36] The term 'moral economy' is used here rhetorically in order to highlight the nature of the claims made by some scholars working from an embeddedness perspective. For debates concerning extension of the moral economy concept, see A. Randall and A. Charlesworth (eds), *Moral Economy and Popular Protest: Crowds, Conflict and Authority* (Clarendon, 2000).

[37] A. Rinaldi, 'The Emilian Model Revisited (and revised) Twenty Years Later', paper presented at *Responses to Innovation: The 2001 Annual Conference of the Association of Business Historians*, 29–30 July 2001, Portsmouth.

[38] A. Colli, 'Networking the Market: Evidence and Conjectures from the History of the Italian Districts' in W. Feldenkirchen and T. Gourvish (eds), *European Yearbook of Business History*, No. 1 (1998), p. 80 (emphasis in the original).

network organizations that are 'composed of sets of independent actors who co-operate frequently for mutual advantage and create a community of practice'.[39] Frequently, though, stress is placed not on the sort of leadership provided by hub firms in Japan, but on the importance of strengthening value systems, such as those provided by ethnicity, religion or local political cultures.[40] Here, the ability of networks to facilitate or constrain the actions of economic actors in clustered industries is to be interpreted not from the position of those actors within networks, but from their attributes, such as 'artisanal' or 'non-conformist', attributes that are derived primarily from their membership of wider groupings within the community. The concept of the network is readily collapsed into the concept of the community, rendering it oversocialized and with a poorly defined model of how change either occurs or is accommodated. As Staber notes, the social embeddedness perspective remains 'silent on the content of social relations [and] on the *mechanisms* by which social structures constrain and facilitate economic action'.[41] It is also possible that at times strong networking reinforced the legitimation of organisational forms that market signals were urging entrepreneurs to abandon or extensively modify.

The concept of trust as a necessary component of these communal frameworks is a further central element of the embeddedness perspective, particularly with regard to signalling and co-ordination. This particular emphasis is shared by Casson, who defines networks according to the presence of 'warranted mutual trust'.[42] At the same time, there is also a tendency for issues such as power, prominent in other forms of network analysis, to be somewhat downgraded or even ignored, and for the conditions under which trust emerges and persists to remain poorly-specified. Studies have shown that this kind of high-trust equilibrium can be hard to maintain in the face of the firm population dynamics flowing from the uncontrolled patterns of entry and exit sometimes associated with clustered industries. Scranton, for example, demonstrates clear evidence of a damaging lack of cohesion within the Philadelphia textile industries, given the propensity of large numbers of marginal new ventures to emerge in boom periods, frustrating the efforts of longer-established firms to stabilise the trade through various co-operative measures.[43] Popp has also provided further support for this view, highlighting how in the English Potteries little cohesion was achieved by a business community that in many other ways provided the classic example of an

---

[39] M. Fruin, *The Japanese Enterprise System* (Oxford University Press, 1992).

[40] Even Powell and Smith-Doerr resort to similar generalizations when discussing districts, noting that exchange 'embedded in local social relationships cemented by kinship, religion and politics, encourages reciprocity. Monitoring is facilitated by these social ties ... Indeed, trust-based governance seems easy to sustain when it is spatially clustered'.

[41] Staber, 'Social Embeddedness', p. 157 (emphasis in the original).

[42] See M.C. Casson, 'An economic approach to regional business networks', in this volume.

[43] P. Scranton, *Figured Tapestry: Production, Markets and Power in Philadelphia Textiles, 1885–1941* (Cambridge University Press, 1989).

industrial district.[44] Alternatively, high-trust networking could shade into collusive behaviours and attitudes, reducing the responsiveness of firms and districts.

The relationship between regional business networks and local growth and development is, in part, one of facilitation. At a practical level, networks provide entrepreneurs with access to valuable resources and information. However, and equally importantly, the moral economy of district development validates the growth and innovation-stimulating aspects of entrepreneurship, whilst also ensuring that its conduct conforms to those '*collective* beliefs about economic exchange' claimed by Staber. From a 'strong' embeddedness perspective, then, networks lie at the heart of governance systems in districts and clusters, drawing their power and effectiveness from systems of meaning deeply rooted in communities.

Networks, markets and hierarchies

The identification of the regionally-embedded network as an important governance form is both promising and problematical. It has been enthusiastically embraced in some quarters, leading to its promotion as a distinct *alternative* to the market on the one hand and the hierarchy on the other.[45] Rose, for example, highlights how 'the notion that networks represent a competitive alternative to integration is an important conclusion'.[46] As Nohria ruefully notes, however, 'the network organization has been reified as a new ideal type of organization'.[47] How useful is this line of development to the historian, and how may the historian contribute to its further elaboration?

Firstly, we must note that there are real problems of definition attached to the view of the network as a distinct, alternative governance form. In particular, how do we meaningfully distinguish between the idealized, regional network, with its low-cost information and ready co-ordination of resources, from the market on the one hand and, on the other, the hierarchy? Appealing to the notion of social 'content' does not distinguish networks from any but the most rigid and abstract models of the market. At the same time, unless we adhere to the strongest and most deterministic of embeddedness perspectives, we must recognize that an issue such as power is as germane to networks as it is to hierarchies.

A solution might lie in acknowledging the extent to which these governance forms are not analytically separable, but instead lie on a continuum, each form interpenetrating the others. Firms and industries and districts, clusters and

---

[44]   Popp, *Business Structure, Business Culture*.
[45]   See W. Mark Fruin, 'Analyzing Pacific Rim Networks and Markets', in W. Mark Fruin (ed.), *Networks, Markets, and the Pacific Rim. Studies in Strategy* (Oxford University Press, 1998), pp. 3–7.
[46]   Rose, *Firms, Networks and Business Values*, p. 6.
[47]   Nohria, 'Introduction', p. 12.

regional economic systems, simultaneously and at all times employ a blend of these governance forms, a blend that changes over time as the structure of relationships is cast and recast and the external environment changes. Charting this constant shifting, and the context in which it occurred, provides the historian with a framework for an analysis of the impact of networks on attitudes and behaviours of actors and on the growth and development of districts and clusters.

Conclusion

We began this chapter by noting the persistence and frequency with which firms and industries clustered together at a range of geographical scales during industrialisation in England, and by indicating just some of the questions that this observation prompts. We may now reflect on how a dialogue with other social sciences allows us to identify the key questions we need to ask of the historical record if we are to gain a better understanding of the significance of districts and clusters to industrial England from the eighteenth century onwards.

Staber has observed that '[w]hile the theoretical logic of the district model stresses [their] dynamic and innovative aspects ... researchers have generally performed empirical analyses with static data sets that assume stability and equilibrium'.[48] Similarly, Soda, seeking as we do a rapprochement between history and other social sciences, notes that lacking the 'sensitivity and know-how possessed by most historians ... the most serious weakness of network analysis [has been the] absence of the diachronical, the historical dimension', a weakness that limits the ability to 'take account of development and transformation'.[49]

Clearly, discontinuity, as well as continuity, must be a central motif of any rounded analysis. At the same time, this should not be interpreted as an interest in constructing sweeping periodizations that are assumed to hold true across space. Instead, we have to remain sensitive to the specificities of particular places and stories. Nor should a concern with *process* be mistaken for a conception of *progress*. We should not be bound by the essentially teleological perspectives of either the Chandlerian paradigm or its counterpoint, Sabel and Zeitlin's 'historical alternative to mass production'. The districts and clusters studied here were neither fated to be anachronisms in a progressively globalising and placeless world nor blueprints for a future resurgence of the local. Firms, industries and regions made their own destinies.

Nevertheless, it is possible to explore processes of transformation, and with them 'the durability of regions', in a systematic fashion, despite their different

---

[48] U. Staber, 'An Ecological Perspective on Entrepreneurship in Industrial Districts', *Entrepreneurship and Regional Development*, 9 (1997), p. 45.
[49] Soda, 'The Convergence of History', p. 246.

outcomes in different places and at different times. As Hudson asserts, it is quite possible through 'small-scale and disaggregated research ... to answer big theoretically informed questions'.[50] Our reading of the literature from a range of disciplines in the social sciences also suggests that from a concern with process there flow three distinct but interrelated sub-sets of questions.

Firstly, what forces drive, and impede, the process of change and transformation. From Marshall, we would highlight the imperatives of changes in markets and technology. Of course, these should not be conceived of as purely exogenous forces. Instead, actors in districts and clusters constantly strove to reshape the factors of production available to them. Nor were they simply passive in the face of the market. Capabilities had to match what the market demanded, but markets could also be stimulated to accept new desires. Capabilities and demands existed in a symbiotic relationship. Moreover, life-cycle models proposed by economic geography, and indeed the evolutionary models of economists such as Nelson and Winter, suggest that this emerging elaboration of capabilities takes place in a path-dependent fashion at the level of both the firm and the district or cluster. Indeed, given the importance of external economies to the logic of agglomeration, the capabilities of the firm must be understood as being set within and related to those of the cluster as a whole. The systemic nature of districts and clusters is further reflected in a propensity to form networks. These, too, evolve in a path-dependent fashion. Here, we stress the structural and structuring nature of networks; that is, as institutions that both constrain and facilitate actors according to the position they occupy. The structures of networks consequently need to be carefully specified over time. At the same time, regard for both the path-dependent evolution of clusters as systems and for the structuring properties of networks should be tempered by a healthy, empirically-informed acknowledgement of contingency and narrative.

Secondly, to what extent and in what ways are change processes affected by the wider context in which that transformation occurs? What is the influence of wider macro-economic, socio-cultural and political contexts? It is not possible to examine any district or cluster in isolation from larger systems. For example, it may be important to establish the extent to which local networks were able to intersect with, learn from and influence other systems operating at a range of geographical scales, be they regional, national or even international. These systems might relate to technology, commerce, politics or the law.

Thirdly, through what mechanisms are the forces for and against change mediated and accommodated? Especially important here is the issue of governance systems and, in particular, the extent to which we can identify networks as effective institutions of governance at the local level. In doing so, we must carefully assess two balances. First, networks, defined as structures of relationships that exist within and between individual actors, firms and other

---

[50] P. Hudson, 'Regional and Local History: Globalisation, Postmodernism and the Future', *Journal of Regional and Local Studies*, Vol. 20, No. 1 (1999), pp. 6 and 8.

organisations, necessarily contain elements derived from markets on the one hand and from hierarchies on the other. This involves an exploration of how networks interpenetrated and interacted with other governance systems and how these patterns of interdependence changed over time. Second, contrary to the 'strong embeddedness position', we argue in favour of a concern with how actors constructed their network positions. In other words, networks should be viewed not simply as structuring institutions, constraining or facilitating in particular directions, but as vehicles for agency, and thus for power and influence. This is not to argue that social context has no bearing on actors. Systems of norms, values and meaning had real impact on behaviours and attitudes. At the same time, it is important to argue against the reification of networks as a distinct and ideal governance form, and against a retreat from close specification of networks in favour of an appeal to notions of 'community'. Again, this concern for agency in the local context can only be fully appreciated when followed over time.

As we have indicated, there is a high degree of interdependence between these three areas of enquiry. In the essays that follow, the authors each have their own particular focus, but behind each lies a central interest, a broad concern with how districts, networks and clusters emerge, adapt and evolve. Our hope is that by taking the spatiality of English industrialisation seriously, we are together able to contribute new insights to that analytical process.

Chapter 2

An economic approach to regional business networks

M.C. Casson

Introduction

This chapter presents an economic perspective on regional business networks (RBNs). The aim is to explore the contribution that economic theory can make to the analysis of the historical evolution of industrial districts, regional networks and clusters of firms. Economics is a continually evolving discipline, and some non-economists judge the subject using an old-fashioned stereotype which is no longer true (if it ever was). This chapter therefore begins by setting out the gist of an economic approach to historical subjects and distinguishing this from the neoclassical 'straw man' used by critics of economics.

It is important to appreciate what kinds of phenomena economics can explain and what kinds it cannot. Given the way that economics is set up, in terms of the assumptions that it makes, there are certain things that it can do well, other things that it can only do badly, and a few things that it cannot do at all. Economics is good at explaining the measurable behaviour of a group or population of firms, but not so good at explaining the qualitative behaviour of an individual firm, although there are many cases in which this can also be done. Economics makes no attempt to explain factors which cannot be perceived by a detached observer – for example, it makes no attempt to explain what it *feels* like to be an employer or employee in a particular firm, or to be a member of a particular business network. Criticising economic theory for not doing things that it has never set out to do is not very helpful. Conversely, valuing economics for the things that it can do, and combining it with other perspectives which can do what economics cannot do, is a much more constructive approach.

Methodological individualism is an important feature of modern economics. Social and economic phenomena are explained as outcomes generated by the interaction of numerous individual decisions. Economics does not regard organic concepts such as 'community' as fundamental, but rather as derivative from individual actions. A community exists if people behave differently towards people whom they perceive as belonging to the same community, but otherwise it does not. A community does not have a will of its own. To explain an outcome by saying that the community willed it is invalid, but to say, for example, that it happened because a majority of individuals voted for it is perfectly valid.

A similar point applies to firms. Although it is sometimes useful, as a form of 'shorthand', to describe a firm as having taken a decision, in reality key decisions are typically taken by the managing director or the members of the board (through consensus or majority vote). Again, the behaviour of an inter-firm network is in reality the behaviour of a group of representatives of firms, and how the network behaves may well depend upon who is representing a given firm at a particular time (see below).

This rejection of organic concepts as explanatory factors can be regarded as a special case of Occam's Razor: the principle that conceptual distinctions should not be multiplied without good reason. Eliminating organic actors in a model means that only one type of actor – the individual – needs to be considered. The disadvantage, though, is that there are sometimes many different actors of this particular type. Economists put a premium on the internal logical consistency of explanation: the structural simplicity achieved by applying Occam's Razor gives economic reasoning a logical transparency which ensures that any contradictions will be quickly exposed.

Economics postulates that individuals are rational. Rationality is instrumental, in the sense that rational individuals choose the best means of achieving given objectives. It is not the case that some objectives are more rational than others – any set of objectives is rational so long as the individual has a consistent set of priorities in view. Contrary to common misperceptions, there is nothing rational about being selfish. A rational individual could aim to improve the welfare of the community instead. This would mean, for example, that they behaved altruistically towards everyone whom they perceived as belonging to the same community as themselves. Economics is therefore fully able to deal with the altruistic motives that may underpin certain forms of network behaviour.

It is also wrong to suppose that economics assumes that markets are competitive and work perfectly. Modern economics recognises monopolistic and oligopolistic market structures, and transactions costs too. Nevertheless, there are important differences between the way that economists explain market behaviour and the way that other social sciences do. For example, while other social sciences say much about 'power', economists use the word very sparingly. This is not because they deny the reality of the phenomena that others describe with this word, but that they interpret the same phenomena in a different way. In economics, individuals always have a choice of some sort. In economics, a person exercises power when they influence another person's decision in order to further their own objectives. Power is simply a special kind of influence, in other words. For example, if an employer induces a worker to accept a low wage because he is heavily in debt, this may be described as the exercise of 'bargaining power'. But in reality it is the exercise of influence rather than power. The employer cannot compel the worker to take the job. The worker is free to reject it if they would rather starve – the employer is simply offering them an incentive to take the work.

Other forms of 'power' can be included in economic discourse too. If an employer with the 'power of persuasion' induces a worker to believe so much in the social value of the product that the worker works harder for the public good, then this is again an exercise of influence. The employer does not have to resort to physical intimidation, but simply confers emotional value on work which it could not otherwise possess. The worker has a choice of whether to believe the employer or not. It is therefore a mistake to infer that because economists do not mention power very often that they are ignoring an important aspect of economic and social life.

It is sometimes inferred that because of its methodological individualism and commitment to rational action, economics is unable to explain the key phenomena associated with networking. Networking is such an inherently social activity that it seems improbable that a discipline such as economics could shed much light upon it. But networking activity is entirely rational. Networks provide people with access to information through conversations with other members; they 'purchase' the information they need by bartering information of their own. Networking is, however, time-consuming, for the time spent in social activity could be spent in other ways. Spending time with friends and family may well provide emotional benefit, but spending time with a business acquaintance in order to procure commercial intelligence may incur emotional cost. The rational networker will trade off the benefits of networking – in terms of the expected value of the information collected – against the costs, as reflected in the time spent gathering the information and the emotional penalties involved.

A further advantage of the economic approach is that it addresses the viability of networks. Some of the literature on RBNs has a strong ideological dimension. It is often suggested that inter-personal relationships are much healthier within a network than they are within an ordinary market. Network relationships are personal rather than impersonal, co-operative rather than competitive, and democratic rather than domineering, it is said. On this basis, networks certainly sound much cosier than markets, but is such a comfortable existence really viable? Are networks successful because of the 'comfort factor', or in spite of it? An economic approach can help to identify when and where networks are more efficient than markets and, conversely, where markets have the advantage instead. This analysis generates predictions about the types of industry and location at which successful RBNs are likely to be observed, and the form that a successful RBN is likely to take.

An economic approach also provides a valuable antidote to purely political perspectives on RBNs. Support for regional networks is sometimes linked to arguments for the preservation of indigenous regional cultures and minority languages. It is argued that because of the potential vitality of RBNs, regional economies can be self-sufficient – indeed, that they may flourish more in isolation than as 'dependencies' or 'peripheral' units serving some 'imperialist' metropolis. Because of its commitment to logical rigour, economics is well placed to 'deconstruct' and critically examine such contentions. An economic approach of the kind developed in this chapter shows very clearly that regional economies are most likely to flourish when their local networks are strongly integrated with national and international ones. Just as an individual person may suffer from isolation, and flourish within a wider social group, so a regional economy is likely to suffer in isolation and to flourish as part of an interdependent national and international economy.

Path dependence

It is often alleged that economics is unsuitable as a framework for historical analysis because it is inherently static. History is about change over time, and it is clearly inappropriate, it is alleged, to analyse it by means of a framework which does not allow for change. Whilst there is an element of truth in this view, it is only a half-truth at best. Economics does analyse change over time, but in a distinctive way. Although simple economic models of change have important limitations, sophisticated economic models are perfectly adequate for historical purposes – including analysing how networks evolve over time.

Economics is static in the sense that it makes extensive use of the equilibrium concept. An equilibrium is a state in which everyone's immediate expectations about other people's behaviour are fulfilled. Everyone has done as well as they could expect to do, given the way that other people have acted and so, given the chance, everyone would behave in the same way again. The simplest way to apply this concept is to relate behaviour at any given point in time to the conditions prevailing at this time. In a historical context this means, for example, postulating that the way people behaved in, say, 1850 was efficiently adapted to conditions prevailing in 1850, that behaviour in 1860 was well adapted to conditions in 1860, and so on. Hence, if business behaviour changed between 1850 and 1860 it did so simply because the environment changed. It is unnecessary to know what happened in 1850 in order to understand behaviour in 1860, because everything that could be relevant is reflected in the conditions prevailing in 1860.

This approach does not deny that the environment in 1860 is influenced by actions taken in 1850. Suppose, for example, that local business conditions in 1850 encouraged the building of a railway to join a town to the national railway system. The existence of this railway will then influence decisions in 1860, and the equilibrium in 1860 will reflect this. This is an example of what historians describe as 'path dependence'. Path dependence arises in this case because the railway network cannot be costlessly re-configured in 1860 to reflect requirements ten years after it was built. The costs incurred in 1850 cannot be recovered by closing the line, so any new line must be financed from scratch. The investment required to establish a new route is an 'adjustment cost' incurred in adapting the railway network to new conditions.

A similar argument can be applied to business networks. Just as a railway line is part of a physical network – the *tangible infrastructure* of a region – relationships between local businessmen form part of a social network – the *intangible infrastructure* of a region. Both physical and social networks are costly to set up, are long-lived and are costly to change. Thus, the business environment at any given time is determined to a significant extent by investments in business networks that were made in the past.

If the members of a business network are aware that the environment is constantly changing, and that networks are costly to change, rationality implies that networks will be made as flexible as possible. This means that networks designed for one purpose may be adapted for some other purpose later on, because this is cheaper than creating a new network from scratch. Thus, at any given time, a regional economy may comprise a portfolio of different networks, some long-established and others recently formed, some of which are expanding or contracting, whilst others are in the process of adaptation to other purposes. The decisions taken at this given time will reflect the beliefs about the future prevailing at this time. The concept of equilibrium does not imply that beliefs about the distant future are entirely correct, but only that everyone is sufficiently aware of how other people are acting at the same time that they are satisfied with their own behaviour at that time. Equilibrium means simply that the simultaneous decisions of different individuals are reconciled with each other. Each individual is perfectly satisfied that they have chosen the right set of networks to join, in the light of the choices made by others. On the other hand, each individual recognises that their own decisions reflect their personal judgements about the future as well as the present. Membership decisions may be costly to reverse, and so members need to keep their options open as far as possible. Thus, if, say, networks are easier to leave than they are to join, people may belong to networks simply as an option to participate more actively later on should circumstances change. Equilibrium does not, therefore, imply that with the benefit of hindsight no mistakes are made, but rather that no one is dissatisfied with the decisions they have made at the time.

Networks of entrepreneurs

A major benefit of an economic approach is that it makes it possible to relate networking to other economic concepts. This chapter argues that relating networking to entrepreneurship is crucial in understanding how regional business networks (RBNs) really work. Economic historians were quick to see the potential importance of RBNs, but the entrepreneurial aspect has not been consistently stressed.[1] Recent academic literature places most emphasis on informal social interactions within the regional economy.[2]

This chapter argues that both entrepreneurship *and* networking are crucial to the development process. Just as entrepreneurship without networking may prove ineffectual, so networking without entrepreneurship may prove ineffectual too. Networking without entrepreneurship may actually retard regional economic development.

This is a special case of a more general proposition: namely, that the *type* of networking that occurs is more important than whether networking of any sort occurs or not. There is 'good' networking and 'bad' networking so far as regional economic development is concerned. Good networking is typically open, transparent and entrepreneurial, and involves the provision of 'public goods' to industry. Bad networking is typically closed and opaque. It may involve politicians or anti-entrepreneurial social elites, although entrepreneurs may be implicated too. Bad networking is exemplified by 'rent-seeking lobbying' in which entrepreneurs combine with politicians to protect weak regional industries against external competition.

Regions that are poorly endowed with natural resources, and are located away from major trading routes, may have difficulty in attracting entrepreneurs. Able and ambitious local entrepreneurs may well emigrate to the nearest metropolis. Such regions need to possess an 'outward looking' culture if they are to maintain access to the entrepreneurial skills they need to orient their local networks towards successful economic development. Many of the entrepreneurial skills that a region requires will be possessed by individuals who live in the metropolis. For some regions, therefore, 'dependency' on a metropolis may hold the key to successful development.

---

[1] See, for example A.P. Wadsworth and J. de Lacy Mann, *The Cotton Trade and Industrial Lancashire, 1600–1780* (Manchester University Press, 1931); W.H.B. Court, *The Rise of the Midland Industries, 1600–1838*, (Oxford University Press, 1938); J. Prest, *The Industrial Revolution in Coventry*, (Oxford University Press, 1996); G.C. Allen, *The Industrial Development of Birmingham and the Black Country, 1860–1927* (Cass, 1956); R.A. Church, *Economic and Social Change in a Midland Town: Victorian Nottingham, 1815–1900* (Macmillan, 1966).

[2] R.F. Dalzell, Jr., *Enterprising Elite: The Boston Associates and the World They Made* (Harvard University Press, 2000); P. Hudson, 'Capital and Credit in the West Riding Wool Textile Industry c.1750–1850', in P. Hudson (ed), *Regions and Industries* (Cambridge University Press, 1989), pp. 69–99.

Recent literature on RBNs has lost sight of some of these points. Regions are often analysed as isolated economic entities. Local networking between workers and artisans is usually stressed, despite the fact that such networking is often geared towards trade union organisation or local cartelisation, which raise the local costs of production rather than reduce them to inter-regionally competitive levels. This parochial perspective understates the importance of long-distance networking between entrepreneurs. Because of this parochial outlook, it is mainly studies of metropolitan areas, rather than studies of regions, that highlight entrepreneurial links between region and metropolis.[3]

Recognition of the importance of the entrepreneurial dimension to regional networks has major policy implications – particularly in view of the recent establishment of Regional Development Agencies in the UK. Government policies to promote RBNs will not necessarily enhance economic development. There is a real danger of promoting the formation of inward-looking anti-entrepreneurial regional cliques, whose influence will actually inhibit local development. The inward-looking nature of regional cliques tends to be reinforced by nationalist and separatist political parties.[4] By weakening links with the metropolis, these political pressures may deny the region access to the entrepreneurial skills that are necessary to implement the policies that regional politicians are seeking to promote.

Networks – formal and informal

The more informal the process of networking, the more difficult objective evidence is to obtain. Interviews and personal diaries are probably the best sources for the historian. Conversely, the more formal the process of networking, the easier evidence is to obtain. The most obvious way of formalising network relationships is through associations or clubs. Meetings of these associations will normally be minuted, so that the frequency of meetings, the regularity of attendance, and the main topics of discussion can be assessed. What is more difficult to discover, of course, is what is said after the formal business of the meeting has closed.

Writers on RBNs have remarkably little (though see Chapter 10) of this book) to say about formal associations, considering the emphasis that they place on social interaction. Consider trades unions, for example. Given the importance of craft skills in many industrial districts, and the role of craft trades unions in the enforcement of apprenticeship, it might be thought that trades unions would have an important part to play in the promotion of flexible

---

[3]   See, for example, M.C. Casson and H. Cox, 'An Economic Model of Inter-firm Networks' in M. Ebers (ed), *The Formation of Inter-organizational Networks* (Oxford University Press, 1997), pp. 174–96.

[4]   See M.C. Casson, *Entrepreneurship and Business Culture* (Edward Elgar, 1995).

specialisation. In fact, it seems that it is the weakness rather than the strength of trades unions that explains the success of some industrial districts. In many instances, the craft worker is self-employed, and in others he is the non-unionised employee of a paternalistic entrepreneur. Possibly as a response to this, writers on industrial districts seem remarkable reticent about the role of the trade union.

The same is true of employers' associations and trade associations. One of the most detailed series of studies is afforded by Scranton,[5] which is based on Philadelphia, and its textile trades in particular. Scranton's interpretation of flexible specialisation is very broad, encompassing all industries in which customised or batch production is significant relative to mass production. His research demonstrates the negative impact of institutionalised conflict in industrial relations on the performance of a mature industrial district.

Scranton's work also underlines the fact that a great deal of formal networking occurs at a national, rather than a regional, level. Regional conflicts are often a microcosm of national ones. From a policy perspective, the most interesting issue is whether certain types of region are less prone to militancy where industrial disputes are concerned. There is little evidence that 'industrial districts' are less militant than other areas. The concentration of a particular craft in a given region tends to concentrate trade union activity there, with other areas being neglected. Indeed, it could be argued, in the light of UK experience at least, that the vulnerability of mature industrial districts to trade union militancy has been a major factor in promoting the decentralisation of industry away from these areas. In the post-war period, for example, many foreign investors in manufacturing industries have avoided established industrial districts, and selected locations where they can train workers in their own production methods from scratch. It could be argued that it is regional *diversity*, rather than regional specialisation, that holds the key to long-run success.

The fact that many formal associations are national rather than regional highlights the importance of integrating the analysis of RBNs into a discussion of national business systems as a whole. Excessive focus on networking within a region may obscure the importance of external networking. One of the aims of this chapter is to analyse the connection between a region's internal networks and its external ones.

---

[5]   P. Scranton, *Proprietary Capitalism: The Textile Manufacture at Philadelphia, 1800–1885* (Cambridge University Press, 1983); ibid., *Figured Tapestry: Production, Markets and Power in Phiadelphia, 1885–1941* (Cambridge University Press, 1989); ibid., *Endless Novelty: Specialty Production and American Industrialization, 1865–1925* (Princeton University Press, 1997).

Networks – good and bad

One of the reasons why trade union activity can impair regional competitiveness is that the trade union acts as a monopoly supplier of labour. A cartel is an analogue of the trade union operating in the product market. A local cartel can also undermine the competitiveness of a regional economy, by pricing its goods out of international markets. While the local firms benefit from higher profit margins, the local economy loses out as the volume of output and employment contracts. Like trades unions, cartels usually operate on a national basis. Because of regional specialisation, however, the major members of a cartel may all be based in a particular region, and the meetings of the cartel may even take place there. Church has noted the way that domestic cartels contributed to the economic failure of the UK motor industry in the inter-war and early post-war period.[6] This failure was most evident in the West Midlands, which was where the industry was concentrated at the time.

A combination of trades unions and cartels can be a fatal one. This is particularly true where there is multi-stage production, with different employers and different crafts being involved at each stage. Horizontal combinations of workers and of employers at each stage all add a monopoly mark-up to the price of the final product. When consumer resistance asserts itself, conflict may break out between the vested interests at different stages of production, over how the total available profit is to be distributed between them.

This point illustrates a significant difference between the effects of horizontal and vertical networks in multi-stage production. Whilst vertical networks can help to improve coordination of the 'supply chain', by reducing transaction costs in intermediate product markets for components and raw materials, horizontal networks may easily inhibit coordination by promoting conflict over the distribution of profit. Where vertical networking is weak, vertical integration is often effected to mitigate the problems of multi-stage mark-ups and bargaining over the prices of intermediate products.

Olson provides a classic statement of the case against networks.[7] He focuses on networks that are formally organised as clubs. He argues that clubs formed initially for laudable purposes, such as the provision of public goods, like basic research, may easily become corrupted. Considering clubs in very general terms, he shows how they can appropriate economic rents for self-interested members by organising collusion against non-members. It is worth noting that writers who extol the virtues of networking in supporting flexible specialisation rarely mention Olson's seminal work.

---

[6]   R.A. Church, *The Rise and Decline of the British Motor Industry* (Macmillan, 1993).

[7]   M. Olson, *The Rise and Decline of Nations* (Yale University Press, 1982).

There certainly appear to be systematic patterns in the rise and decline of regionally-specialised industries, as noted in Chapter 5 below. In the early days of an industry, the most entrepreneurial firms form an association and actively recruit new members to their club, in order to spread the cost of the facilities that they wish to provide for shared use. As the industry matures, however, and the threat of overcapacity looms, the firms become more concerned with restricting entry to the club as a means of denying entrants access to key facilities. As their profits begin to dry up, and further investment is deferred, the focus of their activities switches to price fixing instead. The owners of the firms reconcile themselves to the decline of the regional industry, but seek to maintain prices, at the expense of jobs, so that their firms can remain solvent until they retire. If no one is prepared to move in to the industry to buy up the firms as their owners quit, then the industry may become extinct in a very short space of time.

A more recent source of criticism of networks has arisen in the wake of the Asian crisis. The informal networks which only recently were hailed as providing a competitive edge to the Asian economies are now described as bastions of cronyism, and are seen as being responsible for their present recent economic decline. This points, once again, to the importance of distinguishing between different types of network.

The role of trust in networks

Another reason why so little is known about RBNs is that propositions about regional networking are often expressed in rather nebulous terms. The term 'network' is used by different writers in very different ways.[8] As indicated in Chapter 1 of this volume, what is required is a consistent set of definitions through which propositions about networks can be unambiguously expressed.

In its everyday use, the term 'network' signifies a collection of entities that are linked up in some way. In the context of RBNs, the term signifies linkages based upon communication. But not just any form of communication will do: the term also signifies that the communication is of high quality. For the purposes of this chapter, *a network may be defined as a set of high-trust linkages connecting a set of people.*

Some networks exist purely for social purposes: a network of friends who gather at a cafe in an evening, for example. From an economic perspective the most interesting networks are those which promote coordination. For example, representatives of firms who share a common interest in changing government

---

[8]   B. Axelsson and G. Easton, *Industrial Networks: A New View of Reality* (Routledge, 1992); M. Best, *The New Competition: Institutions of Industrial Restructuring* (Polity Press, 1990).

policy may network with each other in order to coordinate their lobbying activities. Networks that facilitate coordination are the focus of this chapter.

A *business network* is a network whose membership consists wholly or partly of business people. The members may be acting in their own right – an *inter-personal* network - or on behalf of the firms they represent – an *inter-firm* network. In some cases, the network may consist only of representatives of business interests – for example, a cartel – while in other cases non-business interests may be represented as well – for example, civil servants may be involved in a business-government network used to coordinate industrial policy. An RBN is a *business network whose members are located in a particular region, industrial district or cluster of firms.*

As noted earlier, a region is not an isolated entity, and so when analysing RBNs, it is important to recognise the importance of *inter-regional business networks* (IRBNs) too. IRBNs are important because physical proximity is not the only factor sustaining networks. Mutual advantage from exploiting the gains from inter-regional trade and investment, and shared occupational allegiance, favour networking too. As already indicated, the interplay of RBNs and IRBNs is a major theme of this chapter.

Warranted mutual trust

Defining a network in terms of trust is of little help if the concept of trust is not itself well defined. Unfortunately, different concepts of trust are also used in the literature.[9] Trust is *warranted* when the party who is trusted actually behaves in a trustworthy way. Naive people may place unwarranted trust in other parties, and be taken advantage of as a result. Unwarranted trust is of little economic value, since it merely redistributes income from the naive to the dishonest. The focus in this chapter is therefore on warranted trust.

Trust may be *one-sided* or *mutual*. One-sided trust is not reciprocated, but mutual trust is reciprocated. Mutual trust is sufficient to sustain a transaction, in the sense that both parties are willing to proceed to contract, but one-sided trust is not. Since only mutual trust guarantees that a transaction can proceed, it is mutual trust that is the focus of this chapter.

The definition of trust used in this chapter is therefore *warranted mutual trust*. An important advantage of this definition is that it corresponds to a *high trust equilibrium*.[10] It is an equilibrium because each party's actions fulfils the beliefs of the other party, so that neither party has any reason to change their beliefs for the future. Transactions can therefore be repeated indefinitely

---

[9]   G. Dei Ottati, 'Trust, Inter-linking Transactions and Credit in the Industrial District', *Cambridge Journal of Economics*, Vol. 18 (1994), pp. 529–46.

[10]   M.C. Casson, *The Economics of Business Culture* (Oxford University Press, 1991).

because the outcome of each transaction creates a climate of opinion in which further transactions can take place.

When defined in this way, trust becomes a special type of reputation. Each party has a reputation with the other party for behaving in an honest way. A network is a natural generalisation of trust to the case of several parties. If everyone has a reputation for honesty, then everyone will be willing to trade with everyone else. The question then arises as to whether everyone needs to know everyone else on a personal basis. *Personal trust* is based on beliefs about a specific individual, derived from face-to-face contact with them. *Impersonal trust* is based on more limited information – typically about the group to which the individual belongs, or the circumstances under which they are acting. If it is known that members of a certain group are morally committed to honesty in all their business dealings – such as Quakers at the time of the Industrial Revolution – then it is sufficient to know that someone belongs to this group; it is unnecessary to have met them face-to-face.[11] Impersonal trust is often based on the fact that the individual belongs to the *same* social group as oneself; in this context, the crucial group-specific value is loyalty to other members of the group.

Some writers extend the concept of impersonal trust to trust that is mediated by the force of law. Many economists have noted that an ideal legal system allows trade to take place between anonymous individuals. It is sufficient for transactors to know that the other party is operating under sanctions which punish dishonest behaviour. Defining impersonal trust as broadly as this, however, makes it difficult to distinguish between networks and markets, since both become high-trust coordination mechanisms. For the purposes of this chapter, therefore, *impersonal trust is confined to trust sustained by moral and social sanctions.*

The sanctions imposed by law are generally of a material form, such as fines or imprisonment. The sanctions imposed by morality, by contrast, are of an emotional kind. A person can be trusted on moral grounds because they fear self-inflicted emotional sanctions – such as guilt – if they cheat. Guilt involves a person losing reputation with themselves. It is an extremely effective sanction from an economic point of view because the punishment is inflicted by the person who is in the best position to detect the dishonesty – namely the offender themselves. Social sanctions rely on a mixture of emotional and material factors. The main emotional factor is fear of shame and humiliation. Shame involves a loss of reputation with other people. The main material sanction operating in a social context is the risk of being excluded from future transactions.

Social sanctions only work if the offender is detected, however. This may be fairly easy in a small group, where the potential suspects are few, but it is more

---

[11]   See Chapter 8 in this book.

difficult in large groups. This is one reason why large groups tend to rely heavily on general moral systems backed up by legal sanctions, whilst small groups tend to rely more on social sanctions instead.

A successful network confers on its members a degree of self-respect. Members retain this self-respect by behaving in an honest way. Individuals may occasionally lapse, however, due to loss of 'self-control'.[12] It may be possible, however, for an individual to regain reputation through some suitable act of penance – such as a public apology, or restitution of the damage they have done. A network is *forgiving* if it provides a mechanism for restoring reputation in this way.

When everyone is prone to lapses in behaviour, a forgiving group is more attractive than an unforgiving group. It will also enjoy greater success in retaining members. On the other hand, if it is too *lenient* then it may attract people who are immune to moral sanctions or have little capacity for self-control. Their disruptive influence will induce other members of the group to quit. If a group is forgiving, therefore, it also needs to be sufficiently *tough*.

The efficacy of a network thus depends upon the mixture of moral and social sanctions it employs. Where social sanctions are involved, the mixture of material punishment, shaming and exclusion is important too. Where shaming is involved, a tough but forgiving approach is likely to perform particularly well.

Leadership in networks

Some writers talk about trust as though it were just 'something in the air'.[13] It is either present or absent, and there is nothing that anyone can do about it. This chapter takes a rather different view. As already noted, trust is a valuable asset, because it provides access to information and reduces transaction costs. Given the benefits that flow from trust, it is rational to invest in it, provided that the value of the benefits exceeds the initial cost. Investment in trust generates 'social capital'.[14]

But how exactly is social capital created? Some writers argue that it emerges spontaneously under suitable conditions. The view in this chapter is rather different. It is suggested that trust can be engineered. Networks tend to be built by individual leaders. These leaders recognise an opportunity to develop a set

---

[12] R.H. Thaler and H.M. Sheffrin, 'An Economic Theory of Self-control', *Journal of Political Economy*, Vol. 89, No. 2 (1981), pp. 392–406.

[13] For example, A. Marshall, *Principles of Economics* (Macmillan, 1890). See also 'atmosphere' as described by O.E. Williamson, *Economic Institutions of Capitalism* (Free Press, 1985).

[14] J.S. Coleman, 'Social Capital in the Creation of Human Capital', *American Journal of Sociology* (Special supplement), Vol. 94 (1988), pp. S95–S120.

of linkages for the purposes of coordination. The rewards may accrue to the leaders themselves, or to the members of the group that they help to form. Thus, there is scope for both selfish and altruistic motives where leadership is concerned.

Leaders play an intermediating role. Leaders help to establish high-trust links between people who previously either had no link, or who did not trust each other sufficiently to put their link to economic use. Each member of the group trusts the leader, and the leader trusts them. They trust him because of his substantial reputation for integrity – a reputation which is reflected in the fact that he enjoys a higher status than any other member the group. He trusts them because he has engineered a culture based on strong moral sanctions such that no one wants to cheat.

Some writers on networks do not like the leadership concept. There are overtones of 'dictatorship' and 'propaganda' in the account of moral leadership given above. It is important to recognise, however, that leadership is a role, and that the leader described above is simply a personification of that role. In practice, there may be several people that fulfil this role. The group may have a constitution which distributes the power of leadership amongst different people. A common practice is to separate the formulation of policy and the conduct of external relations from day-to-day administration. The network is thus coordinated through a partnership between two leaders, one of whom initiates proposals, whilst the other implements agreed decisions. These people may be appointed by the membership as a whole. In the limiting case of a democratic group, everyone participates equally in the leadership role. In a large group, however, democracy is normally institutionalised through a system of elected representatives, leaving ordinary members to play a passive role.

Rival leaders may form different groups and then compete for members. Provided individuals are free to decide which group (if any) they wish to join, competition between leaders will tend to distribute most of the benefits of the groups to their individual members. It is mainly when a group enjoys a monopoly that the power of the leader is to be feared. When everyone in a region is satisfied that they belong to the most appropriate set of groups (given the costs of membership subscriptions, where applicable, and the commitment of time involved) then there exists a network equilibrium of the kind described above.

The region and the metropolis

A region is a very appropriate unit for networking because geographical proximity promotes face-to-face contact. In this context, it is useful to distinguish between an ordinary region and a metropolis. A metropolis is also a region, in the sense that it occupies a well-defined geographical area, but it is clearly a region of a very special type. The working population of an ordinary region will contain many production workers, owner-managers of small enterprises, and so on. Networks will tend to be harnessed for the coordination of production, as explained above.

The working population of a metropolis comprises bankers, lawyers, accountants, journalists and academic experts, in addition to many other workers in supporting services. The predominance of financial services means that metropolitan networks are heavily involved in the coordination of financial flows between banks and industry. Export and import marketing also tend to be concentrated in the metropolis, and this gives metropolitan networks an important role in coordinating international product flows as well. The metropolis may also coordinate inter-regional domestic distribution by acting as a transport hub.

If the metropolis is also a capital city, it will contain politicians, civil servants, lobbyists, and so on. Its networks will also coordinate government-industry linkages, and financial relations between government and banks.

It is important to note that the value of resources which is controlled by metropolitan business networks (MBNs) is far greater than that which is normally controlled by an ordinary RBN. It is also important to recognise that the geographical extent of a metropolis is smaller than that of many regions, and its population density is consequently much higher. It is equipped with mass transit systems and relatively sophisticated telecommunications facilities. All of this reflects the fact that the metropolis specialises in processing information. Whilst the ordinary region specialises in handling goods and raw materials of a particular type, the metropolis specialises in handling information instead.

The importance of information handling in the metropolis means that networking is of greater economic significance in a metropolis than it is in an ordinary region. Why then does the literature place so much emphasis on networking within an ordinary region? One explanation may be that networking in the metropolis involves a lot of bilateral contacts between network members, which is not visible to outsiders, whereas networking in an ordinary region involves multi-lateral contact of a more visible form. Yet metropolitan social life is often highly visible, with journalists reporting on glittering social functions. The main difference between the metropolis and the ordinary region appears to lie in the fact that the metropolis has both visible and invisible networking in abundance, whereas the ordinary region has much less invisible networking than the metropolis does. The reason why the metropolis has more invisible networking is probably that more commercial information of a confidential nature changes hands. The invisible networks emphasise confidentiality because the information relates to profit opportunities which could be pre-empted by other people, so that the information would lose its value if other people got to know it as well. On the other hand, the symptoms of these invisible networks can be detected in the phenomenon of interlocking directorates on the boards of metropolitan companies, which attest to the networking activity which must have gone on behind the scenes.[15]

Another difference is that networking in the metropolis is likely to be less spontaneous and more pre-planned. Many social events in the metropolis are organised well in advance, so that busy people can make the best use of their valuable time. The diversity of social contacts that people maintain in a metropolis is also likely to be a factor. A person who goes to the same pub every night, or the same club on a given date of the week, has little need to organise their diary. But a person who belongs to numerous different social groups needs to prioritise conflicting dates, and to optimise their schedule in travelling from one meeting to another on the same day.

The attitude to social networking may also be a more instrumental one in the metropolis. Everyone is seeking to extend their circle of contacts by making new introductions. In many cases, people have moved to the metropolis because they are ambitious to make money, and have already decided that they are willing to sacrifice the pleasures of spontaneous social intercourse for material ends.

The implication of all this is that networking is more intense, and of greater economic significance, in the metropolis than it is in an ordinary region. The emphasis in the literature on the economic value of networking in ordinary regions may actually reflect a nostalgic desire of the writers for the pre-capitalist age. The appeal of regional networks lies in the fact that they have *not* been adapted for narrow economic uses. It is the fact that they involve small networks in which the same people meet to discuss social rather than economic topics which make these networks appeal to the writers concerned. It is likely that networks organised in this way are not of much economic significance when compared to the metropolitan networks described above.

An information systems view of networking

An economic system consists of many different types of network connected up together. Indeed, it could be said that the entire economy is a single gigantic network in this sense. Connections between networks are effected by a special type of intermediator. These intermediators pass on information gathered from one network to the members of other networks to which they also belong. Kipping uses the term 'connector' to denote this special type of intermediator.[16]

---

[15]   See, for example, M. Wilkins, 'The Free-standing Company: An Important Type of British Foreign Direct Investment', *Economic History Review*, Vol. 41 (1988), pp. 259–82.

[16]   M. Kipping, 'American Management Consulting Companies in Western Europe 1920–1990: Products, Reputation, and Relationships', *Business History Review*, Vol. 73

Sometimes the connector may fulfil other intermediating roles as well. Connectors between business networks are often mobile entrepreneurs who belong to several business networks rather than just a single one. Leaders are usually connectors too. Most leaders take overall responsibility for the external relations of their network. They socialise with the leaders of other networks in elite social groups. Many connections are established through these elite groups. A person in one network who needs to establish trust with a person in another network will ask their leader to speak to the leader of the other network at a meeting of the elite. This leads to an introduction in which each leader endorses the integrity of his own followers.

The more networks a given connector belongs to, the greater their influence is likely to be. There are definite limits to the number of connections that a single connector can sustain, however. To begin with, each connection requires a minimum commitment of time, for in the absence of any contact trust will tend to obsolesce, and so a maximum number of connections is set by the fact that there are only twenty-four hours in each day. Connectors also need to be versatile. Each network to which they belong will have its own moral and social norms. Diversity amongst these norms may make it impossible to simultaneously satisfy the requirements of certain groups. The connector needs to learn the requirements of each group to which he belongs. Indeed, membership of certain groups is mutually exclusive; it is impossible to be a true supporter of two rival football teams, or to subscribe to two different religions at once. The connector may need to be secretive about his membership of one group if he wishes to belong to another. The more groups he belongs to, the more likely are conflicts of this nature to appear.

There are many different connectors within an economic system, and so long chains of trust can be created, and these can be harnessed for the promotion of long-distance trade. Thus, a local entrepreneur in an industrial district may possess a high-trust link to another entrepreneur in a neighbouring metropolis. This link may have been established on the initiative of the metropolitan entrepreneur. The metropolitan entrepreneur may also belong to an elite group of international entrepreneurs which includes metropolitan entrepreneurs in other countries. These entrepreneurs, in turn, belong to national networks of entrepreneurs, which put them in touch with retail distributors in the regions of their countries. Thus, the connections forged by the metropolitan entrepreneurs create a set of links which hold the world economy together.[17] Because the metropolitan entrepreneurs belong both to their own national networks and to the international network, they provide a gateway to the world for the exports of each of the regions with which they

(1999), pp. 191–222.
    [17] M.C. Casson, 'Entrepreneurial Networks in International Business', *Business and Economic History*, Vol. 26, No. 2 (1998), pp. 811–23.

deal.

Connections can be made, not only in series, but also in parallel. There may be several paths from one part of the global system to another. Thus, a local entrepreneur may have a choice of the metropolis through which he routes his export trade. For example, a Yorkshire merchant might use contacts in either Hull, Liverpool or London to reach a customer in a remote part of the world. Some parallel paths may be shorter than others because fewer connectors are involved. One way of shortening a path is to 'cut out the middleman'. For example, a local entrepreneur could visit an overseas market in order to by-pass intermediation by a metropolitan entrepreneur.

The performance of a regional economy is likely to be better, the wider the range of connections it possesses. The more strongly it is embedded in the global trading system, the better it is likely to perform. The regional economy needs connectors who maintain links with the elite networks that coordinate international trade. Some of these connectors may be local leaders and entrepreneurs who live in the region, but many will reside in the metropolis. Indeed, some of the most successful regional entrepreneurs may emigrate to the metropolis because the members of the elites are concentrated there. While it may seem ideal that members of the entrepreneurial elite should reside in the region, this is not always a practical possibility. In this case, it is better to tolerate the influence of a metropolitan elite, than to cut the region off from the rest of the world altogether.

The relationship between region and metropolis

The preceding discussion may be conveniently summarised with the aid of the schematic diagram presented in Figure 2.1.[18] Information flows within a network are represented by thin lines, and arrows are used to indicate the direction of information flow. Since most information flows within a network are two-way, the lines normally carry two arrows each. Product flow is distinguished by the use of a thick black line. These flows are usually one-way. Flows of factor services are shown as well. Labour services are represented by a thick grey line, whilst the flow of risk capital is represented by a 'spring' symbol; this symbol indicates that the suppliers of risk capital buffer other factor suppliers such as labour against fluctuations in business conditions by assuming financial risks.

Processes involving physical transformation are represented by square boxes. These processes include production, consumption, physical distribution, and so on. Processes involving the handling of information are indicated by

---

[18] The diagram follows the conventions set out in M.C. Casson, *Information and Organization* (Oxford University Press, 1997), Chapter 1.

circles. It is assumed that information processing is effected by individuals; thus, the circles represent people in their capacity as decision-makers. Where a circle appears inside a square, this indicates that an individual decision maker is in charge of a process of material transformation too. Education is treated as both information and material transformation, since substantial plant and equipment is utilised in the process.

The representation of the processes is effected using two main axes. The vertical axis represents a sequence that begins with the household as supplier of labour, and follows that labour through the process of education to its use in the economy. The economy involves two stages of production – upstream production (including primary industries such as mining, and possibly the early stages of manufacturing, such as component production too), followed by downstream production (such as the later stages of manufacturing, like assembly and packaging). The output from downstream production is then passed on to physical distribution, which encompasses transport, warehousing and retailing. The final stage of this sequence is household consumption. Complications relating to the purchase of goods by government, and the supply of machinery for investment are ignored.

The horizontal axis captures the spatial dimension. Three zones are distinguished: a representative region on the left hand side, a metropolis serving the needs of the region in the middle, and the rest of the world on the right. The rest of the world may be identified with the international export market for the purposes of this discussion. There are several different types of metropolis; some are pure service centres with offices and speciality retail functions only, some are also major ports, and others are seats of national government too. The metropolis portrayed in Figure 2.1 is a port, but not a capital city. If it were a capital city, then government would have to be introduced into the picture, and this would further complicate the figure.

The diagram focuses on an export industry in which the region is specialised. This aligns the theory with the concept of an 'industrial district' described in Chapter 1. Each square represents a specific function connected with this industry. Thus, the square labelled 'upstream production' represents all the upstream plants in the local export industry. The thick black line connecting this square to 'downstream production' represents the set of all intermediate product flows linking successive stages of production in the region. Thus, the existence of just a single square at each stage of production does not mean that there is just a single plant at that stage in the entire regional economy.

The different plants at a given stage are normally heterogeneous. They are located in different parts of the region, and are of different capacities. The coordination of product flow therefore involves not merely adjusting total supply to total demand, but matching supplies from the upstream plants to the demands of the downstream plants in such a way that local transport costs and

Figure 2.1
Regional business networks

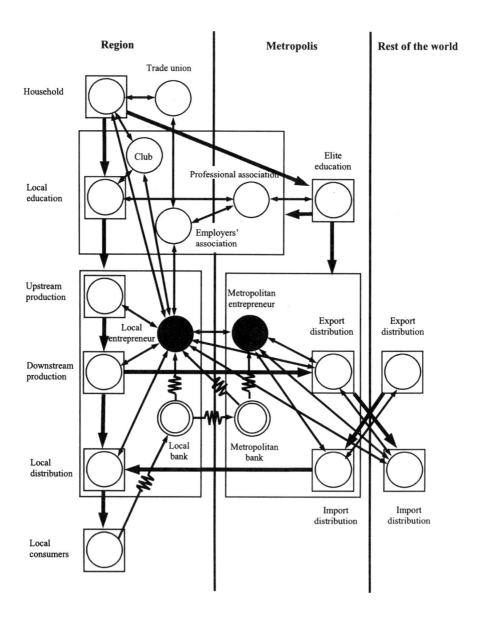

inventory costs are minimised for the industry as a whole. The heterogeneity of individual plants explains why coordination requires an intensive flow of information.

The figure identifies the local entrepreneur as a hub of regional communication. A representative local entrepreneur is indicated in the figure by a shaded circle on the left-hand side of the figure. By acting as a hub of local information flow, the representative entrepreneur is able to coordinate the regional production process. He procures labour services from the households, coordinates the flow of intermediate product from upstream to downstream production, and places the finished output in the hands of distributors. ˙

A metropolitan entrepreneur is also shown, indicated by the right-hand shaded circle. The metropolitan entrepreneur also acts as an information hub, but specialises in coordinating international trade rather than local trade. He handles the distribution of goods for export, and he coordinates flows of imports too. He is part of the international elite. The local entrepreneur can use the services of the metropolitan entrepreneur for the conduct of his export trade if he wishes. Many local entrepreneurs may not have sufficient expertise to deal directly with import merchants in foreign countries, and may not even be familiar with warehousing arrangements in the metropolis.[19] The skills of the local entrepreneur relative to those of the metropolitan entrepreneur is one of the major factors that determines the degree of 'dependency' of the region on the metropolis.

The figure also illustrates the role of banks as financial intermediaries: they take savings accumulated by households and channel them to the entrepreneurs. The households could in principle lend directly to the entrepreneurs, but if they did so they would be unable to spread their risks, they would reduce their liquidity, and they would lack the specialised knowledge of the bank about which entrepreneurs to back. There is a local bank and a metropolitan bank, just as there was a local entrepreneur and a metropolitan entrepreneur. Metropolitan banks can allocate funds between different regions, allowing 'deficit' regions with a high level of entrepreneurial activity, but a lack of wealthy investors, to borrow funds from 'surplus' regions.

From a network perspective, non-profit associations are of particular interest. Several types of association are illustrated in the figure. Some are *representative* associations, such as trades unions and employers associations, whilst others are *accrediting* associations, such as professional associations which screen their members for competence. Another important form of association is the *club*; this includes churches, political parties, as well as sporting and leisure clubs. All of these associations have an important role in coordinating the flow of labour services. They discharge this role in connection

---

[19] A. Popp, *Business Structure, Business Culture and the Industrial District: The Potteries, c.1850–1914* (Ashgate, 2001).

with educational institutions. The figure distinguishes between local educational institutions, such as schools and teaching universities, and elite educational institutions such as research universities. The latter tend to be based near to the metropolis (though not invariably so). These elite institutions supply labour to metropolitan activities such as entrepreneurship and banking, and also provide the individuals who determine policy in the professional associations. The policies of these associations in turn feed through to employers and local educational institutions.

Cordial relations between institutions in the not-for-profit sector are important for economic success, because they help to overcome potential coordination failures in the labour market. Good relations between not-for-profit institutions and for-profit institutions such as firms are also important - for example, in promoting good industrial relations. The figure shows that the economy depends upon a complex web of inter-institutional relations, and all of these relations need to be maintained in good working order if the regional economy is to prosper.

By and large, the type of networking that promotes coordination of this kind is vertical networking of an open, visible and transparent form based on a tough but forgiving morality. Indeed, most horizontal networks are suppressed in a figure of this kind, since only one representative entity of each type is shown. The focus of the figure, therefore, is on those types of network that enhance overall economic performance, rather than those which inhibit it.

The economic logic of RBNs

Although the diagram presented above is very useful as a descriptive tool, its main purpose is to predict a network structure to which all successful regions will be found to conform, whether they have yet been studied or not. In other words, it encapsulates the theory of RBNs developed in this chapter. Popperian methodology indicates that one of the tasks of future research is to attempt to refute this theory – if it can.[20]

Unsuccessful regions will tend to have fewer network linkages than those shown in the figure. Although they may have information flowing along similar channels, it will not be high-trust communication sustained by a network, and so coordination will be weak, and this will lead the economy to underperform.

A weakness in one link may not be a serious problem if another parallel link is available to replace it. Thus, a lack of trust between local entrepreneurs

---

[20] Namely, the objective of theory is to derive a mutually consistent set of hypotheses each of which can, in principle, be refuted using available evidence but which will hopefully survive the process of attempted refutation.

and metropolitan entrepreneurs may not be a problem if the region possesses able local entrepreneurs who can organise a direct export trade. But if there is a lack of trust between regional entrepreneurs and metropolitan entrepreneurs, and local entrepreneurs are incapable of organising a direct export trade, then the economy will underperform because export marketing will be weak. Again, some economies may rely on collective bargaining to coordinate the labour market, whilst others may rely on intermediation by local clubs instead. But if an economy has no local clubs, and collective bargaining is adversarial, then there is no mechanism for labour market coordination at all. This economy too will underperform. Thus, the fewer the vertical networks, the more likely are such coordination failures, and the poorer regional economic performance will be.

Conclusion

This chapter has demonstrated the value of modern economics in developing a simple yet rigorous theory of regional business networks. A schematic representation of a regional economy has been developed to facilitate the testing of the theory. Although the theory postulates rationality and equilibrium, it is still highly relevant to the interpretation of historical evidence, and has, indeed, been developed with this particular application in mind.

The analysis in this chapter indicates that the strength of the links with the metropolis is a crucial factor in channelling the specialised expertise of the metropolis into the region, particularly in connection with the export trade. It is unrealistic to expect a region to have a large amount of specialised expertise when it is not a natural hub of communication. If a region is to survive without significant dependence on the metropolis then it must have substantial entrepreneurial resources of its own. It is no good trying to make do without such resources altogether.

The metropolis tends to be a magnet for ambitious entrepreneurs, because it is there that the biggest profit opportunities are to be found. As a result, there is a natural tendency for able young people to migrate to the metropolis. If a region is to become a centre of entrepreneurship in its own right then it must be sufficiently attractive to retain its local entrepreneurs. A congenial political climate, with low taxation, and social attitudes that accord respect to 'new money' as well as 'old', will encourage entrepreneurs to settle in the region. On the other hand, excessive industrialisation may cause them to leave in search of a better quality of life. Social isolation caused by a very remote location will be a deterrent too.

If the climate is right, and local entrepreneurs remain, then networking will flourish. The entrepreneurs will invest in strong RBNs and IRBNs because they have strategic reasons for doing so. Networks will develop without government intervention because they promote the interests of the entrepreneurs. Without strong local entrepreneurs, on the other hand, there will be less incentive to invest in RBNs because the majority of local business people can derive only limited economic benefit from them. The RBNs that do emerge are more likely to be collusive; their aim will not be to promote efficiency, but to redistribute income to vested interested groups instead.

The idea that the quality of local entrepreneurship holds the key to regional prosperity is, of course, simply an application to a region of a proposition which has already achieved widespread recognition in the field of economic development, when applied to the nation state. It is an obvious and rather unsurprising conclusion. There are sound economic reasons for believing that entrepreneurship is a more fundamental factor in regional economic performance than is the network structure. It makes more sense to see network structure as a complement to entrepreneurship rather than as a substitute for it. The most able entrepreneurs invest in both RBNs and IRBNs because they need the networks to access the information required to maximise the potential of the regional export trade. Network structure is therefore best regarded as part of the transmission mechanism by which entrepreneurship impacts on performance, rather than a completely independent determinant of performance in its own right.

One reason why this result has not been properly recognised is that many economists retain a prejudice that entrepreneurship only flourishes under conditions of impersonal atomistic competition. According to this view, each firm is an isolated economic unit, converting factors of production into finished product independently of other firms as suppliers of inputs or distributors of its output. Once the interdependence between firms at different stages of production is recognised, however, the crucial issue of inter-firm coordination comes to the fore. The potential advantage of vertical networks over arm's length trade or vertical integration becomes apparent. It can be seen that competition takes place, not so much between firms, as between different networks. Each vertical network represents an alternative path linking raw materials and factors of production to consumers of finished goods. Within each network, firms 'cooperate in order to compete'.

Recent literature on RBNs takes account of this insight, but tends to distort it, by focusing on cooperation between artisans, rather than on cooperation between merchants, who are the true entrepreneurs. A self-employed artisan in an industrial district may be a totally passive recipient of orders, competing intensely against other local artisans for the work that the merchants put out. Lacking scientific education, he may be highly secretive about the 'tricks of the trade' that he believes he has learned from experience, and which he sees as the basis for any cost advantage that he possesses over local rivals. As the owner-manager of a small business, subject to strong competitive discipline, the artisan does in fact operate under the kind of isolation depicted above.

It is the merchant who is the true 'networker'. The merchant processes information rather than the product itself. He obtains his information through contact with other merchants operating at adjacent stages of production or distribution. These sources of information provide the merchant with a wider view of competition than the artisan possesses. A successful merchant realises that, at the global level, the region from which he sources his production is competing with other specialised regions around the world, whilst his particular network is competing with other networks rooted in the same region for its share of the regional export trade. The merchant therefore has the breadth of vision to recognise both the importance of vertical networks in maintaining export market share, and the value of local horizontal networks in which competing merchants cooperate to maintain the export base on which they all depend. Focusing on the merchant, rather than the artisan, has the added advantage that merchants record much of the information they receive, in day books, ledgers and diaries, whereas artisans normally do not. This provides a reliable source of evidence on networking which is missing in the other case.

In conclusion, it is recommended that future historical research on RBNs should concentrate on testing propositions which are grounded in rigorous economic reasoning. Research should focus on the observable aspects of networking, such as the behaviour of merchant networks and local not-for-profit associations, rather than unobservable aspects, such as informal socialisation amongst self-employed artisans. Future research should also pay more attention to the different types of network that can emerge in a regional economy, and their different implications for economic performance.

Chapter 3

The Manchester industrial district, 1750–1939: Clustering, networking and performance[1]

John F. Wilson and John Singleton

Introduction

When Britain emerged as the world's 'First Industrial Nation', one of its principal engines of growth was located within a thirty-mile radius of Manchester in North West England. While by the mid-twentieth century this industrial district was still a significant economic centre, not only had its prominent position been successfully challenged by a host of late-comers, but also relatively little effort had been made to adapt to a range of exogenous pressures. Of course, one might question whether these challenges were beyond the control of a single business community, given the general problems faced by the British economy after 1880. On the other hand, it is vital to consider the co-ordination and signalling mechanisms devised by the Manchester business elite, as well as the actual responses implemented at varying stages in the region's life-cycle. This will provide a better understanding of the regional dynamics that contributed to the evolutionary pattern of Manchester's industrial district.

Central to our work will be an application of Swann's notion that four stages can be identified in the life-cycle of a region.[2] Overlapping this analysis, we shall then investigate whom the key 'change agents' were at varying times in the evolutionary process. In particular, it is vital to stress that as the region passed through Swann's stages the regional business elite would appear to have metamorphosed. Initially, the mercantile community played a key role in

---

[1] In completing this chapter, the authors would like to acknowledge the advice offered by John Walton, Andrew Popp and the other contributors to this collection.

[2] G.M. Peter Swann, 'Towards a Model of Clustering in High-technology Industries', in G.M. Peter Swann, M. Prevezer and D. Stout (eds), *The Dynamics of Industrial Clustering* (Oxford University Press, 1998).

building the industrial district. By the 1880s, however, industrialists were far more prominent, only to be usurped by bankers and politicians during the increasingly difficult interwar decades. Whatever the reasons behind these changes, an issue we shall address at varying points in the chapter, it is clear that the elite failed to adapt established patterns of networking to the changing environment, creating major problems when market signals had to be interpreted and fresh messages disseminated to the broader community. As a result, the business networks became increasingly dysfunctional, frequently relying on defensive collusion as an alternative to aggressive change. This challenges the excessive optimism voiced by those analysts of business networking who regard these informal institutions as essential to the viability of industrial districts. Above all, it is apparent that to be successful in the long term industrial districts must adapt all aspects of both their working practices and economic structure, posing enormous challenges to the incumbent business elite. It was in this crucial respect that the Manchester industrial district failed, initiating a series of problems that persisted throughout the twentieth century.

The Manchester industrial district and a life-cycle typology

Sited at the confluence of the rivers Mersey and Irwell, Manchester nestles into the foothills of the Pennine mountain range at the southern-most edge of Lancashire amidst over 200 towns and villages in northern Cheshire and southern Lancashire. Extending from Stockport and Macclesfield to the south, as far as Preston, Blackburn and Burnley in the north, and east to Oldham, Rochdale and the Rossendale Valley, one can claim that at least up to the early-twentieth century a distinctive Manchester industrial district existed. While most people living in Preston or Burnley would have been surprised to learn that their economic destinies revolved around Manchester, up to the 1930s certainly the business community would have acknowledged the heavy dependence upon this city as the driving force behind the district's economic performance.

Before going on to explain the reasons behind its emergence, it is vital to stress that the Manchester industrial district has never embraced Liverpool and the Merseyside region (including towns like Warrington, St. Helens and Widnes). Indeed, even though there were strong links through the cotton trade, Liverpool developed into one of the world's leading ports independently of Manchester, while its immediate hinterland was a base for coal and chemicals.[3] One might even stress that the rivalry between Liverpool and Manchester acted as an important stimulus to the respective business communities, especially from the 1880s when the latter was trying to break the stranglehold the former held on the importation of raw cotton and export of finished goods. At the

---

[3]   Kenneth Warren, *Chemical Foundations: The Alkali Industry in Britain to 1926* (Oxford University Press, 1983).

same time, having access to an international port like Liverpool was one of the key agglomeration factors to which one would be obliged to point when explaining the rise of the Manchester industrial district.

In explaining these agglomeration factors, while space constraints limit the extent to which one can elaborate on each factor, it is important to list the principal reasons why the Manchester industrial district evolved into such an economic power-house from the eighteenth century.[4] The key factors were:

- access to an international port (Liverpool);
- the complementary development of textiles (linen and fustians) and engineering from the sixteenth century;
- the availability of adequate supplies of skilled and unskilled labour;
- the emergence of other support industries and services;
- the construction of an extensive transport infrastructure: turnpike trusts in the eighteenth century; canals, starting with the Bridgewater Canal connecting Manchester and local coalfields in the 1760s; and by 1830 the world's first commercial railway linking Manchester and Liverpool;
- the rapid development of a major coalfield in South Lancashire;
- *and, above all*, the expertise and resources of a local mercantile community.

Given the emphasis placed on the last point, it will be important to return to this factor. At this stage, though, we can conclude that the Manchester industrial district was beginning to reap rich rewards from what Alfred Marshall described as 'the localization of industry'.[5] It was this combination of factors that provided enormous advantages in allowing the exploitation of external economies of scale and of scope in marketing, in labour, in the supply of inputs and in many other transaction costs. Once cotton spinning had become economically feasible, due to the technological innovations introduced between 1770 and 1790, the district was launched into the 'take-off' phase, attracting an even larger number of suppliers, sub-contractors and essential factors of production into the vicinity.[6] These agglomeration effects made Manchester into one of the era's most dynamic centres of industrial capitalism, exerting large multiplier effects on the rest of the region. 'Manchester at this

---

[4]   For more detailed work on these factors, see G. Timmins, *Made in Lancashire. A History of Regional Industrialisation* (Manchester University Press, 1998), and John K. Walton, *Lancashire. A Social History, 1558–1939* (Manchester University Press, 1987).

[5]   Alfred Marshall, *Principles of Economics* (Macmillan, 1890), p. 221.

[6]   For more detailed work on this subject, see D.A. Farnie, *The English Cotton Industry and the World Markets 1815–1896* (Oxford University Press, 1979), and Mary B. Rose, *Firms, Networks and Business Values. The British and American Cotton Industries since 1750* (Cambridge University Press, 2000).

time was more than a factory town; it was an industrial metropolis, the capital of a manufacturing empire with world markets.'[7]

A useful way of explaining the evolution of this particular industrial district is to apply Swann's work on life-cycles. Although others have adapted the standard product life-cycle typology to describe different issues, Swann has rightly claimed that most industrial districts pass through four distinct stages, namely, critical mass, take-off, saturation, and maturity.[8] These stages have been tracked in Table 3.1, where more detailed information has been provided to illustrate the practical impact of each stage's characteristics. Again, it is difficult to devote much space to a full explanation of how each stage materialised, other than to note that the Manchester industrial district would provide rich material to support the work not only of Swann, but also of Enright and of Scott.[9] Above all, though, the main conclusion one can draw from Table 3.1 is that there is no simple relationship between the establishment of an industrial district and long-term economic success. While firms might be capable of developing and extracting agglomeration economies in one period, this does not necessarily equip the region with an ability to cope with major changes. Indeed, the evolutionary process contains dangers, as well as advantages, with significant 'agglomeration diseconomies' arising from, for example, the failure to adapt to either exogenous pressures or the internal problems associated with what Olson describes as 'institutional sclerosis'.[10]

Linked to this issue is another key dimension of Swann's work on regional life-cycles, namely, the contention that in the 'saturation' stage clusters ought to diversify their industrial structure, rather than compete head-on with emerging rivals. This indicates the crucial importance of a district's principal 'change-agents',[11] given that they must play a major role in detecting signals and transmitting reliable information to the rest of the business community. Which groups performed this role in the Manchester industrial district? Did the identities of these groups change over time? To what extent did contemporaries respond to their messages? These are the key issues to which we must now turn.

---

[7]   L.S. Marshall, 'The Emergence of the First Industrial City: Manchester, 1780–1850', in C.F. Ware (ed), *The Cultural Approach to History* (Oxford University Press, 1940).

[8]   Swann, 'Towards a Model of Clustering'.

[9]   Ibid.

[10]   M. Olson, *The Rise and Decline of Nations* (Yale University Press, 1982).

[11]   This term has been borrowed from A. Pettigrew, *The Awakening Giant. Continuity and Change in ICI* (Blackwell, 1985).

Table 3.1
The life-cycle of the Manchester industrial district

Stage	Characteristics	Manchester's Experience
Critical Mass	Clustering of expertise and factors of production	**Up to 1780:** development of linen and fustian production, controlled by Manchester merchants. Heavy investment in turnpikes and (from 1760s) canals
Take-off	Often associated with key inventions and innovations, which alongside clustering of expertise and factors of production give the region competitive advantage	**1780–1850:** Cotton spinning and, later, weaving becomes technologically feasible, resulting in rapid growth of factory production. Royal Exchange takes on role of regional co-ordination. Mercantile community augmented by foreign merchants. Manchester Chamber of Commerce influences national trade policy debates. Multiplier effects result in complimentary development of engineering, bleaching and dyeing. Further expansion of canal network and rail transport pioneered in North West
Peak Entry	Cost of clustering start to outweigh benefits, with rate of growth falling away, innovation rare and competition increasing from low-cost producers	**1850–1920:** Cotton industry expands to become major British exporter. Growing sophistication of Manchester mercantile community, Royal Exchange expanding and local stock exchange linked with industrial investment. Little diversification into Second Industrial Revolution industries, in spite of Trafford Park and Manchester Ship Canal
Saturation	Rivals offer superior advantages for new firms and decline sets in across the older district	**1920–1939:** (continuing over the four decades), rapid decline of cotton and heavy engineering in spite (because?) of 1919 investment boom. Banks gain stronger grip of strategy. Very limited diversification of industrial base and integration of old sectors

The 'change agents'

It was already apparent by the early seventeenth century that a wealthy and extensively connected mercantile community was coming to be regarded as the lynchpin connecting many aspects of the Lancashire economy. By that time, the introduction of fustian cloth (combining linen and cotton) was rapidly overhauling the well-established linen trade. Furthermore, Manchester merchants were the acknowledged masters of manufacturing and selling textiles.[12] As Walton suggests, in explaining why Lancashire became the major centre for cotton textiles, arguments based on mercantile traditions carry more weight than assertions about the climate or the unregulated political scene.[13] In effect, merchants were the district's 'change-agents'. It was this group which created the 'critical mass' required at stage one of the life-cycle (see Table 3.1), providing not only commercial expertise and business contacts, but also a significant proportion of the capital required for its industrial, transport and marketing activities.[14]

Having stressed that the Manchester mercantile community was the pivot around which much of the region's economy revolved, one should remember that Manchester was always portrayed as the factory town *par excellence*. For example, reference is frequently made to the famous lithographic reproduction featured in the *Illustrated London News* of 4 July 1857 showing over a hundred factory chimneys belching out clouds of black smoke. Indeed, until the 1850s Manchester remained the world's largest cotton manufacturing town. At the same time, as Lloyd-Jones and Lewis have shown, Manchester's economic fortunes depended much more on the commercial operations of merchants, transport firms and financiers.[15] While in 1825 cotton factories accounted for 12 per cent of all capital invested in Manchester property, warehousing had absorbed 43 per cent. Moreover, not only did most of the North West's cotton industrialists and merchants establish a warehouse in Manchester, traders from all over the world used the town as a base, indicating how the mercantile community was highly cosmopolitan in character and connections.[16] As Farnie and Nakaoka note about the period up to 1880: 'The dominant figure in Victorian Manchester always remained the merchant, its central institution the [Royal] *Exchange*, and its most typical building the warehouse'.[17]

---

[12]   Rose, *Firms, Networks and Business Values*, pp. 72–4.

[13]   Walton, *Lancashire*, pp. 65–6.

[14]   S.D. Chapman, *Merchant Enterprise in Britain: From the Industrial Revolution to World War II* (Cambridge University Press, 1992).

[15]   R. Lloyd-Jones and M.J. Lewis, *Manchester and the Age of the Factory: The Business Structure of Cottonopolis in the Industrial Revolution* (Croom Helm, 1988), pp. 107 and 115.

[16]   Chapman, *Merchant Enterprise*, pp. 4–9.

[17]   D.A. Farnie and T. Nakaoka (2000), 'Region and Nation', in D.A. Farnie, T. Nakaoka, D.J. Jeremy, J.F. Wilson and T. Abe (eds), *Region and Strategy in Britain and Japan. Business in Lancashire and Kansai, 1890–1990* (Routledge, 2000), p. 14.

In this context, it is also vital to discuss the role of the *Royal Exchange*. An informal cotton exchange had been operating in the coffee-houses and taverns around Market Street since the 1720s. So important was this informal institution that in 1809 a purpose-built Exchange was opened. In 1851, it was renamed the *Royal Exchange*, while in 1874 a much-expanded facility was built to accommodate the several thousand registered members.[18] Although its principal function was the buying and selling of cotton goods, others associated with the industry also traded there, including dyers and engineering firms. Above all, the *Exchange* provided an essential medium of communication concerning all aspects of local and international trade, making it essential that all those involved in the industry should either attend regularly or send representatives capable of transmitting vital information.[19]

Another central institution linking the regional business community was the *Manchester Chamber of Commerce*. Founded in 1820 as a vehicle to further the interests of local trade, the *Chamber* has been described as the district's business parliament.[20] Although its membership was dominated by the cotton industry, and especially cotton merchants, the *Chamber* brought together the elites of most local industries and services, facilitating the exchange of opinion and information on a range of matters. In particular, there emerged a 'Manchester School' of economics built around demands for free trade and reduced governmental interference in the economy. The founders of the Anti-Corn Law League, Richard Cobden and John Bright, were prominent members of the *Manchester Chamber of Commerce*.[21] Although there were many reasons why Britain adopted Free Trade policies, the 'Manchester School' played such a prominent role in lobbying for this ideology that throughout the nineteenth century the North West was regarded as the home of liberal policies.

In between 1780 and 1850, the Manchester industrial district was clearly experiencing a 'take-off' phase that spread from its core city to many of the smaller towns and villages. At the heart of this activity was a community of merchants that had been largely responsible for generating the successes achieved by Manchester and its hinterland. With specific reference to its core industry, this industrial district was also highly successful, because by 1883 the twenty-one principal centres of the Lancashire cotton industry operated just over thirty-nine million spindles, or approximately forty per cent of the world total. Such was the commercial importance of Manchester that 4.8 million visitors attended its Royal Jubilee Exhibition in 1887, while by that time thirty

---

[18] D.A. Farnie, 'An Index of Commercial Activity: The Membership of the Manchester Royal Exchange, 1809–1948', *Business History*, ol. 21 (1979), pp. 97–106.

[19] Rose, *Firms, Networks and Business Values*, pp. 73–4.

[20] A. Redford, *Manchester Merchants and Foreign Trade, 1794–1858* (Manchester University Press, 1956), p. 73.

[21] R. Lloyd-Jones, 'Merchant City: The Manchester Business Community, the Trade Cycle and Commercial Policy, c.1820–1846', in A. Marrison (ed), *Free Trade and Its Reception, 1815–1860. Vol. I, Freedom and Trade* (Routledge, 1998), pp. 86–104.

foreign consulates had been established in the city.[22] At the same time, in fuelling this expansion, the established business elite was also attracting other groups into the region, laying the basis for what was a subtle shift in the balance of power between 1880 and 1920.

Networks and change agents

Having outlined the 'take-off' stage, and especially the role played by the 'change-agents' in stimulating regional economic development, it is important to benchmark Manchester against Marshall's definition of an industrial district. In particular, Marshall recognized that industrial districts possessed a *genius locii*, or distinct social structure, that 'cannot be quickly acquired ... [but] yields *gratis* to the manufacturers ... great advantages that are not easily to be had elsewhere'.[23] This emphasises how co-ordination occurred through a range of mechanisms that existed on a continuum stretching from markets to hierarchies. In the case of Manchester and its surrounding district, Marshall observed that vertical specialisation arose largely out of the role played by such institutions as the *Royal Exchange*. Indeed, by the 1850s any move towards vertical integration of spinning, weaving and selling had waned dramatically, indicating how reliance upon externalities became a hallmark of the Lancashire cotton industry. Larger firms were also likely to trade exclusively with a narrow range of sub-contractors and suppliers, indicating that while Lancashire markets remained highly competitive, they were intensely personalised.[24] It was also a structure that persisted for many decades, because Broadberry and Marrison have demonstrated that the reliance upon external economies of scale in cotton textiles continued to be vital to the industry's performance right up to the Second World War.[25]

The personal character of commercial relationships requires further explanation, because in highlighting how there was an air of 'collegiality' to the *Exchange's* activities one comes closer to understanding the dynamics of intra-district operations.[26] In this context, it is interesting to see how McGovern and Mottiar have outlined a system of 'co-operative competition', drawing on the Foucauldian concept of networking in which co-operation and competition exist symbiotically.[27] Such is the extent to which each sub-group relies on the others that the dominant group accepts the need to compromise or share power

---

[22] Farnie and Nakaoka, 'Region and Nation', p. 23.
[23] Marshall, *Trade and Industry*, pp. 284–7.
[24] Ibid., pp. 599–603.
[25] S. Broadberry and A. Marrison, 'External Economies of Scale in the Lancashire Cotton Industry, 1900–1950', *Economic History Review*, Vol. LV, No. 1 (2002), pp. 51–77.
[26] A. Howe, 'The Business Community', in M. Rose (ed), *The Lancashire Cotton Industry* (Carnegie Publishing, 1996).
[27] S. McGovern and Z. Mottiar, 'Co-operative Competition: A Foucauldian Perspective', Dublin City University Business School Research Papers, No. 20 (1997), pp. 7–9.

in the interests of improving the district's competitive advantage. In Foucauldian terms, 'power is the network itself'. With all firms operating according to established norms, they become embedded in the local socio-cultural system, accepting the need for a degree of self-regulation that limits opportunistic activity. In effect, then, each firm and entrepreneur recognised that regional prosperity depended upon the health of the network as a whole, giving rise to collective endeavour that sustained the competitive advantages achieved through either technological innovation or industrial agglomeration.

Foucauldian theory throws new light on the North West's co-operative structure. Casson would prefer to emphasise 'warranted mutual trust' as the essence of how business communities operate, with moral and social sanctions providing the necessary discipline,[28] but trust may in part have its basis in the recognition of a common interest in the survival of the network. This highlights once again what Staber has called the 'key feature of the industrial district model', namely, the 'embeddedness of firms in a distinctive social fabric'.[29] In Manchester's case, the business community was not only bound by the norms of the *Royal Exchange*, but also by a strong sense of community. Furthermore, by 1800 what Walton refers to as the 'gentry-industrialists' were extensively linked through marriage to the major families of the North West, creating a dense social network that flourished throughout this era.[30]

When one also examines the non-economic impact of this elite, it had clearly been extremely active. For example, exactly the same businessmen had also been responsible for establishing other permanent institutional features of the Manchester scene, including the *Manchester Literary and Philosophical Society* (1781), the *Portico Library* (1806), the *Royal Manchester Institution* (1825), the *Manchester Statistical Society* (1834), and a host of charitable and philanthropic ventures.[31] By the late-nineteenth century, Manchester also possessed a range of educational institutions of considerable merit, including the Manchester Technical School (1882) and Owen's College (1851). Aped by their contemporaries in most of the major North West towns like Bolton, Blackburn and Preston, the regional bourgeoisie displayed all the scientific and philanthropic interests of their counterparts in other major European cities. This was a further means of embedding the bourgeoisie into the local socio-cultural infrastructure, confirming their value as 'change-agents' at a time of constant flux.

---

[28] See the Chapter 2 in this volume.

[29] U. Staber, 'The Social Embeddedness of Industrial District Networks', in U. Staber, N. Schaefer and B. Sharma (eds), *Business Networks: Prospects for Regional Development* (de Gruyter, 1996), p. 148

[30] Walton, *Lancashire*, p. 129. See also Rose, *Firms, Networks and Business Values*, pp. 74–5.

[31] M.E. Rose, 'Culture, Philanthropy and the Manchester Middles Classes', in Alan J. Kidd and K.W. Roberts (eds), *City, Class and Culture. Studies of Social Policy and Cultural Production in Victorian Manchester* (Manchester University Press, 1985), pp. 103–14.

This image of a cohesive regional business community working within a system based on 'co-operative competition' would appear to support the claims of those who believe that networking has been a central reason why industrial clusters have been so successful. Of course, one must question the degree of cohesion arising from these linkages. In the first place, at least until the 1840s an intense rivalry characterised relations between the Tory and liberal factions within the business community.[32] In simple terms, the Tory faction was Anglican and allied to big business interests (the Peels and Birleys), while the liberal group was dominated by religious dissent (Unitarians) and small-scale enterprise. Naturally, there were exceptions to these rules, because several large-scale industrialists and merchants (Philips, Heywood, Greg and Potter) supported the liberal cause. The *Manchester Chamber of Commerce* also helped to smooth party differences during the 1840s, creating an unprecedented degree of cohesion within the local bourgeoisie based on an allegiance to Free Trade.[33] In effect, then, while there were extensive kinship networks reinforced by intermarriage, the North West business community would appear to have had as many fissures as linkages. On the other hand, it seems unlikely that these political and religious divisions were anything other than tangential to the manner in which the regional economy functioned. Under the dominating influence of a mercantile elite, the Manchester industrial district managed to sustain its growth in spite of these fissures, reflecting the sanctity of economic over any other interests.

The multiplier effect and networking

With cotton textile production growing rapidly from the 1770s, and Manchester's mercantile community controlling the whole process from their warehouses and the *Royal Exchange*, it was clear to contemporaries that enormous opportunities were being created for complementary industries. Indeed, just as it would be a mistake to see Manchester as primarily an industrial town, it would be wrong to classify the North West as solely a cotton textile district (see Table 3.1). In this context, it is vital to stress the growing importance of engineering to the North West, building on an established artisanal tradition linked to clock- and watch-making.[34] Many of the early cotton entrepreneurs – McConnell & Kennedy, Andrew Murray, Robert Owen and Peter Ewart – had actually started in business as textile machine-makers.

---

[32] See V.A.C. Gatrell, 'The Commercial Middle Class in Manchester, 1820–57', unpublished Ph.D. thesis (Cambridge University, 1971).

[33] A. Kidd, 'Introduction: The Middle Class in Nineteenth Century Manchester', in Kidd and Roberts (eds), *City, Class and Culture*, pp. 12–13; A. Marrison, *British Business and Protection, 1903–32* (Oxford University Press, 1996), p. 52.

[34] A.E. Musson and E. Robinson, 'The Origins of Engineering in Lancashire', in A.E. Musson and E. Robinson, *Science and Technology in the Industrial Revolution* (Manchester University Press, 1969), pp. 440–55 and 473–6.

By the 1820s, though, a specialised engineering industry had emerged, with pioneering names like William Fairbairn, James Nasmyth, Joseph Whitworth and Richard Roberts introducing radically new techniques and machine tools.

As a result, the Manchester region became Britain's largest centre for engineering, outpacing Birmingham and London by the 1820s and maintaining that status for at least a century. A highly diversified product portfolio also evolved, with famous firms like Beyer, Peacock (locomotives), Mather & Platt (pumps and engines) and Crossley's (general engineering) sustaining the earlier achievements of Whitworth and Roberts.[35] Furthermore, this diversity was certainly not confined to Manchester, because engineering became a major employer in its own right in towns like Oldham, Stockport, Bolton, Hyde, Blackburn and Preston. While much of this activity was linked to the production of textile machinery, with world-class firms like Platt Brothers (Oldham) exporting equipment to mills all over the world,[36] the region developed a wide range of engineering sectors that competed aggressively in British and international markets.

In addition to engineering, leading firms in other sectors were attracted to the North West by the cotton industry's expansion. For example, having developed his famous rubber-coated material in Glasgow, in the 1820s Charles Mackintosh established a complex of factories in central Manchester to produce rainwear. In 1856, following William Perkin's discovery that aniline dye could be extracted from coal-tar, a synthetic dyestuffs industry emerged in Manchester. Although weaker than their German counterparts, firms like the Clayton Aniline Co. and Levinstein's played an important role in supplying local cotton manufacturers with dyes and chemicals used in the finishing trades. Other finishing trades like bleaching also clustered around the cotton industry, while by 1911 over 40,000 people worked in clothing manufacture.[37]

Of course, the emergence of these industries at the 'take-off' stage was highly dependent upon the success of cotton textiles as the district's core sector. At the same time, as they matured over the course of the nineteenth century their leading figures came to play significant roles within the formal and informal institutions. Subtle changes also occurred within cotton textiles, with some concentration of ownership and the emergence of an increasingly powerful group of industrialists. Toms has outlined these changes in greatest detail, noting how: 'By the 1900s "empires" of mills, controlled by individuals and cliques [of share-owning directors]' came to dominate the industry.[38] This

---

[35] A.E. Musson, *The Growth of British Industry* (Batsford, 1978), pp. 114–8 and 183–6.

[36] D.A. Farnie, 'The Textile Machine-making Industry and the World Market, 1870-1960', *Business History*, Vol. 32 (1990), pp. 150–65; Timmins, *Made in Lancashire*, pp. 299–309.

[37] Timmins, *Made in Lancashire*, p. 310.

[38] J.S. Toms, 'The Rise of Modern Accounting and the Fall of the Public Company: the Lancashire Cotton Mills 1870–1914', *Accounting, Organizations and Society*, Vol. 27 (2002), p. 71.

trend is further reinforced in the chapter contributed by Toms and Filatotchev, where clear evidence of 'hierarchical networks of companies and their amalgamated structures' is presented.[39] The apogee of this movement occurred around the turn of the century, when as we shall see in the next section a series of mergers created giant concerns like English Sewing Cotton, Fine Cotton Spinners' & Doublers' Association and the Calico Printers' Association.[40] With headquarters in Manchester, and using predominantly Manchester capital and management, this further reinforced the city's control over the district's core industry, albeit no longer under mercantile control. Furthermore, as Berghoff concludes: 'This unparalleled degree of regional integration led to the formation of a regional rather than an urban elite, whose business and private interests ignored municipal boundaries'.[41]

When one combines the emergence of a vibrant and growing range of industries with the major changes that occurred within cotton textiles after the 1880s, it is apparent that the industrialists had usurped the 'change-agent' role formerly played by Manchester merchants across the district as a whole. Of course, as we stressed earlier, such was the reliance upon external economies of scale within cotton textiles especially, that merchants remained important components within the industry, not least at the *Royal Exchange*. However, their former dominance was successfully challenged by the increasingly powerful industrialists. The key issue to address, then, is whether the industrialists were able both to sustain the economic momentum achieved in the 'take-off' and 'peak entry' phases (see Table 3.1), and to cope with the mounting problems associated with 'saturation'.

The challenge of change

From the 1880s, the Manchester industrial district was faced with a series of challenges. In the first place, diseconomies like the increased price of land and labour were beginning to threaten competitiveness. At the same time, competition was also intensifying, especially in overseas markets, as both established and new districts started to mount a strong challenge to Britain's economic dominance. In addition, the 'Second Industrial Revolution', associated with electricity, synthetic chemicals and the internal combustion engine, was presenting new opportunities to the world economy. Finally, the First World War and its aftermath had a devastating impact on Britain's traditional export markets, materially affecting industries like cotton, engineering and coal. How would the business community cope with such

---

[39] See Chapter 4 in this volume.

[40] Rose, *Firms, Networks and Business Values*, pp. 173–5.

[41] H. Berghoff, 'Regional Variations in Provincial Business Biography: The Case of Birmingham, Bristol and Manchester, 1870–1914', *Business History*, Vol. 37, No. 1 (1995), pp. 71–2.

challenges? To what extent would they either 'stick to their knitting' or convert wholesale to the new industries so extensively developed in countries like the USA and Germany? How would the district's co-ordination and signalling mechanisms cope with these challenges? These were the issues confronting entrepreneurs between 1880 and 1940.

According to Swann's life-cycle typology, at the 'saturation' stage a business community must decide whether it needs to diversify away from its original activities.[42] While this begs an important question about the optimal level of diversification required, in terms of the challenge facing North West business by the late-nineteenth century it was evident that new strategies were required. In particular, it was incumbent upon the regional business network that had performed so well over the previous hundred years to respond effectively to the challenges and opportunities at later stages in the evolutionary cycle. At the same time, as we noted at the end of the last section, industrialists had only recently replaced merchants as the main 'change-agents' within the Manchester industrial district. It is also clear that when faced with intensifying competition and increasingly rapid technological change, the district's networks were increasingly tempted into collusive action of a highly defensive kind. Of course, Victorian Lancashire businessmen have always been described as fiercely individualistic, brooking no interference with the management of their enterprises.[43] On the other hand, during the period 1880–1950 many were willing to sacrifice certain aspects of their independence and participate in a wide range of organisations linked to labour and pricing issues.[44] For example, powerful employers' associations were formed in several industries as a means of dealing with the rise of strong trade unions.[45] While these bodies were generally successful in reinforcing managerial prerogatives, price cartels and loose holding company arrangements proved to be disastrous.[46]

The contrast between employers' associations and cartels illustrates the pervasive reluctance to allow outsiders any influence over management strategy. While businessmen were happy to combine with others in the interests of thwarting trade unionism, as they baulked at allowing outsiders influence over such matters as pricing or market share, cartels and holding companies lacked rigour.[47] For example, there appeared firms like the Fine Cotton Spinners' and Doublers' Association (in 1898, involving 31 firms), the Calico Printers' Association (1899; 46 firms), the Bleachers' Association (1900; 53 firms), and the British Cotton and Wool Dyers' Association (1900; 46 firms).

---

[42]   Swann, 'Towards a Model of Clustering', pp. 53–5 and 62–6.

[43]   John F. Wilson, *British Business History, 1720–1994* (Manchester University Press, 1995) p. 45.

[44]   Rose, *Firms, Networks and Business Values*, pp. 222–4.

[45]   Arthur McIvor, *Organised Capital: Employers' Associations and Industrial Relations in Northern England, 1880–1939* (Cambridge University Press, 1996).

[46]   Wilson, *British Business History*, pp. 100–2.

[47]   Ibid., pp. 103–6.

However, even though each of these firms could have exploited internal economies of scale by rationalising production and management, each constituent firm was given almost complete autonomy, thereby limiting the group's ability to capture the potential benefits of merger. Although by 1914 they had all been reorganised, and more integrated structures implemented by smaller executive bodies based in Manchester, they still failed to effect much improvement in the industry's competitive performance. At the same time, such were the cost advantages enjoyed in particular by Japanese competitors that it was unlikely these mergers could have staved off the loss of export markets.[48]

Whether or not the North West cotton textiles industry could have overcome the onslaught from Japanese competition is an issue we shall return to in the next section, when the dismal interwar decades are assessed. It is clear, though, that local businessmen only entered into merger arrangements in a half-hearted fashion. Similarly, mergers in engineering and brewing failed to produce the synergies anticipated by their promoters.[49] This failure reveals some fundamental flaws within the regional business network's 'software',[50] given the apparent failure to respond effectively to information on market trends and technological change. More generally, it is possible that at the 'saturation' stage (see Table 3.1) long-established institutions and linkages began to decay as the industrialists took over from the merchants as the peak of the district's business elite. While retaining most of the traditional means of interpreting and transmitting information, these systems were not suited to the discovery and exploitation of unfamiliar opportunities. This dysfunctionality was further compounded by the highly defensive nature of the responses devised by industrialists to the mounting problems, setting in train a longer-term decline.

Before examining this critical thesis further, however, it is worthwhile considering in more detail the two most successful initiatives taken in Manchester after the confidence-sapping trade depressions of the late-1870s and mid-1880s. These were the construction of the Manchester Ship Canal and consequent establishment of the world's first industrial estate in Trafford Park. In this context, the rivalry with Liverpool was central to Manchester's preoccupations, given the prevailing belief that if the cotton textiles industry was to regain a competitive edge in export markets, then transport costs would have to be reduced.[51] While at a later stage this rivalry limited the North West's ability to develop a pan-regional consensus on economic policy, it prompted a major initiative when in 1887 the Manchester Ship Canal Co. was created. It is important to note that much of the Manchester Ship Canal Co.'s

---

[48] D.A. Farnie and T. Abe, 'Japan, Lancashire and the Asian Market for Cotton Manufactures, 1890–1990', in Farnie et al, *Region and Strategy*, pp. 131–6.

[49] Wilson, *British Business History*, p. 108.

[50] The term 'network software' was first used in R.N. Langlois and P. Robertson, *Firms, Markets and Economic Change* (Routledge, 1995).

[51] D.A. Farnie, *The Manchester Ship Canal and the Rise of the Port of Manchester, 1894–1975* (Manchester University Press, 1980), pp. 2–6.

£10 million share capital had to be raised in London by the merchant bank of N.M. Rothschilds.[52] This City institution was also obliged to intervene in 1891 when a liquidity crisis threatened the construction programme. At the same time, Manchester businessmen dominated the company's management, while in 1891 Manchester City Corporation was persuaded to invest £5 million in the venture, as a means of extending local interest and control.

When it opened in 1894, the Manchester Ship Canal represented one of the world's most impressive engineering triumphs. Coming just five years after Manchester had extended its municipal boundaries to encompass a population of two million people, the city's influence was now felt in parts of the region formerly dominated by Liverpool. Under the dynamic leadership of its first chairman, the prominent cotton merchant John K. Bythell, by 1906 Manchester's Pomona Docks was Britain's fourth largest port, reinforcing the city's role in serving a hinterland that was struggling to come to terms with the changing economic environment. It was also in 1894 that Manchester established its own *Cotton Association*. While this venture failed to match the influence of its Liverpool counterpart, it was a further reflection of the business community's desire to improve performance by focusing the provision of basic services in Manchester.

Of perhaps even greater significance, however, was the establishment of the world's first industrial estate directly opposite Pomona Docks.[53] The ship canal provided equal encouragement to both old and new industries, but the focus of the industrial estate was on diversification. Run by one of the era's most influential businessmen, Marshall Stevens, Trafford Park Estate was a carefully planned network of interconnecting roads, railways and utility supply networks. While the Manchester Ship Canal reinforced the city's position as the economic hub of North West England, the vital importance of Trafford Park was its role in creating a new industrial order almost totally distinct from *Cottonopolis*. Inevitably, there were cotton warehouses on the Pomona Docks, used for storing imported raw cotton and exporting finished goods. However, apart from the large cotton mill owned by Sir Richard Haworth & Sons, located directly opposite the docks, not a single cotton mill could be found in Trafford Park. Instead, contractors and transporters moved in, followed by the milling operations of the Co-operative Wholesale Society and Hovis, and by 1912 chemical processors and a number of light engineering firms. By the First World War, in stark contrast to the old-fashioned family firms in the region's traditional engineering and cotton industries, many of the estate's occupants were 'limited companies, employing the most modern technology, capital-intensive methods of production and skilled labour'.[54]

One of the most telling features of Trafford Park was the influx of American subsidiaries, one hundred of which had settled there by 1915. The most notable

---

[52]   This section is based on Farnie, *Manchester Ship Canal*, pp. 9–14 and 84.
[53]   Farnie, *Manchester Ship Canal*, pp. 118–40.
[54]   Ibid, p. 129.

of these ventures were British Westinghouse (1899) and the Ford Motor Co. (1910). Although the latter was only an assembly operation, with Ford shipping all its components from Detroit, production increased to such an extent that by 1930, 2000 people worked for Ford. After some early difficulties, British Westinghouse also became a major Manchester employer, with 6000 skilled engineers and technicians working for the firm in 1920, many of whom had passed through its highly regarded training school. In 1917, the original British Westinghouse operation had also been absorbed into the much stronger Metropolitan-Vickers Electrical Co. (hereafter, Metro-Vicks), creating one of Europe's most progressive electrical and electronics manufacturers. By 1933, over 200 American firms had set up subsidiaries in Trafford Park, indicating how local business was provided with a shining example of the potential gains from diversifying into the new industries of the Second Industrial Revolution.

While during the early twentieth century both the Manchester Ship Canal and Trafford Park cushioned the district from some violent economic storms, one must still question the extent to which local entrepreneurs recognised the need for a wholesale conversion from traditional methods and activities. Faced with the dual challenges outlined earlier, of intensifying foreign competition and rapid technological change, the Manchester business community should have devised radically new strategies, whether by overhauling the cotton industry's traditional practices, or by moving into new sectors offering greater commercial opportunities. Of course, some members of the established business elite did acknowledge the need for diversification, because by 1914 some of the great cotton dynasties were diversifying their investments, especially into electric tramways and other utilities, using the services offered by the Manchester Stock Exchange. In 1901, the Prestwich family also invested £320,000 in Dick, Kerr & Co., in Preston, one of the new generation of electrical engineering enterprises.[55] However, this was very much the exception rather than the rule, because at the heart of the Manchester business network cotton remained king until well after the First World War.

In assessing the extent to which the North West should have responded to exogenous challenges, it is clear that while this region witnessed some impressive attempts at diversification, especially when compared with other old industrial regions (Central Scotland, South Wales, and North East England), by world standards the process was inadequate. Of course, it is always difficult comparing regions in different countries, given the stark contrasts in, for example, central government roles, the provision of capital, and entrepreneurial traditions. Nevertheless, there are serious questions to consider, especially with regard to the region's preference for 'sticking to the knitting' and the failure of new industries (electrical engineering, automobiles,

[55] John F. Wilson, 'A Strategy of Expansion and Combination: Dick, Kerr & Co., 1897–1914', *Business History*, Vol. 37, No. 1 (1985). For evidence of investment strategies, see J.S. Toms, 'Windows of Opportunity in the Textile Industry: The Business Strategies of Lancashire Entrepreneurs, 1880–1914', *Business History*, Vol. 40, No. 1 (1997), pp. 1–25.

synthetic chemicals, light engineering and aerospace) to develop as rapidly in the North West as in other British and overseas regions. In particular, one must consider whether the Manchester business community developed dangerously sclerotic tendencies, severely inhibiting the emergence of more radical solutions to the district's problems.

The impact of war and network stagnation

Quite clearly, the Manchester business elite was slow to move beyond the familiar, treating diversification as a secondary issue to the central problem of reviving the cotton textiles industry.[56] In effect, at the 'saturation' stage this elite was failing to perform its role as 'change-agents'. In many ways, one might argue that this hesitancy was understandable. The regional business network's beliefs, attitudes and routines, or 'network software',[57] were geared towards collecting and evaluating information in specific ways that were not conducive to flexibility. Alternatively, one might state that the 'network software' was attuned mostly to the established industries, rather than to the wider market signals. This implies the existence of serious weaknesses in the district's co-ordination and signalling mechanisms, making it increasingly difficult for the business community to respond effectively to the emerging challenges. J.M. Keynes was rather more dismissive in his analysis of the cotton industry's lack of vision, claiming that its intensely individualistic leaders were 'boneheads ... who want to live the rest of their lives in peace'.[58] While Keynes was both harsh and simplistic in his analysis of Lancashire's difficulties, his views reflected a strong contemporary feeling that Lancashire was struggling to come to terms with its problems.

Britain was plunged into war in 1914 at a crucial stage in its economic development, just as the need for speedier diversification in the old industrial regions was becoming obvious. While the North West's ageing 'network software' would have posed some obstacles to the recognition of new opportunities even in the absence of war, capital would have been more readily available to entrepreneurs than it actually was in the depressed 1920s. In effect, the war and its aftermath both weakened the old industrial structure and hindered risk-taking and diversification. Furthermore, both during and immediately after the War key industries like engineering and cotton textiles were misled by confusing market signals into pursuing disastrous strategies. In the first place, as a result of wartime government encouragement, engineering had enormously expanded its capacity, albeit in the form of defence-oriented products. Secondly, between 1918 and 1920 false signals were received by the

---

[56] This is stressed especially in Sir Raymond Streat, *Lancashire and Whitehall: The Diary of Sir Raymond Streat*, 2 Vols, edited by M. Dupree (Manchester University Press, 1985).

[57] Langlois and Robertson, *Firms, Markets and Economic Change*, pp. 124–7.

[58] Quoted in Streat, *Lancashire and Whitehall*, Vol. 2, p. 181.

cotton industry, which mistakenly anticipated a renewed era of expansion in view of the disruption experienced by its European rivals. Investment and takeover decisions taken on the basis of this mirage not only rendered the industry's subsequent crisis all the more serious, but also compromised the stability of the regional banking network. Furthermore, the depressed regional business climate of the 1920s and 1930s discouraged risk-taking in new sectors. Instead, fear and uncertainty encouraged a rash of defensive mergers and cartel agreements in the old sectors, significantly hampering the region's ability to respond to new challenges. Crucially, in these circumstances financiers and politicians came to prominence within the Manchester industrial district, overshadowing the merchants and industrialists who had formerly been so dominant.

Pursuing the case of cotton textiles further, it is clear that World War One and its aftermath proved disastrous. A boom in mill construction, accompanied by frantic takeover activity, occurred at the end of World War One. Largely as a result of wartime inflation, 1920 marked the all-time maximum values for the production and export of cotton, as well as for profits and dividends made from investments in cotton companies. While 1920 also marked the peak year for membership of both the *Royal Exchange* and the *Manchester Chamber of Commerce*,[59] the boom was transitory. The British government deflated the economy in the early-1920s, in order to reduce inflation and prepare for a return to the Gold Standard at the pre-war exchange rate (of $4.84 to the pound sterling). Likewise, overseas markets for British cottons and other staple manufactures collapsed in the 1920s, at least partly because the World War had encouraged the expansion of cotton industries in developing countries formerly supplied by Lancashire. In particular, the Japanese cotton industry forged ahead, exporting to markets in Asia and Latin America. At the same time, infant industry protection in key overseas markets like India created even greater problems. As a result, in volume terms, British exports of cotton piece goods fell by eighty per cent between 1913 and 1938.[60]

Rationalisation of capacity was piecemeal in the industry as a whole, indicating that the network software was only partially successful in transmitting the right kind of message to a much-troubled industry. Moreover, Higgins and Toms argue that the nature of the constraint on key decision-makers within cotton firms changed after the 1918–20 investment mania, with external stakeholders, especially the banks, exerting a much stronger influence over planning horizons.[61] As Keynes noted, the banks' determination to secure their original advances with fresh loans not only reduced the exit of inefficient firms, but also thereby starved the industry of re-equipment finance for the

[59] Farnie and Nakaoka, 'Region and Nation', p. 24.
[60] For further insights into these trends, see the chapters by Sandberg and by Dupree in Rose (ed), *Lancashire Cotton Industry*.
[61] D. Higgins and J.S. Toms, 'Capital Ownership, Capital Structure and Capital markets: Financial Constraints and the Decline of the Lancashire Cotton Textile Industry, 1880–1965', *Journal of Industrial History*, Vol. 4, No. 1 (2001), pp. 48–64.

installation of high draft ring frames and automatic looms. Higgins and Toms conclude that: 'Without adequate finance, technological advances were always threats and never opportunities for Lancashire firms'. This also confirms the changing status of financiers within the Manchester industrial district, because such was their involvement in various sectors that their decisions became crucial to the way in which events would move.

Did the local banks' involvement in propping up the cotton industry contribute to the lack of diversification within the Manchester industrial district? Of course, one must be wary when describing the banks as local, given that most had been absorbed by London-controlled operations like the Midland Bank and the Westminster Bank. Nevertheless, both North West and London-controlled institutions were intrinsically tied into the local economy's fortunes, and several leading cotton men, including William Holland of the Fine Cotton Spinners' and Doublers' Association and Alan Sykes of the Bleachers' Association, sat on the boards of Williams Deacons Bank.[62] In 1931, Professor Sir Henry Clay stressed in evidence to the Macmillan Committee that the Lancashire bankers had failed to initiate a severe rationalisation programme in the 1920s, adopting a passive stance at a time when radical measures were required.[63] At the same time, while it was not the custom for British commercial banks to provide venture capital, their commitment to the ailing cotton industry reduced the availability of working capital for new firms in other industries. Of course, it could be argued that after the debacle of 1919–20 the banks could not afford to cut off their debtors. On the other hand, it is interesting to note that the banks also refused to support Raymond Streat's proposed Lancashire General Industries Investment Corporation, blandly claiming that they were already doing everything possible to support the region's industrial base.[64]

Although history has yet to pass a conclusive judgement on the role played by bankers in the interwar period, it is apparent that in linking their fortunes inextricably with cotton their flexibility was severely constrained as that industry's performance spiralled downwards. Far from being 'change-agents' in the conventional sense, the financiers failed to use their undoubted influence to effect change. However, it would be misleading to focus entirely on the financial community in the search for alternative strategies, because it is clear that industrialists and merchants pursued diversification in a most desultory manner. The Lancashire Industrial Development Corporation (LIDC), formed in 1931 at the nadir of the depression, came into being only after the

---

[62] J.J. Mason, 'William Henry Holland', in D.J. Jeremy (ed), *Dictionary of Business Biography, Vol. 3* (Butterworths, 1985), pp. 303–7; A.C. Howe, 'Sir Alan John Sykes', in D.J. Jeremy (ed), *Dictionary of Business Biography, Vol. 5* (Butterworths, 1986), p. 422.

[63] *Minutes of Evidence taken before the Committee on Finance and Industry*, Vol. 2 (1931), pp. 256, 260, 263 and 270.

[64] *The Times*, 31 March 1931, p. 9; Streat, *Lancashire and Whitehall*, Vol. 1, pp. xxv, 64, 129–33 and 243–4.

government's chief industrial advisor (Sir Horace Wilson) had persuaded the competing business factions of Liverpool and Manchester to work together.[65] The aim of this body was to entice new firms, and especially American or European operations with access to new technologies, into the region. Heim suggests that many foreign firms using LIDC's services would have invested in the region in any case, given the proximity of similar operations. Others were motivated by a desire to avoid the protective duties imposed by central government in 1932, rather than by the attractions of the North West. On the other hand, the example of Trafford Park showed that the North West was already regarded as a suitable location by many multinationals, which provides convincing evidence that the region's economic potential was not being exploited effectively by the indigenous business community.[66] Here again, while one can see how politicians and officials created an opportunity to influence events, they failed as miserably as the financiers to exploit an opening.

Significantly, certain sections of the engineering industry were also beginning to lose their dynamism. The engineering industry had since the 1820s transcended a narrow dependence on cotton. Locomotives, machine tools and general equipment emerged from factories located in almost every North West town. Nevertheless, exactly the same problems that beset the cotton industry – the onset of foreign competition, rapid technological change and protectionism – were from the 1880s undermining the engineering industry's prospects.[67] Similar strategies were also pursued in dealing with these challenges, in particular specialisation in niche sectors of the engineering market. Although there were some important mergers, for example between Whitworth's and the Newcastle firm of Armstrong in 1897, such was the poor quality of management at the top of this company that by 1930 it had been absorbed by the Sheffield steel and engineering firm, Vickers.

Just as with the cotton industry, however, the quality of management in the engineering industry left much to be desired. Predominantly family firms, most engineering concerns relied on a limited pool for senior management, resisting the temptation to hire from the further and higher education institutions that had appeared in the region since the late-nineteenth century. These technical and managerial constraints were compounded by a desire to retain ownership within the family, curtailing access to external sources of capital, other than in the form of bank loans or mortgage debentures. At a time when profits came under intense pressure from foreign competition and severe fluctuations in demand, engineering firms' restricted access to capital hindered the development of new products and processes. Of course, there was little

[65] R. Lowe and R. Roberts, 'Sir Horace Wilson, 1900–1935: The Making of a Mandarin', *Historical Journal*, Vol. 30, No. 3 (1987), p. 657.
[66] C. Heim, 'Industrial Organization and Regional Development in Interwar Britain', *Journal of Economic History*, Vol. 34, No. 4 (1983), pp. 931–52.
[67] Musson, *Growth of British Industry*, pp. 312–6; Timmins, *Made in Lancashire*, pp. 299–300.

individual firms could do about general market trends and the cyclical nature of capital equipment purchases. On the other hand, especially in sectors like machine tools, textile machinery and steam engineering there is clear evidence of 'weaknesses in industrial organisation, production methods, research, and marketing'.[68] This demonstrates once again a failure of both individual firms and the regional business network to transmit the right kind of signals capable of effecting a radical improvement in competitiveness. Just as with cotton and its allied trades, the interwar engineering industrialists failed to devise adequate recovery strategies, creating difficulties that later generations found impossible to overcome.

One of the major weaknesses of North West engineering was the failure to nurture more automobile firms. If cotton was the catalyst for much of what happened in the North West between 1770 and 1914, automobiles could have assumed a similarly beneficial role during the twentieth century, substantially boosting output and exerting robust multiplier effects on related sectors. Sadly, though, apart from Leyland Motors near Preston, few automobile firms used the North West as a base. Indeed, several firms that started in the North West moved to other regions. For example, while the earliest Rolls-Royce cars were made in a cramped Manchester factory, after negotiating favourable terms with Derby Corporation production was moved to that town in 1908.[69] An even greater loss was the Ford assembly plant at Trafford Park. Having established the Ford name in British markets, in 1931 the firm decided to relocate in Dagenham, London. Given the automobile's importance to the 'Second Industrial Revolution', and the enormous growth in demand for motorised transport since the 1920s, the failure to develop this industry was a handicap to the North West as it struggled to survive on the basis of an older technological base.

Despite this catalogue of mishaps and false starts, the engineering sector was not entirely moribund and some successful firms emerged in the electrical, electronic and aerospace branches of this industry. Electrical manufacturers like Westinghouse (later Metro-Vicks) and Ferranti flourished in the interwar period as demand for electricity increased substantially. The Metro-Vicks story has already been related, indicating how the Trafford Park industrial estate was capable of nurturing world-class operations. Out in Oldham and Moston, Ferranti became one of Europe's most innovative electrical and electronics firms, diversifying away from its original product base of meters and transformers into domestic appliances, avionics and electronic devices. This

---

[68] T. Gourvish, 'British Business and the Transition to a Corporate Economy: Entrepreneurship and Management Structures', *Business History*, Vol. 29, No. 4 (1987), p. 145.

[69] Peter Pugh, *The Magic of a Name: The Rolls-Royce Story. The First Forty Years* (Icon Books, 2000), pp. 39–52.

firm employed over 6000 people by 1939, providing steady employment for many people affected adversely by the contraction of cotton.[70]

While electrical and electronic engineering was laying down solid foundations, an aerospace industry was also successfully established. A.V. Roe Ltd. (or Avro) became one of Britain's leading aeroplane manufacturers, having established a plant in Miles Platting three years after starting business in the premises of a Manchester braces manufacturers in 1910.[71] Avro's most successful early product was the *504*, nearly 10,000 of which were made during World War One. The Manchester engineering firm of Crossley Motors purchased a controlling interest in Avro in 1920, selling it on to Armstrong-Siddeley in 1928. Hawker acquired Armstrong-Siddeley in 1935, forming Hawker-Siddeley, and subsequently financed the design of a new generation of aircraft including the highly successful *Lancaster* bomber. At the same time, Ferranti developed a flourishing avionics operation, supplying gyroscopically-controlled instruments for civil and military aircraft. English Electric also started aircraft development and production in Preston during the 1930s, while Rolls-Royce returned to the region to produce aircraft engines in Burnley, and Lucas established a major business in motor and aircraft components in north-east Lancashire.

The drawback, of course, was that there were too few firms like Metro-Vicks, Ferranti, and Avro, both in the North West and across the economy as a whole. Excessive quantities of resources continued to be expended by the region's supposed 'change agents' in a futile attempt to save the cotton industry from total collapse. The regional business elite was locked into the defence of older industries by past investment decisions, and to some extent by 'network software', that failed to recognise the full potential of newer industries.

Faced with this scenario, it is clear that not only did the incumbent regional business network fail to respond effectively, but also those who offered new solutions lacked sufficient influence to persuade the established business community to change direction. The destruction of this old business network and its associated 'software' would at least have released factors of production for recombination in more creative ways. As it was, the old network retained sufficient strength to commandeer factors of production throughout the 1920s and 1930s, in a desperate attempt at self-preservation. Consequently, the use of these factors was denied to new enterprises, while business was faced with a combination of pressures about which they could do very little, individually or collectively.

---

[70] J.F. Wilson, *Ferranti. A History. Building A Family Firm, 1882–1975* (Carnegie, 2000).

[71] R. Higham and R.P.T. Davenport-Hines, 'J.D. Siddeley', *Dictionary of Business Biography*, Vol. 5 (Butterworth, 1986), pp. 136–9.

Conclusions

The world's first modern industrial district provides a fascinating insight into how externalities and agglomeration effects created a highly dynamic environment for the first generations of Manchester entrepreneurs. It is also clear that the Manchester industrial district passed through a variety of stages between 1750 and 1939. Certainly, one can detect the four stages outlined by Swann – critical mass (1720–80), take-off (1780–1850), peak entry (1850–80) and saturation (1880–1939).[72] Similarly, it is clear that the 'change-agents' metamorphosed from merchants (who were dominant up to the 1880s) into industrialists (1880–1920) and ultimately on to financiers and politicians (1920 onwards). At the same time, it is difficult to see how the district's 'network software' altered much, because even in the 1920s and 1930s there was no evidence that the business leaders had effectively interpreted market signals and devised viable alternative strategies. Indeed, from the 1880s the Manchester industrial district was in rapid retreat. Aspects of the old 'network software', in the form of routines, habits and traditions, were hard to cast off, because in Manchester they had existed for well over 100 years and had fed a long period of expansion. This helps to explain why in spite of the changing composition of the business elite the district coped feebly with the 'saturation' stage after 1920. Even when the local community (with assistance from the government and the Bank of England), formed bodies like LIDC (1931) and firms like Lancashire Cotton Corporation and Combined Egyptian Mills (1929), the region continued to experience grave economic difficulties.[73] The dynamic business network that had facilitated the creation and rapid development of the world's first modern industrial district had fossilised and developed sclerotic tendencies, hampering the work of those like Raymond Streat and J.M. Keynes who were advocating new strategies.

That there was an alternative to this miserable tale is confirmed by the vigour of such ventures as Trafford Park, where over 200 American firms were operating by 1932. In addition, by the 1920s vibrant electrical and aerospace firms were operating across the Manchester district. Overall, though, the 'Second Industrial Revolution' created enormous opportunities that this district simply did not grasp in their entirety, principally because Manchester's network software failed to identify and appreciate the potential of these trends. Any advantages stemming from a strong commercial sector, skilled labour and finance were only seized half-heartedly. While contemporaries like Streat and Keynes put forward radical programmes for dealing with the interwar crises, few key actors within the network were willing to devote time, let alone resources, to their implementation. Clay's assertion, that a purge of all but the most efficient cotton firms was a precondition of the industry's revival, was regarded as blasphemy by many. The prevailing elite was too preoccupied with

---

[72]   Swann, 'Towards a Model of Clustering'.

[73]   For further information on these initiatives, see Chapter 4 in this volume.

its own problems to consider anything other than palliative measures that simply delayed the inevitable, indicating how the network had become so dysfunctional by the 1920s that rationality was denied a hearing.

Chapter 4

Networks, corporate governance and the decline of the Lancashire textile industry, 1860–1980

Steve Toms and Igor Filatotchev

Introduction

This chapter is concerned with the role played by business networks in the supremacy and subsequent decline of the cotton textile industry in industrial Lancashire. It will begin by developing a theoretical model of industrial and corporate change. It will draw on agency theory, the resource based view of the firm and strategic restructuring. The decline issue has dominated the historiography of the Lancashire textile industry in recent decades. Specific aspects of this are whether or not entrepreneurs were rational in the light of the constraints they faced and, related to that issue, whether this or other causes were more important in loss of competitiveness. It is not the purpose of the chapter to deal with the details of these debates, although the theoretical framework implies constraints other than those identified in prior literature. Thus it will seek to comment upon them in the light of research into governance and resource based constraints suggested by the theoretical framework and the additional empirical evidence presented in the chapter.[2] Also the chapter will aim to show that ownership and governance structures placed financial constraints on decision-makers, and in the crisis of the 1920s prevented the organisation of ameliorative and recovery strategies, condemning the industry to a protracted death. Also, because the governance structure of the Lancashire cotton textile industry developed during the nineteenth century, the later inability to adapt to crisis can be traced historically to the previous century. At that time the rise of the Lancashire's industrial district and 'flexible

---

[1]   The principal empirical sources used in the study are the annual returns for samples of companies from the period 1880-1960. Stock exchange and press sources were also used. These were used to measure family and institutional shareholdings, board membership and characteristics, directors' shareholdings, access to financial resources, capital structure, financial performance etc.

specialisation' appeared to underpin the cotton industry's route to international competitive advantage.[3]

To summarise, the theoretical model described above will be explained in detail and then used to explain the rise of managerial and shareholding networks within the corporate economy of Lancashire. The chapter will then go on to explain how these governance structures prevented flexible and timely responses to the requirements of restructuring and re-equipment. It will offer evidence on the broader question of perhaps why in the British case clustering did not seem to aid declining industries like cotton textiles.

Theoretical background

This section provides a brief overview of corporate governance, strategic resources and the characteristics of networks in industrial districts. It then provides an analytical model describing the inter-relationships between them.

Ownership and governance structures provide an important context that moderates strategic response to expanding markets and the kind of crisis situations repeatedly faced by the Lancashire textile industry after 1920, and that affects the firm's survival in the long-run. Previous studies of ownership structure, strategy and performance have shown that large outside stockholders have the incentive and the power to ensure that managers operate the firm efficiently.[4] Research from a resource-dependence perspective has also emphasised that outside institutional investors play a crucial role in providing the firm with the resources needed to survive and function efficiently.[5] In particular, the links that directors have with the firm's environment can be used to obtain financial resources needed for effective restructuring.[6] This may also influence the restructuring expertise directly related to board diversity measured in terms of board size, the number of outside directors, and the

---

[3]   For further explanation of the notion of flexible specialisation, see M. Piore and C. Sabel, *The Second Industrial Divide* (Basic Books, 1984).

[4]   S.J. Nickell, D. Nicolitsas and N. Dryden, 'What Makes a Firm Perform Well?', *European Economic Review*, Vol. 41, No. 5 (1997), pp. 783–96; R.E. Hoskisson, R.A. Johnson, and D.D. Moesel, 'Corporate Divestiture Intensity in Restructuring Firms: Effects of Governance, Strategy and Performance', *Academy of Management Journal*, Vol. 37 (1994), pp. 1207–51. J.E. Bethel and J. Liebeskind, 'The Effects of Ownership Structure on Corporate Restructuring', *Strategic Management Journal*, Vol. 14 (special issue), (1993), pp. 15–31.

[5]   J. Pfeffer, 'Size and Composition of Corporate Boards of Directors: The Organization and its Environment', *Administrative Science Quarterly*, Vol. 17 (1972), pp. 218–22; J.A. Wagner, J.L. Stimpert, E.I Fubara, 'Board Composition and Organizational Performance: Two Studies of Insider/Outsider Effects', *Journal of Management Studies*, Vol. 35, No. 5 (1998), pp. 655–77.

[6]   J.A. Pearce and S.A Zahra, 'The Relative Power of CEOs and Boards of Directors: Associations with Corporate Performance', *Strategic Management Journal*, Vol. 12 (1991), pp. 135–53; Pfeffer, 'Size and Composition of Corporate Boards'; K. Provan, 'Board Power and Organisational Efficiency Among Human Service Agencies', *Academy of Management Journal*, Vol. 23 (1980), pp. 221–36.

number of outside directorships ('interlocks') each individual board member holds in other organisations both within the industry and outside. To summarise, it may be assumed that strategic restructuring and long-term survival in declining industries such as textiles may be impeded by a managerial unwillingness and/or lack of capacity to undertake change. These attitudes may be a function of governance and resource based constraints, especially financial constraints. Part of this argument is based on a synthesis of evidence from recent research into the ownership of the industry, its financial performance and its decline.[7]

Share ownership, the role of the board and other governance attributes can be generalised into the notion of accountability. Hence accountability refers to the processes whereby the stewards of the business are held accountable to its owners and other external stakeholders through the processes of corporate governance. From the network perspective, according to Casson's typology,[8] the notion of accountability translates readily into the transparency or opacity of the network. Accountability also suggests an emphasis on the quality of information flow and facilitates a broader perspective than merely emphasising the Chandlerian view of technology and the exploitation of associated scale and scope economies.[9]

In addition to accountability, the second important dimension of the analytical framework presented in this chapter is the strategic resource content of business activities. According to this view, managerial and entrepreneurial resources drive growth and diversification.[10] Such resources might include specialised production facilities, trade secrets and engineering experience.[11] They might also include firm-specific idiosyncratic knowledge assets.[12] Such firm-specific factors are traditionally considered as the major drivers of strategic change according to the resource-based view.[13] At the same time specialisation may in certain periods of history and stages of economic development promote flexibility, replacing standardisation and scale

---

[7]   I. Filatotchev, and J.S. Toms, 'Corporate Governance, Strategy and Survival in a Declining Industry: A Study of UK Cotton Textile Companies', *Birkbeck College Discussion Paper*, University of London (2000).

[8]   See Chapter 2 in this volume.

[9]   G. Hamilton and R. Feenstra, 'Varieties of Hierarchies and Markets: An Introduction', *Industrial and Corporate Change*, Vol. 4 (1995), pp. 51–91. R.N. Langlois and P.L. Robertson, *Firms, Markets and Economic Change: A Dynamic Theory of Business Institutions* (Routledge, 1995), p. 150. M. Casson, 'Institutional Economics and Business History: A Way Forward', *Business History*, Vol. 39, No. 4 (1997), pp. 149–71.

[10]   R. Whittington and M. Mayer, *The European Corporation: Strategy, Structure and Social Science* (OUP, 2000), pp. 56–7; E. Penrose, *The Theory of the Growth of the Firm* (Oxford, 1959).

[11]   D. Teece, G. Pisano, and A. Sheun, 'Dynamic Capabilities and Strategic Management', *Strategic Management Journal*, Vol. 18, No. 7 (1997), pp. 509–33.

[12]   R. Castanias and C. Helfat, 'Managerial Rents', *Journal of Management*, Vol. 17, No. 1 (1991), pp. 155–71.

[13]   J.B. Barney, *Gaining and Sustaining Competitive Advantage* (Addison-Wesley, 1997).

economies.[14] Meanwhile, industrial districts, trade associations and other networked organisations may be promoted through sharing trade secrets and drawing on local pools of experience and skilled labour. These resemble knowledge pools or agglomeration based external economies of scale originally described by Alfred Marshall.[15] Synthesising these relationships, organisational diversity and network characteristics are likely to be closely influenced by the firm's access to resources.

If organisational diversity is combined with the earlier perspective on accountability, this now provides a more detailed understanding of network characteristics and the processes that might influence their evolution through time. Table 4.1 provides a summary of these relationships. The matrix columns characterise accountability as transparent or opaque and the degree of organisational diversity or the resource base of the firm as narrow or extensive. The matrix quadrants describe the network characteristics. Comparing the two columns, the degree of transparency will be a function of the degree of dependency on external stakeholders for resources, especially financial resources, which create reciprocal agency costs. Opaque networks are unaccountable to external stakeholders and more likely to be self sufficient in resource terms. Transparent networks on the other hand demonstrate accountability and are more likely to be resource dependent. At the same time, large and diverse organisations by definition have control over a wider resource base and have the option of internalising them using a hierarchic structure. Similarly, small-scale and specialised firms draw on a narrow resource base and will draw on market inputs for non-specialised functions. Following Williamson[16] and Fruin and taking a markets and hierarchies perspective on the rows of the matrix, if networks are assumed to combine elements of both, then they will tend to replace one or the other.[17] Thus, if there is a pure market and a network develops, it will tend to substitute market processes. Examples might include inter-firm arrangements to control supply and price, particularly where firms with narrow resource bases lack the market power to do so singly. Similarly if there is hierarchy, network development substitutes for the original.[18] Examples might include outsourcing to associated companies, enforcement of supply via dedicated contracts, and horizontal amalgamation of semi-independent firms within a federal combine structure.

---

[14]   Piore and Sabel, *The Second Industrial Divide.*

[15]   M. Kamien, E. Mueller and I. Zang, 'Research Joint Ventures and R&D Cartels', *American Economic Review*, Vol. 82, No. 5 (1992), pp. 1293–306; A. Marshall, *Principles of Economics*, (London, 1890); C. Oughton and G. Whittam, 'Competition and Co-operation in the Small Firm Sector', *Scottish Journal of Political Economy*, Vol. 44, No. 1 (1997), pp. 1–30.

[16]   O.E. Williamson, *Market and Hierarchies: Analysis and Antitrust Implications*, (Free Press, 1975); ibid., *Economic Institutions of Capitalism*, (Free Press, 1985); ibid., 'Markets, Hierarchies and the Modern Corporation: An Unfolding Perspective', *Journal of Economic Behaviour and Organisation*, 17 (1992).

[17]   W.M. Fruin, *Networks, Markets and the Pacific Rim: Studies in Strategy* (OUP, 1998).

[18]   Ibid., p. 9.

Where networks replace markets or hierarchies, ownership ties and inter-locking directorships might be used to police arrangements.

Table 4.1
Dynamic determinants of network characteristics

		Strategic Context: Degree of Accountability	
		Transparent	*Opaque*
Strategic Content: Organisational Resource Base	*Extensive*	**Quadrant 4** Hierarchy substituting, high external resource dependency networks	**Quadrant 3** Hierarchy substituting, low external resource dependency networks
	Narrow	**Quadrant 2** Market substituting, high external resource dependency networks	**Quadrant 1** Market substituting, low external resource dependency networks

In this taxonomy, resource dependency impacts on the social construction of networks. Thus there are differences with Fruin's typology where networks are not substitutes for markets and hierarchies. According to Fruin, where they exist as complementary extensions of markets or hierarchies they are either naturally occurring or socially constructed. If an institutional and social constructivist view is taken of accountability structures,[19] self-sufficient and resource dependent networks correspond to these. Transparent governance and accountability is more likely to be socially constructed whereas self-sufficiency

---

[19] N. Fligstein, *The Transformation of Corporate Control* (Harvard University Press, 1990). From an accounting perspective, Hopwood, p. 213, suggests, 'Rather than seeing organisational accounts as a technical reflection of the pregiven economic imperatives facing organisational administration, they are ... more actively constructed in order to create a particular economic visibility ... and a powerful means for positively enabling the governance and control of the organisation along economic lines'. A.G. Hopwood, 'The Archaeology of Accounting Systems', *Accounting, Organisations and Society*, Vol. 12, No. 3 (1997), pp. 207–34.

is more likely to be naturally occurring. In other words economic action is 'embedded'[20] by *ex ante* resource distribution and accountability structures. This suggests the following network typology corresponding to the matrix quadrants:

1. Market substituting, low external resource dependency (self-sufficient) networks.
2. Market substituting, high external resource dependency (resource dependent) networks.
3. Hierarchy substituting, low external resource dependency (self-sufficient) networks.
4. Hierarchy substituting, high external resource dependency (resource dependent) networks.

Table 4.1 is a dynamic model to explain network development and changes in network structure. Pure markets and pure hierarchies, which lie at either end of the vertical continuum in the Table 4.1 matrix are useful theoretical abstractions but rarely found in practice. Similarly information is always costly to acquire but valueless if never exploited commercially, suggesting the impossibility of the horizontal extremes of total and zero accountability.[21] Networks are hence common and easy to identify in most business situations. More interesting than mere identification, however are the cause and effect relationships governing their time dependent dynamics. There are four forces governing these changes, illustrated in Figure 4.1. The firm's ability to internalise resources, including knowledge assets that underpin managerial economies of scope is a function of the firm's resource base and therefore the presence of internal economies of scale and scope. Conversely narrow resource bases and external economies of scale and scope exert a pull towards markets. At the same time, if firms are self sufficient in resources or if a network can be used to share resources on such a basis, the network will have no recourse to outside resource providers and monitors. On the side of the transparency continuum, the use of a network to secure access to outside resources requires the construction of structures of governance and accountability and submission to those rules by network members. From this analysis, it can be seen that trust tends to be low on the left-hand side of Table 4.1 and Figure 4.1 and high on the right. This is broadly consistent with Casson's view, which sees trust as based on personal contacts in a context of repeat transactions.[22] Game theoretic analysis also suggests that co-operation is a more likely result when

---

[20] M. Granovetter, 'Economic Action and Social Structure: The Problem of Embeddedness', *American Journal of Sociology*, Vol. 91 (1985), pp. 481–501.

[21] S. Grossman and J. Stiglitz, 'On the Impossibility of Efficient Capital Markets', *American Economic Review*, Vol. 70, No. 3 (1980), pp. 393–408.

[22] Chapter 2 in this volume.

transactions are repeated through time.[23] More specifically, whilst Marshall's discussion of industrial districts has little room for concepts such as business networks and trust, as suggested in Chapter 1, the model in Table 4.1 and Figure 4.1 provides a clear and explicit linkage between trust, Marshallian external economies and network characteristics.[24]

Perhaps an even more important determinant of network characteristics is the rate of growth. This in itself is a function of the rate of technological change, which establishes the available internal and external economies of scale within the industry, district or economy. Self-sufficient networks are almost by definition unconcerned with growth and may be appropriate to low-growth industries or to support rationalisation, patent based monopoly production, etc. Conversely in high growth industries, firms and networks require funds for production facilities, advertising, research and development that can only be obtained externally. In general past growth influences the current resource base whilst future growth impacts on the degree of resource dependence. Low past growth equates to narrow resources base but with the option of high future growth if cash flow can be accessed from outside stakeholders. Future growth might be secured also for firms with high past growth, which therefore have a broader current resource base. Alternatively, if the firm has reached the peak of its growth cycle, with positive cash flow, managers no longer require access to external sources of funds. In the network typology corresponding to the matrix quadrants in Table 4.1:

1. Market substituting, external resource dependency (self-sufficient) networks, underpinned by low past growth and low future growth.
2. Market substituting, high external resource dependency (resource dependent) networks, underpinned by low past growth and with high future growth prospects.
3. Hierarchy substituting, low external resource dependency (self-sufficient) networks, underpinned by high past growth and with low future growth prospects.
4. Hierarchy substituting, high external resource dependency (resource dependent) networks, underpinned by high past growth and with high future growth prospects.

Finally self sufficiency and resource dependence may reflect the politics of regulation and ideology.[25] Competition policy, company law and rules governing financial institutions are the obvious examples.[26] The absence or

---

[23]   R. Axelrod, *The Evolution of Co-operation* (Basic Books, 1984).

[24]   See Chapter 1 in this volume; Langlois and Robertson, *Firms, Markets and Economic Change*, p. 125.

[25]   G. Davis, K. Diekmann and C. Tinsley, 'The Decline and Fall of the Conglomerate Firm in the 1980s: the Deinstitutionalisation of an Organisational Form', *American Sociological Review*, Vol. 59, No. 4 (1994), pp. 547–70.

[26]   Fligstein, *The Transformation of Corporate Control*.

presence of such rules influences the viability of secretive cartels and the level of protection offered to external stakeholders. Meanwhile prevailing ideology may influence the extent to which managers acquiesce to or promote accountability to external stakeholders.[27]

Figure 4.1
Forces determining network structure

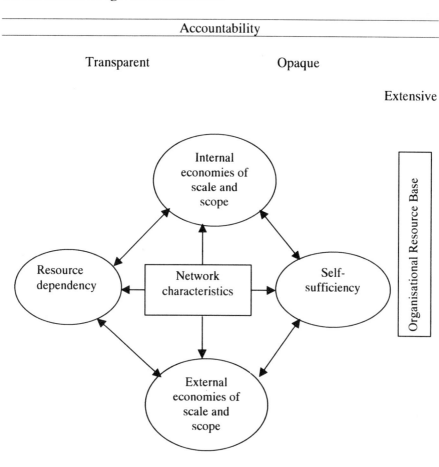

The above discussion has suggested many possible relationships based on the network literature outlined in Chapter 1. They are summarised in Table 4.1 and Figure 4.1. The remainder of this chapter will assess the utility of these

[27] W. Lazonick and M. O'Sullivan, 'Maximising Shareholder Value: A New Ideology for Corporate Governance', *Economy and Society*, Vol. 29, No. 1 (2000), pp. 13–35.

frameworks with reference to the long run changes in governance structures and organisational resource characteristics of the Lancashire textile industry.

Networks and governance in an expanding industry, 1860–1920

In this period the industry resembled the classic Marshallian industrial district, with an apparently high degree of competition and market based co-ordination.[28] Specialisation and atomisation of the industry occurred on the basis of external economies of scale and narrow resource base at the level of the individual firm. However, networks were used to internalise these economies and the network structures adopted reflected this, with the appearance of trade associations to regulate prices, wages and output. At the same time there was a revolution in corporate governance based on directoral cliques and centralisation of ownership, which had important consequences for the structure of accountability. As the industry diverged in terms of equipment, product range, specialist knowledge and network linkages, it converged in governance terms.

The growth of organisational diversity

The second half of the nineteenth century witnessed a growth in specialisation. In the late nineteenth century the smaller horizontally specialised firms were increasingly based around regional centres of specialisation.[29] Each area possessed its own distinctive technical education and machinery,[30] providing firms with access to agglomeration economies such as pools of specialised labour. For example the coarse spinners of the Oldham district, the fine spinners around Bolton and the weavers of North-East Lancashire.[31] Within each sub-region employers' federations and trade unions imposed uniform wages on local firms using a system of regional lists.[32] The development of futures exchanges in Manchester and Liverpool played an important role in the development of the region's network of entrepreneurs. Judgement of prices, and hence margin, in the difficult futures markets of Liverpool and Manchester was

---

[28]   Langlois and Robertson, *Firms, Markets and Economic Change*, p. 125.

[29]   S. Kenney, 'Sub-regional Specialization in the Lancashire Cotton Industry, 1884–1914: A Study in Organizational and Locational Change', *Journal of Historical Geography*, Vol. 8, No. 1 (1982), pp. 41–63.

[30]   E. Lorenz, 'Organizational Inertia and Competitive Decline: The British Cotton, Shipbuilding and Car Industries, 1945–1975', *Industrial and Corporate Change*, Vol. 3, No. 2 (1994), pp. 379–404

[31]   D. Farnie, *The English Cotton Industry and the World Market* (Oxford, 1979). A. Marrison, 'Indian Summer', in M.B. Rose (ed), *The Lancashire Cotton Industry* (Lancashire County Books, 1996).

[32]   J. Jewkes, and E.M. Gray, *Wages and Labour in the Lancashire Cotton Spinning Industry* (Manchester University Press, 1935).

the crucial ingredient of entrepreneurial success for the cotton spinner.[33] *Exchange* membership and linkages with broker and warehousing firms developed around these functions.[34]

What had resembled a Marshallian industrial district in the nineteenth century was transformed further by developments in the twentieth. These tended to increase organisational diversity by giving powerful managerial groups control over large numbers of firms performing similar if specialised functions. With increased managerial economies of scope came greater market power. In a wave of mergers at the turn of the century, federal combines, such as the Fine Cotton Spinners and Doublers Association (FCSDA) and Bleachers' Associations were created on the basis of horizontal specialisation.[35] Meanwhile other groups such as Horrockses, Tootals and Ashton Brothers consolidated vertical structures.[36] Therefore, at this stage the industry consisted of two types of overlapping networks. On the one hand, there was a large number of independent, small mills that formed a core of Lancashire's industrial district by sharing the same pool of technical knowledge, local labour resources, and distribution networks. On the other hand, there was a growing importance of hierarchical networks of companies that were forming amalgamated structures, such as FCDA, LCC, etc. Further restructuring in the twentieth century was closely linked to changes in ownership and management, discussed below, rather than product range and industry structure.

Convergence in corporate governance and accountability

In 1850, although the industrial north dominated the British economy, it was poorly integrated in terms of corporate governance and capital markets. This enhanced transparency at regional level but opacity from the perspective of outsiders. Southern investors lamented their lack of investment opportunities in the profitable companies created during the industrial revolution.[37] Even within

---

[33] For an individual firm case study of these practices at Fielden Brothers, see B. Law, *Fieldens of Todmorden: A Nineteenth Century Business Dynasty* (George Kelsall, 1995). J.S. Toms, 'Integration, Innovation, and the Progress of a Pennine Cotton Enterprise: Fielden Brothers Ltd. 1889–1914', *Textile History*, Vol. 27 (1996).

[34] D. Farnie, 'Region and Nation' in D. Farnie, T. Nakaoka, D. Jeremy, J. Wilson and T. Abe (eds), *Region and Strategy in Britain and Japan: Business in Lancashire and Kansai, 1890–1990* (Routledge, 2000).

[35] H. Macrosty, *The Trust Movement in British Industry* (Longmans, 1907).

[36] J.S. Toms, 'The Profitability of the First Lancashire Merger: The Case of Horrocks Crewdson, 1887–1905', *Textile History*, Vol. 24, No. 2, (1993), pp. 129–46; J.S. Toms, 'The Finance and Growth of the Lancashire Textile Industry, 1870–1914', unpublished PhD thesis (University of Nottingham, 1996); ibid., 'Windows of Opportunity in the Textile Industry: The Business Strategies of Lancashire Entrepreneurs 1880–1914', *Business History*, Vol. 40, No. 1 (1998), pp. 1–25.

[37] J.B. Jefferys, 'Trends in Business Organisation in Great Britain since 1856, with Special Reference to the Financial Structure of Companies, the Mechanism of Investment and the Relations between the Shareholder and the Company', PhD thesis (University of London).

the North-West, however, there were distinct regional differences in the approach towards governance. The Oldham system was founded on an ideological tradition of co-operation and common ownership.[38] Such ownership was locally based and it was only the larger firms based around Manchester that sought capital on regional and metropolitan stock markets.[39] Meanwhile in Preston and elsewhere in Lancashire, private ownership was the norm.[40] The second half of the nineteenth century witnessed a convergence in governance in significant sections of the industry as groups of directors set about consolidating private control.

This was most dramatic in Oldham, where cliques of financial capitalists replaced dispersed co-operative share ownership. The principal feature of the Oldham system was the establishment of limited liability companies under the 1862 Companies Act, whose permissive governance rules allowed the Oldham co-operative societies to open share lists to the local population using a one shareholder one vote system. Directors and auditors in these new mills exercised an intermediary accountability function between the mill manager and salesman and well attended quarterly shareholder meetings, earning nominal fees in return. This system promoted transparent governance structures and a relatively efficient stock market promoted managerial accountability.[41] From around the 1880s several processes undermined this system. New institutions, particularly cotton and yarn futures markets complicated the directors' task whilst trade cycle effects exposed them to risk and the opprobrium of shareholders when things went wrong.[42] Poor remuneration and managerial economies of scope based on deal networks in Manchester and Liverpool provided incentives for building cross directorships whilst the prolonged slump of the early 1890s provided the opportunity to buy blocks of cheap shares and secure control of mills from the co-operators.[43]

These financial capitalists were increasingly able to organise and benefit from wealth transfers through repeated flotations of companies. A Preston commentator speaking to the Royal Commission of 1886 condemned the system of public ownership of shares prevalent in the cotton mills of Oldham because mill promotions created excess capacity.[44] John Bunting best

[38] B. Jones, *Co-operative Production* (Clarendon Press, 1894); W. Marcroft, *The Companies Circular* (Oldham, 1879).
[39] For example, Ashton Brothers of Hyde, Tootal Broadhurst and Lee. Toms, 'Windows of Opportunity'.
[40] Kenney, 'Sub-regional Specialisation'.
[41] J.S. Toms, 'The Supply of and Demand for Accounting Information in an Unregulated Market: Examples from the Lancashire Cotton Mills', *Accounting, Organizations and Society*, Vol. 23, No. 2 (1998), pp. 217–38.
[42] J.S. Toms, 'The Rise of Modern Accounting and the Fall of the Public Company', *Accounting, Organizations and Society*, Vol. 27, No. 1/2 (2002).
[43] Ibid.; J.S. Toms, 'Information Content of Earnings in an Unregulated Market: The Co-operative Cotton Mills of Lancashire, 1880–1900', *Accounting and Business Research*, Vol. 31, No. 3 (2000), pp. 175–90.
[44] *Oldham Standard*, 20th February, 1886.

exemplified the mill promoter and multiple director.[45] These promoters raised finance from known contacts.[46] Finance was also raised using spare cash from existing companies. These processes cemented director's interlocks. At the Honeywell Spinning Company, John Bunting having been a promoter, became the chairman and his son, James Henry Bunting, the auditor.[47] The result was that companies that had previously been controlled by a broad shareholder base were consolidated into business empires controlled by cliques of directors and cross share-holdings.

The same pattern was repeated elsewhere in the industry. Where profits were made in private concerns from single mill enterprises, a common pattern was reinvestment in the construction of new mills or the purchase of existing enterprises as going concerns. This process of accumulation allowed the family controlled company to remain an important feature of the business landscape. For example William Birtwistle (1855–1936) and his emergent group of companies (hereafter the Birtwistle group) provided a good example of the type of empire building associated with entrepreneurs prepared to take over existing businesses as going concerns, thereby pulling together a loose federation of companies.[48] Assembled in the late 1890s, these companies shared the proprietorship of William Birtwistle, a Blackburn based entrepreneur, but little else, remaining a loose association of relatively small and independent operating companies. Although the managements of these companies often overlapped, and were under the day to day control of Birtwistle himself, there were no apparent transfers of goods or cash from one business to the other and no other signs of mutual interdependence.[49] The remarkable feature of the Birtwistle 'empire' was the rapidity with which it was constructed. Treated collectively, the business in 1913 was on a par with the largest Lancashire enterprises,[50] and by

---

[45] Other examples included Thomas Henthorn, Harry Dixon, William Hopwood, Ralph Morton, John S. Hammersley, and Sam Firth Mellor. D. Gurr and J. Hunt, *The Cotton Mills of Oldham* (Oldham, 1985), pp. 9–10. Examples of companies floated by Bunting include the Empire, Summervale and Times Spinning Companies. The Times No. 2 mill floated in 1907 was the largest mill in the area at 174,000 spindles, financed almost exclusively by loans raised by Bunting (*Oldham Chronicle*, 28th December, 1907; F. Jones, 'The Cotton Spinning Industry in the Oldham District from 1896–1914', M.A. thesis (University of Manchester, 1959), p. 88.

[46] Private spinners, for example Ralph Bagley, and Manchester-based tradesmen such as William Kenyon appeared on the share registers of Bunting's new companies. Public Record Office, BT/31 company files, Summervale Spinning Company, Empire Spinning Company and Times Spinning Company.

[47] *Oldham Standard*, 9th October, 1897.

[48] For more detail on this group, see Toms, 'Finance and Growth', Chapter 9.

[49] Eccles, Lancashire County Record Office (LCRO), DDX/868/7/1, Profit and loss accounts and balance sheets, Whiteley, LCRO, DDX/868/21/5, Balance sheets.

[50] The company was approximately the same size as Horrockses, having slightly less spinning capacity, but slightly more weaving, *The Cotton Spinners' and Manufacturers' Directory for Lancashire* (Oldham, Worrall, 1913).

the beginning of World War One, Birtwistle was 'one of the most powerful men in the trade',[51] although none of the individual firms were particularly large.[52]

In the North-East of the county, where weaving and even smaller firms predominated similar patterns of entrepreneurship emerged. In Burnley a prominent example was Thomas Burrows (1839–1906).[53] Although the companies he floated were on a far smaller scale, Burrows was a Burnley equivalent of Oldham's John Bunting. Thomas Burrows and Company Ltd was the most important successor to the Haggate Joint Stock Commercial Company, which like Mitchell Hey at Rochdale and Sun Mill at Oldham had been an attempt at co-operative manufacturing in the 1850s.[54] Between 1887 and 1905 the company acquired control of mills at Calder Vale, Gannow, Queensgate, and Westgate. None of these were significant in their own right, but their combined size added to Burrows's significance as an entrepreneur.[55] Burrows also became chairman of the Calder Vale Room and Power Company and of Healey Wood Mill. Like Edward Fielden, he also pursued a career in local politics and on the bench.[56] As a Liberal, he was immensely active in Burnley municipal politics, becoming Mayor in 1891.[57] However, Burrows's activities resembled closest those of William Birtwistle. Again capital accumulation occurred at an individual rather than corporate level. Like Bunting, Birtwistle, and other such individuals, this type of entrepreneur needed to see profits distributed as dividends rather than accumulated. Previously distributed personal wealth could then be used to reinvest in new concerns. The pattern of business organisation and development followed by Birtwistle was typical and similar to other multi-business enterprises, for example Fielden, Horrockses, Osbourne and Tootals.[58]

Whilst these processes led to the centralisation of capital in Lancashire the crucial effect of the merger waves of 1898–1900 was to draw in finance from metropolitan sources. Again, however, these federations were vehicles for creating powerful networks of directors. This process of attracting outside finance culminated in the recapitalisation boom of 1919–20, when London and

[51]   Birtwistle Group, *The William Birtwistle Group of Mills, Centenary, 1851–1951* (undated and privately published, available in Manchester Central Library).
[52]   Elsewhere, William was recognised as a significant figure. He continued his acquisitive strategy into the 1920s, for example with the acquisition of Ewood mills in 1928 (*The Times*, 17th December, 1928 p. 11g), and by the time of his death in 1936, controlled 16 mills, 'forming one of the largest combinations under the same management in Lancashire', *The Times*, 15th June, 1936, p. 17d.
[53]   For more detail on this group, see Toms, 'Finance and Growth', Chapter 9.
[54]   R. Frost, *A Lancashire Township: The History of Briercliffe with Extwistle*, (Rieve Edge Press, 1982) p. 65.
[55]   Britannia and Belle Vue Mills at Westgate had 1527 looms; Worrall, *The Cotton Spinners' and Manufacturers' Directory*, 1913.
[56]   Frost, *A Lancashire Township*, p. 66.
[57]   *Burnley Express*, 27th June, 1906.
[58]   Toms, 'The First Lancashire Merger'; J.S. Toms 'Financial Constraints on Economic Growth: Profits, Capital Accumulation, and the Development of the Lancashire Cotton Spinning Industry, 1885–1914', *Accounting, Business and Financial History*, Vol. 4, No. 3 (1994), pp. 364–83; ibid., 'The Finance and Growth'; ibid., 'Fielden Brothers'.

other outside syndicates invested in specialised companies or new amalgamations such as Amalgamated Cotton Mills Trust (ACMT) and Crosses and Heatons.[59] These re-flotations were speculative and depended heavily on the reputations and contacts of the entrepreneur.[60] Hence new capital was used to finance high dividends to equity shareholders, in particular those promotional capitalists who used stock market quotations as fast exit routes for their own investments.[61] However, money was attracted from syndicates from outside the local area. [62]

An important reason for the emergence of this governance structure was the industry's reliance on the mill as the basic technical unit of organisation. This facilitated diversity of output, but at the same time contained available economies of scope and limited opportunities for the professionalisation of management. Thus although increasingly controlled by cross directorships and share holdings, each mill was structured by the necessary activities to fulfil the specialised productive task. Hierarchies within the work force, exemplified by the minder-piecer system helped guarantee a narrow span of control. At the strategic apex, the financial capitalist had little need for management hierarchy *per se* and managerial economies of scope developed through cross directorships and financial linkages. For these reasons, a special type of individual capitalism had emerged in parts of Lancashire by the early 1900s. In summary, Lancashire firms retained only narrow resource bases within the company whilst directors were able to amass financial resources, promoting network self-sufficiency and opaque accountability.

Networks and governance in a declining industry, 1920–1980

Although the directors of Lancashire firms might have been reasonably self-sufficient, other aspects of the industry's network structure created a great deal of vulnerability. In particular the network of overseas merchants and selling agencies that linked Lancashire via the Manchester metropolis to the far reaches of the world market. As suggested in the previous section, when markets expanded metropolitan investors supported Lancashire directors in new mill financing. However, the end of the growth phase in 1920 ushered in a new period of interdependence. As the industry's markets contracted the

---

[59]   W. Thomas, *The Provincial Stock Exchanges* (Frank Cass, 1973).
[60]   Samuel Firth Mellor and Frank Platt were examples of the entrepreneurs involved. Thomas, *The Provincial Stock Exchanges,* p. 157; J.H. Bamberg, 'The Government, the Banks, and the Lancashire Cotton Industry, 1918–1939', PhD thesis (University of Cambridge, 1984), p. 6.
[61]   For example the premature retirement of Frank Platt. J.H. Bamberg, 'Sir Frank Platt', in D. Jeremy (ed), *Dictionary of Business Biography* (Butterworths, 1984–6); Thomas, *The Provincial Stock Exchanges*, p. 158.
[62]   Thomas, *The Provincial Stock Exchanges*, p. 157.

opacity of the industrial network and specialised resource base prevented exit and made restructuring more difficult.

Before 1914 Lancashire textiles companies had been subjected to speculative booms prompted by the activities of groups of promoters. In 1919–20, there was a similar boom based on the reflotation of existing capacity and a post war shortage of material and factor inputs.[63] However world demand remained depressed and Lancashire lost its dominance in key export markets. Consequently the restructuring of 1919–20 resulted in a disastrous over-valuation of assets, a trend related to another infusion of London and metropolitan influences into an industry that to date had been locally owned and managed.[64] Like the merger boom of 1898–1900 this new boom also attracted outside financial support from London syndicates for certain restructuring companies, such as the Amalgamated Cotton Mills Trust, whilst other large sections of the industry, particularly Oldham, were re-capitalised by local syndicates.[65] The overvaluation in the boom of 1919–20 was so serious that it thwarted all attempts to engineer recovery at the level of the single mill company. The specialised marketing and production structures that had created competitive advantage before 1914 were by the 1920s and 1930s the subject of increasing criticism from contemporaries.[66] Reformers were advocating the fabrication of a more concentrated industry, as a means of driving down unit costs, whilst retaining the advantages of external economies.[67]

These trends did little to undermine the pre-1914 governance system. The equity market became illiquid, preventing disposal of depreciated shares. Whilst many mills became heavily indebted to the banks, there was little debt to equity conversion at the level of the individual firm. Instead, as much to rescue the banks as rescue the mills, the Bank of England underwrote the formation of the Lancashire Cotton Corporation (LCC) in 1929. Its objective was to buy up the least efficient and most indebted mills in order to close them down. Loan creditors would receive new equity in the company in return.[68] At the behest of these outside financial backers a new management structure was imposed and decisions previously made at plant level, for example on product range were centralised.[69] Despite (and because of) the importation of outside

---

[63] Ibid.

[64] D. Higgins and J.S. Toms, 'Capital Ownership, Capital Structure, and Capital Markets: Financial Constraints and the Decline of the Lancashire Cotton Textile Industry, 1880–1965', *Journal of Industrial History*, Vol. 4, No. 1 (2001), pp. 48–64.

[65] M. Rose, *Firms, Networks and Business Values: the British and American Cotton Industries Since 1750*, (Cambridge University Press, 2000), p. 208.

[66] W. Lazonick, 'Industrial Organization and Technological Change: The Decline of the British Cotton Industry', *Business History Review*, Vol. 57 (1983) pp. 195–236.

[67] J.M. Keynes, *The Return to Gold and Industrial Policy II*, (Collected works, Cambridge, 1981), Vol. XIX, p. 583.

[68] J.H. Bamberg, 'The Rationalisation of the British Cotton Industry in the Inter-war Years', *Textile History*, Vol. 19, No. 1 (1988), pp. 83–102.

[69] G. Bennett, 'The Present Position of the Cotton Industry in Britain', MA thesis (University of Manchester, 1933).

managers, the company found the process of matching production in individual mills to the large number of small orders very difficult relative to the efficiency by which this had been traditionally carried out using the markets of Liverpool and Manchester. Under the new leadership of Frank Platt the LCC reverted to the federal model practised elsewhere by the FCSDA and the Bleachers Association.[70] In these companies local directors retained power. The net result of these processes was to reinforce the cliques of interlocking directorships that controlled much of the industry.[71] This control remained a crucial feature of the industry in its decline phase, and is detailed in Table 4.2.

Table 4.2
The distribution of directorships in British enterprises, 1950

	Cotton Textile (%)[a]	All British Enterprises (%)[b]
No. of directorships per person		
1	19.2	87.4
2	13.2	8.5
3-5	43.7	3.9
6 or more	23.9	0.2
Total	100	100

Note: [a] % of directors in each category from a sample of 167 directors from 45 quoted textile companies.

[b] % of directors in each category from the top 250 British enterprises. The % is estimated from Scott (1997), p. 117 which provides breakdowns for the years 1938 and 1976. The figures shown here are a simple average for those two years.

Sources: Annual Returns (form E) Companies House and PRO files. Scott, 1997, p. 117.

---

[70]   Bamberg, 'Sir Frank Platt'.
[71]   The following discussion on directors and shareholders is based on an analysis of annual returns for over 50 companies in the period 1880-1960, located at the Public Record Office (file BT/31) and Companies House. For further sample details and analysis of these variables, see Toms, 'The Rise of Modern Financial Reporting'; ibid., 'Information Content of Earnings'; Filatotchev and Toms, 'Corporate Governance, Strategy and Survival'.

A survey using annual returns of these companies in the 1950s has revealed interlocking directorships and a rump of residual small private shareholders.[72] Table 4.2 shows that the typical Lancashire director sat on the boards of far more other companies in comparison to national averages. The average director of the typical large British company in 1950 held just that one board position. In contrast the Lancashire director held three or four board positions with a significant minority holding more than six. This governance structure reflected the nineteenth and the early twentieth century developments referred to above. Hence the most common type of interlock was in other cotton industry companies. The average age of each director in the Table 4.2 sample was 59 years, suggesting that whilst many had served during the crisis years of the inter-war period, a minority had also participated in the development of earlier Bunting style groups. At the same time, it is suggestive that centralisation of directors' power acted as a barrier to the development of new managerial talent.

Meanwhile share-ownership was individual rather than institutional. Although the financial syndicates attracted institutional investors in the re-floatation boom of 1919–20 and the banks were left with a lot of worthless equity after the crisis of 1922, individual ownership re-asserted itself after 1945. There were several reasons for this. With Bank of England support, the LCC proved a useful vehicle for the commercial banks to liquidate their positions in the 1930s. Also the positions of many institutional investors were speculative, temporary and limited to the larger firms. Finally share quotations were based on thin local stock markets, and this was the case for the larger conglomerates and the larger number of smaller quoted firms. Instead of institutional ownership there was substantial share-ownership by directors, their families and members of founding families. Only where there had been previous history of amalgamation was there evidence of a modern model of corporate governance, that is characterised by an increase of institutional shareholding and growing importance of board interlocks with firms outside the industry. To summarise, the majority of firms in the industry were classic 'Berle and Means' companies, with powerful, networked directors and weak, inactive shareholders.[73]

To what extent did this system of governance and opaque accountability explain the decline of the industry and failure to rationalise, compared to traditional explanations? Following the immediate post-war boom of the late 1940s, the expected effects of increased international competition, import penetration and excess capacity should have been that firms began to exit the industry. However, the actual exit rate was low. That weak companies were not short of cash and could stay in the industry is paradoxical. However, the reluctance of firms to exit was a function of the system of corporate

---

[72]   Filatotchev and Toms, 'Corporate Governance, Strategy and Survival'.

[73]   A. Berle and G.C. Means, *The Modern Corporation and Private Property* (Commercial Clearing House, 1932).

governance and the narrow, specialised and increasingly obsolete resource base. In this sense the situation in the 1950s was similar to the 1920s when Keynes and others pointed out the banks' refusal to allow their debtor companies to exit.[74] In the 1950s, bank and other forms of debt had largely disappeared, but equity stakeholders inherited a similar set of problems. Realisable values were low as shrinking markets created over-capacity and undermined the second hand market. Assets involved were highly specific, especially machinery, and in most cases were of old vintage.[75] Re-equipment meant investment in new but more expensive technology with high replacement cost. Thus the only alternative valuation available to financial claim holders was economic value of the assets in use. Specialised firms survived on meagre but positive cash flow, shared out according to the price fixing rules enforced by employers' organisations such as the Yarn Spinners' Association. In this fashion, self-sufficient cliques of directors substituted market processes, shared resources and prevented exit from the industry. Regulatory intervention, in the form of the Cotton Industry Act 1959 was necessary in order to achieve a more rational distribution of resources, concentrated in fewer more competitive units.[76]

Another legacy of the restructuring of the early twentieth century and inter-war years was the larger and more diverse firm. Access to a larger resource base created a different set of strategic opportunities. Slow exit and continuing over-capacity had led to the creation of the LCC, with the express purpose of rationalising the industry.[77] Its strategy in the 1930s was to purchase weaker mills in order to close them down. It did so under the close scrutiny of the Bank of England and other representatives of the layers of structured debt finance that dominated the company's balance sheet.[78] By the 1950s, it had freed itself of debt and pursued a different strategy. It now proceeded to 'cherry pick' the best mills as take-over targets.[79] The company obtained agreement in target mills by exploiting the structure of cross directorships. Cyril Lord followed a similar strategy. Other amalgamations, such as the Shiloh group proceeded on the same lines. The annual report of the LCC described Eagle and Durban mills as 'very satisfactory acquisitions' with modern machinery. When the Eagle Spinning Company was taken over by the LCC in 1956, J.B. Whitehead was a director of the former company for several years prior to being appointed to the LCC board as well in 1955. Acquisitions were value destructive from the perspective of LCC shareholders. This reflected poor

---

[74] Keynes, 'Industrial Policy'; Bamberg, 'The Rationalisation of the British Cotton Industry', pp. 83-102.

[75] C. Miles, *Lancashire Textiles: A Case Study of Industrial Change* (Cambridge University Press, 1968), pp. 38-9.

[76] For details of the Act's provisions, see Miles, *Lancashire Textiles.*

[77] Bamberg, 'The Rationalisation of the British Cotton Industry'.

[78] Ibid.

[79] D.M. Higgins, 'Structure-Conduct-Performance: Lancashire Spinning Firms, 1945–65', PhD thesis (Cambridge, 1991).

monitoring by inactive shareholders in an illiquid and inefficient capital market.[80] Unrelated diversification, for example the acquisition of brick making and electrical companies lacked strategic fit and again reflected poor monitoring from financial stakeholders. Whilst LCC managers had little incentive to maximise value on the basis of their relatively small shareholdings, there were other managerial reasons for such a diversification policy. In a tight managerial labour market, there was a problem of attracting and retaining managerial talent. This explained diversification into brick making and ladies woollen fabrics in the late 1950s. Where investment opportunities stagnate in the core business, diversification may help retain ambitious executives. The process also reduced financial risk.[81]

Despite these apparent advantages, such investments were no solution to the problems of the industry. Diversification reflected existing networks and promoted further interlocks, and these tended to exploit only local business contacts. In the case of the Bleacher's Association, new ventures were confined to Lancashire because its directors preferred to do business over drinks and on the golf course.[82] Nowhere did these transactions promote greater accountability. Notwithstanding the scale of merger and restructuring, the market for corporate control was under-developed for textile companies, whose shares were often thinly traded.[83] In general the stock market was incapable of sustaining hostile take-over activity until the late 1950s.[84] Instead of relying on large, professionally managed hierarchies, these firms continued to reflect the network relationships of the directoral cliques that had come to dominate the industry.

The last years of the LCC illustrate that widening the resource based through diversification was a necessary but not sufficient condition of effective long-term strategic restructuring. Such strategies also required extending the network of business contacts beyond the traditional industrial district, particularly to secure the support of City based financial backers. By 1962 it had become apparent that the reduction in capacity brought about by the 1959 Cotton Industry Act had been offset by the substantial rise in imports, and excess capacity remained a problem. In these circumstances the LCC board proposed to accelerate its programme of acquiring other mills, possibly in collaboration with other combines. Although the strategy continued to reflect interlocking directorships, its political lobbying power remained weak. In the face of take-over threats the objective of the LCC board was to create powerful groupings that could lobby

---

[80] D.M. Higgins and J.S. Toms, 'Public Subsidy and Private Divestment: The Lancashire Cotton Textile Industry', *Business History*, Vol. 42, No. 1 (2000), pp. 59–84.
[81] I. Hill, 'The Structure and Organisation of the British Textile Industry', in F. Brech (ed), *Management in the Textile Industry* (London, 1968) pp. 28–9.
[82] D. Jeremy, 'Survival strategies in Lancashire textiles: Bleachers Association to Whitecroft plc, 1900–1980s', *Textile History*, Vol. 24, No. 2 (1993), pp. 163–209; J. Singleton, 'The Decline of the British Cotton Industry Since 1940', in Rose (ed), *The Lancashire Cotton Industry*.
[83] Higgins and Toms, 'Public Subsidy and Private Divestment'.
[84] J. Littlewood, *The Stock Market* (Pitman, 1998).

government to defend Lancashire's dwindling share of the domestic market based on the directors' power base of local networks. Lack of political influence undermined the financial viability of the LCCs restructuring plan and paved the way for the Courtaulds take-over of the LCC. The need to create powerful groupings also explains Courtauld's take-over of FCSDA subsequent to its acquisition of the LCC[85] and also why the rationalised industry that emerged after 1965 was one of the most concentrated in the world.

Courtaulds and other firms such as Smith and Nephew lacked the obstacles imposed by traditional Lancashire governance structures and instead used their professional hierarchies and already extensive resource base to enter the industry and as upstream and downstream diversification strategies.[86] Some textile firms diversified within the industry downstream (e.g., ACMT started production of bandages), but in general few firms within the industry were able to generate survival strategies. Exceptions, such as Smith and Nephew, Shiloh and the Bleachers' Association (later Whitecroft plc) used City contacts to raise financial resources, which in turn facilitated diversification and widened the resource base of the firm. Managerial economies of scope now reflected techniques of financial control in portfolio businesses rather than the traditional specialised knowledge of the Lancashire region.[87] Diversification meant that the survivors became less and less like mainstream textile companies and more conglomerate in appearance.

The role of networks in the rise and fall of the Lancashire textile industry: Some conclusions

The above discussion has emphasised the role of external economies of scale, coupled with the development of specialisation in production. In this respect it has certain commonality with other explanations for the rise and fall of the Lancashire textile industry. In the above narrative, the role of accountability and governance has also been emphasised. Combined with an analysis of the resource base of participant companies, this has been used to analyse the principal features of the dominant business networks. In particular the concentration of power among directors and its parallel dispersal amongst shareholders played a significant role in the evolution of the industry.

---

[85] Rose, *Firms, Networks and Business Values*, p. 287–8.

[86] J. Foreman-Peck, *Smith and Nephew in the Health Care Industry* (Edward Elgar, 1995)

[87] For example A.M. Alfred's promotion of discounted cash flow at Courtaulds and to a wider corporate audience. A.M. Alfred, 'Investment in Development Districts in the United Kingdom', *Journal of Accounting Research*, Autumn (1964), pp.172–82; P. Miller, 'Accounting Innovation Beyond the Enterprise: Problematizing Investment Decisions and Programming Investment Growth in the UK in the 1960s', *Accounting, Organizations and Society*, Vol. 16, No. 8 (1991), pp. 743–5.

Table 4.3 reprises the grid first presented above in Table 4.1. The grid can now be used to summarise the history of the industry as revealed in detail by the earlier narrative. For the majority of the period 1860–1960, most firms were part of an industrial district whose principal characteristics were their specialised resource base, internalisation of external economies of scale using a network structure of directors that promoted self-sufficiency, secrecy and independence from external stakeholder groups.

Table 4.3
Dynamic determinants of network characteristics in the Lancashire textile industry, 1860–1980

		Strategic Context: Degree of Accountability	
		Transparent	*Opaque*
Strategic Content: Organisational Resource Base	*Extensive*	**Quadrant 4** Surviving companies, 1950–80.	**Quadrant 3** Lancashire Cotton Corporation, 1950–62; Other federal combines (e.g., FCSDA)
	Narrow	**Quadrant 2** Oldham Limiteds, 1860–90	**Quadrant 1** Industrial district, 1860–1959

Quadrant 1, market substituting, low external resource dependency networks summarises the position of most firms. Some firms for limited periods did not conform to this Lancashire model of network capitalism. In Oldham, in the period 1860–90, a co-operative ideology and democratic governance structure promoted transparent accountability. This was a temporary phenomenon, since the principle method of raising finance, new stock exchange share issues, facilitated manipulation by insider groups and the usurpation of control by cliques of directors. Oldham had moved from quadrant 2 to quadrant 1 by the mid-1890s. The LCC, from its inception in 1929 was intended to be a centralised, professional hierarchy. This was never a substitute for the relatively efficient markets of Manchester and Liverpool and until 1960, the LCC operated as a more decentralised organisation, allowing autonomy to the managers of individual mills and basing its acquisition strategy on local knowledge and contacts. Other larger firms such as the FCDSA had adopted this model since the beginning of the twentieth century. They represented a tightly related network of firms that was held together by cross-ownership of shares and directors' interlocks. For the period 1900–60, most of these firms operated in quadrant 3. Surviving firms in the later period were able to diversify away from cotton as the industry declined and sustain a wider resource base. To do this they had to secure outside finance and secure new structures of accountability and governance. Quadrant 4 describes the networking characteristics of this strategy.

For the majority of firms characterised by the Lancashire model of network capitalism, industry growth encouraged the concentration of directors' power. In turn this undermined accountability and acted as a barrier to restructuring during decline. Whilst emphasising the role of accountability, the above discussion has also showed how the ownership and management structure of the industry interacted with organisational diversity. Hence in the nineteenth century, the rise of specialisation also promoted the informal interlocked group of firms. In the twentieth century interlocks reinforced specialisation and acted as a constraint on restructuring. Only in the minority of cases where board diversity was associated with organisational diversity were recovery strategies achieved.

From the 1890s onwards the Lancashire textile industrial district developed a highly unusual system of governance. It was based on diversified directors and non-diversified shareholders (in the conventional model of Anglo Saxon economies it is the other way round). Hence the rise of powerful directors was not consistent with the rise of managerial capitalism, rather an unusual Lancashire variant of personal capitalism.

Chapter 5

Much ado about nothing? Regional business networks and the performance of the cotton and woollen textile industries, c.1919–c.1939[1]

Sue Bowden and David Higgins

Introduction

As the introductory chapter to this book indicates, networks have had a rather ambiguous role in the development of particular industries and regions.[2] In addition, at different points in time, networks have been shown to exercise first a positive and subsequently a negative effect on the development of specific industries.[3] Ordinarily, we would expect both that the transmission of information between agents and the formation of networks to facilitate this transmission would be highly desirable. However, there can be little, if any, guarantee that firms and their supporting networks will use this information for the common good. This is clearly an important consideration because the issues of trust and consensus are pivotal to the successful operation of networks. This chapter seeks to provide a re-appraisal of the positive view of networks by examining the break-up of consensus and the undermining of networks in depressed industries.[4]

[1]   Parts of the research embodied in this chapter were made possible by the award of a Hallsworth Fellowship to Sue Bowden, and a Nuffield grant to David Higgins, Ref: SGS/00108/C. In addition, we have received useful comments from participants at seminars given at the LSE, Manchester University, Manchester Metropolitan University, and the other contributing authors at a conference in Preston, 2001. The usual disclaimer applies.

[2]   See Chapter 1 in this volume.

[3]   For example, financial syndicates accelerated growth of the industry pre-1914 but hampered its subsequent development in the inter-war years and post-1945. See, for example, Chapter 4, in this volume. For a much broader discussion of the role of networks in the Lancashire textile industry see, for example, M.B. Rose, *Firms, Networks and Business Values: the British and American Cotton Industries since 1750* (Cambridge University Press, 2000).

[4]   We recognise that a distinction can be drawn between networks and network

Focusing on the main branches of the English cotton and wool textile industries during the inter-war years, this chapter provides case studies of the conflicts that can arise between the interests of networks and their members. In two of the case studies, cotton spinning and cotton weaving, we find that, at times, this conflict proved almost impossible to resolve. In the other case study, wool textiles, we find that attempts by networks to seek and impose agreements that operated on an industry-wide basis were quickly abandoned in the 1920s. This left each section free to pursue its own interests. The central theme that emerges from this chapter is that the *assumption* that networks are advantageous may be very misleading. In industries that are characterised by a high degree of vertical specialisation, and with each section experiencing different market conditions, the ability of agents to work towards a *common* purpose is undermined. The breakdown of trust appears to be central to this. So, too, are the difficulties of co-operating for mutual advantage when the interests of one section of the industry are incompatible with the interests of others.

This chapter is organised as follows. Section I sets out the market structures of the cotton and wool textile industries and provides a brief overview of their relative performance during this period. Despite similarities in market structure, these industries experienced very different economic fortunes. Sections II and III present findings from the Lancashire cotton textile industry which highlight the conflict between networks and the firms that belonged to them. We examine why networks acted to restrict reaction to depressed demand (cotton spinning) and to preclude productivity enhancing changes in work practices (cotton weaving). Section IV examines the experiences of the Yorkshire wool textile industry and indicates why, in this industry, networks appear to have exercised a more positive influence. Section V presents the conclusions of this chapter and its implications.

Overview of the cotton and wool textile industries during the inter-war years

Our case studies focus on the cotton and wool textile industries in England during the inter-war years. Both had a long and distinguished history, contributing much to national output, employment and export performance. The wool textile industry had played a long and important role in the economic history of Britain, dating back in its earliest recorded times to the Roman era

organisations. The former term has been interpreted as referring to the means by which information is transmitted, whereas the latter term has been interpreted as the formation of institutions in which independent actors co-operate frequently for mutual advantage. Because we are principally concerned with formal organisations in the form of, for example, employers associations, we use the term network to refer to network organisations.

until, by the beginning of the eighteenth century, the industry had become the world's largest manufacturer and exporter of woollen cloth.[5] The late nineteenth century was characterised by a contraction of world trade in woollen goods, as countries increasingly met their own requirements. Of the diminished volume of trade, however, Britain retained a large and increasing share.[6] Likewise, the cotton industry had become synonymous with Britain's early Industrial Revolution success, setting the scene for her dominance of world trade in cotton textiles throughout the nineteenth century.

The first two issues that need to be addressed concern the presence of networks in these industries, together with a discussion of their similarities in terms of industrial structure. It is well established in the literature that the institutional framework is vital to the formation of regional and industrial business networks. For example, networking among firms is enabled and supported by regionally embedded institutions such as chambers of commerce, provincial banks and insurance companies, as well as local employers' and employee associations. In addition, inter-firm networking has been traced to the spatial clustering of specialised resources and know-how in regional/industrial districts.[7]

Both the cotton and wool textile industries had employer and employee networks. Cotton spinning employers were networked through district and industry associations. At the industry level, the *Federation of Master Cotton Spinners Association* (hereafter, FMCSA) and *The Cotton Spinners and Manufacturers Association* (hereafter, CSMA) were the key networks. At the district level, there were networks such as the *Oldham and the Bolton Master Cotton Spinners Association* (hereafter, OMCSA and BMCSA). Employee interests were networked through industry level organisations, namely the *Amalgamated Association of Operative Cotton Spinners and Twisters* (hereinafter AAOCST) and *The United Textile Factory Workers Association* (hereafter, UTFWA), while at the district level there were networks such as *The Bolton and District Operative Cotton Spinners Provincial Association* (hereafter, BDOCS).

Wool had its own national *Wool and Allied Textile Joint Industrial Council* (JIC), with two English (the West Riding of Yorkshire and the West of England) and one Welsh district councils.[8] Given the fact that the West Riding

---

[5] Board of Trade, Working Party Reports, *Wool* (HMSO, 1947), p. 1.

[6] The United Kingdom's share of the combined exports of the United Kingdom, France and Germany was 41.6 per cent in 1880–83 and 53.9 per cent in 1909–13. Working Party Reports, *Wool*, p. 6.

[7] See, for example, M. Ebers, (ed), *The Formation of Inter-organisational Networks* (Oxford University Press, 1997), p. 9.

[8] C. Wrigley, *Cosy Co-operation Under Strain: Industrial Relations in the Yorkshire Woollen Industry*, 1919–39, University of York Borthwick Paper, No. 71 (York, 1987), p. 1.

Council covered about 80 per cent of industry employment, the Northern District JIC was the decisive body, receiving support from both sides of the industry.[9] Wrigley has described the war years as having brought 'a fragmented industry together' with the unions gaining 'prestige from participation in the running of the industry in wartime'.[10] The JIC had its own monthly journal, which started in 1920, and regular meetings. In addition, employers networked through the more specialist sectional *Wool Textile Manufacturers Federation*, the *Woollen and Worsted Trades Federation* and the *Worsted Spinners Federation*, all of which had regular meetings and produced documentation and reports. The umbrella network for the workers was the *National Union of Textile Workers*, which encompassed a large number of specialist (including, *inter alia*, the *Worsted and Woollen Warpers Association*, the *Wool, Yarn and Warehouse Workers Union* and the *National Society of Woolcombers*) and regional (including *inter alia*, the *Huddersfield and District Healders and Twisters Society*, the *Leeds and District Warp Dressers and Twisters Association*) groups of workers.[11]

Although networks had a long history, a key impetus to the formalisation of their members' interests were Government-imposed requirements during the First World War, as a result of which both the cotton and wool textile industries operated on a centralised, collective wage bargaining basis. To a large extent, this collectivisation was both inevitable and necessary during the war years, when there was a need to avoid industrial unrest. Indeed, in wool textiles, this collectivisation was enshrined under the auspices of a JIC, which received widespread support from both employers and workers alike.[12] Employer and union networks persisted throughout the inter-war years in both industries. Both had a formal identity, and both met on a regular basis at national, district and local levels.

In addition, both the cotton and wool textile industries possessed remarkably similar industrial structures, with high degrees of geographical and product specialisation, together with a preponderance of small firms in each stage of production. Individualism had been advantageous for the cotton industry when it experienced expanding export markets prior to 1914. Substantial external economies in the form of specialised labour, raw cotton and yarn exchanges, and a sophisticated distribution network, had developed to cater for the large number of independent firms. Expanding markets had encouraged high levels of specialisation in each sector and the external economies generated made it easier for new firms to enter, thereby reinforcing specialisation and external

---

[9] Ibid.

[10] Ibid., p. 3.

[11] Minutes of a Court of Inquiry into the matters in dispute between the parties to the Northern Counties District Wool (and Allied) Textile Industrial Council, Vol. 3, No. 29 January, 1930, Bradford Archive Office, File Ref: 3D86:9/3/3. Hereafter, *Minutes of Inquiry*.

[12] Wrigley, *Cosy Co-operation*, p. 16.

economies. This vertical specialisation appears to have accelerated during the inter-war years.[13] The single biggest cotton weaving town, Burnley, was heavily engaged in the production of medium 'grey' cloth for printing or for export in the grey state to the East. Blackburn and Darwen concentrated on the production of finer quality 'grey' cloths for the Indian market. Nelson and Colne specialised in finely-woven cloths and coloured cloths. Bolton and its neighbourhood concentrated on fine cloths, and were especially renowned for high-quality bedding and quilt products.[14]

The pattern of geographic and product specialisation which existed in Lancashire's cotton industry was mirrored in the wool textile industry.[15] Halifax and Keighley specialised in the production of a variety of worsted yarns and dress goods; Dewsbury and Batley were the main centres of the heavy woollen industry, concentrating especially on rugs and blankets; Huddersfield produced fine woollen cloths as well as high quality worsteds for men's wear, whilst Leeds had both worsted and woollen activities ranging from fine cloth to plain woollen goods.[16]

Both the cotton and wool textile industries were also remarkably similar in terms of industrial concentration. In 1930, over 60 per cent of returns in cotton to the Census were made by firms which employed less than 200 workers. These firms accounted for nearly a quarter of all those employed and of net output in cotton spinning.[17] Large firms, namely, those employing over 1000, by contrast accounted for less than one per cent of the total returns, 14 per cent of net output and 10.6 per cent of employment. In the woollen industry, small-scale undertakings were prevalent in nearly all branches, with the large majority being privately owned and personally conducted businesses. In the early 1920s, 56.4 per cent of the 1384 companies in wool textiles were private firms; of those, 78.6 per cent employed less than 100 people.[18] This was to remain the dominant structure throughout the inter-war years.[19]

---

[13]   Ibid.

[14]   H. Clay, *Report on the Position of the English Cotton Industry* (Confidential Report for Securities Management Trust Ltd, 1931), p. 20; Political and Economic Planning, *Report on the British Cotton Industry* (1934), p. 61.

[15]   The geographical specialisation which existed in the cotton industry is well documented. This division, by which spinning was largely concentrated in the south and west, and weaving largely concentrated in the north and east of Lancashire, was reinforced by product specialisation. See, for example, S. Kenny, 'Sub-regional Specialisation in the Lancashire Cotton Industry, 1884–1914: A Study in Organisational and Locational Change', *Journal of Historical Geography*, Vol. 8 (1982), pp. 41–63.

[16]   Working Party Reports, *Wool*, pp. 2-3; A. Frobisher, *Report on Wages in the Woollen and Worsted Industries*, 1880-1920, Bradford Archive Office, File Ref: 20D81:78, pp. 7, 18 and 22 (hereafter, Frobisher *Report*).

[17]   Board of Trade, *Census of Production*, 1933, p. 32.

[18]   Committee on Industry and Trade, *Survey of Textile Industries*, (HMSO, 1928), pp. 175–6.

[19]   Working Party Reports, *Wool*, p. 15.

However, despite their many similarities, these industries experienced markedly different performances during the inter-war years, despite the fact that both initially confronted similar external conditions. For example, cotton textiles experienced severe problems as export markets collapsed, but wool textiles gained new overseas markets and generated increased domestic demand. The broad trends in output and exports in each of the major sections of the cotton and wool textile industries are shown in Tables 5.1, 5.2, 5.3 and 5.4. Comparing 1912 with 1937, the percentage decline in production of cotton yarn and cotton manufactures, was –30.5 and –46.7 per cent respectively. For wool textiles, the relevant figures are: woollen yarn, 2.85 per cent, worsted yarn, -3.3 per cent and tissues, -1.3 per cent.

By 1937, despite a collapse in exports, the output of each section of the woollen industry was very close to that of 1924 and 'all the ground lost in the intervening depression had been recovered'.[20] The same, however, could not be said of the cotton textile industry.

Table 5.1
Output volumes in the principal sections of the cotton textile industries, 1912–1937

	Cotton Yarn[a]	Cotton Mfgs[b]
Year		
1912	1983	8050
1924	1395	6074
1930	1047	3500
1933	n.a	n.a
1935	1167	3766
1937	1377	4288

Notes: [a] Expressed as million pounds.

[b] Expressed as million square yards, except, 1912, which is in linear yards.

Source: R. Robson, *The Cotton Industry in Britain* (Macmillan, 1957), p. 345.

---

[20]   Ibid.

Table 5.2
Output volumes in the principal sections of the wool textile industries, 1912–1937

	Woolen Yarn[a]	Worsted Yarn[b]	Tissue Output[c]
Year			
1912	315.7	249.4	481.0
1924	312.0	242.5	475.7
1930	200.3	185.6	343.9
1933	283.4	238.6	413.3
1935	298.6	244.4	439.2
1937	324.7	241.1	474.6

Notes: [a] Expressed as million pounds.
[b] Expressed as million pounds.
[c] Expressed as million pounds.

Source: Board of Trade Working Party Reports, *Wool* (HMSO), p. 5; Foster Collection, Box 275–7, Brotherton Library, University of Leeds.

Table 5.3
Export volumes in the principal sections of the cotton textile industries, 1912–1937

	Cotton Yarn[a]	Cotton Mfgs[b]
Year		
1912	2142	6913
1924	1369	4585
1930	1272	2491
1933	1177	2177
1935	1261	2013
1937	1431	2023

Notes: [a] Expressed as millions of pounds.
[b] Expressed as millions of pounds.

Source: Robson, *The Cotton Industry*, p. 333.

Table 5.4
Export volumes in the principal section of the wool textile industries, 1912–1937

	Woolen Yarn[a]	Worsted Yarn[b]	Tissue Output[c]
Year			
1912	6.25	56.8	235.0
1924	8.30	54.0	221.5
1930	5.40	32.0	113.7
1933	7.50	35.0	94.20
1935	7.80	33.0	109.6
1937	6.80	29.7	122.7

Notes: [a] Expressed as million pounds.
[b] Expressed as million pounds.
[c] Expressed as million pounds.

Source: Board of Trade, *Wool*, p. 5; Foster Collection, Box 275–6.

How can we explain these differences and to what extent, if any, did networks play a role? The key issue that needs to be addressed is the role that networks played in determining the response of agents to the conditions they faced. In our first case study, that of cotton spinning, we demonstrate that networks did have a role to play in determining the range of strategies pursued by firms as they laboured under heavy debt levels caused by the re-floatation boom of 1919–20. However, this role was not always consistently or successfully applied. In fact, to the extent that networks did have a role to play in cotton spinning, it was often reactionary and defensive. In our second case study, the cotton weaving industry, we examine the role that networks played in limiting changes in working practices. These changes, often referred to as the More Loom System (MLS), had the potential to improve the competitiveness of firms in the most depressed sectors of this industry. However, the need of the CSMA to preserve employer solidarity undermined, indeed, practically eradicated, any advantages that adoption of MLS would have had. In this case, we demonstrate that networks exercised a disabling effect. Our final case study is the wool textile industry. While this industry shared many of the structural and network characteristics of the cotton spinning and weaving industry, unlike the cotton spinning industry its agents were not labouring under debt levels. The consequence of this, we argue, was that there was less pressure in this industry for networks to try and protect a common interest: no such interest existed in this highly fragmented industry and so individual firms and individual sections were free to pursue their own interests.

In other words, in the wool textile industry, the role of networks varied from passive (when there was recognised implementation of a common policy this was impossible) to positive (for example, in facilitating vertical links, especially between manufacturers and retailers).[21]

The cotton spinning industry

The crucial difference between the cotton spinning and the wool textile industry was their financial circumstances. We are not referring here to *physical plant*, since much of this in both industries was very old and fully depreciated.[22] The financial implication of this was that the fixed costs of operation were virtually zero. However, in the cotton spinning industry the high levels of debt accumulated as a *direct* result of the 1919–20 boom, together with their high fixed interest charges, meant that it was no longer sufficient only to cover variable costs in order to remain viable. During this boom, the response of many cotton firms was to re-float: owners of spinning firms issued new shares in their companies and these were bought by speculators at a high price in the expectation of forming a new company with a capitalisation based on the exceptional profits that were being made and which seemed likely to continue.[23] A total of 217 companies in the spinning industry, and 110 firms in the weaving industry, were involved in this boom.[24] The problems were exacerbated by the methods employed to finance the boom. Shareholders were called upon to provide only 55 per cent of the finance, the remainder being raised by loans, bank overdrafts and debentures. Such finance bears fixed interest that had to be paid irrespective of whether profits were being made. Effectively, the means used to finance the re-floatation augmented

---

[21] The qualification to this statement concerns the high degree of unanimity which existed when the Whitley Councils were in force, up to the mid 1920s. In addition, there is evidence that networks operated to reinforce suitable vertical, not horizontal, relationships. These are detailed in part four of this chapter.

[22] In the cotton industry, a survey of plant in 1934 revealed that 36.7 per cent of mule spindles and 41.7 per cent of looms had been installed before 1900: Calculated from Political and Economic Planning, *Report*, pp. 54 and 62. In wool textiles a similar picture appears. A survey of machinery in 1946 revealed that almost twenty-five per cent of worsted spindles and a higher proportion of woollen spindles were installed before 1900, and that, 'many of the looms have been in use for 50 years or more'. Working Party Reports, *Wool*, p. 76.

[23] Between August 1919 and April, 1920, the average price paid per 1,000 spindles increased from £1400 to £4160. G.W. Daniels and J. Jewkes, 'The post-war depression in the Lancashire Cotton Industry', *Journal of the Royal Statistical Society*, XCI (1928), pp. 170–72.

[24] Between them, these firms accounted for forty-six and fourteen per cent respectively of their industry's capacity. Ibid., p. 174.

the debt of the cotton industry. When the post war boom collapsed, the new owners of the industry were saddled with massive, fixed-interest bearing debt.[25]

The new owners of the cotton industry could not easily exit, because their financial resources were intricately tied up in the fortunes of the industry: exit would have required owners to forego any opportunity they had of recovering their investments should the trading environment improve.[26] However, by refusing to exit, abnormal and prolonged levels of excess capacity were maintained and this, by increasing the incentive to 'weak selling', increased financial fragility and uncertainty in the industry.[27]

The presence of substantial debt meant that all firms in the cotton spinning industry had to consider themselves financially vulnerable and potentially marginal.[28] This, in turn, generated defensive pressures to pursue collective decision making, especially on the key issues of industry output (regulated by collective short-time working) and industry price (regulated by industry-wide price associations). During the inter-war years, the network representing employers, the FMCSA, enacted these strategies. Two issues arise. First, why

---

[25] Calculated as follows. Pre-decimalisation, there were 240 pence per pound and so a figure of £1710 equates to 410,000 pence. To express this per spindle, we divide 410,000 pence by 1000 spindles, which yields 410 pence. Recalling that one shilling was worth 12 pence, we arrive at the figure given in the text. Calculated from data given in Daniels and Jewkes, 'The Post War Depression', Table 20, p. 177. Data for scrap value per spindle taken from J. Bamberg, 'The Government, the Banks, and the Lancashire Cotton Industry, 1918–1939', unpublished Ph.D thesis, (University of Cambridge, 1984), p. 256.

[26] In any case, being heavily indebted to the banks, the choice of exit was no longer their own. As Bamberg has shown, the banks, in order to safeguard their previous lending, were just as keen that heavily indebted firms should continue. Sometimes, the vested interests of the banks worked to delay absorption of mills by the LCC. See Bamberg, 'The Government, the Banks', especially pp. 17–30 and 91–103. For a detailed analysis of the impact of the boom and its persistence throughout the inter-war years on the balance sheets of representative companies, see D.M. Higgins and J.S. Toms, 'Capital Ownership, Capital Structure and Capital Markets: Financial Constraints and the Decline of the Lancashire Cotton Textile Industry, 1880–1965', *Journal of Industrial History*, Vol. 4, No. 1 (2001), pp. 48–65.

[27] Such exits as did occur were largely involuntary in the spinning section. The Lancashire Cotton Corporation, for example, established in 1929 as an amalgamation of approximately 100 firms in the coarse and medium American sections, had support from both the banks and the government to coerce firms into the amalgamation as a vital first step to scrapping excess capacity. See, Bamberg, 'The Government, The Banks'. By 1939, the Lancashire Cotton Corporation had scrapped about 4.5m spindles which it had brought under its control. W. Lazonick, 'The Cotton Industry' in B. Elbaum and W. Lazonick, *The Decline of the British Economy* (Oxford University Press, 1986), p. 33.

[28] Firms which re-equipped had heavy fixed costs to bear. Firms which had re-floated had incurred heavy fixed interest payments. Both these types of firms were vulnerable to 'weak selling' which threatened to set prices in the industry to ruinous levels. For a further discussion, see S. Bowden and D.M. Higgins, 'Short-time Working and Price Maintenance: Collusive Tendencies in the Cotton Spinning Industry, 1918–1939', *Economic History Review*, LI (1998), pp. 326–32.

did the federation chose these options and, secondly, to what extent was the federation successful in pursuing this strategy?[29]

In the cotton spinning industry debt, and the added risk it generated, played a substantial part in determining the role played by the FMCSA. This role was to contain uncertainty and to reduce the risk of financial collapse, expressed by enacting short-time working and price maintenance schemes.[30] Although there are different explanations why supposedly efficient and over-capitalised firms had to bear high fixed costs, both had an incentive to engage in output regulation and price maintenance because in a situation of rapidly falling prices, both would incur proportionately bigger losses compared to firms which did not have these fixed costs. In a sense, therefore, the interests of the technically strong (but financially weak) coincided with the interests of the technically weak (and financially weak). Moreover, given the scale with which export markets contracted, and given the pervasive uncertainty about future levels of demand, neither type of firm could be confident that price levels would remain at a financially viable level. Such firms, therefore, could consider themselves financially vulnerable and potentially marginal, and neither type of firm could be certain which would exit first. This was the main reason why the FMCSA tried to enforce output allocation and price maintenance schemes. Establishing and maintaining a united approach to the resolution of the industry's problems was the task of the FMCSA.[31]

The FMCSA provided the essential network through which such practices were imposed. From the employers' point of view, the stated reason was to bring output into equilibrium with a shortfall in demand. The underlying and real aim, however, was to spread reduced demand between existing firms: everyone received less, but no one would be forced to exit the industry. Equalising the burden meant 'they can apparently produce a situation of comparative safety from their point of view by producing on a restricted scale and selling at profitable prices'.[32] If output was not shared and the industry struggled to secure what business there was available, this would lead to the trade 'giving away its margins until financial ruin was obvious'.[33] Short-time work was openly seen by employer networks as 'the only effective remedy ...

---

[29] 'Success' refers to the ability of the FMCSA to persuade firms to agree to and abide by a collective strategy for the good of the industry as a whole.

[30] Bowden and Higgins, 'Short time working', pp. 326–43.

[31] H. Levy, *Monopolies, Cartels and Trusts in British Industry* (Macmillan, 1927), p. 202.

[32] Amalgamated Association of Operative Cotton Spinners and Twiners (AAOCST), Quarterly Report No 220, p 4: ACA/1/2/(16). John Rylands Library, University of Manchester.

[33] Federation of Master Cotton Spinners Associations (FMCSA), Report, 1926, p. 64. John Rylands Library, University of Manchester.

for preventing a financial calamity of unprecedented disaster ... it has ... [rescued] American spinning from such a disaster'.[34]

Short-time working was the industry's initial response to the collapse in demand in 1920.[35] Thereafter, for most of the inter-war years, short-time working was introduced on various occasions and for various lengths. On average, throughout the inter-war years, 15 per cent of operatives were on short-time work. This conceals important fluctuations, as employers regularly increased the percentage of operatives on short-time working in periods of acute difficulty, for example, 1924–6 and 1930–1.[36] The incidence of short-time working was especially pronounced in the American section of the industry.

How successful was the FMCSA in this policy? Networks operate most effectively when members perceive common reason for participation and co-operation. Balancing the different and sometimes conflicting aspirations of members made consistent and long-run support for short-time working difficult, if not impossible. Even during the six relatively successful years, 1920–26, difficulties were experienced in sustaining *organised* short-time working. Often, short-time would disappear as soon as economic conditions improved. In 1926, for example, the FMCSA noted that there were 'so many firms not acting in accordance' that it cancelled short-time working. Increasingly by the mid-1920s, there was a reluctance to back organised schemes. In August 1927, March 1929, and 1930, the FMCSA's recommendations for the introduction of short-time working were defeated in ballots. Between 1927 and 1933, the industry moved away from consecutive periods of organised short-time working, and thereafter, there were no attempts to introduce organised short-time working.

Similar problems were experienced when price maintenance schemes were introduced. But these schemes, too, experienced the same problems as short-time working. A *Cotton Yarn Association* was formed in January 1927, but collapsed in November of the same year. Between 1928–33, it proved impossible for *any* minimum price scheme to operate effectively. When an effective price maintenance scheme was introduced in the American section, its success depended not on a growing convergence of views among cotton spinners but fear of the credible threat by the industry's price leader, the Lancashire Cotton Corporation, that at the first sign of the scheme being

---

[34] Oldham Master Cotton Spinners Association (OMCSA), Statement by Mr. Mills, Chairman, Federation Short Time Organisation Committee, Reprinted from Manchester Evening Chronicle (31 March 1925), Annual Reports Attachment, Annual Report for 1925. John Rylands Library, University of Manchester.

[35] For a further discussion of the role of the FMCSA in relation to the policies pursued by cotton spinning industry see, Bowden and Higgins, 'Short-time working', pp. 319–43.

[36] Ibid., p. 333.

eroded, it would flood the market with stocks and force the ruling price down to 'rock-bottom' levels.[37]

Enactment of price maintenance schemes by the FMCSA could only be successful if *every* member ignored the temptation to breakaway and cut prices. Frequently, though, during the 1920s especially, this temptation proved irresistible. It was stated that price maintenance schemes were broken by 'those firms who are the most clamorous for the Federation to take action (who) ... are often those who soonest succumb to the temptation to take unauthorised advantage of any improvement effected'. In fact, as Keynes demonstrated, the greater the degree of capacity under-utilisation in the spinning industry, the greater was the temptation for firms to breakaway from price maintenance schemes.[38]

Our case study on cotton spinning indicates both the strengths and weaknesses inherent in networks. They are strong only when all members perceive benefits from complying with the network. However, they are weak and will frequently be undermined when incentives emerge for members to breakaway from the policies prescribed by the network. Collective action taken in the cotton spinning industry during the inter-war years was directed toward protecting the marginal firm. However, the means taken to ensure this, regulation of output and price, were rarely truly successful: the individualistic ethos which prevailed in the industry and the temptation for individual firms to succumb to short-term profit effectively precluded any binding consensus.

The cotton weaving industry

Networks may impede productivity-enhancing change when and if these changes are perceived to favour one group of members at the expense of others. Our second case study of the negative consequences of networks derives from the cotton weaving industry. Our research suggests the final outcome of limited change was a reflection of an understandable, if costly, predisposition to sacrifice productivity-enhancing schemes with long term potential, for more modest schemes that preserved some degree of consensus in the industry during the short-term.[39]

---

[37] Bamberg, 'The Government, the Banks', pp. 310–12.

[38] J.M. Keynes, 'Industrial reorganisation: cotton', in ibid., *The Collected Writings of John Maynard Keynes, Vol. XIX, Part II, Activities, 1922–29: The Return to Gold and Industrial Policy* (Macmillan, 1981), p. 612.

[39] For a full exposition of this research, see Sue Bowden and David Higgins, 'Productivity on the Cheap? The "More Looms" Experiment and the Lancashire Weaving Industry during the inter-War Years', *Business History*, Vol. 41, No. 3 (July, 1999), pp. 21–41.

As Tables 5.1 and 5.2 indicate, the fortunes of the weaving industry mirrored those of spinning during the inter-war years. However, although broadly similar in terms of industrial structure and the existence of networks, the weaving industry differed from the spinning industry in one important respect: it did not participate to any great extent in the re-floatation boom of 1919–20, and consequently it was not saddled with comparable levels of debt.[40] Unlike the spinning industry, one might assume that this absence of debt would have allowed the principal employers' network, the CSMA, greater freedom of manoeuvre in pursuing productivity enhancing schemes. However, as we demonstrate below, the need to preserve some façade of industry solidarity meant that this network could not give its unreserved support to this scheme.

During the inter-war years, the *main* scheme entertained by the CSMA to improve productivity and thereby alleviating the trade depression was the MLS.[41] Traditionally, weavers in Lancashire tended four looms.[42] In 1928, representatives of the *Burnley Cotton Spinners Manufacturers Association* sought CSMA approval for an experiment to increase to eight the number of looms attended by each weaver.[43] The scheme was designed to improve competitiveness in the bulk trade which was most severely affected by foreign competition. The experiment focused on the production of traditional, Burnley plain cloths, to evaluate the cost savings of setting weavers to eight looms.

Initial findings appeared to confirm the viability of the scheme. One estimate was that the direct saving in labour costs was between 20 and 30 per cent, which amounted to a saving in the total production costs of cloth of between two and seven per cent.[44] Other estimates suggested the cost saving in

---

[40] Contemporary estimates indicate that, at most, fourteen per cent of looms were owned by firms re-floated. However, most of these were owned by combines engaged in spinning and weaving. It appears that among firms engaged solely in weaving, participation in re-floatation was negligible. Daniels and Jewkes, 'The Post-war Depression', pp. 174–5.

[41] Other schemes, involving the replacement of ordinary looms with automatic looms, were considered. However, the greater capital costs of automatics when compared with ordinary looms (much of which were fully depreciated) meant that the latter type of loom was at a total cost advantage. For a further discussion of the issues involved, see Bowden and Higgins, 'Productivity on the Cheap?', pp. 25–6.

[42] In 1906, only 2.8 per cent of British weavers were engaged on six looms, and little attempt was made to raise that figure prior to 1914. Lazonick, 'The Cotton Industry', p. 28.

[43] (CSMA), *Minutes*, 28 June, 1928. Greater Manchester Country Record Office (GMCRO).

[44] Board of Trade, *Industrial Survey of Lancashire*, p. 139. The issue of capital costs is not important in this context. The explanation for this is that the comparison now is not between ordinary looms and automatic looms, but between different systems of work-allocation on ordinary looms. Since no new capital expenditure was involved, and since a large proportion of the ordinary looms were fully depreciated anyway, the issue of capital costs therefore disappears.

weaving were nearer to 18 per cent.[45] In the depressed conditions of the inter-
war years, the possibility of achieving significant reductions in labour costs,
without having to undertake heavy expenditure on re-equipment, must have
seemed very attractive.[46]

Despite the attractions of the MLS system, it proved difficult to implement.
There were two reasons for this. Firstly, adoption of MLS was not suitable for
all weaving firms. This necessarily threatened consensus in the industry. In
addition, though, there was a second factor at work: if the CSMA was to
support firms wishing to adopt MLS, it risked losing the support of firms that
could not. Each of these two factors, therefore, had the potential to undermine
the role and credibility of the CSMA. Both are considered below.

In broad terms, the impact of foreign competition was most acutely felt in
those towns that produced 'grey' cloths. These were, principally, Blackburn,
Burnley, and Darwen. Other towns, such as Bolton, Colne, and Nelson,
specialised in finer cloths and 'fancies'. Between 1922–30, the decline in
looms in the former group of towns averaged 12.5 per cent, compared to 8.8
per cent for the latter.[47] However, the difference between individual towns was
particularly striking. During the same period, Burnley experienced an 18.2 per
cent decline in looms, whereas Bolton and Nelson experienced a decline of just
six and 6.7 per cent respectively.[48] The towns most badly hit by foreign
competition, therefore, had the greatest incentive and ability to adopt the MLS.

But what of those firms whose products were not amenable to the MLS?
This problem presented a dilemma to the CSMA. This network was keen to
stress that employers should be at liberty to effect schemes that would improve
their competitiveness. But if the industry fragmented into a division between
those firms that could adopt MLS and those that could not, its central position
and credibility would be undermined. The dilemma was compounded by the
fact that introduction of the MLS was closely bound up with industry wage
agreements. In fact, the CSMA was intending to use the MLS as a vehicle to
revolutionise the payments system prevailing in the industry.[49] Clearly, if
unanimity among employers on wages was thought desirable, so, too, would

[45] 'More Looms per Weaver', *Textile Weekly* (20 June, 1930). This figure was
given by Mr. Ashurst, secretary of CSMA. Precise estimates of the extent to which savings in
weaving were translated into actual savings in the final cloth varied according to the type of
cloth produced (finer and more intricate cloths required more labour input, but are less
amenable to MLS), and movements in the exchange rate.
[46] This point requires elaboration. The fundamental principle behind the MLS was
that, although the wages of individual weavers increased, total labour costs would fall because
of the displacement of labour.
[47] Calculated from Clay, *Report*, Table XI, p. 20.
[48] Ibid.
[49] Traditionally, wages in the industry were governed by the 'Uniform List'.
However, introduction of the MLS required a new scheme of wage payments - the More
Looms List.

some degree of unanimity on the MLS - even though not all employers could adopt it.

Signs of the disunity among the employers became apparent during the earliest attempts to introduce the scheme in 1931.[50] The lock-out which ensued lasted for four weeks, but even during this relatively short period, breakaways and the threat of breakaways from the CSMA increased.[51] A number of fissures revealed themselves. One problem was that some of the mills in the most depressed towns, for example Blackburn, simply couldn't afford to prolong the lock-out. Conversely, mills in some of the more prosperous towns, for example, Nelson, indicated they were resolutely in favour of continuing the lock-out. In between these extremes, the degree of support in towns such as Bolton, Chorley, Heywood, Padiham and Skipton, was undermined by resignations from the CSMA and the irresistible temptation to break ranks and secure orders while competitor mills were shut.[52] Accordingly, the CSMA, cancelled the lock-out.[53]

Thereafter, *unofficial* attempts to introduce the MLS were attempted. However, because firms adopting MLS would be in a more favourable position compared to those that did not, there was always the risk that the CSMA would be unable to achieve a wage agreement which was acceptable to MLS firms and which did not simultaneously antagonise non-MLS firms. However, even as the depression intensified in the early 1930s, attempts to introduce a uniform reduction in wages from the Uniform List were undermined by the fear that this would aggravate cost differences between MLS and non-MLS firms, and the planned reduction had to be postponed.[54]

The essential dilemma of trying to maintain consensus when the economic conditions confronting its members and their ability to adopt the MLS were so very different, was to remain with the CSMA until the introduction of a legalised list in 1935. Until that date, firms were increasingly breaking away from the Uniform List and forging their own individual agreements on the

---

[50] The MLS was originally introduced on an experimental basis only by a group of firms in Burnley in 1928. Subsequently, in 1931, the CSMA decided that firms who wished to adopt the MLS should be free to do so. The weavers' association, the Amalgamated Weavers Association (AWA), responded by striking mills in Burnley which attempted to introduce the MLS. Eventually, an industry-wide lockout ensued. A.J. Bullen, 'The Cotton Spinners and Manufacturers Association and the Breakdown of the Collective Bargaining System, 1928–35', unpublished MA thesis, (University of Warwick, 1980), pp. 27-37.

[51] Ibid., CSMA, *Minutes*, January 15, 1931; 13 February, 1931.

[52] CSMA, *Minutes*, 13 February, 1931. When the lock-out ended, the CSMA was unwilling to fine breakaway firms because this would have increased the risk of their resignation from the CSMA and undermined even further its grip on an increasingly fragmented industry. Bullen, *The Cotton Spinners*, p. 35.

[53] CSMA, *Minutes*, 13 Feb, 1931.

[54] CSMA, *Minutes*, Dec 4, 1931.

MLS.[55] The incentives to do this were understandable. For example, one tactic was to pay MLS rates of wages while operatives only worked a complement of four looms. This offered a means by which unscrupulous firms could steal a march over their rivals. It was estimated that if four looms were worked on the MLS basis, firms could save fifteen per cent of their wage costs compared to firms working four looms on the Uniform List.[56] This not only increased divisions between MLS and non-MLS firms, but also threatened to introduce divisions *between* firms adopting the MLS. Effectively, two wage systems were in operation, with the non-MLS firms facing bankruptcy and placing even greater pressure on the CSMA to reduce wages on the Uniform List to improve their competitiveness.[57]

The effect of the 1935 legalised list was to solve the difficulty of securing a wages policy that would satisfy both MLS and non-MLS firms that had haunted the CSMA for so long. This list reduced the basic rate of pay for weavers on four looms by 5.7 per cent, and increased the basic rate of pay for weavers on the six-loom system by four per cent. In effect, therefore, the wage costs of the two systems were made more equal and gains that MLS firms would have achieved over their non-MLS rivals were partly cancelled. Although there were to remain significant differences between individual towns in the adoption of the MLS system, as far as the industry as a whole was concerned, the general adoption of the MLS was very poor: by 1937, less than sixteen per cent of all weavers were employed on the MLS.[58]

In the Lancashire weaving industry, productivity growth was constrained by attempts of the CSMA to preserve industry consensus. The need to maintain as much solidarity and consensus at the industry level (as much a problem for the employers as it was for the operatives), meant that the original experiment had to be sufficiently weakened to make it palatable. As in the case of the cotton spinning industry, our evidence for weaving suggests that when industries are composed of many sections, each of which experienced different economic conditions, attempts to preserve the authority of networks will be undermined. Productivity-enhancing schemes beneficial to certain sections of the industry promoted conflict and division and increased the incentive to undermine network policy. In such conditions, networks can engender satisficing behaviour. In these terms, Olson's[59] warnings of the damage caused to long run growth by institutional rigidity seem appropriate and act as an important

[55] CSMA, *Minutes of Joint Meetings*, 24 November, 1931.
[56] Political and Economic Planning, *Report*, p. 88.
[57] Bullen, *The Cotton Spinners*, pp. 49 and 51.
[58] E.M. Gray, *The Weaver's Wage* (Manchester University Press, 1937), Table 7, p. 17.
[59] M. Olson, *The Rise and Fall of Nations: Economic Growth, Stagflation and Social Rigidities* (Yale University Press, 1982).

warning to any tendency to view networks as a positive force in isolation from the economic conditions in which they operate.

The wool textile industries

The cotton spinning and weaving industries provide case study evidence of the negative consequences of networks. Our final case study, wool textiles, shows networks in a different light. In this industry, networks also existed and uncertain economic conditions applied, but the absence of substantial levels of debt meant that these networks did not have to seek and impose *industry-wide* policies.[60] In wool textiles we have a case study of flexible specialisation, and a resultant success in withstanding the depressed trading conditions of the inter-war years.

The wool textile industry was not immune from the post-war re-floatation boom. Like the cotton industry, it was recognised that exceptional profits were made in the immediate post war years.[61] However, and unlike the cotton industry, profits made in the wool textile industry in the post-war boom years were not read as a signal for large-scale re-capitalisation. This industry chose to ignore the 'disastrous re-capitalisation of the cotton industry'.[62] We suggest that the key explanation for this was that re-capitalisation would have involved a switch away from privately owned and managed firms on which the industry was traditionally based. The consequence of this, therefore, was that the wool textile industry had a much more favourable cost structure.

In 1926, 56 per cent of firms in the woollen industry were private firms.[63] There were only 15 publicly quoted companies in existence, and even here it is

---

[60] Even where a consensus had emerged on the need for wage cuts, the differing sectional interests of the industry led, eventually, to fragmentation. By the mid-1920s, it was recognised that employers were finding it increasingly difficult to respond to disparate trading experiences with uniform policies. I. Magrath, 'Protecting the Interests of the Trade: Wool Textile Employers' Organisations in the 1920s' in J.A. Jowitt and A. McIvor, *Employers and Labour*, pp. 44-63; J.A. Jowett and K. Laybourn, 'The Wool Textile Dispute of 1925', *Journal of Local Studies*, Vol. 2 (1982), pp. 10–27.

[61] Investigations were made compulsory under the Profiteering Acts, in 1920 and 1921. These investigations revealed the following trends. In the wool top and yarn making industry, the average profit per pound (weight) was fifteen times the pre-war figure: 3D86/9/2/1. This corresponded to an increase in net profits as a percentage of total capital employed from 15.7 per cent in 1912 to 59.44 per cent in 1919. *Minutes of Inquiry*, Section 2, p. 43. By June 1919, profits for the industry as a whole stood at 5.7 per cent of the selling price after deducting taxation, raw materials making up 52 per cent of the selling price, wages 14 per cent and expenses 17 per cent: Analysis of Costings of Five Cloths, *Minutes of Inquiry*, Section 2, p. 46.

[62] Working Party Reports, *Wool*, p. 15.

[63] Committee on Industry and Trade, *Survey*, p. 176. This figure should be regarded as a considerable under-estimate of the number of companies which did not issue

not clear that all of these were re-floatations.[64] Although there was some movement towards the formation of joint stock companies, it was not on any large scale 'and did not seriously disturb the existing pattern of organisation and ownership'.[65] Privately owned and managed firms remained the dominant method of organisation in the industry throughout the inter-war years. The available evidence did not suggest the superior efficiency of the large over the small firm and, as such, there was no overriding incentive for owners to float firms on the market in any attempt to build large-scale production units. Wide variations in efficiency in the industry were not the result of any size effect.[66]

This industry adopted a strategy of flexible specialisation and price competition in reaction to the problematic trading conditions of the inter-war years. Its ability to do so may be traced back to the absence of debt overhang. Although there was some movement towards the formation of joint stock companies, it was not on any large scale 'and did not seriously disturb the existing pattern of organisation and ownership'.[67] Privately owned and managed firms remained the dominant method of organisation in the industry throughout the inter-war years. The available evidence did not suggest the superior efficiency of the large over the small firm and, as such, there was no overriding incentive for owners to float firms on the market in any attempt to build large-scale production units. Wide variations in efficiency in the industry were not the result of any size effect. The outcome was an absence of any incentive to re-float.

This released wool textiles from the endemic and ultimately destructive behaviour of its neighbours over the Pennines. Differences in the level of debt that had to be borne by the wool and cotton spinning industries allowed firms in the former much greater freedom to pursue their own production, sales and marketing policies. Firms in the wool textile industry were relatively free, therefore, to develop their own strategies of product specialisation and quality, niche marketing, unconstrained by the need to observe any collective, industry-wide, policy. Indeed, as a result of the disastrous attempts to secure industry consensus on wage cuts in the 1920s, by 1930 it was admitted that 'each Section will have to fight and ask for what they want on their own. I do not see

---

shares. According to the Committee on Industry and Trade, many of the 603 firms described as limited liability companies were, in fact, private companies.

[64] *Minutes of Inquiry*, Appendix One.

[65] Working Party Reports, *Wool*, p. 16.

[66] The direct savings in production costs from large runs were rarely large. In the heavy woollen districts costs may have ranged from 11 per cent above to 21 per cent above the average, but size was not the explanation: 'they are lowest in one very large firm and highest in the next lowest firm'. Small firms had costs near the average. Similar details were reported for the worsted weaving sector. Working Party Reports, *Wool*, p. 70–1.

[67] Ibid., p. 16.

how the trade can all come together at the same time, as the conditions between the woollen and worsted trades are totally different'.[68]

Firms in the wool textile industry did not pursue price fixing arrangements because they had little incentive to do so. There was 'a perpetual tendency throughout the trade ... for competition through the operation of price to drive out the inefficient'.[69] Firms in this industry could and did compete through product market specialisation and exploiting market niches. The very idea of price fixing was abhorrent to the industry as a whole, and pressure from subsidiary trades was successfully resisted.[70] In any case, recognition of the vastly different trading conditions of each section meant a common policy toward price fixing would have been impossible. Networks did exist in wool textiles, but their purpose had never been to propose and still less implement and monitor price fixing arrangements.

Instead, firms in the wool textile industry pursued an entrepreneurial strategy of flexible specialisation manifested in a policy based on the pursuit of high quality, niche markets abroad, and on cultivation of the domestic market. As world demand shifted in the more highly developed countries from lower grade goods to those of a higher class, wool adapted its production strategy. In these terms, wool behaved as product cycle theories of trade would predict. Exports of low-grade goods declined to be replaced by those of finer grade goods.[71] Overseas, many old markets were retained and new ones developed, largely as a result of market niche specialisation in finer goods in the more highly developed countries.[72] The standard practice in the inter-war years was for firms in the industry to build up a reputation for quality in their own special lines in both home and export markets.[73] Product ranges were extended and new styles introduced.[74] As such, although exports to China and Japan fell, those to the developed economies of Europe, South Africa and the USA held up well.[75] Even in Japan, where demand had fallen overall, it remained buoyant

---

[68]   Magrath, 'Protecting the interests', p. 61.

[69]   Working Party Report, *Wool*, 1947, p. 91; Labour Research Department, Supplementary Memorandum prepared by the Labour Research Department for the Woollen and Worsted Enquiry, 18 September, 1925, Bradford Archive Office. File Ref: 3D86/9/2/3, Part 5.

[70]   Working Party Reports, *Wool*, 1947, p. 91.

[71]   Minutes of a Court of Enquiry into the Matters in Dispute between the Parties to the Northern Counties District Wool (and Allied) Textile Industrial Council, Vol. 1, 27 January, 1930, Bradford Archive Office. File Ref: 3D86/9/3/1, p. 88.

[72]   Ibid., pp. 87–8.

[73]   Committee on Industry and Trade, *Survey*, p. 184.

[74]   Working Party Reports, *Wool*, p. 15.

[75]   Trade with Portugal, the Netherlands and Sweden all grew in these years. Germany had been a major exporter before the war, but the loss of Alsace and Lorraine to France, meant that Germany became 'not so much a competitor ... as a customer' of British goods'. Transcript of Court of Investigation into the Wool Textile Industry, Vol. 2, 22 September, 1925. Bradford Archive Office. File Ref: 3D86/9/2/5, p. 32.

in the finer goods since its native industry was 'in a backward conditions as regards quality owing to the difficulty experienced in blending and mixing'.[76] By contrast, the cotton industry was unable to make up for the loss of its principal, Indian, market and singularly failed to adopt wool's product niche specialisation and developed markets strategy.

The wool textile industry, however, did not depend on overseas markets alone for its relative prosperity. Had it done so, it would have been ruined. Specialisation in developed export markets cushioned the industry against the kind of collapse experienced by cotton textiles, but it was not sufficient to sustain the industry. Survival also depended to a large extent on the industry's strategy of developing the home market.

Success in the home market followed from the explicit policy of establishing close relations between the wool manufacturers and the retailers. Here, networks did play a key role in instigating such relations and maintaining contact and communications. The aim was to induce buyers to demand and give preference to specific firms and to enable manufacturers and retailers to 'understand the requirements and problems of each other and thus to co-operate more effectively' in the distribution of woollen goods.[77] This was partly the result of the slump in prices in 1920–1 which left many merchant houses in a crippled condition and which, in turn, forced manufacturers to develop their own machinery to secure distribution.[78] It was also the result of an explicit policy of developing close ties with the growing retailing market. Only in these terms can we view networks as having some positive force on the wool textile industry.

The woollen textile industry shared a similar degree of regional and firm specialisation as the Lancashire cotton textile industries. In addition, the wool textile industry experienced a similar collapse in export markets. As far as networks were concerned, though, the crucial difference between this industry and Lancashire was the growing recognition of the impossibility of cajoling all sections of the industry to pursue a common policy. No such policy existed after the mid-1920s and there was an increasing acceptance that each section of the industry would have to 'go it alone'. In this regard, the wool textile industry may have benefited from the passive role played by its networks.

---

[76]   Ibid., p. 37.

[77]   Ibid., p. 183. See also, S. Bowden and D.M. Higgins, 'Quiet Successes and Loud Failure: The UK Textile Industries in the Inter-war Years', *Journal of Industrial History*, Vol. 3 (2000), pp. 91–111.

[78]   Ibid., p. 181.

Conclusion

This chapter has examined the role of business networks in relation to case studies of the cotton spinning, cotton weaving, and wool textile industries during the inter-war years. It will be apparent that we are highly critical of the alleged benefits that are supposed to flow automatically from networks *per se*. A number of conclusions suggest themselves.

Irrespective of whether networks are a necessary or sufficient condition for industrial success, the role of trust and consensus in the literature has been given special significance. However, in light of the preceding analysis we would argue that trust is an attribute which will itself depend on the prevailing economic environment. In a market scenario of expanding markets and high profitability, the break-down of trust is likely only to affect the relative, not absolute, positions of firms. However, in highly depressed market conditions, characterised by uncertainty and financial instability, the breakdown of trust could spell irrevocable collapse for particular firms. In these conditions, although there are strong grounds for maintaining trust, there are equally compelling grounds for undermining it. The more uncertain the environment and the more unstable the industry, the more likely it is that trust breaks down and the less feasible it is to sustain networks. The case of the cotton spinning and weaving industries suggests that networks, as embodied by the principal employers' associations, were trying to achieve the impossible.

Of course, it might be argued that some pro-active role for networks is always to be preferred to a passive role. This, too, has some merit, but is not without its critical aspects. Networks in the cotton spinning and weaving industries adopted a pro-active stance, but the policies they recommended were ultimately of little benefit to the industry. In situations where a policy for the common good cannot be perceived or implemented, it may be more desirable for networks to be passive.

Finally, while much of the recent literature on networks has emphasised their benefits, especially in expanding industries, there is an equally good case to be made for examining the potentially destructive consequences of networks in depressed industries. We hope the evidence herein presented of the cotton spinning and cotton weaving industries during the inter war period provides a useful counterweight to this literature.

Chapter 6

Banks, communities and manufacturing in West Yorkshire textiles, c.1800–1830

Steven Caunce

Introduction

Wool textiles were the first global consumer goods industry of England, though they have been overshadowed after 1780 by the even greater success of cotton. Between 1750 and 1830, West Yorkshire became the most dynamic and successful wool textile region ever seen. Links to the old trading system based around London had helped to start growth off, but new markets and new products, marketed and shipped independently, became the rule, with production set within an atomised domestic network. Proto-industrialisation theory briefly seemed to have defined the process whereby this system was transformed into factory-based mass production, but few historians who have worked closely on the north of England now accept this model of a merchant-dominated, poverty-stricken, extensive system that depended upon agricultural failure for its labour force. The Yorkshire manufacturing region certainly never had a mass of people excluded from farming, and it became increasingly geographically concentrated. It became a cluster of specialised production districts which collectively produced woollen and worsted cloth of all qualities, instead of low quality woollens with little diversity or fashionability. Merchants traditionally held back from manufacturing, dealing instead with large numbers of independent clothiers in public markets, and urbanisation came late and in a fragmented manner.[1]

This network developed without role models in a region that initially lacked sophisticated commercial institutions, and in a world unsuited to the mass production of consumer goods. Final markets were extremely volatile and often had to be made, rather than taken, communications were difficult, and no practical model of centralised management of large-scale operations existed. Even after factories arrived, wool textiles, and especially woollens, were

---

[1] S. Caunce, 'Urban Systems, Identity and Development in Lancashire and Yorkshire: A Complex Question', in N. Kirk (ed), *Northern Identities* (Manchester University Press, 2000).

characterised by small firm sizes compared to cotton and most other industries, and in 1830 the domestic network's central negotiating venues, the great cloth halls, still flourished, even though merchants were less detached, and making to contract had increased.[2] Indeed, we must be wary even of the word 'firm', since the production system of Yorkshire was so well integrated that viable operational units could be too small to possess real autonomy or functionality, while still combining into a dynamic system.

Many modern networks are dominated by key actors through size or strategic location, and markets for subcontracted goods and services can become artificial if they lack independent consumers and competing purchasers. This network, however, really was defined by market relationships, which were embedded in a strong cultural matrix whose rules and limits stopped it becoming a free-for-all. Whereas modern businesses try to mimic networks through notional internal markets, most production costs here were really charged to and from independent units, before and after the coming of the factory. Competition was rife, though rivalry would describe it better, and while mutuality was also constantly evident, it functioned to promote business among those who operated efficiently, while the inefficient were left to fail.[3] This proved an ideal evolutionary matrix, approximating closely to Adam Smith's conception of perfect competition and the 'invisible hand of market forces'. Marshall's concept of the industrial district, where general involvement occurred without formal co-ordination, similarly fits the area well, though it is important to stress that mining and engineering, and many other trades, were stimulated by textiles, giving the region a very complex economic structure, including a new and vital role for agriculture. Most things producers needed could be obtained readily on the open market, much of it made or mined locally.

Increasing production was paralleled by rapid growth of local banks, and this chapter considers the links between them and the traders and manufacturers of this unusual region. Banks designed primarily to mobilise large quantities of capital were irrelevant, for as yet there was no need for large, long-term loans, which inevitably carried substantial overheads. Domestic manufacturers, and early mills and factories as well, were adequately financed by loans from family connections, neighbours and members of religious networks, and by ploughing back the profits that success brought.[4]

---

[2]   H. Heaton, *The Yorkshire Woollen and Worsted Industries* (Oxford University Press, 1920), remains the classic account of these institutions and their place in the system, see especially Chapter 11. A brief modern account of the Yorkshire wool textile industry is P. Hudson, 'Proto-industrialisation: The Case of the West Riding Wool Textile Industry in the Late 18th and Early 19th Centuries', *History Workshop*, 12 (1981).

[3]   S. Caunce, 'Not Sprung from Princes: The Nature of Middling Society in Eighteenth-century West Yorkshire', in D. Nicholls (ed), *The Making of the British Middle Class? Studies in Regional and Cultural History Since 1750* (Harvester Press, 1998).

[4]   P. Hudson, *Genesis of Industrial Capital: A Study of the West Riding Wool Textile Industry, c. 1725–1850* (Cambridge University Press, 1986), pp. 265 and 268–9. L. Neal, 'The Finance of Business During the Industrial Revolution', in R. Floud and D.

What was needed instead was an extension of the assessment of credit-worthiness of individuals beyond traditional methods, and support for the innumerable internal transactions which functioned as the central information transmission system, showing clothiers, via the prices ultimately offered by merchants, how to adapt their activities.[5] A generally acceptable, freely available and stable medium of exchange was lacking.

This was a time when the English currency system was itself in transition, when the mint had been largely inactive for long periods, and when few mechanisms existed to move cash out from the centre as a counter to the centripetal forces of taxation. Informal credit had sufficed for many decades, but after 1800 the increasing pace of business created growing uncertainties, and so threatened the network's ability to maintain its development. To understand this vital aspect of the internal structure of the network, we will examine the pragmatic efforts of a typical Yorkshire woollen merchant, Joshua Taylor, to facilitate the production process by establishing his own bank in 1800 or thereabouts.[6] It chiefly issued small notes, since his own very successful and innovative enterprises needed any family capital available for investment.[7] His family, indeed, had been mercantile entrepreneurs for generations. Gomersal, where they lived, lies half way between Leeds and Halifax and at the heart of the woollen-manufacturing district.[8] It formed part of the parish of Birstall, a prominent domestic production area which was unusual in also having a substantial resident group of merchants.[9] The Taylors epitomised the development of that domestic system perfectly.

The Gomersal Bank failed in the general economic crisis of 1825–6, without ever evolving beyond its original role, and was therefore unimportant in the long run. However, the press reports its failure prompted allow us to observe Taylor's activities, suggesting that as a bridge between the older system and something more developed this type of banking played a temporary, unspectacular, but vital role. They also allow us some insight into contemporary views of ordinary producers which would otherwise be lost, because one of the network's strengths was that most members accounted to

---

McCloskey (eds), *The Economic History of Britain Since 1700, Vol. 1, 1700–1860*, 2nd ed. (Cambridge University Press, 1994), p. 152.

[5]   S. Caunce, 'Complexity, Community Structure, and Competitive Advantage Within the West Yorkshire Woollen Industry', *Business History*, Vol. 39, No. 1 (1997), pp. 26–43.

[6]   This forms part of a long-term research project into the Taylors, c. 1550–1900. Hudson mentions the bank, *Genesis*, p. 220, but the facts are incorrect.

[7]   Such banks probably concentrated capital in the hands of the operator rather than distributing it, L.S. Pressnell, *Country Banking in the Industrial Revolution* (Oxford University Press, 1956).

[8]   C. Bronte, *Shirley*, 1842, contains a portrait of Taylor very thinly disguised as Hiram Yorke. *Briarmains* was his residence, Red House.

[9]   H. Heaton, 'Yorkshire Cloth Traders in the United States, 1770–1840', *Thoresby Society Miscellany*, XXXVII (1944), pp. 225–87, discusses the significant role of Gomersal merchants in the USA, for instance.

no-one, and so few records were created, and fewer survive. This is as true of early banks as of production units.[10]

Banking and the network

A bullion-based coinage restrains economic growth, since its prime virtues include its fixed extent and centralised authentication. Bank-issued currency, in contrast, keeps trade moving, and can be adjusted constantly to the needs of local trade where note issuing is locally based. Wealth and economic dynamism are persistently confused, and the concern of historians with capital formation has meant that banks' role as the beating heart of any sophisticated commercial system rarely receives sufficient attention.[11] Even Pressnell neglected this, and most existing accounts imply a teleological inevitability about the absorption of local banks into hierarchical organisations.[12] The collapse of around a hundred English country banks in 1825–6 seems eloquent proof of weakness, especially given the stability achieved after the subsequent centralising reforms, which many accounts treat as the real start of effective banking.[13] However, a literature on network-based 'free' banking, arising from modern debates about central banking, disagrees. While it has been largely divorced from analyses of British industrialisation, White has argued that early Scottish banks, which evolved quite independently and were unaffected by the storm of 1825–6, and self-evidently provided excellent support to Scottish industrialisation, were of this type. The areas Pressnell focussed upon were de-industrialised.[14] A special issue of *Business History* drew attention to the need to consider what banks do within networks, and Hudson's exhaustive work on capital formation in the domestic system can thus be developed by considering country banks as liquidity providers.[15]

[10] Pressnell, *Country Banking*, p. 3.

[11] T.G. Burnard, "'Prodigious Riches": The Wealth of Jamaica Before the American Revolution', *Economic History Review*, LIV (2001), pp. 506–24, for instance, shows that, in the vital late eighteenth century, wealth and income streams from plantation trade in the British Atlantic trading world related inversely to economic development potential.

[12] R. Cameron, *Banking in the Early Stages of Industrialization: A Study of Comparative Economic History* (Oxford University Press, 1967); P. Cottrell, *Industrial Finance, 1830–1914. The Finance and Organization of English Manufacturing Industry* (Methuen, 1980); F. Crouzet, *Capital Formation in the Industrial Revolution* (Methuen, 1972); P. Mathias, 'Capital, Credit and Enterprise in the Industrial Revolution', *Journal of European Economic History*, Vol. 2 (1973), pp. 121–43. As, for instance, in the standard account by E.V. Morgan, *A History of Money* (Pelican, 1965), pp. 61–4.

[13] M. Collins, *Money and Banking in the U.K.*, 1988.

[14] L.H. White, *Free Banking in Britain: Theory, Experience, and Debate, 1800–1845* (Oxford University Press, 1995).

[15] Hudson, *Genesis*; ibid., 'The Role of Banks in the Finance of the West Riding Wool Textile Industry, c. 1750–1850', *Business History Review*, Vol. 55 (1983), pp. 379–402; A. Godley and D.M. Ross (eds), *Business History*, Vol. 38, (1996), Special Issue on Banks, Networks and Small Firm Finance.

The woollen industry's production chain was more complex and fragmented than that of either worsted or cotton, creating a particular need for liquidity. Fleeces had to be produced, collected, and transported to West Yorkshire, since local production was insignificant. After cleaning, sorting and opening, they were carded and spun, woven into a loose web, fulled into a solid cloth, tentered and dyed, raised and sheared to a high finish, possibly given specialist cosmetic treatments, and finally passed to appropriate but distant markets. Many production units were involved, even though the central processes were performed within clothiers' households. There, sorted wool was converted into woven pieces which were ready for fulling, but unsaleable as yet. The traditional equipment used was simple, and as early spinning machines were hand-powered, they were incorporated easily into household production. Fulling was generally done in water-powered public mills for a fee, and carding and scribbling were added to this after 1780. Steam-driven pumps economised on the water usage of water-wheels, as at Taylor's fulling and scribbling mill, but even by 1830 woollen yarn was too full and soft for the crude, uncertain power-driven machinery available for other processes. However, room-and-power letting systems allowed small operations a share in early steam-powered mills when they began to spread.

The industry formed the principal means by which most people in West Yorkshire could make a good living, so participation was both general and voluntary either in textiles themselves, or in the provision of goods, buildings, food and services to those in textiles. Individual failures were common, but the system as a whole did well and rewards were shared relatively widely, allowing clothiers to remain fiercely independent, both as individuals and as a group.[16] A strong common culture did not mean loss of individual initiative here. By holding aloof from controlling production, merchants gave up part of the profits, but they also shed a great deal of risk, almost all responsibility for overheads, and freed themselves to concentrate on marketing. Some merchants, including the Taylor family, had always involved themselves in finishing, because in the final stages intervention could increase quality control and responsiveness to market trends, and hence increase revenue dramatically, but otherwise flexibility increased their usefulness within the network, and avoided them becoming over-committed to existing firms and methods.[17]

Investment was as dispersed as production, so confidence in future profits and the simple nature of most equipment usually allowed it to be funded by relatively informal credit from suppliers. Fulling mills were over-crowded and paid for themselves rapidly, so men like Joshua Taylor readily undertook their

[16] See Royal Commission on Historical Monuments of England, *Rural Houses of West Yorkshire*, 1986, pp. 178–83, and A. Randall, 'Work, Culture and Resistance to Machinery in the West of England Woollen Industry', in P. Hudson (ed), *Regions and Industries* (Cambridge University Press, 1989), p. 180–1.
[17] See J. Ottosson and A. Lundgren, 'AB Gust Carlsson, 1880–1990, Networks and Survival in the Swedish Printing Industry', *Business History*, Vol. 38, (1996), pp. 117–26 for a discussion of a similar relationship between merchants and a network.

construction and modernisation. Generally, anyone would wait for payment unless bad intent was suspected, and as many debts were cleared by labour or by goods, the pound sterling often functioned mostly as a money of account.[18] The diaries for 1811–12 of Joseph Rogerson, a fulling and scribbling miller at Bramley (about six miles north east of Gomersal) reveal a high degree of mutual respect both between competing millers, and between the millers and their customers, without suggesting altruism or general affection.[19] Quarterly pay-days saw letters sent requesting settlement of all outstanding debts, but currency was often lacking. He only cleared his debts when others paid him, and cash ricocheted rapidly through the system as one person after another straightened out their affairs.

This informal management of the system was reaching its limits by 1800, but it did not collapse. Even in 1826, a Huddersfield correspondent of the *Leeds Mercury* could write:

> The dealers in Wool, Oil, and dye Wares, make their purchases on various terms - a time of payment is appointed, and if not adhered to, the purchaser must satisfy his Creditors by an explanation of his affairs, or suffer the consequences of his neglect ... Business is conducted upon the same principle in other trades but [there] the credit is usually much shorter than for Woollens ... There are many merchants who purchase Woollen Cloths and make their payment with punctuality, but there are others, who, when the day of payment arrives, put off the clothiers from week to week, and from month to month, without seeming to feel that they are as much bound both in honour and in honesty to keep their engagements with the poor clothier as with their accepting Banker. The clothier, notwithstanding his utmost exertion, cannot satisfy the demands upon him, while his own property and that of the persons with whom he trades, is locked up in the hands of those who retain the capital of others to suit their own convenience, without making the requisite efforts to relieve the distress of their Creditors, and do not hesitate to say, in answer to the application made to them for payment – 'We shall pay nothing *this* month,' and in some cases to repeat the observation, month after month.[20]

Debt can form the lynch-pin of many oppressive relationships, such as the permanent entitlement to a share in a production system characteristic of proto-industrialisation. Bankers in England had, however, already realised that in an open economy large debts simply tied a bank to a customer who would

---

[18] G. Cookson, 'Millwrights, Clockmakers and the Origins of Textile Machine-Making in Yorkshire', *Textile History*, Vol. 27, No. 1 (1996), pp. 43–57, shows Hattersley's of Keighley, the early and very successful textile engineers, waiting very long periods, and also accepting payment in very unorthodox media. See also B.W. Clapp, *John Owens: Manchester Merchant* (Free Press, 1967), pp. 33–4, 83–6 and 114.

[19] Most easily consulted in W.B. Crump (ed), *The Leeds Woollen Industry 1780–1820* (Leeds University Press, 1931).

[20] *Leeds Mercury*, 11 February 1826.

probably fail sooner or later.[21] Historians have begun to understand that unspectacular credit networks could unlock the capital referred to above, and the cellular structure of this industrial district contributed to a paradoxical but effective mix of financial simplicity and sophistication.[22] Credit-worthiness was easy to assess where most commercial obligations were incurred either within a community, or between members of a close-knit regional business network, or even between substantial merchants who vouched for each other and regularly dealt over long distances through agents.[23] The bankruptcy law was draconian, but more importantly, debtors knew that reneging on commitments meant constantly facing those they had let down.[24] One clothier's prospective father-in-law fled to London, for instance, while he sorted out his affairs, leaving his family to stay with the prospective husband and cope with the consequences.[25] Exclusion from religious communities was normal, and families of disgraced men lost status, with sons' and daughters' marriage prospects suffering especially. The marriage just mentioned broke down.

Credit persisted partly because of the chronic shortage of actual coins. In West Yorkshire, the Halifax Coiners' activities illustrated the problem's special significance in textiles. A notorious group of at least 70 men, they operated in the 1760s in and around the rugged and inaccessible Cragg Vale, about a dozen miles west of Gomersal. Gold was clipped from good guineas collected legitimately at the active markets of Halifax, and then cast as imitation Portuguese moidores. They were legal tender, but rare enough for forgeries to pass normal scrutiny despite a content of 22s worth of gold, instead of 27s. Intermittent action by the authorities provoked the murder of an exciseman in 1769, which led in turn to imprisonments, transportations, and the execution of three men. Coining continued, however, since local manufacturers regarded the perpetrators as friends providing the token currency they needed for internal trade. Long distance traders and the

---

[21] See G. Rae, *The Country Banker*, 5th edn, (1885), reissued in different format, 1902, pp. 24–5, 47–51 and 235. First published as T. Bullion, *The Internal Management of a Country Bank, in a Series of Letters on the Functions and Duties of a Branch Manager*, it is used here as the best guide to the principles underlying early country banking. A country bank manager from around 1845, Rae also had experience of the times before the Bank Charter Act of 1844. This was the basic bank staff training manual for decades. See also J.K. Horsefield, 'The Duties of a Banker. 1. The Eighteenth Century View', in T.S. Ashton and R.S. Sayers (eds), *Papers in English Monetary History* (Oxford University Press, 1953), pp. 1–15.

[22] D.A. Kent, 'Small Businessmen and their Credit Transactions in Early Nineteenth-Century Britain', *Business History*, Vol. 35, No. 1 (1994), pp. 47–64; M. Zell, 'Credit in the Pre-industrial English Woollen Industry', *Economic History Review*, XLIX, (1996), pp. 667–91.

[23] Clapp, *Owens*, p. 114, shows this successful merchant recruiting agents entirely on trust through other merchants, often through remote connections.

[24] R. Hoppit, *Risk and Failure in English Business, 1700–1800* (Cambridge University Press, 1987), Chapter 3.

[25] T. Wright (ed), *The Autobiography of Thomas Wright of Birkenshaw, in the County of York, 1736–1797*, (J.R. Smith, 1864), p. 68.

government, in contrast, were primarily concerned with protecting the coinage's bullion value because they used coins as stores of value.[26]

Large enterprises sometimes produced tokens, but people disliked their associations with truck systems, but bills of exchange provided a more widespread and entirely legal resolution to part of the currency problem.[27] When endorsed, and thus guaranteed against default by the person who accepted it, a reputable bill became 'the highest form of banking security', since the amount due was paid in full on a set date.[28] They took on a quite different character if simply passed on, rather than held to maturity or discounted, however, as was general in the eighteenth-century north. Created through trade, they were normally directly proportionate to traders' needs and the more endorsements, the better the protection. However, they were essentially a makeshift and the *Leeds Intelligencer* commented in 1826 upon 'the determined unanimity and resoluteness with which [Yorkshire bankers] set their face against all mere accommodation bills.[29] Some years ago, these "kites" were exceedingly rife at Liverpool, and produced ... great disaster and ruin'.[30] Bank of England notes became widely used in Lancashire thereafter, but were distrusted elsewhere since they were only available for five pounds or above, were unfamiliar to ordinary people, and were easily forged.[31]

The suspension of payments during the French Wars showed people that paper had advantages over gold coins. Joshua Taylor was one of many merchants who used his reputation for honest dealing and substantial wealth as the basis of issuing his own notes.[32] Operating from the counting house behind his residence, with an underground vault for secure storage of money and documents, he facilitated transactions for those who made cloth for him and supplied him with goods or services. Banking thus evolved naturally within this rapidly-growing business network, rather than arriving as opportunistic or parasitic extensions of the older elite financial system. Not initially intended for general, long-term circulation, such notes went to approved customers on request, and resembled a hybrid between modern notes and cheques. The familiarity of the issuer and their low denominations, frequently one pound, worked in their favour. Just as the global trading value of gold provided an independent measure of any coin's intrinsic value, local banks used the pound

---

[26] A straightforward narrative account of the coiners is given in T.W. Hanson, *The Story of Old Halifax*, 1st ed. (King, 1920), 3rd (David and Charles, 1985), pp. 189–96.

[27] T.S. Ashton, 'The Bill of Exchange and Private Banks in Lancashire, 1790–1830', in Ashton and Sayers, *Papers*, pp. 37–49. Cameron, *Banking*, states that bills probably formed the majority of the English money supply.

[28] Rae, *Country Banker*, p. 243.

[29] These fictitious bills of exchange were created either as a form of loan, paid by the discounter but guaranteed by a friend, or as outright fraud. Rae was vitriolic against them, *Country Banker*, pp. 243–56.

[30] *Leeds Intelligencer*, reprinted in *Times*, 4 January 1826.

[31] Rae, *Country Banker*, pp. 157–8.

[32] See Pressnell, *Country Banking*, pp. 19–35, though this ignores Yorkshire. See also White, *Free Banking*, pp. 90–91.

sterling without affecting its value. Therefore, no speculative market could arise, such as we see today in different national currencies, despite the lack of central controls. By stretching and distorting the link between currency and gold, while retaining its psychological impact, they allowed business to operate at levels far above those that cash trading would support and with greater security than credit or bills could offer. The amount of currency available in each region effectively became self-regulating and locally-determined, as no-one could be compelled to take notes. When they judged matters correctly, country bankers like Taylor prospered, but their own personal fortune had to be mobilised to meet unusual demands and the threat of personal bankruptcy guarded against speculative issuing.

Credit continued, as we have seen, but where clothiers' personal judgment ceased to be reliable, George Rae advised such bankers, 'to the good people of [your town] you will stand in the delicate relation of the arbiter of credit ... The leading subject of your daily education will be to learn who to trust ... Credit given [must be] based upon an intimate knowledge of the parties themselves, their habits of life, their business capacities, their liabilities and their resources'.[33] He stressed that the banks' function was to create and sustain liquidity, building their profits through minute charges of a fraction of a penny on innumerable transactions, rather than seeking large rewards by taking partnerships in enterprises. Small bankers thus endorsed the good name of account holders, not their business plans, and took full collateral against overdrafts. They acted like pawnbrokers and guarantors, not venture capitalists, allowing men to buy land, goods and property and still use much of their wealth in business, with the banker secured from the consequences of failure.[34]

Northern country banks were simply commercial institutions, with few linkages to national or local government, either overt or covert. They sprang up entirely due to need and opportunity, and traded much as they wished.[35] French financial institutions did not achieve this separation, in contrast, and Rothschild has shown that in Angouleme in the 1760s, for instance, overtly political manipulation of the local judicial system through a spurious action against bankers over breaches of the usury laws turned into a seven-year battle

---

[33]   Rae, *Country Banker*, pp. 1, 6 and 251. Outside his own district he said a banker could not expect anything like the same level of knowledge, and so should operate very cautiously, p. 75.

[34]   Rae, *Country Banker*, pp. 269–73. M.P. Silverman, 'The Role of Banks in Industrial Finance in Yorkshire, 1895–1914', unpublished M.A. thesis, (University of Leeds, 1997), discovered that this was still largely true for her period. Her research first made drew my attention to the extent and clarity of these attitudes. Rae, *Country Banker*, Chapter 2 especially. Hudson, *Genesis*, p. 261–2, shows the roots of this practice in the distinctive attitude of Yorkshire clothiers towards ownership of land, mostly seen as collateral rather than a patrimony. She says 'to be known and trusted in the locality and to have some form of property or security were *the* vital elements in procuring a lifeline to the capital and credit markets'.

[35]   W.C.E. Hartley, *Banking in Yorkshire* (Clapham, 1975), is a thorough and useful, if unacademic, survey of early Yorkshire banks, showing their number and variety.

between competing and well-connected cliques, who included members of the national government. There was widespread financial panic, as well as opportunist efforts by many debtors to ruin their creditors, so that credit became almost unobtainable in Lyon for many textile firms, leading to bankruptcies and cash-only dealings. Finally, merchants were prevented from organising the importation of corn during a famine in 1769–70.[36]

Again, English rural banks linked agrarian elites to the London system, transferring their surpluses to the capital after harvest sales and providing for both their regular and exceptional needs for cash in spring or when they contemplated investment.[37] It has been held that these surpluses were transferred on to manufacturers, but evidence for this on any large or consistent scale is lacking, and it is not consistent with their real needs. Instead, enterprising customers of banks like Taylor's were enabled to try ideas out, and speedier settlement of debts encouraged everyone to trade more vigorously. Instead of the small clothier being driven out or turned into a disguised employee, high levels of local, small-scale involvement were encouraged, maintaining the character of the expanding production network.

The Gomersal Bank and the banking system

West Yorkshire has always been unusually lacking in urban concentration relative to population, and its banks reflected the dispersed nature of manufacturing. In *Baines's Directory* of 1822, Huddersfield had five banks, Leeds had four, Wakefield three, Halifax and Bradford two each and even Dewsbury had one.[38] Gomersal was thus literally surrounded by nearby urban centres, and with no nucleus or village institutions, such as a parish church or manor house, it not only had its own bank, but various other features usually associated with towns, including (for a time) a cloth hall that threatened those of Leeds.[39] This combination of some urban attributes with dispersed settlement was paralleled in another woollen centre, Saddleworth, between Huddersfield and Oldham, which had two banks.[40] However, some manufacturing towns, like Keighley, and many market towns, like Tadcaster, Otley and Pontefract, had none. The Taylor family had an unblemished record of spotting and promoting innovations, such as turnpike roads, that made them

---

[36] E. Rothschild, 'An Alarming Commercial Crisis in Eighteenth-century Angouleme: Sentiments in Economic History', *Economic History Review*, LI, (1998), pp. 268–93.

[37] Rae recognised the fundamental difference between banking in agricultural and manufacturing areas. See, for instance, *Country Banker*, pp. 222–3.

[38] E. Baines, *Baines's Yorkshire*, Vol. 1 (Baines, 1822).

[39] G. and N. Cookson, *Gomersal: A Window on the Past* (Kirklees Cultural Services, 1992), pp. 92–5 and 111–7. This disproves Pressnell's contention that banks of this type usually required isolation to work, *Country Banking*, p. 18.

[40] Heaton, 'Yorkshire Cloth Traders', shows Saddleworth merchants taking over from those of Gomersal in the USA.

money by improving the effectiveness of the production network, and the bank's survival for two and a half decades in a free market suggests that this was not merely a personal initiative.

Banks seemed to seek niches rather than competition, in fact, suggesting that they also operated like a network. Thus, the *Leeds Intelligencer* compared the policies of Leeds banks with Wakefield's aggressively expansionist Wentworth and Co.:

> In several of the neighbouring towns ... their issues of notes to manufacturers were very extensive. A person who had a certain sum to expend on building a new mill, or enlarging an old one, if he thought or discovered that the undertaking would require an outlay greater than he possessed, went to the Wakefield bank, stated his intentions and his wants, and, did matters appear satisfactory on depositing or mortgaging the title deeds of his premises, or other adequate securities, the deficiency of capital was supplied in the notes of the establishment.[41] These issues were, of course, disbursed to the different tradesmen employed, and formed part of the currency of the county. Other accommodations were afforded in a similar manner, either for wages to workmen, or funds to meet necessary demands, and thus a great portion of the business of the community centred in Messrs. Wentworth and Co.'s bank. The notes, distributed in the mode just described, fell almost necessarily, in large quantities into the hands of retail trades people; but ... particularly into the hands of the Yorkshire butchers ... The Leeds banks pursue an opposite policy. They issue comparatively a trifling number of small notes, and ... do not attempt, as it is technically said, to "force" their paper into circulation – their customers are for the most part the higher order of merchants, manufacturers, and trades people, and in the aggregate, generally speaking, the occasions which these respectable persons have to draw out and disburse quantities of 1£ or even 5£ notes are few. Their transactions at the banks are on the contrary, mostly heavy, and they themselves being of high character, large property, and undoubted credit, unceremoniously sometimes overdraw their accounts almost ad libitum, and without any previous warning to the bankers – on the recognised understanding that every customer is entitled to an advance not exceeding one-tenth of the total annual amount of his money transactions with his banker. We understand that advances in the form of bankers' acceptances or draughts are thus occasionally made of 10,000£ to a single house, and higher sums, indeed as far as ... 15,000£ and upwards![42]

Leeds banks thus disdained one pound notes, and the Bank of England saw them as inflationary, but they were vital for manufacturers in 1826:

---

[41] Note that this is not a loan, but the provision of liquidity against assets of equivalent worth.

[42] *Leeds Intelligencer*, reprinted in *Times*, 4 January 1826.

Such is the scarcity of money owing to the disinclination of the banks to issue their notes, which are almost immediately returned to them, that on Saturday last, a considerable manufacturer of this place, instead of money gave to his work people, orders on the butchers, bakers and other dealers in the necessaries of life, having previously congregated the people in the mill and explained to them the difficulties under which persons in trade laboured, owing to the disposition now so prevalent amongst the working classes to hurry their notes into the banks. Several of the manufacturers in the neighbourhood of Halifax have made a deduction of 3½d in the pound from the amount of their workmen's wages to indemnify themselves from the expense of obtaining discount for their Bills, under the present deficiency of the currency. This appears to us like correcting folly by usury.[43]

Other employers acted differently, but further proved the monetised nature of the local economy: 'the firm of Messrs Nussey and Sykes of Mirfield Lowmill, having paid a portion of their workmen's wages on Friday week, with notes of the Gomersal Bank, liberally exchanged such of them as were not paid away when the bank stopped on Saturday'.[44] The Nusseys were distantly related to the Taylors and the two families were friends. Local tradition also recalled that small shopkeepers who held Gomersal Bank notes were repaid personally by Joshua Taylor. When the government asked that small notes be withdrawn, 'the respectable firm of Messrs Rawsons and Co. of Halifax, Huddersfield, and Rochdale, have announced their determination to receive and discharge [them] and to supply their place with specie'.[45] However, in practice the notes were in circulation because the coin to do this did not exist and notes worked better.

The crisis

During 1825 the north smugly watched southern country banking collapse, but by February 1826 it seemed the whole commercial system was failing. The *Mercury* noted after the worst week that 'the bankrupts inserted in the [London] Gazette of last Saturday night amounted to 60! Being a larger number probably than was ever advertised in that paper ... The average annual number for the last twenty years is about 1500, or 15 in each Gazette'.[46] On 28 January, Joshua Taylor had contributed to the sense of doom by stopping payments. He issued this statement in the *Leeds Mercury*:

---

[43] *Leeds Mercury*, 11 February 1826.
[44] *Leeds Mercury*, 12 February 1826. It was also reported that pensioners around Halifax had been paid their quarterly allowance in Saddleworth Bank notes, which were changed for gold when the bank stopped payment.
[45] *Leeds Mercury*, 12 February 1826.
[46] *Leeds Mercury*, 4 January 1826.

It is now my painful duty to inform you that the recent failure of the house of ABRAM DIXON and Co. of London, has involved me and my family in ruin; and what is still more distressing to me, has withdrawn from me the means of paying my Creditors the whole of their just demands.

Under these most distressing and afflicting circumstances, which I have not had the means of averting, my most anxious wish is that all which is left to me, shall be fairly and equally divided, at the least possible expense amongst my suffering creditors.

To attain this end, I will devote my unceasing, undivided exertions; and I earnestly request you to attend a General Meeting of my Creditors, when a statement of my affairs will be produced, and a plan submitted to the meeting, for winding them up in what appears to me the most advantageous manner for the benefit of the creditors.[47]

This heartfelt notice, more personal than any others that appeared, could imply that his bank was simply too small to survive, and reaction was initially muted: 'Mr Taylor is well known to be a man of real property – with an unencumbered estate we hear of the value of thirty thousand pounds, and as his bills and provincial notes are said not to exceed that amount, the public will probably sustain no other loss than that which arises out of the delayed payment, and from the interruption of his manufacturing and mercantile concerns in the woollen line, which were rather considerable. Mr Taylor's transactions as a banker were upon a very small scale'.[48] The Taylor estate was indeed substantial for an ordinary merchant, but much of his capital was tied up in the business and the *Liverpool Advertiser* added more realistically that 'much local inconvenience will be sustained by the stoppage'.[49] Taylor was thus known outside his own locality, though the undoubtedly strong local bias explains the use of Dixon as a factor in London instead of an arrangement with a bank. This proved to be a fatal mistake.

This clarifies the importance and the limits of private wealth in the Yorkshire system: the bank's credibility had rested comfortably upon Taylor's reputation, but the actual strain was too much, vindicating Rae's consistent warnings that a tenth of rumoured wealth was the basis on which to deal with bank customers.[50] The interim settlement of five shillings in the pound showed the scale of the immediate shortfall, but as the rest of the business was very profitable, especially Hunsworth Mill, the creditors allowed everything except

---

[47] *Leeds Mercury*, 11 February 1826. The same issue contained the more impersonal announcement of stoppage at the Saddleworth Union Bank, for instance.

[48] *Leeds Mercury*, 4 January 1826.

[49] Quoted in *The Times*, 3 February 1826.

[50] Rae, *Country Banker*, pp. 6–9.

the bank to proceed.[51] Taylor and his son therefore endured genteel poverty for many years, and the business was crippled because the surplus it generated could not be used for modernisation.[52] Moreover, the interconnection of banks and businesses might also become negative, for the *Leeds Mercury* reported:

> The stoppage of the Gomersal Bank renewed the run upon SHAKESPEARE B. SIKES, Esq., of Huddersfield, with increased vigour on Monday ... On Wednesday morning, ... the alarming news that it had finally closed circulated very generally ... and the consequence has been, that persons who are going about the country increasing the alarm by spreading wicked rumours, to the prejudice of all the banks in the neighbourhood, found believers in every town in the riding. On Tuesday Mr Sikes put forth a hand bill of which the following is a copy:-

> "S. G. Sikes, in consequence of the unexampled distress of the present period, has the painful task to announce that, *for a short time*, He is placed under the necessity of suspending his payments: but, if favoured with the indulgence of the public, he feels confident that ultimately, he shall honourably discharge all the claims on his establishment."

> The stoppage ... has increased to a great degree the distress already prevailing in the town and neighbourhood of Huddersfield, and the calamity is much heightened by the failure of Messrs Taylor and Dixon of that place, who were extensive dealers in the fancy manufacturers.[53]

This refers to a partnership between Dixon and one of Joshua's brothers, William. Later events suggest instability and bad judgement, for Dixon failed several times. Another *Mercury* report shows Taylor's failure triggering off a small business revolt:

> At Bradford the Bank of Messrs C H and A Harris has of late received the notes of other Bankers from their customers, subject to a guarantee of twenty-one days, and when the Gomersal Bank stopped last Saturday, they returned to their connexion such notes on that Bank as had been paid to them from the middle of the month till the time of the stoppage of the Bank ... The quantity of Gomersal notes in circulation was so small as not to lead to a regular exchange [and] the tradesmen of Bradford ... called a meeting ... Two propositions were submitted ... one that depots should be established in that town to which all country notes should be taken every Monday morning, by those who had received them during the past week, – and that they should immediately be sent to their

---

[51] Similarly, but much more formally, the creditors of Messrs Lord, Robinson, and Co., woollen cloth merchants and manufacturers, allowed the company to continue trading under the inspection of five gentlemen, appointed as trustees, since the accounts showed the firm to be solvent. Eighteen months were allowed for repayment of all debts.
[52] G. and N. Cookson, *Gomersal*, Chapter 11.
[53] *Leeds Mercury*, 4 February 1826.

respective banks to be exchanged for Gold or Bank paper: the other proposition was that a deputation should wait upon Messrs Harris, to learn, whether they were disposed to accommodate the trade of the town, by limiting the guarantee on country notes from those who took them in, to one week, or to some shorter period than at present demanded ... The former was very [soon] abandoned on its being suggested ... that ... it would banish from the town and neighbourhood almost the only circulating medium, as no Banker would issue notes which would be returned to his counter weekly ... After some further discussion, ... [a] deputation waited upon the Bank, and represented the great risk and insecurity felt by the tradesmen of the town, ... adding that if a weekly exchange of notes would subject them to expense, they would willingly pay [it].' However, terms could not be agreed with Harris's, 'who simply expressed their readiness to facilitate early exchange of notes paid to them as far as was in their power'.[54]

In fact, Sikes recovered and the system proved very robust: 'in Leeds we have not had a Bankruptcy of any consequence for the last three months ... Bradford and Halifax have, with the exception of Wentworth and Co.'s Bank, escaped equally well. At Wakefield, the principal seat of that great but unfortunate Banking establishment, we have only heard of one single failure of consequence; and at Huddersfield, where two banks have failed, no house of any great consequence, with the exception of Messrs Dixon & Co. has become bankrupt. This cheering retrospect is attributable ... to the indulgent consideration of tradesman towards each other; ... and the ... character of the present embarrassment, which is rather that of suspended credit than of actual insolvency'.[55]

The heart of the Yorkshire manufacturing network was thus proved fundamentally strong, apart from cases like Wentworth's, who seem to have operated on unsound principles, and Taylor, who relied too much on one related business partner.[56] Generally, the old sense persisted, that waiting for payment was better than punitive action. This proved more important in keeping things afloat. It mattered more than the developing role of the Bank of England as lender of last resort, which was invaluable during normal business, but did nothing to build confidence in local notes, nor allowed the fast, dramatic support needed to end a run on a bank.

The crisis certainly does not compare with that in the south in 1825, much less Rothschild's earlier French disaster. However, Scotland survived even better, because large, stable banking partnerships emerged naturally there, whereas in England the legal maximum of six partners per note-issuing bank prevented it.[57] Scottish banks did fail, but far less often than in England, and

---

[54]   *Leeds Mercury*, 11 February 1826.

[55]   *Leeds Mercury,* 11 February 1826.

[56]   Pressnell, *Country Banking*, p. 486, endorses this view of Wentworth's.

[57]   S.G. Checkland, *Scottish Banking: A History, 1695–1973* (Glasgow University Press, 1975) is the classic account of Scottish banking, though White takes issue with many of

with virtually no loss to customers. The most spectacular early collapse, the Ayr Bank in 1772, left liabilities of over one million pounds, but the 241 shareholders met them so well that England was more inconvenienced than Scotland.[58] Moreover, without a dominant central bank, companies saw that competition was dangerous. Their many individual issues became one as far as customers were concerned, as they remain today, for they collectively guaranteed customers against failure, which in turn forced them to police each other. A banker who moved to England in 1826 said that, 'the Scottish system is one of entire confidence, and devoid of fear; while the English system is rather one of fear'.[59] Scottish notes were therefore the currency of choice in the far north of England.[60]

The existence of local clearing schemes like that revealed in Bradford meant that Yorkshire banks should have been disciplined by market forces, since any which persistently had disproportionate numbers of notes returned through other banks would have to hand over in return other local notes, Bank of England notes, and even gold. Fellow bankers would put extreme pressure on recalcitrants, lest they should be left holding worthless paper. However, Wentworth's eventual bankruptcy stemmed from prolonged over-expansion of their note issue, hidden by an 'expedient for recalling the small notes of the firm and preventing those heavy weekly balances from being payable to the neighbouring bankers'. They effectively paid customers to return the notes directly, and as Wakefield had become the centre of trade in grain and meat for the manufacturing district, 'great numbers of their engagements [are] now in the hands of the graziers and farmers in the North of England, and which will, in due course, return upon the butchers, corn-dealers, and other retailers of the West Riding, at no distant period'.[61] Thus, while Yorkshire had a feeling of groping towards a Scottish mutuality in banking, the network of banks was never allowed to consolidate itself and the resulting lack of certainty hurt the manufacturers.

Conclusion

The essence of this highly successful manufacturing network cannot be the quality of individual firms or entrepreneurs, who had little power. Instead, the links between units encouraged widespread, frequent and effective interaction in structured but not predetermined ways, guided by practical testing in open markets. Transactions thus took on a developmental role alongside their

---

his interpretations. See also C.W. Munn, *The Scottish Provincial Banking Companies, 1747–1864* (Edinburgh University Press, 1981).

[58] White, *Free Banking*, p. 29.

[59] Quoted in White, *Free Banking*, p. 143. The Co-operative Movement used a similar device to support its many small members, with equal success.

[60] White, *Free Banking*; p. 35.

[61] *Leeds Intelligencer*, reprinted in *Times*, January 4, 1826.

obvious function of exchange and a sort of incremental, generalised entrepreneurialism emerged. However, none of this can be taken for granted, and network functions are likely to decay naturally as particular linkages become rigid and dominant, or because of changing external circumstances. Only when everything works effectively will the result be an evolving mix of goods that consumers really want, at prices they can pay, and delivered to the places where they are most in demand, but that is what Yorkshire delivered for several decades, and the remaking of the system did not interfere. As part of the network, banks effectively allowed Yorkshire manufacturers to borrow from the future, encouraging and facilitating a wide-ranging but unfocussed push towards a new model of manufacturing.

Thus, after the crisis was over the Chancellor of the Exchequer told the House of Commons that though 'the issues of country banks may have in some cases encouraged enterprise, and thus have promoted our manufacturing and agricultural prosperity, ... with a proper degree of feeling, that for such advantages we ought not to risk the ruin of thousands of families who had been deprived of their daily bread by the imprudent management and consequent failure of such establishments'.[62] However, most historians now see local currency-issuing as unrelated to the difficulties, an attitude supported by the Scottish experience, and Taylor's failure was actually exceptional. Moreover, if local note issuing might once have been taken as a temporary expedient, or a relic of a primitive system, it is now again a live issue. Disputes over joining a common European currency are often based on worries over losing sensitivity to the needs of particular manufacturing areas. Local Exchange and Trading Systems and Credit Unions are promoted in deprived parts of advanced countries to break log-jams where needs and the ability to meet them both exist, but cannot be brought together within the conventional economy, and the Grameen Bank movement offers micro-credit in the Third World.[63]

We should not take for granted the existence of a business culture behind a developing network, or the support systems needed to allow networks to function creatively. Certainly, the ability of West Yorkshire to develop both spontaneously deserves more study. Local banking clearly espoused the 'needs-of-trade' theory which equated the correct level of currency in the economy with that which allowed business to be done at the level at which businessmen wished to do it.[64] Institutions like the Gomersal Bank were insignificant alone, but collectively they reinforced trust within the manufacturing network through dispassionate assessments of credit-worthiness, based on performance, not status. Collateral was the key to borrowing, not likely success, while informal credit within communities and a general willingness to form partnerships still kept barriers to entry low. Banks

---

[62] *Times*, February 3, 1826.

[63] Thus, the *Guardian*, 5 January 2002, reported that Argentina's current problems have led to ten thousand people a week joining barter clubs for the exchange of goods and services without money being required.

[64] White, *Free Banking*, Chapter 4.

were themselves businesses dependent on public confidence, constantly feeding the region's own energies back into the system to enlarge it further, rather than dominating it or draining profits out to a metropolitan centre, a recognised facet of modern underdevelopment. This turned the region into a business hot-spot, rather than encouraging the widespread, lower-intensity activity of neo-classical theory.

Chapter 7

Capital networks in the Sheffield region, 1850–1885[1]

Lucy Newton

Introduction

Recent literature in business history has focused upon the viability of an alternative model of capitalist development to that put forward by Chandler. Rather than championing the 'big business', US-orientated approach, others have argued in favour of capitalist development in the form of industrial districts or 'clusters', involving small and medium-sized business units and flexible specialisation.[2] A key element of such districts is that they possess an internal homogeneity in comparison with other regions, and have well-developed networks of internal connections. They also manufacture a variety of products for domestic and international consumption utilising flexible technology. Furthermore, within these districts the formations of institutions occur that promote both cooperation and competition among enterprises, therefore stimulating innovation in the business environment.

This paper aims to examine such an industrial district, but with the focus upon internal connections, most particularly business and capital networks. While business networks are notoriously difficult to define and research, they are characterised here as 'high-trust linkages connecting to a series of entities',

---

[1] I would like to thank the following people for the support given and helpful comments made in the writing of this chapter: Phil Cottrell, John Wilson, Josephine Maltby and all those present at the Preston 'Networks and Clusters' conference in September 2001. All errors and omissions are my own.

[2] M.J. Piore and C.F. Sabel, *The Second Industrial Divide: Possibilities for Prosperity* (Basic Books, 1984); M.E. Porter, *The Competitive Advantage of Nations* (Macmillan, 1990); C. Sabel and J. Zeitlin, 'Historical Alternatives to Mass Production: Markets, Politics and Production in the Nineteenth Century', *Past and Present*, No. 108 (1985); P. Scranton, *Figured Tapestry: Production, Markets and Power in Philadelphia Textiles, 1855–1941* (Cambridge University Press, 1989); P. Scranton, 'Diversity in Diversity: Flexible Production and American Industrialisation, 1880–1930', *Business History Review*, 65, (Spring 1991); P. Scranton, '"Build a Firm, Start Another": The Bromley's and Family Entrepreneurship in the Philadelphia Region', *Business History*, 35 (Oct. 1993); M. Storper and S. Christopherson, 'Flexible Specialisation and Regional Industrial Agglomerations: The Case of the U.S. Motion Picture Industry', *Annals of the Association of American Geographers*, Vol. 77, No. 1 (1987).

with linkages based on information flow.[3] As the intricate networks amongst business elites and supplies of capital have important repercussions upon both individual enterprises and the economic performance of a region as a whole, they are therefore worthy of closer inspection.

The region under examination here is that of Sheffield and its surrounding towns and villages in South Yorkshire and North Derbyshire. The city, towns and villages were all involved in the same manufacturing and mining industries of iron, steel, engineering, secondary metals and coal mining. It was a region defined by common economic activity, rather than by geographical or political boundaries. Sheffield and its neighbours formed a specialist centre for domestic production and international exports during the nineteenth century, and into the twentieth. Its manufacture of special steels, tools and cutlery involved a highly differentiated system of production that required flexibility of labour and technology. Such flexibility, along with an emphasis on quality, ensured that the region remained an international leader in these products into the twentieth century.

During the period under examination, business within the region experienced boom and slump, large variations in demand for their products, growing competition from abroad, important innovations in technology and changes in the scale and organisation of production. This paper aims to analyse the role of business networks in managing changing economic and institutional conditions, especially the ability to obtain finance in order to expand, to purchase new technology, or merely to survive. In particular, companies that adopted limited liability during the period are considered.

Following the Joint Stock Companies Act of 1855, enterprises were allowed to adopt limited liability and call upon shareholders as a source of finance. Sheffield, along with Oldham, was a centre of limited liability company formations, following the liberalisation of company law, whereas much of the rest of England was slow to adopt joint-stock form. This paper considers groups of individuals who consistently purchased shares in the region's joint stock companies to form a 'capital network'. Networks of investors are especially pertinent when examining issues of financial provision in an era when funds from family and friends formed a crucial source of supply. In this way, social networks can be seen to impact upon business networks. The aim of the paper is to provide a rigorous analysis, based upon empirical evidence, of the operation of networks as channels of information and resources (in this case, finance) and their impact upon the economic performance of a particular industrial district.

Initially, the paper will examine the institutional framework of share ownership in England and Wales during the period under consideration, namely, the changes in company law and the uptake of limited liability. The following sections will then analyse limited company promotion and

---

[3]   Chapter 2, in this volume.

shareholding patterns in the Sheffield region. A final section will attempt to draw some conclusions from the analysis.

Institutional framework

Following the liberalisation of company law in 1855 and 1856, limited liability became increasingly adopted in Great Britain as a form of company organisation.[4] With limited liability, a company's shareholders were only liable for its debts to the extent of the nominal value of their shareholdings and, furthermore, each shareholder could freely transfer his/her holding in such a company without reference to any other shareholder. This method of company organisation also, potentially, allowed a firm to raise capital publicly and therefore, in theory, to draw upon a broader capital market than had hitherto been available. However, despite the ruling permissive code of company law from 1855, the use made of limited liability by English manufacturing concerns was not very widespread before 1885. Within industry there was some concentration of conversions in the cotton, iron, steel, and coal sectors, while, more rapidly and generally, the number of joint-stock companies only increased from the 1880s. In addition, conversion to the limited form was not always accompanied by public appeals for capital; in an effort to prevent the divorce of ownership from management, those previously in control of the firm and/or their friends and relatives often retained shares.[5] The majority of firms in England and Wales relied upon internal sources of finance, usually the plough-back of company profits.

By 1886, Sheffield and Oldham had become two of the most important centres of joint stock company formation in England.[6] By the mid-1880s, contemporaries estimated that Sheffield had a total of 44 limited companies with a paid up capital of just over £12 million.[7] In this study, a sample of 90

---

[4]   For a full discussion of nineteenth century company law reform see P.L. Cottrell, *Industrial Finance 1830–1914: The Finance and Organisation of English Manufacturing Industry* (Methuen, 1980), pp. 39–79; J.B. Jefferys, *Trends in Business Organisation in Great Britain since 1856* (1938. Reprinted by Arnos Press, 1977), pp. 19–53; H.A. Shannon, 'The Coming of General Limited Liability' (1931) in E.M. Carus Wilson (ed), *Essays in Economic and Social History* (Edward Arnold, 1946), pp. 358–79.

[5]   P.L. Payne, 'Family Business in Britain: An Historical and Analytical Survey' in A. Okochi and S. Yasuoka (eds), *Family Business in the Era of Industrial Growth* (Tokyo University Press, 1984), pp. 171–3.

[6]   L.A. Newton, *Credit and Capital in Sheffield: The Finance of Industry in Nineteenth Century England* (Ashgate, forthcoming); W.A. Thomas, *The Provincial Stock Exchanges* (Frank Cass, 1973); D.A. Farnie, *The English Cotton Industry and the World Market, 1815–1896* (Oxford University Press, 1979).

[7]   *The Accountant*, 1887, p. 17.

companies based in and around Sheffield that adopted limited liability between 1855 and 1885 have been identified and their shareholders analysed.[8]

Company promoters played an important role in the adoption of the new limited liability company form. Firms wishing to adopt joint-stock status could call upon the services of such individuals, who would then market the company and its shares through a prospectus, and by utilising their personal and business contacts in order to ensure that adequate subscriptions were raised. In examining the 90 companies that adopted limited liability in Sheffield during the third quarter of the nineteenth century, three such promoters have been identified and will be discussed in detail below.

Despite the comparatively rapid uptake of limited liability in Sheffield, as compared to the rest of England and Wales, the mixed industrial structure of Sheffield, with a predominance of small-scale operations alongside large-scale industrial concerns, must be emphasised. Flexible production; family control; low barriers to entry; and a cheap supply of highly skilled labour all impacted upon the structure of Sheffield's manufacturing industry, in that it encouraged small-scale, niche manufacturers, rather than large-scale mass producers. Moreover, large-scale operations were not necessarily fully integrated factories of the 'modern' type. The system of production in Sheffield remained dependent upon the mixed system of large-scale production, middlemen and outworkers. A highly differentiated and flexible manufacturing system, particularly in the secondary metal trades, thus dominated production in the Sheffield area in during the nineteenth century and beyond.[9] This is a classic portrait of an industrial district, first identified by Marshall, and one which has been studied in detail by Lloyd-Jones and Lewis.[10] Therefore, by 1885 a very complex industrial structure had developed in the Sheffield region, whereby small-scale firms which required only low levels of capital investment existed in considerable numbers alongside a relatively few large joint stock concerns, mainly in heavy industries, which required large capital investments. Methods of business also remained parochial for large and small-scale firms alike.

---

[8] The companies from this particular study were initially selected by viewing the summary Parliamentary Papers concerned with London registrations of limited liability companies. *British Parliamentary Papers*, 'Returns of the names, objects, places of business, date of registration, nominal capital, number of shares etc. of all joint-stock companies formed or registered...': 1864, LVIII; 1866, LXVI; 1867, LXIV; 1867-68, LIV; 1868-9, LVI; 1874, LXII; 1875, LXXI; 1876, LXVIII; 1877, LXXVI; 1878, LXVIII; 1878-80, LXVII; 1881, LXXXIII; 1881-82, LXIV; 1882-83, LXIV; 1884, LXXII; 1884-85, LXXI. Further companies were consequently identified during searches in the Public Record Office indexes and file series. The sources consulted for the subsequent analysis are located at the Public Record Office, Kew, London: Board of Trade Papers, file series 31. These files include the following documents: Articles of Association, Memorandum of Association, a Summary of Capital and Shares and any Articles of Agreement associated with the conversion of an existing company, all of which were returned to the Registrar of Joint Stock Companies.

[9] Newton, *Credit and Capital*.

[10] R. Lloyd-Jones and M.J. Lewis, 'Personal Capitalism and British Industrial Decline: The Personally Managed Firm and Business Strategy in Sheffield, 1880–1920', *Business History Review*, Vol. 68 (1994), pp. 364–411.

Conducting business in the fluctuating economic climate of nineteenth century Britain was a risky affair.[11] The introduction of limited liability was one method by which those companies wishing to expand their capital bases could reduce their personal risk. However, the persistence of the 'private' limited company in Britain demonstrated the reluctance of owners to fully relinquish control of their enterprises. 'Private' limited companies tended to sell their shares to family members, friends or business associates from the local area. Even many of the 'true' public companies in Britain maintained a high degree of family control.[12] Managers of nineteenth century limited companies were thus ensuring a degree of continuity between the new joint-stock firm and the private partnership.

In addition to maintaining control of their companies, it is likely that the managements of limited companies were attempting to reduce the potential risks that resulted from calling upon external sources of funding. Shareholders known by the promoter or vendor, and who were knowledgeable of, and participated in, the region's industry would have been likely to engender a greater sense of commitment to an enterprise than would be demonstrated by a shareholder from outside the region. Retaining control amongst family and friends meant the maintenance of trust in a business environment which remained uncertain. The entry into a business of persons who stood outside such a circle of kinship or friendship ties would probably be viewed as an increase in risk.[13]

Casson has highlighted the benefits that such 'committed' shareholders could bring to a company, especially with regard to financial support. He has argued that 'if shareholders themselves experience a sense of moral obligation then they may consent to sacrifices over and above this level'. This may be contrasted with 'shareholders who are concerned purely with profit-maximisation [who] will, of course, require that any financial sacrifices made' must generate savings and benefits for the investor.[14]

> Shareholders are ... unlikely to participate emotionally in the goals of the enterprise if they only hold a small shareholding for speculative purposes, which they can liquidate at any time ... In small firms, where each shareholder usually holds a significant stake on a long-term basis, emotional rewards to owners are likely to be much greater. Greatest of all are likely to be the rewards in the owner-managed firm, and in the family firm.[15]

[11] M. Lester, *Victorian Insolvency* (Oxford University Press, 1995); J. Maltby, 'UK Joint Stock Companies Legislation 1844–1900: Accounting Publicity and "Mercantile Caution"', *Accounting History*, Vol. 3, No. 3 (1998), p. 15.
[12] M.B. Rose, 'The Family Firm in British Business, 1780–1914' in M.W. Kirby and M.B. Rose (eds), *Business Enterprise in Modern Britain* (Routledge, 1994), p. 68.
[13] Ibid., p. 67.
[14] M. Casson, 'Culture as an Economic Asset' in A.C. Godley and O.M. Westall (eds), *Business History and Business Culture* (Manchester University Press, 1996), p. 68.
[15] Ibid.

This is not to say that those investing in limited concerns in the Sheffield region were not concerned with making a profit upon their shareholdings. However, Casson's analysis highlights the potential benefits of attracting investors who had a greater commitment to the company – through personal or business contacts – and to the region's industry through their participation in local business networks. This can be applied to large nineteenth century joint-stock firms as equally as to small-scale, modern enterprises.

The concept of business networks has been examined in the introduction to this volume. Such theories appear to be applicable to a nineteenth century business environment in which transactions frequently occurred at a local level and consequently often took place amongst those who were known to each other. Wilson has stressed that the 'highly localised and personal nature of relationships was the bedrock of eighteenth and nineteenth century organisation and finance'.[16] Despite the international nature of Sheffield's export trade, production took place at a local level and would have frequently involved face-to-face contact between economic actors. Indeed, Tweedale's comprehensive studies of Sheffield have emphasised the localised/parochial nature of nineteenth century business in and around the city.

The stamping ground of these men was not the national scene, but their own locality, where they could pursue their personal values and maintain their old-established networks.[17] Tweedale thus confirms the highly embedded nature of the networks that existed in Sheffield.

> Sheffield's cluster of steel firms ... nurtured a close-knit community of shared values. The fact that few of these men ran totally integrated mills intensified an industrial network of complex linkages. These linkages were of course reflected socially, by intermarriage and a complex networking of families ... that often extended into the banking and financial scene in the city.[18]

Institutions such as the *Company of Cutlers*, the *Sheffield Assay Office*, *Sheffield Chamber of Commerce*, the *Freemasons* and the *Sheffield Club*, along with religious and political affiliations, were part of the fabric that constituted a complex network structure of the business community in the region.[19] How did these networks apply to the limited companies under examination here?

---

[16] J.F. Wilson, *British Business History, 1720–1994* (Manchester University Press, 1995), p. 47.

[17] G. Tweedale, *Steel City: Entrepreneurship, Strategy and Technology in Sheffield, 1743–1993* (Oxford University Press, 1995), p. 144.

[18] Ibid., p. 145.

[19] C. Binfield and D. Hey (eds), *Mesters to Masters: A History of the Company of Cutlers in Hallamshire* (Oxford University Press, 1997); C. Binfield, R. Childs, G. Harper, D. Hey, D. Martin and G. Tweedale (eds) *The History of the City of Sheffield, 1883–1993*, 3 Vols. (Sheffield Academic Press, 1993).

Company promoters

Company promoters were responsible for bringing joint-stock firms 'to life' and were crucial to the spread of limited liability during the second half of the nineteenth century. Potentially, such individuals could draw upon considerable networks of contacts in order to facilitate the uptake of company shares in particular and limited liability in general. They could therefore improve the efficiency of the new form of company organisation and capital flows.

However, promoters had a notoriously bad reputation. Fear of the corrupt company promoter had been voiced in the debates concerning the reform of company law in the first half of the nineteenth century. An article in *The Times* in 1844 gave a dramatic warning to the innocent investor of the unscrupulous promoter's ability to:

> stimulate avarice by representations of unimpeachable security, and hope by the promise of boundless wealth – to lull the suspicions of the aged, and rouse the cupidity of the young – to guaranty secrecy and large dividends to all. As director, he must simply lie ... always lie.[20]

The freedom granted promoters to establish limited companies by the reform of company law between 1855 and 1862 increased the activity of promoters. Cottrell has argued that:

> It is highly likely that the extreme freedom that the law gave to company promoters led ironically to limited companies getting a 'bad name', with their formation being regarded with disfavour by manufacturers and industrialists.[21]

Indeed, Armstrong has emphasised that, in terms of regulation: '[t]here were few rules. Neither company law nor the regulations of the Stock Exchange placed many restrictions on the methods the predatory promoter might employ'.[22] The system was thus open to abuse and unscrupulous company promoters furnished the occupation with a rather dubious reputation. Burn assesses the record of the company promoter, arguing that public prejudices against them after the 1870s 'were clearly well grounded, though some of the promoter's errors were doubtless the result not of knavery but of a pardonable failure to forecast the change of price trend in the 'seventies'.[23] Kynaston has

---

[20] Quoted in B.C. Hunt, *The Development of the Business Corporation in England 1800–1867* (Harvard University Press, 1936), p. 90–2.

[21] Cottrell, *Industrial Finance*, p. 54.

[22] J. Armstrong, 'The Rise and Fall of the Company Promoter and the Financing of British Industry', in J.J. van Helten and Y. Cassis (eds), *Capitalism in a Mature Economy. Financial Institutions, Capital Exports and British Industry, 1870–1939* (Ashgate, 1990), p. 115.

[23] D.L. Burn, *The Economic History of Steelmaking* (Cambridge University Press, 1940, reprinted 1961), p. 256.

been more critical, surmising of company promoters that: 'Some ... were more or less honourable; most were not'.[24]

Despite their tarnished reputation, promoters played an increasing and important role in promoting joint-stock companies. 'The period 1870 to 1914 was the heyday of the individual company promoter working on domestic industrial floatations.'[25] The growing numbers of investors and growth in demand for capital from business called for professional intermediation in the establishment of joint-stock concerns.[26] Unfamiliarity with the new company legislation was also a reason to turn to the promoter.[27]

The employment of company promoters grew from the 1860s onwards, especially by enterprises where capital requirements were large and more public calls for capital were required, or where a business was new and the connections necessary to sell shares were inadequate. Promoters did not usually persuade companies to convert to joint-stock status, but rather assisted the process of conversion. Indeed, the company that was to adopt limited liability would usually be a conversion, rather than a brand new venture.[28] Company promoters were engaged in order to utilise their networks of contacts and raise the necessary capital. As the volume of capital required for these conversions rose, the importance of promoters in securing adequate subscriptions from public sources and/or their contacts grew correspondingly. Armstrong has emphasised the importance of such a role when asserting that: '[f]loating a company was primarily a marketing exercise'.[29] As the marketer of company shares, it was important for the promoter to have 'an appreciation of the mood of the market', but Armstrong has also stressed that 'a market could be stimulated, in shares as in any other commodity, and the company promoter needed to be adept at this if he was to be successful'.[30] The prospectus was an important document to be utilised in the attempt to enhance the sales of shares and it was here that 'the company promoter had a fairly free rein to indulge his creative-writing talents'.[31] Promoters would also frequently attempt to ensure the success of a joint-stock venture by the 'underwriting' of floatations, either formally or informally. This was usually achieved through a group of affluent associates who would invest money in a promoter's conversions. A successful history of conversions enhanced the reputation of the promoter and his associated investors.[32]

---

[24] D. Kynaston, *The City of London, Vol. 1. A World of its Own, 1815–1890* (Chatto and Windus, 1994), p. 344.

[25] Armstrong, 'The Rise and Fall of the Company Promoter', p. 115.

[26] Jefferys, *Trends in Business Organisation*, pp. 294–5.

[27] Armstrong, 'The Rise and Fall of the Company Promoter', p. 115.

[28] Ibid., p. 116; Newton, *Credit and Capital*, Chapter 5.

[29] Armstrong, 'The Rise and Fall of the Company Promoter', p. 117.

[30] Ibid., p. 117.

[31] Ibid., p. 117 and 124; Cottrell, *Industrial Finance*, pp. 62–3 and 68–9.

[32] Armstrong, 'The Rise and Fall of the Company Promoter', pp. 117–18 and 126–7.

In terms of the type of industry in which these promoters operated, in the 1860s and 1870s 'the most conspicuous industry of the first type in which the embryo promoter or agent appeared, was iron and steel'.[33] Indeed, such company promoters operated in the iron and steel trades in the Sheffield region. The involvement of promoters in the floatation of a limited company may be discerned by examining the legal documentation contained in the Board of Trade files. These documents also included the names of vendors and initial subscribers to the company, revealing an interesting portrait of a group of capitalists/entrepreneurs operating in the region. This is the initial step in identifying those involved in a network of capital provision for the region's industry.

Promoters of Sheffield companies

When reviewing the names of vendors and promoters of companies adopting limited liability in the Sheffield region, three dominant promoters were identified: Alfred Allott, John Unwin Wing and David Chadwick, all accountants. Alfred Allott, from Sheffield, was the sole promoter of eight companies[34] and a joint promoter of one other[35] – all were conversions of existing undertakings. Four of Allott's promotions took place in 1872, four in 1873 and one in 1874 – a concentrated burst of activity, occurring during the boom years in the iron and steel industries. All the companies with which Allott was involved were iron or steel firms, eight located in Sheffield and one in Rotherham. John Unwin Wing, also from Sheffield, was the promoter of seven companies – one in 1872, three in 1873, two in 1874 and one in 1876.[36] Again, all were conversions. Wing's period of promotions activity was also intense, although not as concentrated as that of Allott, and his promotions again mainly coincided with the iron and steel boom of the early 1870s. Six of the companies were manufacturers and processors of iron, steel or other metals and metal goods, and one was located just over the county border on the Derbyshire coalfield. Of the other Wing companies, four were located in Sheffield and two in Rotherham. The Manchester accountant David Chadwick promoted four companies: Charles Cammell, Parkgate Iron, Yorkshire Engine Company and Vickers. These flotations took place in 1864, 1865 and 1867, involving iron, steel and engineering firms in Sheffield and Rotherham. Thus, the activities of the promoter who was based outside the region took place in the 1860s, in

---

[33] Jefferys, *Trends in Business Organization*, p. 297.

[34] Albion Steel & Wire & Co. Ltd., Charlton Iron Works Ltd., Davy Bros. Ltd., Hallamshire Steel & File Co. Ltd., Hydes & Wigfull Ltd., Phoenix Bessemer Steel Co. Ltd., Saville St Foundry & Engineering Co. Ltd. and William Cooke & Co. Ltd..

[35] Jarvis William Barber was the joint promoter of Henry Wilkinson & Co. Ltd. with Alfred Allott.

[36] Cardigan Iron & Steel, G & J Brown, James Fairbrother, Kelham Rolling Mills, Sheffield Nickel & Silver Plate, Tinsley Rolling Mills, and Whittington Silkstone Colliery Ltd.

contrast to the local promotions of the 1870s, and one of Chadwick's undertakings was not a conversion but a completely new venture (Yorkshire Engine Company Ltd.).

Who were these men that played such a prominent role in the movement towards limited liability by manufacturing industry in the Sheffield region before 1885? Much has already been written about David Chadwick.[37] He was not only an accountant, with offices in both Manchester and London, but had been the Treasurer to the Corporation of Salford, a writer on urban living conditions and a statistician. He was involved in the creation of 47 limited companies, most importantly iron, steel and coal concerns, and was a forceful advocate of limited liability as a method of industrial organisation and finance. Jefferys estimated that the total share capital involved in these floatations was over £40 million. His firm of Chadwick, Adamson and Collier 'was the most important financial agent for industrial companies in the first twenty-five years of the Limited Liability Act'.[38] Morgan and Thomas also argue that 'Chadwick's business was a very conservative one', in that he would check the accounts of a company before taking on its conversion and 'he admitted that other promoters were less strict in their selection'.[39] Chadwick's firm was 'in touch with some of the most important investors in the country'.[40] In 1867, Chadwick claimed that his contacts numbered in the hundreds; in 1874, he claimed that they had reached 4000, and by 1878 the figure was 5000.[41] Even allowing for some exaggeration for the sake of publicity, the volume of such contacts remains impressive. Jefferys estimates that the investors in all of Chadwick's promotions, not only those in Sheffield, provided approximately £10,000,000 to £15,000,000 for domestic manufacturing companies up to 1877.[42] He utilised prospectuses and letters in order to generate subscriptions. In evidence to a parliamentary committee investigating the progress of the 1862 and 1867 Companies Acts, he asserted that: 'We have no connection with the Stock Exchange, no jobbing, and very seldom any advertising'.[43] Rather, he sent out prospectuses and letters marked 'private and confidential' which invited his 'friends to subscribe'.[44] The reputation of Chadwick preceded him and companies using his services were virtually guaranteed to raise sufficient external capital.

---

[37] Cottrell, *Industrial Finance*, pp. 113–4, 153, 186–7 and 252; D.J. Jeremy (ed), *Dictionary of Business Biography* (Butterworths, 1984), pp. 652–3.

[38] Jefferys, *Trends in Business Organization*, p. 298.

[39] E.V. Morgan and W.A. Thomas, *The Stock Exchange. Its History and Functions* (Elek Books, 1962), p. 136.

[40] Jefferys, *Trends in Business Organization*, p. 317.

[41] *British Parliamentary Papers*, 'Report of the Select Committee on the Companies Acts', X (1867), q. 869 and *British Parliamentary Papers*, 'Report of the Select Committee on the Companies' Acts' of 1862 and 1867, VIII (1877), q. 2079.

[42] Jefferys, *Trends in Business Organization*, p. 318.

[43] *PP Report*, 1877: q. 2045.

[44] Jefferys, *Trends in Business Organization*, p. 318.

The backgrounds of John Unwin Wing and Alfred Allott are harder to discern. Alfred Allott was an accountant and partner in Allott, Hadfield, Kidner & Hawson, 'auditors, financial agents, and public accountants' and insurance agents, a firm with an office in both Sheffield and London. He also had a private residence in London.[45] John Unwin Wing was a partner in Wing, Wing & Co., 'accountants, auditors, etc.' of Sheffield and London. John Wing was also secretary to the Sheffield Wagon Co. Ltd., author of *Mercantile Book-keeping* (published in 1865) and resided in Abbeydale, an affluent Sheffield suburb.[46] Both Allott and Wing were active members of the Society of Accountants in England and served on its council during the Council's formative years.[47] They were also founding Fellows of the Sheffield Institute of Accountants, established in 1877, and Allott was the first President of this organisation.[48] John Unwin Wing's career failed to develop smoothly, as in July 1882 he was convicted at Leeds Assizes for felony.[49] This must have been a major setback to the career of an accountant and company promoter. Indeed, Wing did not promote any companies in the 1880s and no information has been found about him after this date.

Sheffield accountants were unusual in their 'very close affiliation and virtual dominance of the Stock Exchange in Sheffield'.[50] Early nineteenth century sharebrokers in Sheffield operated as accountants and this practice continued into the twentieth century. In 1880, almost half of the membership of the Sheffield Stock Exchange offered accountancy services.[51] The importance of such individuals in the region's industrial and financial networks was therefore long-standing. In the case of Allott, Wing and Chadwick, their significance is also apparent by the number of industrial companies in which they participated – 20 of the 90 companies examined – and by the volume of capital involved in their Sheffield promotions (see Table 7.1). These three men taken together were responsible for the promotion of twenty companies with a combined nominal capital of £2,885,000. Chadwick promoted the fewest companies numerically, but they involved the greatest volume of nominal capital. They were therefore financially powerful individuals within the region during the 1860s and 1870s and the volume of capital involved in their promotions implies an importance within this industrial sector on a national level. In addition, their influence was crucial in the success, or failure, of the new limited companies, most particularly in the initial sale of their shares.

[45] *White's Directory of Sheffield* (White, 1962 and 1879).
[46] A.M. Hoe, *The Sheffield & District Society of Chartered Accountants. The First Hundred Years Centenary, 1877–1977* (The Sheffield & District Society of Chartered Accountants, 1977), p. 6; *White's Directory of Sheffield* (1962 and 1879).
[47] Hoe, *Sheffield and District Society of Chartered Accountants*, pp. 3–4.
[48] Ibid., pp. 7–9.
[49] HSBC Group Archives: AD5, Sheffield Union Banking Company, Board of Directors Minutes, f. 227.
[50] Hoe, *Sheffield and District Society of Chartered Accountants*, p. 4.
[51] Ibid., p. 4; Thomas, *Provincial Stock Exchanges*, p. 50.

Table 7.1
Capital involved in promotions by Allott, Wing and Chadwick

	No. of Companies	Total Nominal Capital (£)	Average Nominal Capital (£)
Name			
Allott	9	795,000	88,333
Wing	7	435,000	62,143
Chadwick	4	1,655,000	413,750

The three promoters also often owned shares in their prodigies, once a full allotment had been made, such shares being then potentially available on the open market. Table 7.2 shows the shareholdings of Allott, Wing and Chadwick in their companies following initial subscription. This gives some indication as to the extent of their interest once a company was established. These have been extracted from the first available annual return made to the Registrar of Joint Stock Companies from the summary of capital and shares of the company following registration. It should be emphasised that these figures show actual subscribed capital, rather than nominal capital, thus demonstrating their 'real' involvement in the listed companies. In addition, the Table shows the investments of these promoters in companies other than those in which they were involved in floating.

Chadwick subscribed a total of £12,500 to three of the companies he promoted, a sizeable amount of personal capital. However, £9000 of this was invested in vendors' shares of Yorkshire Engine Co. Ltd., an indication of Chadwick's commitment to the success of this new company. A relatively large amount of capital was also subscribed by Alfred Allott - £4838 to seven out of the nine companies he promoted – but, in addition, £4504 to four where he was not the promoter and to which he made large subscriptions.[52] Therefore, Allott appears to have been committed to investing in Sheffield's manufacturing industry *per se*, rather than merely confining his funds to his own promotions. In contrast, John Unwin Wing was not as supportive to the companies that he had promoted in terms of funds he subscribed once they had been registered. He took up shares in five out of seven companies he promoted, but the total amount of money involved was only £2985.[53] Thus, Wing's involvement appears to have been with regard to the legal and financial aspects

---

[52] £1000 to Brown Bayley & Dixon, £1280 to London & Sheffield Nickel Silver Plate, and £2200 to The Whittington Freehold Colliery.
[53] He also subscribed £150 to The Sheffield Steel & Manufacturing Co. Ltd., a company he did not promote.

of promotion, and less to actual personal investment in the companies themselves.

Table 7.2
Shareholdings of Allott, Wing and Chadwick

	Year	Type of Share	No. of Shares	Capital Subscribed by Promoter (£)	Capital Subscribed by Promoter as % of Total Subscribed Capital per Co.
Company					
Allott					
Whittington Freehold Colliery	1864	Ordinary	500	2200	14.6
Midland Iron Co.	1865	Ordinary	160	1280	6.4
Joseph Peace & Co.	1869	Ordinary	12	24	0.2
Albion Steel & Wire	1873	Ordinary	100	500	0.8
Brown, Bayley & Dixon	1873	Ordinary	50	1000	0.6
Charlton Iron Works	1873	Ordinary	20	550	0.8
Davy Bros.	1873	Ordinary	50	750	2.5
Henry Wilkinson	1873	Ordinary	20	100	0.5
Hydes & Wigfull	1873	Ordinary	50	188	1.5
Phoenix Bessmer	1873	Ordinary	50	2000	2.5
William Cooke	1873	Ordinary	50	750	1.1
Wing					
James Fairbrother	1869	Ordinary	100	100	6.7
G. & J. Brown	1873	Ordinary	2	90	0.2
Sheffield Nickel & Silver Plate	1873	Ordinary	20	80	0.8
Sheffield Steel & Manufacturing Co.	1874	Ordinary	25	150	1.2
Chadwick					
Charles Cammell	1865	Vendors	180	9000	2.3
Parkgate Iron	1865	Ordinary	100	2000	3.3
Yorkshire Engine	1865	Ordinary	100	1500	8.1

The involvement of Allott, Wing and Chadwick in their promotions clearly went beyond merely registration. Jefferys has described a commitment whereby promoters 'did not collect their commission and pass on to another company, but stayed with the company as auditors and felt to a certain degree responsible to their clients whom they had persuaded to invest'.[54] Indeed, of the 20 companies that Allott, Wing and Chadwick were involved in promoting, all bar one utilised the services of the men's accountancy firms as their company auditors.[55] Such responsibility was also demonstrated in the Monthly Circular that Chadwick's accounting firm sent to all its clients.[56] However, it is difficult to assess the extent to which they influenced the subsequent success of the companies they had promoted.

Chadwick claimed that nine out of every ten companies he promoted were a success, when the overall failure rate of joint-stock firms during the 1860s and 1870s was being calculated at between 30 and 50 per cent.[57] However, it was unlikely that Chadwick himself would provide an accurate measurement of success, given the need to publicise his activities in a positive light. An attempt has been made to measure the success of the promoters' companies from the data available in the Board of Trade files.

None of the companies promoted by Allott, Wing or Chadwick were 'abortive' or rather did not commence operations. This would indicate success for the companies in terms of initial promotion. The viability of a company might also be gauged by the proportion of capital subscribed from its first share issue, possibly indicating how attractive the venture was to investors. The promoter was likely to have had a major influence upon the sale of the first issue of shares, although the precise extent cannot be measured. All three promoters under discussion were accountants and therefore were likely to have had well-developed networks of financial contacts and potential investors.

The actual amount of capital subscribed to Allott's, Wing's and Chadwick's promotions in the Sheffield region, as a percentage of nominal capital, is shown in Table 7.3. This indicates that for each of the three groups of companies, the subscribed capital amounted to less than half of the aggregate nominal capital. Cottrell found that the limited companies he sampled between 1866 and 1882 had, on average, only 25 per cent of their nominal capital called up, whilst during the 1860s boom the average was even lower at 18.9 per cent.[58] Chadwick himself claimed that 25 per cent paid on shares was common for industrial concerns.[59] Therefore, comparatively, the amount of capital called by the companies of Chadwick, Wing and Allott was high. The willingness of investors to subscribe to these companies and fulfil the relatively high calls made on the shares would indicate that these promotions were successful.

---

[54] Jefferys, *Trends in Business Organization*, pp. 298–9.

[55] The only firm not to use the services of its company promoter as auditor was Davy Bros. Ltd, promoted by Allott, who instead used the services of John Watson & Son, a Sheffield practice.

[56] Jefferys, *Trends in Business Organization*, pp. 298–9.

[57] Ibid., p. 320.

[58] Cottrell, *Industrial Finance*, pp. 84–5.

[59] Maltby, 'UK Joint Stock Companies Legislation', p. 20.

Table 7.3
Capital subscribed to industrial promotions of Allott, Wing and Chadwick

	Total Nominal Capital (£)	Capital subscribed as % of Nominal Capital (£)	Average Share denomination
Name			
Allott	435,000	40.7	24
Wing	795,000	48.4	17.5
Chadwick	1,655,000	34.2	100

Share denominations had an impact upon their attractiveness to investors. Jefferys has argued that share denominations were high in the early days of the general availability of limited liability, but thereafter gradually decreased. The introduction of lower denominations made shares potentially more widely available, especially with the increase in denominations of £5 or less. The earlier company registrations of Chadwick had a high average share denomination of £100, whereas the later registrations of Wing and Allott had lower average share denomination of £24 and £34 respectively. Yet, despite their relatively high nominal values – not one average share denomination for any set of the promoters companies is below £20 – there does not appear to have been a reluctance to subscribe to shares offered by these companies. The attraction of investing in these companies must, in some part, have been due to Wing, Allott and Chadwick acting as financial agents, using both business and personal connections to ensure that subscriptions were plentiful. There may also have been an element of trust involved in purchasing shares of this nature; either trust in the promoter of the firm and its management. The role of Allott, Wing and Chadwick in the consequent success, or otherwise, of the companies that they promoted is impossible to gauge, but providing a successful floatation and attracting 'solid' investors was likely to have provided a positive contribution to the future progress of the newly converted businesses.

Shareholders in nineteenth century limited companies

What of those that purchased shares in the limited companies – the men and women who 'owned' the concerns? Before considering the shareowners of the 'Sheffield' companies, it is important to consider some general trends in share ownership during the nineteenth century.

Due to the existence of limited companies before 1855, most notably railways that had been incorporated through Acts of Parliament, by the mid-century: 'Investment had become a fairly respectable occupation for landed gentry and merchant alike'.[60] Who were the investing classes? High share denominations meant that only the wealthy, those with money to invest over the long-term, could purchase such shares.[61] Wealthy shareholders were the type most desired by limited companies. They were a high 'quality', safe type of investor, with plenty of money to spend and credentials that were known in the locality or by brokers and financial agents. For industrial companies, who rarely applied for a quotation on the London Stock Exchange, large shares and stable investors were the aim in the early days of limited liability.[62]

Yet the wealthy investor was not the only type who purchased shares in industrial concerns. The middle classes, professionals and traders were also investors in limited companies and, according to Jefferys, tended to be interested in regular dividends and marketable shares.[63] Spinsters, widows and the gentry were another group of investors who gradually came to purchase shares in domestic industrial companies. Jefferys described this group as the 'rentier', 'safe' or 'steady and legitimate' investor, believing that they formed 'the base of the Victorian investment market'.[64] Such investors would usually shy away from riskier enterprises such as new industrial concerns: 'Limited liability only affected them indirectly'. In contrast, it was 'the more enterprising "commercial classes" and members of the "native trading" community which had to lead the way in the new limited companies before the "safe" investor would follow'.[65] While these 'commercial classes' were to be found in large commercial centres and had accumulated volumes of capital, they were not familiar enough with industrial enterprise to set up such ventures by themselves. They tended to be far more adventurous than the 'safe' investor.[66]

The industrial capitalist was another type of shareholder. They were usually entrepreneurs who had conducted businesses on a partnership basis before the coming of general limited liability and who, following the 1855, 1856 and 1862 Companies Acts, were able to convert to limited liability and to potentially raise some level of external finance.

> The typical shareholders of the early joint stock companies was wealthy, tended to confine his investments to two or three companies and was

---

[60] S.A. Broadbridge, 'The Sources of Railway Share Capital', in M.C. Reed (ed), *Railways in the Victorian Economy: Studies in Finance and Economic Growth* (David and Charles, 1968); Jefferys, *Trends in Business Organization*, p. 47–8; J.R. Killick and W.A. Thomas, 'The Provincial Stock Exchanges', *Economic History Review*, XXIII (1970); M.C. Reed, *Investment in Railways in Britain, 1820–1844: A Study in the Development of the Capital Market* (Oxford University Press, 1975).
[61] Jefferys, *Trends in Business Organization*, p. 384.
[62] Ibid., pp. 173–4.
[63] Ibid., p. 175.
[64] Ibid., p. 385.
[65] Ibid., p. 387.
[66] Ibid., pp. 389–90.

interested to a certain degree in the running of these companies. This
applied particularly to the shareholders in industrial concerns.[67]

Thus, the investment of these individuals was largely personal; they invested in
the firms in which they had been proprietors or sometimes extended their
shareholdings to other industrial concerns in the sector or location with which
they were familiar. By delegating the floatation of a limited company to
promoters such as Chadwick, Allott and Wing, a less 'personal' element to
investment in industrial firms was sometimes introduced. The type of company
in which this type of investor took shares, according to Jefferys, tended to be
iron, steel, coal and shipping firms; they had few shareholders per company;
they had large individual shareholdings; and larger enterprises in which they
were involved were likely to have been quoted on the London or provincial
stock exchange lists, although the buying and selling of shares in these
enterprises tended to be restricted.[68] Jefferys went on to argue that: 'As a whole
... the home industrial companies retained their "personal" investment
character and that despite the role of the company promoter, investors in these
domestic manufacturing concerns tended to be the vendors and their friends
and families'.[69]

The work of Maltby confirms these findings. She has argued that, from the
perspective of accounting history, any financial publicity concerning a limited
company was not only undesirable for those large investors who wished to
keep details of their personal wealth private, but also unnecessary due to the
close relationships between many shareholders and the directors of these
concerns. Accounting publicity was not important for large investors who
possessed:

> financial expertise and ready access to management ... Personal
> knowledge, fostered by a shared background and membership of the same
> social network, did the same job, and did not have the drawback of
> exposing shareholders' financial affairs to the world at large.[70]

Moreover, the accounting profession was encouraged to underplay the profits
of limited companies, again in the interests of limited company directors and
their large investors and to the detriment of the small, 'outside' investor.
Maltby argues that 'corporate governance was designed to accommodate the
interests of large "insider" shareholders'.[71] Directors would also vet share

---

[67] Ibid., p. 173.
[68] Ibid., pp. 391-2.
[69] Ibid., p. 393; *Chadwick's Investment Circular*, 1871: p.115.
[70] Maltby, 'UK joint Stock Companies Legislation', p. 26.
[71] J. Maltby, 'The Origins of Prudence in Accounting', *Critical Perspectives on Accounting*, Vol. 11 (2000), p. 63.

applications in order to ensure that shares were allocated to desirable or known individuals.[72]

Was this the case in the Sheffield region? In order to answer this question, the shareholders in those companies promoted by Allott, Wing and Chadwick have been analysed. The data used were taken from the Memorandum of Association and the first annual return of the 'Summary of Capital and Shares' made by each company to the Registrar of Joint Stock Companies.

Firstly, the seven signatories to the Memoranda of Association, or initial shareholders, will be considered. Chadwick regarded initial shareholders in a company as the 'promoters' of the company.[73] They were often important to the management of the company, as they usually included the vendors, if it was a conversion; sometimes the promoter; the Directors of the company; and, if additional names were required, family members or business colleagues of the vendors. Certain 'names' recurred amongst the signatories to the Memoranda of Association of the companies being examined. How active they would be in terms of management is hard to discern, but many were owners of the companies prior to conversion and maintained such involvement after floatation.

Alfred Allott was an initial subscriber to only two of his promotions, but he appears to have used a group of people to sign the Memorandum of Association for his companies. Five names appear as initial subscribers for more than one company – William Cooke (ironmaster), David Davy (engineer), Alfred Davy (engineer), George Haywood (ironfounder), and Joseph Pickering (polish manufacturer). Considering these individuals will provide a better picture of the financial networks operating in the region.

Both Alfred and David Davy were the vendors of Davy Bros. & Co. Ltd., but only David was an initial subscriber to that company. David also signed the Memorandum of Association of another of Allott's companies – the Charlton Iron Works – and Alfred gave his signature to two others – Phoenix Bessemer and Albion Steel & Wire. William Cooke, an ironmaster, was a vendor of William Cooke and Co. Ltd., a company converted in 1873 and for which he was a signatory. He was also an initial subscriber to the Charlton Iron Works, first promoted in 1872. George Haywood was owner of Yates Haywood & Co., which merged with the Rotherham Foundry Co. in 1879 to form a limited concern, a conversion in which Allott was not involved.[74] His connection with Allott's promotions appears, rather, to have been a result of involvement in the iron industry or possibly through a personal connection. Joseph Pickering was a Sheffield polish manufacturer. Unlike the other individuals involved with Allott's companies, he does not appear to have been directly connected with the iron and steel industry. His link with Allott may have arisen through either

---

[72] Maltby, 'UK Joint Stock Companies Legislation', p. 17.

[73] Cottrell, *Industrial Finance*, p. 115.

[74] *White's Directory of Sheffield* (1879), p. 154. The company formed was Yates Haywood & Co. & the Rotherham Foundry Co. Ltd., PRO: BT31/2533/13127.

Allott's accountancy practice, or a personal relationship. However, all those used by Allott in the formation of limited companies as signatures to the Memorandum of Association originated from either Sheffield or Rotherham. Thus, the business and personal contacts of Allott were local.

The companies promoted by John Unwin Wing do not contain the same cluster of common initial subscribers. Wing himself made initial subscriptions to five of the seven companies he promoted, but only two other names appear more than once on the Memoranda of Association of his companies. They are John Easterbrook, signatory to three companies, and John James Brown, signatory to two. Easterbrook was an engineer from Sheffield, a member of the firm of Easterbrook & Allcard, machinists and engineers' tool manufacturers. Brown, an ironmaster from Rotherham, was manager of one of Wing's promotions – G. & J. Brown Co. Ltd. – to which he was an initial subscriber. Brown was also a signatory to Tinsley Rolling Mills, a company that Wing promoted in 1874, two years after G. & J. Brown.

Only two names appear more than once amongst the Memoranda of Association of the 'Sheffield' companies promoted by David Chadwick. William Landsdowne Beale, an ironmaster with a London address and a director/owner of Parkgate Iron and Steel, and George Wood, a Manchester merchant. Both were signatories to two of Chadwick's companies. In terms of initial subscribers, the companies promoted by Chadwick do not show a clear group of men used by the promoter to 'found' or manage these firms, but only four companies are being considered here. However, both Beale and Wood were from outside the Sheffield region and demonstrate the use made by Chadwick of extra-regional capital and management skills, especially that from Manchester and London. This contrasts with Allott's and Wing's multiple signatories, who were all from the Sheffield locality.

To expand upon the exploration of interlocking ownership within the 20 companies promoted by Wing, Allott, and Chadwick, the shareholders, as found in the first summaries of capital and shares returned to the Registrar, have also been analysed. Interlocking shareholdings between the companies promoted by the same financial agent can thereby be established.

Chadwick's four promotions involved 413 shareholdings held by 384 investors. Two men that had been initial subscribers to Chadwick's companies – William Landsdowne Beale and George Wood – retained multiple shareholdings in these companies on the first issue of shares proper. Beale held shares in Yorkshire Engine and Parkgate Iron & Steel, the two companies for which he was an initial subscriber. George Wood, and other individuals with the same surname, figure prominently amongst the shareholdings of Chadwick's companies. George Wood, George Wood Junior and Edward Wood, all cotton dealers from Manchester, each held shares in three of Chadwick's companies. William Newmarch, the economist and manager of the London private bank Glyn Mills, also had shareholdings in three of Chadwick's companies. Eighteen other men held shares in two of Chadwick's companies. Of these, one came from Sheffield, one from Oldham, one from

London, one from Edinburgh, two from Doncaster, with the remaining 12 all from Manchester. Therefore, these multiple shareholders again demonstrate the use of extra-regional capital by Chadwick. There appears to have been a movement of funds generated in the cotton manufacturing North West to the iron, steel and coal producing area of South Yorkshire/North Derbyshire, facilitated by Chadwick and his Manchester associates.

The companies promoted by John Unwin Wing also had a number of investors with cross shareholdings. There were 621 shareholdings in total and 537 investors: thirteen men had shareholdings in three or four of Wing's companies. Of these, seven originated from Sheffield and six from Rotherham, eight were involved in the production of iron and steel and two were colliery proprietors. There were also 50 others that had shareholdings in just two of Wing's companies, of which 38 had Sheffield addresses and nine were from Rotherham. This confirms the local base of Wing's business affiliations.

Alfred Allott's promotions involved the largest amount of subscriptions in numerical terms – 951 shareholdings and 730 investors. The shareholders included individuals with the highest number of multiple shareholdings – 50 people held shares in three to seven companies. Of these multiple shareholders, forty-one originated from Sheffield, three from Rotherham, two from Saltaire, one from Barnsley and only four from outside Yorkshire.[75] All the individuals who were initial subscribers to more than one of Allott's companies retained their shareholdings. William Cooke and George Haywood held shares in three companies and Joseph Pickering held shares in two. The Davy family expanded their investment in Allott's companies after incorporation. Abraham junior, Albert, Charles, Walter Scott and David all had shareholdings in four companies; Dennis in three firms; and Abraham senior, Alfred, and Mary Ann had shareholdings in two companies.[76] All these family members held shares in Davy Bros. Ltd, but their involvement in financial investment in the region's iron and steel production extended to other of Allott's conversions.

Two other men were important investors in the companies promoted by Allott. They were Thomas Hampton and John Kidner, both holders of shares in five of Allott's companies and both co-partners in the same accountancy practice as Allott. The participation of these partners in Allott's accountancy firm demonstrates the personal and professional involvement of accountants in the local share market, as highlighted earlier.

The findings for the 20 companies incorporated by the three promoters came from an initial study of 90 companies floated in and around Sheffield between 1855 and 1885. Multiple shareholdings and cross-holding patterns for all of these 90 companies have also been analysed. Results reveal that there appears to have been a highly localised capital network consisting primarily of iron, steel and engineering industrialists who invested in companies involved in the same manufacturing activities as themselves. Multiple shareholdings and cross-

---

[75] Bridgenorth (Shropshire), London and Worksop (Nottinghamshire).
[76] In addition, four others with the surname Davy held shares in Davy Bros.

shareholdings occurred primarily in 12 firms that were incorporated in 1872, 1873 and 1874 and were undertaken by 63 core investors. Of these 12 firms, seven were promoted by Alfred Allott and two by John Unwin Wing. This indicates that the 'core' membership of the local capital market comprised individuals connected with the two Sheffield promoters. The concentration of this investment activity by the group of individuals occurred in the boom years of the early 1870s, the period in which Allott and Wing were active. Allott himself was owner of multiple shareholdings, making the highest number of separate investments in companies (twelve) to be found in this regional capital network.

Shareholders in Sheffield: Geographical distribution and occupational analysis

The local nature of share subscriptions in manufacturing firms converting to limited liability has already been emphasised. In the case of the companies promoted by Allott, Wing and Chadwick, this can be clarified through the analysis of the addresses of shareholders as detailed in the share returns to the Registrar. The majority of capital invested in the companies of Wing and Allott originated from Yorkshire, 89 per cent and 84 per cent respectively, and over 50 per cent from Sheffield itself. These men were financial agents, originally based in Sheffield, and capital from their local sphere of influence dominated the companies with which they were involved. However, as mentioned previously, the 1879 *White's Sheffield District Trade Directory* shows that both Wing and Allott were by then members of financial practices which had London offices. The predominance of Yorkshire subscriptions could have been due to the promotions taking place before Wing and Allott opened offices in London, or, rather, have been due to their stronger connections in the Sheffield region.

In contrast, the geographical origins of the funds invested in Chadwick's four companies are predominantly Lancashire and London. Chadwick had both Manchester and London offices and the results reflect the difference compared with Wing's and Allott's companies; 29 per cent of the capital invested in Chadwick's firms originated from Yorkshire, whereas a higher amount of capital (33 per cent) came from Lancashire. Much of this finance came from Manchester (26 per cent). In contrast, only five per cent of the capital subscribed to Wing's companies was from Lancashire and one per cent with respect to Allott's companies. In addition, a substantial amount of capital in Chadwick's companies came from London (21 per cent), as opposed to only one per cent for Wing's firms and seven per cent for Allott's. Before the late 1870s, the London connections of Chadwick, therefore, appear to have been far more highly developed than those of the locally-based Sheffield promoters. Chadwick's influence was therefore far more national than either Allott or Wing.

Were shareholders predominantly those involved in local industrial concerns, as identified in the work of Jefferys? In order to answer this question, Table 7.4 shows the occupational origins of shareholders in the companies promoted by Allott, Wing and Chadwick. The majority of shareholders gave their occupation as 'manufacturing'. This is not surprising, given the nature of the companies being considered. The other dominant groups of investors consist of those from commerce, the professions and those with independent means. After manufacturing, 'commerce' constituted the most important occupational group for those investing both in Chadwick's and Wing's industrial concerns, 25 per cent and 20 per cent respectively. More important for the companies promoted by Allott were investors from the 'Professions', which provided 18 per cent of the capital invested, as opposed to 12 per cent of capital from those in commerce. Investors from the professions were less important to Chadwick's companies (nine per cent). Men and women of independent means were an important source of finance for each three promotional groups – 16 per cent in the case of Allott's companies, 11 per cent of Wing's and 17 per cent of Chadwick's. The only other significant occupation, other than the 'top four', occurs in the enterprises promoted by John Unwin Wing, with ten per cent of capital coming from the mining sector. This is probably due to one of his promotions being a coal mining concern, the only such undertaking converted by any of the three. The remaining balance of capital originated from a wide social group of subscribers with varying occupations.

Table 7.4
Allott, Wing and Chadwick promotions: Occupational distributions of shareholdings

	Per cent of subscribed capital		
	Allott	Wing	Chadwick
Occupational category			
Manufacuring	38.9	37.4	40.0
Professional	18.3	13.1	8.8
Independent	15.9	11.0	17.5
Commerce	12.2	20.0	24.7
Unknown management	3.4	5.0	1.8
Unknown workers	2.9	1.3	0.8
Construction	2.8	0.5	0.1
Mining	2.7	9.8	0.1

These results confirm the trend identified by Jefferys: that investors in Sheffield's manufacturing industry tended to be vendors, other local industrialists, and the family, friends and business associates of these individuals. Thus, the promoters could draw upon a 'pool' of knowledgeable investors through their business and social connections and those of the vendors. It is unlikely that Allott or Wing would have had to advertise widely and seek 'outside' investors, as evidenced by the geographical and occupational profile of shareholders in the sample companies. This conforms to the findings of Wilson, who investigated the patterns of investment of the North West gas industry and discovered that before 1880 'the whole process remained a local affair, with the promoters, management and shareholders coming from the business community to be supplied by an undertaking'.[77]

Conclusions

This study has demonstrated that the promoters Allott, Wing and Chadwick had a very important influence upon the movement towards limited liability made by manufacturing industry in the Sheffield region between 1855 and 1885. The number of companies they promoted, and the capital involved in these formations, clearly shows the significance of their roles. Chadwick's promotions in the 1860s introduced extra-regional capital to the local iron and steel industry, mainly from Lancashire, specifically Manchester, and also London. In contrast, local funds constituted the mainstay of Allott's and Wing's promotions in the iron and steel boom of the early 1870s. All of the promoters were involved with the companies they promoted, as auditors, as signatories to the Memoranda of Association or shareholders thereafter, with both Chadwick and Allott retaining considerable shareholdings in their promotions. The development of a management group by the promoters appears to have been most significant in the case of Alfred Allott, who used a group of men involved in the Sheffield and Rotherham iron and steel industries. In each case, Allott, Wing and Chadwick seem to have used their local connections, be they Mancunian or from South Yorkshire, to provide finance for the expansion of iron and steel manufacturing in the Sheffield region. Furthermore, such company promoters were not only important in terms of the funds they generated for the companies that they promoted, but also in their role in the domestic industrial capital market which developed following the 1855 and 1862 Companies Acts. Jefferys stresses that these promoters 'educated a solid core of wealthy investors into the art of investment'.[78]

---

[77] J.F. Wilson, *Lighting the Town. A Study of Management in the North West Gas Industry, 1805–1880* (Paul Chapman Publishing, 1991), p. 103. His results (in Chapters 3 and 4) reveal that shareholders originated from the local area and participated in local trades and professions.

[78] Jefferys, *Trends in Business Organization*, p. 319.

The analysis of shareholders in these companies has revealed a highly localised capital market which was dependent mainly upon subscriptions from four social groups: those engaged in manufacturing, trade, commerce or the 'professions' (members of the former three groups being chiefly occupied in the major Sheffield trades). Within the local financial capital market, there also existed a specific capital network in the Sheffield companies, identified by the existence of multiple shareholders and their cross-holdings in the sample of 90 limited companies promoted in the region between 1855 and 1885. The company promoters were again influential in this phenomenon, as nine of the early 1870s registrations of Allott and Wing contained a common group of local investors. This capital network consisted mainly of local industrialists who were linked with each other, the promoters and the vendors of the limited companies in which they held shares by their occupations and also by kinship and probably social ties. [79]

In terms of the investment patterns identified, network theory may be usefully applied. It is reasonable to argue that the managements of firms adopting a new form of company organisation were attempting to reduce risk and uncertainty by relying upon resources with which the vendors were familiar, in this case shareholders who resided in the local area; who were known to the owners via business or personal networks; or were known to a company promoter via their local networks. The impersonal investor with no links to the firm or the area may be viewed as having less commitment to their investment, and therefore a greater likelihood to withdraw their funds. By deliberately selling shares only to those investors with links to the company and/or the region, managements were acting to reduce potential exit opportunities by ensuring shareholder 'ties' to the company, therefore reducing the risk and uncertainty inherent in broadening their capital bases. This created a 'high trust' environment, one that was likely to have experienced peer monitoring and the consequent restraint of opportunistic behaviour. Indeed, further results have shown that lists of shareholders remained relatively static during the first five to ten years of a limited company's existence, indicating the continuing commitment of investors.[80] It can be further argued that such networks reduced transaction costs and advanced economic efficiency by improving information flows and reducing the risks of opportunistic behaviour.

In addition to providing the company with committed investors, the 'high trust' environment may be considered from the perspective of the shareholder. These investors were usually highly informed, as they were active in and/or connected to local industry and it was unlikely that they would have been 'duped' by a dishonest promoter. They were also purchasing shares of high denominations and with a large amount left unpaid, therefore demonstrating a

---

[79] An examination of institutions such as the *Company of Cutlers*, the *Sheffield Club* and political parties will prove useful in exploring networks in Sheffield in more detail. A comparative examination of financial networks in Oldham would also be fruitful. Such work was beyond the scope of the paper but will be pursued in future.

[80] Newton, *Credit and Capital*, Chapters 5 and 6.

high level of trust in the promoters, vendors and management of the enterprises in which they invested. In turn, it was necessary for those involved in the promotion of such local firms to be known, trustworthy and credible in the eyes of such knowledgeable shareholders and vendors.

This research has therefore demonstrated that capital networks existed in the investing community that developed in the Sheffield region between 1855 and 1885. Such networks were undoubtedly of vital importance to the proliferation of limited liability as a form of company organisation, but also, correspondingly, to the development of the region's industry in terms of its ability to raise finance, to adopt new technology, to increase in scale and to survive cyclical downturns in the economy. Financial networks allowed an initial broadening of the region's capital base, albeit within restricted parameters which maintained local control of industry and a low risk use of external forms of finance. The movement towards a broader capital market was thus tentative but significant, nonetheless.

In this light, these networks may be described as successful: they attracted solid investors and raised finance for local industry. Unfortunately, it has not been possible to measure the 'success' in terms of company performance, such as dividend values, as it has not been possible to consult such data. However, many of the companies considered had a very long lifespan and some survived, in one form or another, into the twenty first century. In considering the success or otherwise of these networks, it is also interesting to note that it was the extra-regional financial network of Chadwick, rather than the local networks of Allott and Wing, which ultimately generated more capital both in the region and on a national level. Even at this early stage of the development of financial markets, the potential limitations of local funding were visible.

Chapter 8

Quaker networks and the industrial development of Darlington, 1780–1870[1]

Gillian Cookson

Introduction

Eighteenth-century Darlington was a prosperous market town in an undeveloped region. The inhabitants were 'abundantly supplied with all the necessaries of life from the adjacent country at a cheap rate', and the local economy was said to thrive on 'foreign money' – profits from trade re-circulating in the town and its surrounds.[2] The main manufacturing industries were linen and worsted manufacture – dominated in Darlington by Quaker masters, both before and after mechanisation – and tanning.[3] A service sector included inns and other facilities for travellers on the Great North Road, as well as professional services and retail businesses associated with the town's position as a market and focus for a large rural hinterland.[4]

In its commercial variety, Darlington differed both from other Tees towns and much of the rest of the North-east region.[5] Despite its own lack of natural resources, it held the key to opening up mineral deposits in the Tees valley,

---

[1]   This chapter is based on research carried out for the Darlington volume of the Victoria County History of Durham, to be published as Durham V.C.H., Vol. IV. Draft text appears online at http://www.durhampast.net.

[2]   B.J. Barber, 'The Economic and Urban Development of Darlington, 1800–1914', M.A. in Victorian Studies, University of Leicester, 1969), p. 6, quoting W. Hutchinson, *The History and Antiquities of the County Palatine of Durham*, III (1794), p. 221.

[3]   For the Pease and Backhouse families and their commercial interests, see Maurice W. Kirby, *Men of Business and Politics: The Rise and Fall of the Quaker Pease Dynasty of North-east England, 1700–1943* (George Allen and Unwin, 1984); Maurice W. Kirby, *The Origins of Railway Enterprise: the Stockton and Darlington Railway, 1821–1863* (Cambridge University Press, 1993); Anne Orde, *Religion, Business and Society in North-East England: the Pease family of Darlington in the Nineteenth Century* (Shaun Tyas, 2000); see Durham V.C.H., IV, forthcoming, for accounts of the textile and leather industries.

[4]   See for instance Peter Barfoot and John Wilkes, *Universal British Directory*, II (1791), pp. 758–9.

[5]   T.J. Nossiter, *Influence, Opinion and Political Idioms in Reformed England: Case Studies from the North-east, 1832–74* (Harvester Press, 1975), p. 14.

thanks to a financial structure which was by 1800 relatively sophisticated.[6] Central to this were banks that had developed as sidelines of two Quaker textile businesses, the Pease bank from worsteds, and Backhouses' from linens.[7] Much of the finance which transformed the region by means of the Stockton and Darlington railway, though, came from outside, from investors who were part of an extended Quaker kinship network. It is these relationships which the chapter will investigate.

The Stockton-Darlington industrial district

The famous railway, foundation of Darlington's nineteenth-century prosperity, opened in 1825, after more than 50 years of efforts to improve Tees valley communications. Events during the decade leading to the establishment of the Stockton and Darlington railway have been thoroughly explored by Kirby.[8] There were problems of organisation, of finance, of geography, of rival schemes based on Stockton which would have marginalised Darlington, and of proposed alternatives involving combinations of canal and rail. Not least of these problems were political difficulties, including opposition by the Earl of Darlington, whose obstructions included an attempt to ruin Backhouses' Bank.[9] After parliamentary defeat in 1819 and delay after the death of George IV, the Act finally passed in 1821, helped substantially by widespread Quaker lobbying of parliamentarians.[10] The legislation was modelled on canal practice, with an emphasis on local, rather than coastal, trade in goods and minerals.[11] As a result, it won support from Tyneside M.P.s who would have opposed coal exports from the Tees. Several changes of route during the planning were necessary, to avoid the Earl's estates and minimise costs. Darlington influence, though, diverted the railway south from its shortest and cheapest line, so that it skimmed the northern fringes of the town. The railway's effect upon coal prices was rapid and dramatic, more than halving the cost of Auckland coal.[12]

The uneasy collaboration between Darlington and Stockton, eleven miles from the sea, did not last. Joseph Pease, son of Edward who was later known as 'father of the railways', was soon arguing that Stockton, with its navigational difficulties and limited capacity, was inadequate for the booming trade. In 1829, in partnership with four other Quakers, he bought the 500-acre Middlesbrough estate for £30,000 and established 'Port Darlington'. The

---

[6]   Kirby, *Origins of Railway Enterprise*, p. 26.
[7]   See John Banham, 'Business Development and Banking in North East England, 1755–1839', unpublished Ph.D. thesis (University of Sunderland, 1997); John Banham, *Backhouses' Bank of Darlington, 1774–1836* (University of Teesside: Paper in North Eastern History No. 9, 1999).
[8]   Kirby, *Origins of Railway Enterprise*, pp. 29–53.
[9]   Banham, *Backhouses' Bank*, p. 23.
[10]   There were no Quakers in parliament before 1832.
[11]   Kirby, *Origins of Railway Enterprise*, pp. 37–9.
[12]   Nossiter, *Influence, Opinion and Political Idioms*, p. 130.

railway was extended there in 1831, a dock built, coal staithes erected, and a town rapidly developed.[13] Joseph Pease (1799–1872) was a man of vast commercial ability and vision. Quickly identifying the potential of the south Durham coalfield as the railway opened the area, he became a partner in the Shildon colliery in 1828, and then acquired one colliery after another until he was 'the largest and most influential coal owner in the whole Division'.[14] Despite the initial fall in coal prices, profits were maintained through the huge increase in volume of sales of Tees coal. The Stockton and Darlington railway was consequently a solid enterprise by the late 1820s. Its £100 share price rose from £80 in 1823, to £315 in 1832, and an eight per cent dividend was paid in 1832 and 1833.[15] By 1839–41, this had reached 15 per cent, the highest of any railway in the country.[16]

Until the 1850s, aside from its effects upon the coal trade, the impact of the railway upon Darlington's industry was limited. The Stockton and Darlington company was itself small, owning under 37 miles of track, and buying in most of its rolling stock.[17] It employed 267 within the town in 1851, about five per cent of the total male population.[18] A few other firms grew up on railway business, the largest being Kitching's engineering works, and there were various related service industries including carriers and professional advisors. But with the opening of the first section of a north-south railway, between Darlington and York in 1841,[19] the town's communications were re-orientated, opening a future as a centre of iron-production and engineering. The Great North of England Railway also undermined Middlesbrough's *raison d'être*, the export of coal by sea, but the discovery of Cleveland iron ore deposits in 1850 presented new possibilities for both towns. Mining the inferior and impure Cleveland ore seams was viable only because of the geological accident that Durham coal, when converted to coke, was superior to any other in Britain. Teesside continued to thrive because the Stockton and Darlington railway was the means of bringing together coal, iron ore and limestone.[20] Pease consolidated the Stockton and Darlington's monopoly by extending branch lines into Cleveland and expanding westwards to create new markets for Durham coal and obtain supplies of haematite ore from Cumberland. Pease himself went into iron ore mining from 1852. An extra 75 miles of railway had been built by the early 1860s; in 1861, the company's mileage was 125, with a further 75 under construction.[21]

---

[13] Barber, 'Development of Darlington', p. 40. The population of Middlesbrough rose from 154 in 1831, to 5463 a decade later, Barber, 'Development of Darlington', p. 41.

[14] J.S. Jeans, *Jubilee Memorial of the Railway System: History of the Stockton and Darlington railway* (Longmans, Green and Co., 1875), pp. 233–6.

[15] Banham, *Backhouses' Bank*, p. 27.

[16] Kirby, *Men of Business and Politics*, p. 26.

[17] Barber, 'Development of Darlington', p. 10.

[18] Ibid., p. 9.

[19] Kirby, *Origins of Railway Enterprise*, Chapter 5.

[20] Barber, 'Development of Darlington', p. 14.

[21] Ibid., pp. 41 and 10.

By the early 1860s, the region was dominant in iron production, a situation deriving as much from international demand for railway capital equipment as from natural endowments.[22] The industrial landscape of both Middlesbrough and Darlington changed markedly as a result. Darlington, where the main north-south railway met a busy mineral line, became a natural location for heavy industry. The Stockton and Darlington directors decided in 1858 to expand and relocate their locomotive works near the original station and close to Kitching, whose business diversified into railway products other than locomotives. The new locomotive works, opened in 1862, had 391 workers three years later.[23] The iron industry itself was more important still. In 1871, when Darlington's population reached a level almost two and a half times that of 20 years earlier, the rise was attributed to 'the introduction of the manufacture of iron, to the erection of blast furnaces, rolling mills, forge works, engine building works and other smaller manufactories'. These activities, with about four per cent of male employees in 1851, employed 14 per cent a decade later, a change largely explained by the establishment of the Darlington Forge.[24] By 1875, 3500 out of a total male population of 15,300 worked in the local iron industry, and a further 1000 in the railway workshops.

The Forge was the first of four firms, together representing all stages of iron manufacture, to locate at Albert Hill, Darlington, between 1854 and 1864.[25] Two of these companies were Quaker-dominated partnerships: the Skerne Ironworks, with four Pease directors; and the South Durham Iron Company, whose partners, including John Harris, Henry Pease and Alfred Kitching, were the same as those of the Albert Hill Land Company which planned and developed Darlington's new industrial quarter.[26] Kitching had retired from active business in 1862, to be succeeded by his cousin and fellow Quaker Charles Ianson at the Whessoe Foundry. Ianson expanded the foundry as well as establishing the Rise Carr Rolling Mills in about 1864 with Sir Theodore Fry, another member of the Society.[27]

The Pease family, and Joseph Pease in particular, was heavily represented in most of the region's industrial activities. On his death in 1872, Joseph Pease's investments included Joseph Pease and Partners, collieries, coke-ovens and fire brick manufacturers; J.W. Pease and Co., ironstone and limestone mining in Cleveland and Weardale; the original family worsted firm, Henry Pease and Co.; Robert Stephenson and Co., locomotive builders; the private bank, J. and J.W. Pease; and the Owners of the Middlesbrough Estate. The bank was, according to Kirby, 'in reality the counting house for the various Pease

[22] Ibid., p. 14.
[23] Ibid., pp. 10 and 14.
[24] Ibid., p. 12.
[25] Ibid., p. 17.
[26] See Durham V.C.H., IV, forthcoming.
[27] Darlington Centre for Local Studies [C.L.S.], acc. E810016282, the History of Whessoe [1958?], p. 16; Durham County Record Office [C.R.O.], D/Ki 332, vol. 2, p. 75; D/Whes 15/14.

enterprises', including the Stockton and Darlington railway. With the exception of the textile firm, the whole of this empire owed its origins to the railway.[28] In Kirby's view, while the impact of railways on the economy's total growth before 1870 was not quantitatively impressive, their effect upon the development of this well-defined regional economy was profound.[29] Darlington's special situation was acknowledged in 1867, when the South Durham MPs pressed for parliamentary borough status for the town:

> situate midway between the extensive coalfields of South Durham and the ironstone deposits of North Yorkshire, and [which] participates largely in the trade of both districts; ... a centre and seat of direction of a system of Railways which bring into communication the eastern and western coasts of the northern counties; ... the seat of extensive woollen, iron and other manufactures [which] ... conducts by various branches the banking of every town in a wide district both in Durham and Yorkshire; and ... supplies a great part of the capital that works the coalfields of South Durham.[30]

Quakers in Darlington industry

Darlington's nineteenth-century prosperity rested on railways, but this was not a railway town as generally understood, rather a 'company town' whose 'board of management' was the Society of Friends.[31] In its dramatic growth and industrial transformation, Darlington was not unusual. What was strikingly different about the locality, Barber argues, was 'the nature of the entrepreneurs who influenced not only the economic structure of the town itself but also the development of the whole region'.[32]

During the middle decades of the nineteenth century, Quaker domination of industry and of every significant aspect of local life was out of all proportion to the size of membership, and at a level possibly unique in England.[33] Nossiter estimates that there were never more than 2000 members of the Society of Friends in the whole region; they remained exclusive and powerful through asceticism and endogamy.[34] Membership of the Society in Darlington amounted to only 160 in 1776, when the town's population was about 3500.[35]

---

[28]   Kirby, *Men of Business and Politics*, pp. 42–4.

[29]   Ibid., p. 45.

[30]   Barber, 'Development of Darlington', pp. 36–7, quoting the *Darlington Mercury*, 30 May 1866.

[31]   Nossiter, *Influence, Opinion and Political Idioms*, p. 129; see Gillian Cookson, 'Quaker Families and Business Networks in Nineteenth-century Darlington', *Quaker Studies* (forthcoming, 2004).

[32]   Barber, 'Development of Darlington', p. 36.

[33]   Nossiter, *Influence, Opinion and Political Idioms*, p. 131.

[34]   Ibid., p. 18.

[35]   W.H.D. Longstaffe, *The History and Antiquities of the Parish of Darlington* (Darlington and Stockton Times, 1854), p. 251; Darlington C.L.S., acc.24034.

In the 1851 religious census, at a time when Darlington had more than 11,500 residents, 187 attended the morning meeting, 167 the evening. There were over 250 in the Society during the 1860s and nearly 400 in 1870, though attendance was higher. Membership was stable and well-recorded, but not completely static, and some who regularly attended meetings could not, or would not, become full members. An analysis of Darlington Quakers registering births shows that almost all were middle-class or white-collar workers: two-fifths shopkeepers, one-third upper or professional, 15 per cent clerks.[36] By 1850, several were very wealthy, collectively owning an area five times greater than the town itself, and their suburban estates surrounded Darlington's population of 11,000.[37] Local commerce – banking, worsted manufacture, industrial finance, railway promotion and direction, coal and iron ore mining – rested largely on Quakers, and especially upon the Pease and Backhouse families.[38] A number of professional men, including engineers, architects and surveyors, who were Friends or on the fringes of the Society, profited from railway business and from the ensuing growth of the town. Among these were the civil engineer John Harris, John Dixon, who was engineer to the Stockton and Darlington Railway, and the architects and conservatory builders Richardson and Ross.[39] Harris, a distant relative of the Pease family, involved in constructing the Middlesbrough docks and in bridge building and extensions to the lines, was appointed contractor to maintain the railway track in 1844, receiving between £11,000 and £12,744 a year for these services over the following decade.[40] Other Quaker industrialists, such as the currier John Hardcastle Bowman, and the Kitching family of engineers, were prominent in various activities relating to urban development, an issue that is further discussed below.[41]

The Darlington Quaker banks, with their external links, were at the centre of industrial activity. Before the railway, both Pease and Backhouse families restricted their activities to textile manufacture, with banking a growing sideline. James Backhouse came to Darlington in 1746 on his marriage to the heir of a linen manufacturer, Jonathan Hedley. Backhouse started holding notes and dealing in bills during the 1750s, and was local agent for Royal Exchange Assurance from 1759. Commercial contacts, nurtured on Quaker business in London, encompassed Norwich, the Midlands and the West Riding.[42] By the

---

[36] Nossiter, *Influence, Opinion and Political Idioms*, p. 131. A contemporary account refers to many Quaker shopkeepers: Henry Spencer, *Men That are Gone From the Households of Darlington* (Rapp and Dresser, 1862). See also James Walvin, *The Quakers: Money and Morals* (John Murray, 1997), p. 30.

[37] Barber, 'Development of Darlington', p. 32.

[38] Ibid., p. 37.

[39] Ibid., p. 44.

[40] Ibid., p. 43. See also H. John Smith, 'John Harris, Quaker Engineer and Investor, 1812–69', *Trans. Cumberland and Westmoreland Antiquarian and Archaeological Society*, LXIX (1969), pp. 330–43.

[41] Durham C.R.O., D/Ki 353 confirms that Bowman was a member of the Society.

[42] Banham, *Backhouses Bank*, pp. 10–1.

early 1760s, Backhouse had taken over his father-in-law's linen firm, whose customers were mainly in Yorkshire, Lancaster and London.[43]

While the Pease bank remained a private concern, Backhouses' grew from short-term lending in linen manufacture to a wide foundation of trade and lending based on national Quaker connections. Catering for more than regional needs, this served to consolidate their wider reputation.[44] There is little evidence that they invested in local industry. James Backhouse certainly helped the Quaker John Kendrew develop and patent a flax-spinning machine and set up a small factory during the 1780s and 1790s.[45] But Banham found no other obvious industrial loans from the bank before 1800 and concludes that its main influence on regional industrial development came between 1815 and 1836.[46] During its first half-century, from the 1750s, the bank had refined its procedures, familiarised itself with the London money market, and developed experience of risk assessment. As a result, industrial support was selective, and the bank later proved very successful in advancing long-term capital to risky projects while avoiding bankruptcy.[47] The Backhouse Bank's success in weathering the storm of 1825–6, and also their experience as shareholders in the Stockton and Darlington railway, gave the family confidence to launch into joint stock banking and to invest more widely in industry.[48]

A further connection between Darlington and the City of London, of great moment in the town's development, came through the Kitching and Ianson families. William Kitching, an ironmonger, married Ann Ianson of Darlington in October 1770, and had a son John (1771–1864) and daughter Mary. By a second marriage, to Hannah Goad of London in 1793, he had other children, including Alfred (1808–82), who established the Railway Foundry in Darlington during the 1830s.[49] When John Kitching was considering his future, he followed the advice of an Ianson uncle to settle in London 'as there seemed few openings for an energetic business career in the north at that time'.[50] Kitching left for the capital, presumably in the late 1780s, with two other young Quakers, Thomas Richardson of Darlington and John Overend, later Richardson's brother-in-law. In London, the three were warmly welcomed by 'south country Friends who were wont to exercise a very real care over the members of their flock'. Richardson and Overend founded a bill-broking business which made their names 'household words in the Banking and

---

[43]   Ibid., p. 13.

[44]   Ibid., pp. 34–5.

[45]   Durham V.C.H., IV, forthcoming.

[46]   Banham, *Backhouses' Bank*, pp. 15–6 and 34–5.

[47]   Ibid., pp. 23 and 34–5.

[48]   Ibid., pp. 28 and 33.

[49]   Durham C.R.O., D/Ki 313, pp. 84–130. Two of William Kitching's sisters also married Iansons, and the two families were much inter-married with Cudworths: Durham C.R.O., D/Ki 332, vol. 2, pp. 81, 99. For the family tree of Iansons in Darlington and London, see Durham C.R.O., D/Ki 290 and 292; Norman Penney, *My Ancestors* (privately published, 1920), pp. 202–18.

[50]   Durham C.R.O., D/Ki 353.

Financial circles of the world', later to become Overend, Gurney & Co. After working for another Ianson uncle, John Kitching joined them in partnership as marine insurance underwriters in 1804. The business rode out the war to 'emerge victorious', and John Kitching retired very young, having made a great deal of money.[51] The links between these families, and between the London money market and Darlington industry, were further cemented when Mary Kitching became Overend's second wife in 1831.[52] By then the capital which this group invested in their home town had ensured that no other young man would have to leave Darlington in order to follow a business career.

Quaker networks in operation

Before 1859, for a Quaker to marry out meant expulsion from the sect.[53] As the local meeting was small, and as it was customary to marry a Friend of similar social and financial standing, many of the more affluent Quakers met their partners through contacts made at Quaker boarding schools and through travels, preaching and trading.[54] By such matches, the industrial and commercial elite reinforced its success. Darlington industrialists allied themselves to bankers in Norwich and London, and with other trades in Bradford and Leeds, and later Falmouth and Bristol, although they seem not to have connected with Cadbury and Rowntree circles.[55] Considering the proximity, similar interests and status, and numbers, of Peases and Backhouses, there were fewer marriages between them than might perhaps have been expected. The railway promoters Edward Pease and Jonathan Backhouse were, however, cousins.[56] Their sons, Jonathan Backhouse and Joseph Pease, married two daughters of Joseph Gurney, the Norwich banker.[57] Pease's lucrative £7000 investment in the Middlesbrough estate was borrowed from his father-in-law at four per cent. The remaining £28,000 came from Gurney himself and from four London Quakers: Thomas Richardson, the bill-broker formerly of Darlington, cousin and friend of Edward Pease; Henry Birkbeck; Simon Martin; and Joseph Pease's brother-in-law Francis Gibson, a brewer.[58] The Darlington families counted among their relatives Frys, Barclays, Birkbecks, Hoares, Hustlers and Foxes, as well as the Richardsons, Overends and Gurneys noted above.[59] Without resources supplied by this extended group, the region's development could not have proceeded so far and so fast.

---

[51] Durham C.R.O., D/Ki 319, pp.60-2; D/Whes 15/16.
[52] Durham C.R.O., D/Ki 353; D/Ki 313.
[53] Orde, *Religion, Business and Society*, pp. 13–4.
[54] See Walvin, *The Quakers*, Chapter 5.
[55] For this idea I am grateful to Helen Roberts.
[56] Banham, 'Business Development', pp. 200–2.
[57] Orde, *Religion, Business and Society*, p. 21.
[58] Kirby, *Men of Business and Politics*, p. 22.
[59] See for instance the introduction to the Backhouse mss., Durham University Library Archives and Special Collections [D.U.L. A.S.C].; Banham, *Backhouses Bank*,

External support, in the form of advice and practical action, as well as finance, was most evident during the years spent planning the Stockton and Darlington railway. Once the principles of route and form had been agreed in 1818, a local committee was set up, with three Backhouses, two Peases and other Quakers, including some from other Tees valley towns. Meanwhile, Thomas Richardson, Samuel Gurney, Robert Barclay and eight others, two of them Ianson cousins, formed a supporting committee in London to obtain subscriptions.[60] Jonathan Backhouse II was treasurer in Darlington, and branches of his family bank in county Durham and the North Riding accepted deposits, as did Quaker banks in London.[61] These arrangements suggest a 'well-established network and a clear strategy'; Banham argues that the Earl of Darlington's attempt to ruin Backhouse confirm the bank's pivotal role.[62] Backhouse was saved during that episode by London contacts willing and able to send £32,000 in gold immediately.[63] Problems completing the railway's subscription list in 1818 were also overcome through the Quaker network.[64] The Pease and Backhouse families pledged £21,300, more than seventeen per cent of the total share capital.[65] Quakers had guaranteed two-thirds of the sum, including £14,000 from Joseph Gurney, by then father-in-law of Jonathan Backhouse, £5000 from Thomas Richardson and £3000 from John Kitching.[66] Equally important to the project's success was extensive lobbying of parliament by Quaker allies from London and elsewhere.[67] The result was a company unique in UK railways, 'a public joint stock concern which was, in effect, a close family partnership'.[68] The purchase of the Middlesbrough property using personalised capital networks provides further dramatic evidence of the strength of these links.[69] By the mid-1840s, the Pease family had built a vast business empire which had never been constrained by lack of finance, the result of 'kinship ties of unusual strength and geographical dispersion'.[70]

After 1850, Darlington's rapid growth offered new possibilities for profit and philanthropy. The Pease family initiated several town centre developments as private enterprises, not all of which were entirely admirable. John Pease, for

---

pp. 10–11; for the Ianson family tree, which shows links by marriage to the Kitchings, see Durham C.R.O., D/Ki 290 and 292.

[60] Jeans, *Jubilee Memorial*, p. 25.

[61] Banham, *Backhouses Bank*, p. 25. The private Pease bank did not have a branch network.

[62] Ibid., p. 26.

[63] Ibid., p. 23.

[64] Kirby, *Origins of Railway Enterprise*, p. 33.

[65] Barber, 'Development of Darlington', p. 39.

[66] See Jeans, *Jubilee Memorial*, pp. 293–5, for a list of subscribers; also Durham C.R.O., D/Ki 319, p. 55; D/Whes 15/16; Kirby, *Men of Business and Politics*, p. 12. Joseph Pease married Emma Gurney later, in 1826: Kirby, *Men of Business and Politics*, p. 21.

[67] Kirby, *Origins of Railway Enterprise*, p. 35.

[68] Ibid., p. 6.

[69] Ibid., pp. 79 and 88.

[70] Ibid., p. 6.

instance, proposed low-quality housing in an already crowded and unhealthy central yard in 1857.[71] More significant in developing the suburbs were a number of new organisations, including three building societies, a freehold land society with political aims, and the land company whose directors were the partners in the South Durham Iron Company. Most of these were Quaker-dominated and with partners in common, although the grander families were increasingly remote and assumed only nominal roles. A lower social group was drawn in, including paid managers such as Thomas MacNay, secretary of the Stockton and Darlington railway, and George Harker, a railway contractor based at Shildon.[72] Alfred Kitching, after retiring from business in 1862, devoted much time to such enterprises and to local politics. He was involved with fellow Quakers in the establishment of the resort of Saltburn, was a member of Darlington's Board of Health until 1867, and its chairman from 1866, then an alderman in the new corporation until his death, serving as Mayor of the town in 1870.[73] He had been a partner in the South Durham Iron Company since 1854;[74] a proprietor of the Albert Hill Land Company from 1853;[75] and a member of the land society which launched the development of the suburb of Eastbourne during the 1850s.[76] John Harris, similarly nearing the end of his business career, was also a driving force in the various urban development and building society schemes of the 1850s and 1860s.

From examples given above, it is clear that Darlington Quaker industrialists enjoyed the advantage of access to large resources at short notice, and perhaps with less formality than a conventional business arrangement. The Backhouse bank provides a striking demonstration of the network's power in combination, having been saved from collapse at least twice by fellow Quakers. The Backhouses lost considerably in other local bank collapses between 1805 and 1816, and made no profit from their linen business in the five years to 1815. Banham argues that they were close to failure in 1815, without the liquidity to meet a run on the bank, which survived only because of its high reputation and the support of prominent customers.[77]

---

[71] Darlington C.L.S., acc. 33878, 33879.
[72] For the Darlington Working Men's Equitable Permanent Building Society, established 1856, see Darlington Building Society archive, passbook of William Berry; for Darlington and District Terminating Building Society, extant 1864, see Durham C.R.O., D/X 905/1/23; for Darlington Building Society, extant 1844, see Durham C.R.O., D/Whes 3/47; for the Darlington and South Durham Freehold Land Society, see Darlington Library, C.L.S., acc. 30517, prospectus of 1849; for the Albert Hill Land Company, founded 1853, see Durham C.R.O., D/XD 108/1/A/73; for the South Durham Iron Co., established 1854, see Durham C.R.O., D/Ki 15A. An account of Darlington's physical development in the nineteenth century is in Durham V.C.H., IV, forthcoming.
[73] Durham C.R.O., D/Whes 15/14; D/Whes 14/46.
[74] Durham C.R.O., D/Ki 15A.
[75] Durham C.R.O., D/XD 108/1/A/73.
[76] Darlington C.L.S., acc. 30517.
[77] Banham, *Backhouses Bank*, pp. 18–22.

Quakers had a reputation for financial integrity, and this, combined with their ability to summon such resources, made them attractive as business connections. Besides being widely considered trustworthy, Quakers were seen as possessing other characteristics which were arguably of advantage in forming commercial and technical judgements. They had a *modus operandi* of thinking, planning and recording; they were curious, willing to innovate, and had a broad view of the world; they were untainted by the extravagance, dishonesty, drunkenness or other forms of debauchery to which many family businesses of the time fell victim.[78] Kirby translates this into economic terms: strong and clearly defined Quaker 'personalised external networks' reduced transaction costs by minimising uncertainty and deficient knowledge.[79]

Not least in this equation was the value of informed and disinterested advice. For Alfred Kitching, the judgment of his financier half-brother John in London may have saved his business. In approximately 1843, the Railway Foundry was facing ruin because of excessive competition and an end to sub-contracting by the railway company. Alfred consulted John for 'consideration and advice' before communicating to another brother 'my intentions to resign and discontinue our business'.[80] John's reply has not survived, but he appears to have encouraged Alfred to continue. The following year new partnership arrangements were in place and the Foundry went on to great success.[81] Edward Pease's letters to his cousin, Thomas Richardson, the London banker, show detailed consultations during the 1820s on a range of technical and commercial matters relating to the railway and other business interests.[82] Pease also sought technical advice from a fellow Quaker, Joseph Price of Neath Abbey, when the railway was under consideration in 1818.[83]

Quaker entrepreneurship under investigation

Yet while this Quaker industrial network offered tangible benefits of finance, advice and practical assistance, other supposed business advantages flowing from membership of the Society may have been greatly overestimated. Although Quakers may in general have been very trustworthy, there was no immunity from disaster. An early recollection of Henry Kitching, nephew of

---

[78] Walvin, *The Quakers*, pp. 4 and 45–50; Kirby, *Origins of Railway Enterprise*, p. 80; David H. Pratt, *English Quakers and the First Industrial Revolution: A Study of the Quaker Community in Four Industrial Counties, Lancashire, York, Warwick and Gloucester, 1750–1830* (Garland, 1985), p. 29.

[79] Kirby, *Origins of Railway Enterprise*, Chapter 3, esp. pp. 52–3.

[80] Durham C.R.O., D/Whes 14/45, undated draft letter, presumed from Alfred Kitching to John in London.

[81] Durham C.R.O., D/Ki 8.

[82] Durham C.R.O., D/Ho/C63/2-15; see Andy Guy, 'North-eastern Locomotive Pioneers 1805 to 1827: a Reassessment', in A. Guy and J. Rees (eds), *Early Railways* (Newcomen Society, 2001), pp. 130–1.

[83] Newcastle City Library, 6749–53.

Mary Overend, was of the failure of Overend, Gurney and Co. in 1866. Kitching's father did not lose money in the bank's collapse, but was severely affected: 'The result was stupefying'.[84] The engineer John Harris was said to have lost substantial assets in the Overend, Gurney collapse, obliging him to sell his railway engineering business quickly and for less than its true value.[85] Later, the problems of the Pease textile business were compounded when Joseph Pease's brother Henry and nephew Henry Fell Pease were brought close to personal ruin through a debt owed by the Quaker owner of the Guisborough Alum Works.[86] At the same time, the firm was hit by losses incurred by their Bradford partners, Quakers and distant relatives, John Thistlethwaite and Co., who had suffered embezzlement by a family member.[87]

What, then, of other personal advantages supposedly enjoyed by Quaker entrepreneurs, their vision, foresight, curiosity and innovative approach? While Quakers found their way into the Smilesian pantheon of Victorian industrial heroes, there is no evidence that they deserved such overblown accolades any more than the rest. Much of the foresight supposedly employed in transforming the Tees valley from backwardness turns out to be a result of hindsight, as in 1875 when Edward Pease was absurdly credited with 'discerning sixty years ago that railways were destined to revolutionise the world'.[88] The truth of how the railway was brought to reality is much more mundane. Although considerable information was collected and projections made, for instance in an 1818 report on its economic feasibility, vision was limited.[89] William Kitching, writing to his son John in London at the end of that year, was pessimistic, as evidently were some of the Pease family. Joseph Pease of Feethams, brother of Edward, had 'taken much pains and seem certain from the calculations he has made that it will not pay', while his brother and others 'seem as positive it will be a good thing ... I cannot say I feel so sanguine as the subscribers, well knowing that in public concerns money goes swimmingly out, but too oft is apt to sink never more to rise'.[90] Jonathan Backhouse made clear during discussions of the joint canal and railway proposal between 1812 and 1818 that he was considering only the economic development of the Darlington area, not a sea-coal trade to rival the Tyne and Wear. In opposing a scheme which would have by-passed Darlington, Backhouse was promoting his family's interests, the coal trade on the Wear served by the Sunderland Branch

---

[84]   Durham C.R.O., D/Ki 353.
[85]   Durham V.C.H., IV, forthcoming; Barber, 'Development of Darlington', p. 44. For Harris see Smith, 'John Harris'; also *Institution of Civil Engineers Minutes of Proceedings*, 31 (1870-1), pp. 219-20.
[86]   See Durham C.R.O., D/Pe 3/43; D/Pe 3/44; D/Pe 3/116; D/Pe 3/65; D/Pe 3/48.
[87]   Durham V.C.H., IV, forthcoming. See Joseph Foster, *Pease of Darlington* (privately published, 1891), p. 28, where Thistlethwaite is described as 'of Bradford and Darlington'.
[88]   *The Kings of British Commerce*, 1875.
[89]   Kirby, *Men of Business and Politics*, p. 10.
[90]   Durham C.R.O., D/Ki 313, pp.118-9, 21 Dec. 1818.

of his bank, as well as textile manufacturing in Darlington.[91] Pease and Backhouse thought only of the sale of coal along the line, with some coal to be shipped out as ballast. They had no idea of any more traffic than used existing turnpikes.[92] The corporate motto on the company seal, 'At private risk for public service', suggests support of a utility on the model of canal and turnpike trusts, rather than entrepreneurial activity in its own right.[93]

In the late eighteenth century, Darlington Quakers offered some support to the innovation thesis, in the shape of John Kendrew's prototype flax-spinning machine. Backhouse backed and patented the experiment, while others in the town planned to buy a licence and open a factory to use it, although that project foundered.[94] Information about the machine was broadcast through Quaker circles, for Thomas Fox of Wellington, Somerset, visited Darlington in May 1789 to investigate its use for wool-spinning.[95] The railway proceeded similarly cautiously on well-tried principles; Kirby confirms that it was radical neither in its technical nor its organisational development. The pioneering railway was almost a geographical accident, the only possibility amidst poor rivers and unsuitable terrain for canals.[96] The original scheme was for a coal and mineral line, with locomotive haulage and passenger carriage essentially afterthoughts.[97] While Edward Pease was instrumental in persuading the committee to build a railway rather than a canal, he told the engineer Stephenson to have 'as little machinery introduced as possible'.[98] The line at first combined horse with steam-power and leased passenger carriages to contractors.[99] When this proved impractical, it was decided in 1828 to phase out horse haulage, which terminated on the main line in 1833, though continuing on branch lines until 1856, when the 'public way' idea finally ended.[100] The Stockton and Darlington's main contribution to technological development may have been as a testing ground for various innovations, notably Hackworth's locomotive in 1828, which led to Stephenson's trial at Rainhill the following year.[101] In this it laid foundations for the more novel steam-drawn Liverpool and Manchester railway of 1830.[102]

---

[91] Banham, *Backhouses' Bank*, p. 25.

[92] Kirby, *Men of Business and Politics*, p. 16.

[93] Kirby, *Origins of Railway Enterprise*, p. 2; Pratt, *English Quakers*, pp. 87–8, discusses the long involvement of Quakers in road-, canal- and bridge-building schemes.

[94] Longstaffe, *History and Antiquities*, pp. 311–2; Durham V.C.H., IV, forthcoming. Banham, *Backhouses' Bank*, cites patent no. 1613 dated 19 June 1787, for the spinning of hemp, tow, flax and wool; also Barclays Bank archives, 388/103; Durham C.R.O., D/Ki 317.

[95] Hubert Fox, *Quaker Homespun* (1958), pp. 51–2. I am grateful to Bob Dunning for this reference.

[96] Kirby, *Origins of Railway Enterprise*, p. 4.

[97] Ibid., p. 2; Idem., *Men of Business and Politics*, p. 16.

[98] Kirby, *Origins of Railway Enterprise*, p. 40.

[99] Kirby, *Men of Business and Politics*, p. 16.

[100] Kirby, *Origins of Railway Enterprise*, pp. 3 and 94.

[101] Ibid., p. 3.

[102] Ibid., p. 16.

Local Quakers proved rather more adept at responding to the railway's possibilities once it was an established fact, in a way better described as pragmatic than visionary. Even before the line opened, in the summer of 1825, encouraged by Backhouse the Tees Coal Company was formed to exploit the coastal market for coal. Two years later, recognising Stockton's inadequacies, the railway directors decided to extend the line to Middlesbrough and achieved that despite parliamentary opposition from Tyne and Wear interests.[103] At the same time, Joseph Pease began his acquisition of coal leases in Auckland and further north.[104] Pease's involvement in promoting the Great North of England Railway from 1835, connecting Leeds and York to Newcastle and Scotland, was apparently at odds with his own interest in the new town of Middlesbrough, for he could not then have anticipated the iron industry developments which would save the redundant port in the 1850s.[105] For the Stockton and Darlington railway, though, a valuable strategic position on the rail network was secured which opened up coal markets in York and the North Riding. The North Eastern Railway, described at the time it merged with the Stockton and Darlington in 1863 as 'the most complete monopoly in the UK', also proved a good investment for many Quaker investors from outside the region, including the Darbys of Coalbrookdale.[106]

If the Quakers' entrepreneurial vision is suspect, so too was the everyday management of their various concerns. Through decades of religious and social ostracism, members had developed enormous self-confidence while representing unpopular causes – a Pease delegation went to the Czar in an attempt to avert the Crimean War. But this, combined with the supposed Quaker attributes of being careful, educated, intelligent, and honest, and to an extent cushioned against financial disaster, did not necessarily translate into efficient business leadership. The long-term decline of the local textile industry, run largely by Quaker family businesses, is a case in point. In the mid-eighteenth century, Darlington had been the leading centre for certain types of fine linen cloth.[107] Backhouse's support for John Kendrew's early, reasonably competent, efforts to mechanise flax-spinning could have maintained this success, and the Iansons invested in modern plant during the 1780s. Ultimately, though, Darlington capitulated to Leeds, Barnsley and Scottish linen centres. By 1830, linen manufacture, lacking the technology available elsewhere, was all but finished in the town.[108]

[103] Kirby, *Men of Business and Politics*, p. 20.

[104] Ibid., pp. 21–2.

[105] Ibid., p. 24.

[106] Nossiter, *Influence, Opinion and Political Idioms*, p. 66; Kirby, *Men of Business and Politics*, p. 42; Kirby, *Origins of Railway Enterprise*, p. 124.

[107] *Universal Magazine*, October 1749, p. 147, quoted in Durham V.C.H., II, p. 316; Longstaffe, *History and Antiquities*, p. 296; Darlington C.L.S., acc 23757; D.U.L. A.S.C., Cosin BB.4.29, *A New and Accurate Description of the Present Great Roads and the Principal Crossroads of England and Wales* (R & J Dodsley, London. 1756), p. 103. See Durham V.C.H., IV, forthcoming.

[108] Durham V.C.H., IV, forthcoming.

The worsted industry in Darlington came to consist only of the original Pease family firm, known as Henry Pease and Co. from about 1833 when Joseph Pease's younger brother took over its management. Although Henry Pease's approach was evidently careful and thoughtful, the business's results were poor. It was sustained only through a sense of responsibility to the workforce, a fear of losing the capital invested, and not least, sentiment, for as long as it could be subsidised by other, spectacularly successful, family interests. Closure was discussed in 1842 and several times after that. Despite continuing sizeable losses, the hard decision was never taken and further large sums were poured into the concern. Several times the firm's appalling management was re-organised, but losses continued to mount. Not until after the Pease crash of 1902 – to which the textile concern had made a major contribution – when the family was removed from all management responsibility, did the worsted business achieve profitability.[109] Decisions on the worsted firm's future were apparently made without reference to the wider Quaker network. The various resolutions to shore up Henry Pease and Co., against the considered views of more business-oriented family members, were based upon a religious notion of protecting the livelihood of the poor, but there was also concern to preserve the family's reputation for political reasons. While Darlington Quakers were bound by conscience on certain issues, for instance against profiting from military contracts,[110] in general they followed a pragmatic line in commerce and closed unprofitable businesses when necessary. With the local linen industry in terminal decline, the Backhouses shifted entirely to banking, while the Iansons turned to engineering. The Peases may have been less charitable towards their textile employees had they not had a portfolio of other investments to support them.

The Stockton and Darlington railway, perhaps surprisingly in view of its extraordinary financial results and its impact upon regional industrialisation, also provides a sorry story of managerial incompetence. In 1845, it was accused of being 'one of the worst-managed undertakings in the Kingdom, and that is saying a great deal'.[111] The railway's 'antediluvian' management practices 'remained ossified at an immature level of development', according to Kirby.[112] The subcontracting of locomotive repairs and servicing, and track maintenance, in the tradition of an eighteenth-century mineral line, could have been 'a rational form of business organisation', but was used rather as 'a method of evading management'.[113] The result was that Hackworth, the most significant subcontractor, became *de facto* general manager, employing the

---

[109] Ibid.

[110] Edward Pease, for instance, refused to accept profits from Stephenson's manufacture of war-ships: Kirby, *Men of Business and Politics*, p. 17.

[111] Kirby, *Origins of Railway Enterprise*, p. 126.

[112] Kirby, *Origins of Railway Enterprise*, pp. 3 and 102.

[113] Ibid., pp. 102–3; see also Sidney Pollard, *The Genesis of Modern Management: a Study of the Industrial Revolution in Great Britain* (Edward Arnold, 1965), p. 38.

Kitchings to do much of the engineering work.[114] Under the circumstances, this arrangement may have cut complications and enabled an otherwise impossible level of technical sophistication.[115] The system persisted for as long as the line was independent, suggesting, as Kirby concedes, that it was manageable and cost effective for a small railway.[116] Nor did it lack direction, for the Pease brothers were always on hand as 'managerial' directors.[117] Joseph Pease in particular, dynamic, forceful and innovative, was known as an autocrat in the 'little railway republic'.[118] In this the railway seems to have received more attention from its directors than was customary for a canal or turnpike undertaking.

The railway's pioneering role, and its continuing domination by Quaker interests, made it a special case among such enterprises, 'more appropriate to a close partnership than to a joint stock company with share capital over £100,000'.[119] While the planning and managing in a sense reflected badly upon its projectors, it cannot be denied that by many criteria the railway was exceptionally successful. The way in which it was organised represented a 'best possible' system for the time and place. It was an 'outstanding commercial success' during the 1830s and 1840s, its shares, which remained concentrated in the hands of Quakers, rose steeply, and the company contributed significantly to the development of the trunk rail network between London and Edinburgh.[120]

Indeed, the network structure sustaining Quaker businesses through the early difficulties of industrialisation may later have proved disadvantageous to continuing success. The committees and sub-contracting which took the place of individual direction could have worked against the development of effective management systems. There were further pitfalls in networks. Their interdependent elements exposed members to the danger of a domino collapse. Banks were especially at risk through the failures of others, as with Backhouses' in 1815, saved from a crash only by its Quaker links.[121] The new industries following in the wake of the railway were particularly vulnerable to external economic downturns. Networks which had sustained promising businesses through the fluctuations of an immature industrial economy could not protect them in a changed business environment. The Stockton and Darlington railway depended upon mineral business, a fluctuating market, with little else to fall back on, so relied upon the goodwill of bankers and of its

[114] Kirby, *Origins of Railway Enterprise*, p. 103.
[115] Contrast with the achievements of the subcontracting system in Keighley; G. Cookson, 'Family Firms and Business Networks: Textile Engineering in Yorkshire, 1780–1830', *Business History*, Vol. 39, No. 1 (1997), pp. 1–20.
[116] Kirby, *Origins of Railway Enterprise*, p. 109.
[117] Ibid., p. 110.
[118] Jeans, *Jubilee Memorial*, p. 233.
[119] Kirby, *Origins of Railway Enterprise*, p. 131, quoting Reed.
[120] Ibid., pp. 102 and 126–8.
[121] Banham, *Backhouses Bank*, pp. 18–22.

Quaker connections.[122] The interdependence of companies meant an overlap of directorships, which in this case brought the advantage of consistent decision-making across the related activities. The disadvantage was an over-reliance on the Peases, so that, for instance, bad speculations by Joseph and Henry Pease in the 1840s threatened the railway's future.[123] The Pease bank later became a huge drain, eventually dragging down the whole empire.[124] Members of the Pease family were also implicated in the failures of the two Quaker ironworks, the South Durham and the Skerne, both out of business by 1882. On the other hand, Kitching and the (non-Quaker) Darlington Forge, with a more flexible approach to their products, managed to survive recession, competition and changing markets.[125]

There were other potential drawbacks with the network's persistence. Although the Quaker network lost its industrial potency over the course of the century, the links of friendship and kinship were still strong, and were increasingly perceived by non-Quakers in a negative light. Obligations to other members, for instance preferment in employment or contracts, may have generated poor commercial judgements. The railway solicitor Francis Mewburn, closely associated with Quaker enterprises in Darlington for 50 years, thought so in 1861:

> The Quakers are more clannish than any other sect, and carry it to such an extent as to cause much dislike to the body. In all cases where they form part of a company and have the ruling or preponderating influence, they not only favour those of their servants who are of their own sect, but in granting favours they select for preference members of their own sect although they may be less deserving than others.[126]

Many Quakers were indeed employed by the Peases, and upon railway projects, but there was no closed shop, for non-Quakers such as George Stephenson, Thomas Summerson,[127] Mewburn himself and Timothy Hackworth[128] were prominent in technological and organisational innovation. Under the circumstances, it was likely that the local candidates best qualified for such positions might be Quakers, who tended to be of the appropriate class and education. In any case, initially there was little choice of supplier of components and services to the railway, as only a limited circle had developed

---

[122] Kirby, *Origins of Railway Enterprise*, pp. 30–1.

[123] Ibid., p. 7.

[124] Ibid., pp. 70–81.

[125] Durham V.C.H., IV, forthcoming.

[126] Francis Mewburn, *The Larchfield Diary* (Simpkin Marshall, 1876). pp. 173–4.

[127] For Summerson, Harris's protégé, see Barbe's, 'Development of Darlington', p. 44; Darlington C.L.S., acc. E810048434, 'The Summerson Story, 1840–1956', and *British Bulletin of Commerce, Histories of Famous Firms*, Teesside Survey (2), vol. 17(3), (Thos Summerson & Sons Ltd).

[128] Hackworth was a Methodist. Thanks to Winifred Stokes for this information.

the necessary expertise.[129] The success of Quakers in attracting investment to Darlington and its region may have been the means of retaining local talent, rather than lose it to London and elsewhere, as shown in the contrasting cases of John Kitching and his much younger half-brother, Alfred.

Conclusion

The supposed special qualities of Quaker entrepreneurs do not detract from the instructive merits of this as a case study of networks. Membership of the Society of Friends, and any notable characteristics and advantages which those conferred in business, can be set clearly in perspective. The 'Quaker' commercial attributes, of foresight, organisational skills, curiosity, innovative energy, and so on, turn out to be largely mythical. The main contribution to regional economic growth by Darlington's Quaker network came through their access to London and Norwich finance and other practical support, operating across a wider range of close kinship and business channels than has generally been recognised. The involvement of external investors in the Stockton and Darlington railway, and in the development of the port of Middlesbrough, has usually been attributed to their shared religious faith, but it is now clear that the main London investors were more than fellow Quakers: they were close relatives of Darlington promoters, and some were themselves of recent Darlington origin. Their participation was fundamental in kick-starting the region's economic growth and sustaining it through early fluctuations to maturity. Combined with the skills and energy of Quakers and others, this enabled Darlington and the wider region to gain an economic advantage. The network, drawing heavily upon its external financial and political connections, without doubt expedited the opening and development of a backward region, sustained it through early fluctuations to maturity, and established a number of exceptionally profitable businesses.

Yet the Quaker features of the Darlington network – the way in which the group's activities spread into all aspects of life in the town – are a reminder that entrepreneurs are never solely profit-maximisers, but have other roles and motivations in the wider world. While Joseph Pease stands out as a bold and energetic individual, neither he nor his associates fits the mould of the identikit entrepreneur of economic theory. All of them had a hinterland, beyond the realms of business. This case-study confirms, moreover, that entrepreneurship was a widespread quality. The idea that a network requires a powerful figure, an organiser or *impannatore*, at its centre entirely misses the point. It confuses a network with the putting-out system, which was essentially a dispersed factory and a quite different phenomenon. It is conceivable that a network would have an individual at its hub for practical – perhaps technical – reasons,

---

[129] Compare with the situation in textile engineering: Cookson, 'Family firms'.

as with the Keighley machine-makers, but this does not necessarily imply leadership.[130]

The way to analyse such formations is by addressing the very complexity which makes networks so difficult to define, but which supplied an essential backdrop to dynamic networking. Complexity – the range of people, skills, products, resources, markets – provided options in rapidly shifting contexts, with networks a matter of contingency between individuals who lacked appropriate institutional frameworks. For the historian, such commercial developments need to be located in social circumstances. This is especially important in understanding relationships before, perhaps, 1850, and certainly before 1800, when most economic activity was outside formal institutions and the community context of industry was of the utmost significance.

The Darlington network was dynamic and far from purposeless; while relatively informal, it was not casual, amounting to more robust connections than simply random business exchanges. Like other such multi-stranded structures, it was founded in contingency, a 'best possible' system to produce a desired result from limited resources. Such networks should be seen as a stage of development, and not as competing with more generally recognised institutional forms. While their initial purposes are limited, their fascination for historians lies in the fact that they seem to achieve more than was ever intended or envisaged at the outset. But their possibilities are finite, so that such networks will become obsolete. That the Darlington example appears to have been relatively long-lasting – though its lifespan is impossible to define exactly – may be explained by the durable family and religious links which were integral to it.

The proof of a network's efficacy is in its economic results. The difficult operation to open up and develop the Tees valley was achieved despite a striking lack of foresight and effective management; the network's contribution was contingent rather than visionary, and was in this case a striking one because of the region's intractable geographical problems and relative backwardness, combined with the extraordinary amounts of capital the network could muster. Once the railway's future was assured, the network became increasingly exclusive and locally autonomous. Different kinds of network developed after 1850, as Darlington grew exponentially; commerce rested on institutions rather than individuals, and a circle of paid managers and servants came to the fore in business and politics. Once its members had gained resources to act independently, the network served no further point, thereafter dissipating in the face of overwhelming economic forces that it had been responsible for initiating.

---

[130] Cookson, 'Family firms'.

Chapter 9

The British glove industry, 1750–1970: The advantages and vulnerability of a regional industry[1]

Richard Coopey

Introduction

This chapter will examine the history of the British glove industry from the mid-eighteenth century to the mid-twentieth. This industry, though relatively insignificant today, was a major sector of the clothing industry before the 1950s. Important in its own right, it is particularly interesting from the perspective of regional or networked industry analysis, since gloving came to be concentrated in two major manufacturing centres, exhibiting pronounced network structures at a number of levels. This chapter will chart the rise and decline of this industry, mapping the nature of networks and the scope of regionality involved. Taking glove making as a case-study, we will also attempt to shed light on the dynamics which lead to regional concentration, and importantly, whether, and in what ways, such an industrial configuration can prove to be an advantage or a disadvantage for the industry involved.

Glove making represents a minor, if important, economic sub-sector of the clothing industry today. Glove manufacture is a multi-faceted industry with a wide range of products and markets. These include work gloves of many specific types, sports gloves (for golfers, skiers or goalkeepers, for example) or general gloves for winter wear, and a limited market for fashion or formal wear. Manufacture is spread across the globe, though Indonesian factories figure prominently in the production of leather sports gloves. The vast majority of production is for utility – function rather than fashion – to protect hands, enhance grip, etc. Though fashion does overlap function in places, for example, the popularity of skiing gloves for everyday wear, the former plays a minor role. This is almost the exact reverse of the situation which pertained before the mid twentieth century when gloves were an essential part of fashion. Glove wearing, like its partner hat wearing, was a central tenet of the code of dress

[1] The author would particularly like to thank the following for their considerable help in researching this chapter: Carole Anderson, Nicole Burnett, Megan Coopey, Jean Harper, Annette Leach, and the late Bob Ring.

throughout British and other industrialising societies.

The gloves that formed the major part of production were very different to those are manufactured today. Predominantly made from leather or silk, they were typically extremely fine garments, very close fitting and called for high degrees of skill in a range of manufacturing processes. An elaborate procedure needed to be followed in putting on or taking off gloves – involving stretching the fingers, rolling (never pulling) over the hand, and so on. This was reputed to take up to 20 minutes on occasion.[2] The fashion for glove wearing did perhaps originate in utility – the avoidance of the domestic and urban dirt and dust of the eighteenth century – but was transcended by aesthetic considerations. Particularly for the middle and upper classes, the condition of the hands became an important and deeply symbolic indicator of social position, status and its attendant etiquette. As one source noted:

> The texture and colour of the skin, and the appearance of the nails, show how much care and culture the possessor has bestowed upon them and consequently, may be regarded as evidence of his or her taste ... a soft white hand ... the palm and tips of the fingers should be the colour of the inner leaves of a moss rose, with the blue veins distinctly visible ... gloves should always be worn on exposure to the atmosphere, and are graceful at all times for a lady of the house.[3]

This fashion for glove wearing extended to both men and women, though the overlap of utility and fashion was more marked in the case of the former. In particular, there existed a very large market for 'driving gloves' – for use in driving horse-drawn carriages and for riding generally. Riding or not, gloves were compulsory. 'Whether in town or country always wear gloves, those for town wear should be of a light and delicate tint, as such a glove has an air of elegance and finish. Gloves for the country may be stouter, but the material must be kid and the fit perfection. A gentleman is known by his gloves.'[4] Gloves of a delicate, pristine and light-coloured nature had a short life, and typically a member of the middle and upper classes would own a great many pairs. This fashion for wearing gloves was ubiquitous throughout society – only the quantity owned and the quality varying through successive social strata.

Glove manufacturing was, then, for over 200 years at least, a major industrial sector – one of the central pillars supporting British clothing culture. By 1820,

---

[2] Fownes', Annual Catalogue (1898), p. 59.

[3] 'How to Dress, or the Etiquette of the Toilette' 1876, quoted in S. Levitt, *Victorians Unbuttoned: Registered Designs for Clothing, Their Makers and Wearers, 1839–1900* (Allen and Unwin, 1986), p. 131. Women in society had for a long time aspired to a white and translucence complexion. Certainly, a ruddy countenance from exposure to the elements was generally frowned upon. See, for example, the attitude towards Elizabeth Bennett's disdain for cosseted convention in Jane Austen's *Pride and Prejudice*.

[4] 'Etiquette for Gentlemen', (1866), quoted in S. Levitt, *Victorians Unbuttoned*, p. 131.

over 15 million pairs of fashion gloves were being manufactured each year in Britain. Leather gloves predominated, being made from a range of fine leathers, including kid, lambskin, chevrette, reindeer, the skin of unborn calves, and some dog-skin. Particularly prized were skins from the mountainous regions of Italy, Spain and Switzerland, though skins were imported from Russia, southern Africa and South America.[5] In the 1830s over three million skins per annum went into the glove industry.[6]

The industry had its origins in antiquity and was firmly established by the medieval period. There was, for example, a Glovemakers Street in Worcester in the thirteenth century. By the eighteenth century, however, a pronounced regional profile could be observed. Centres of glove making were concentrated around Worcester and Yeovil in Somerset, with minor centres around Woodstock in Oxfordshire and Ludlow in Shropshire. There were also pockets of manufacturing around York and in London. In the 1820s, employment figures for towns and their immediate surroundings were 30,000 in Worcester, 20,000 in Yeovil, and 1000 each in Woodstock and Ludlow.[7] The Worcester-Yeovil axis remained by far the most important. Worcester manufacturers alone were producing 50 per cent of national production by the 1820s. There was some regional specialisation in terms of styles, Yeovil becoming renowned for military gloves, for example. Gloves were made for domestic and world markets, exported principally through London for sale in Europe, the USA and throughout the British Empire. Raw materials were also imported via London.

Concentrating on Worcester, we can see how the industry expanded and contracted through a series of changes in the general market, and also the ways in which production went through phases of start-up growth and increasing scale and concentration of firms. By the early decades of the nineteenth century, the industry dominated the Worcester economy. The broadcloth woollen industry, which itself had previously monopolised Worcester's economy, had been in decline into the eighteenth century. Gloving replaced weaving to the extent that the spire on St Andrew's church, the most prominent feature in the City skyline, was generally referred to from the late eighteenth century onwards as the 'glover's needle'. Between 1796 and 1808, the city employed between 5000 and 6000 glove workers in about 70 firms, though many more workers were employed as outworkers in surrounding rural locations. One 1820 Worcester trade directory listed 102 glove masters, and Hull estimated that by 1825 there may have been as many as 150, though other sources put the figure closer to 125. From this peak, when an estimated 30,000 workers were employed, the number of firms follows a

[5]   'A Brief Description of the Manufacture, History and Associations of Gloves', Dent, Allcroft and Co., undated, copy in Bob Ring Collection, (hereafter BRC).
[6]   W. Hull, *The History of the Glove Trade* (Effingham-Wilson, 1834), p. 115.
[7]   W.R. Amphlett, *A History of the Worcester Glove Trade* (Unpublished manuscript, 1954), Worcester City Record Office (hereafter, WCRO); Hull, *History of the Glove Trade,* pp. 58–9; D.C. Lyes, *The Leather Glove Industry of Worcester in the Nineteenth Century* (Worcester City Museum, 1976), pp. 65 and 69.

declining trend, from 108 in 1832, to 85 in 1836, 61 in 1840, 20 in 1844, 24 in 1851 and 16 in 1869.[8] Throughout this decline in the number of firms, there was an expansion in the scale of survivors, however, which eventually saw the emergence of major employers such as Fownes' and Dent Allcroft by the end of the nineteenth century.

The market for gloves went through four broadly defined periods. From the late eighteenth century to the 1820s, output boomed. This was followed by a period of recession and transition, driven by intensive foreign competition from the early 1830s to around 1870. Between 1870 and 1950 the industry recovered and maintained a steady, if declining, market. This was followed by the collapse of the fashion glove market in the post-war period, a period of attrition and elimination for all the major manufacturers in Worcester. This periodisation also encompasses major changes in the structure and organisation of firms. In particular, the transitionary period between the 1830s and 1870 – embodying a phase of classic Schumpeterian 'creative destruction' – saw not only the emergence of a new type of firm, but also heightened technological innovation and changes in the labour process. However, these changes, as we shall see, were contradictory and paradoxical in nature. While we can see the emergence of mechanisation and the factory system, for example, we can also observe the tenacity of gender divisions and the persistence of outworking and handicraft or small scale working side by side with new developments.

Technology and labour, city and countryside

Glove making in the eighteenth century involved an admixture of many trades and skills. The tanning process necessary to produce the fine leathers needed involved many stages of processing and finishing, before the skins were selected by glovers. Skins were then further sorted, processed, dyed and finally cut into the shape required. The latter processes, comprising several specialised stages of cutting, paring, slitting and dressing, called for skill in maximising the use of the leather in order to minimise waste, but also to ensure that the stress points and wearability of the finished glove met required standards. The job of the cutter was central. Highly skilled workers, their job actually involved selecting and stretching and manipulating the skin, finally marking out a rectangular 'trank' for cutting out. The final task of cutting out was actually undertaken by the slitter.[9] These jobs were exclusively the preserve of male workers, most of whom lived in the city, a master cutter often supervising three or four apprentices in the

---

[8]   Hull, *History of the Glove Trade*; V. Green, *A Survey of the City of Worcester* (1764); Amphlett, *History*; Lyes, *Leather Glove Industry*.

[9]   For an excellent guide to the processes involved in glove making, see J. Harper, *Sheep, Donkeys and the Pig* (South Somerset Museum Service, 2000); see also 'A Brief Description of the Manufacture, History and Associations of Gloves', Dent, Allcroft and Co., Worcester, undated copy in WCRO.

workshop.

Sewing the parts of the glove and adding embellishments and finishing was, in contrast, exclusively women's work. Sewing, being the most labour intensive of jobs, was slower and therefore resulted in a high ratio of female to male workers overall. The production of 12,000 dozen pairs of gloves per week in the 1820s employed approximately 3300 cutters, parers, dressers, and slitters, and between 12,000 and 15,000 sewers.[10] Sewing itself was sub-divided into specialist tasks. Separate sewers were responsible for fingers and thumbs, welters hemmed the wrists, and pointers sewed the ubiquitous ornamental lines on the back of the gloves. This outwork was predominantly undertaken on a piecework basis.

Much of the work involved in glove making was undertaken in small domestic units. Indeed, the nature of small-scale craft-based production and its combination with rural life was held up as a paragon by Cobbett as he railed against the encroachment of debilitating factory life. On visiting Worcester in the 1820s, he observed that:

> this glove making is not like that of cottons, a mere gambling concern, making baronets today and bankrupts tomorrow, and making those who do the work slaves. Here there are no masses of people called together by a bell and 'kept to it' by a driver ... glove manufacturing ... cannot be carried on by fire, by wind or by water, and which is therefore carried on by the hands of human beings ... While there is an absolute destruction of life going on in the (Manchester, Leeds and Glasgow) hell holes, there is no visible misery at, or near, Worcester: and I cannot take my leave of this county without observing that I do not recollect to have seen one miserable object in it. The working people all seem to have good large gardens, and pigs in their styes; and this last, say the *feelosophers* what they will about their 'antallectual enjoyments' is the only security for happiness in a labourer's family.[11]

As the firms consolidated into larger scale factories, utilising mechanised processes, the use of outworkers persisted. In 1884, for example, Dent and Allcroft employed 300 factory workers, but also between 10,000 and 15,000 outworkers, many in the villages of Worcestershire. By 1907, the factory had expanded significantly to employ 2455 workers, but outworkers still numbered over 10,000. Similarly, Fownes employed over 7000 'Fownes Ladies' in villages around Worcester.[12] Even after the mechanisation of sewing, many workers, who had often trained in the factory, were provided with a sewing machine at home.

During the nineteenth century, perhaps not surprisingly, employers introduced mechanisation into some of the many processes involved in glove manufacture. Significant innovations included the Jouvin Punch, a French innovation, which

---

[10] S.W. Beck, *Gloves: Their Annals and Associations* (Hamilton Adams, 1883); Lyes, *Leather Glove Industry*, p. 64.

[11] W. Cobbett, *Rural Rides* (Dent, 1924 edn.), pp. 120–1.

[12] Lyes, *Leather Glove Industry*, p. 49.

was introduced in 1835 to mechanise the slitting process. This machine also introduced standardisation into cutting – establishing 14 standard sizes.[13] (There are earlier claims to mechanised slitting. For example, John Burlingham 'partly invented and introduced' a machine designed to cut ten pairs of gloves simultaneously.)[14] During the 1850s, mechanised processes were introduced into the tawing process to replace the trampling method hitherto employed.

As innovations took place in the preparatory stages of glove making, the final stages of manufacture involving the fine, detailed work of sewing proved more difficult to rationalise. This process was partly mechanised by the introduction of the 'donkey' in 1807 – a foot operated vice-like apparatus designed to grip the edges of the leather and provide a guide for sewers to follow. This device was probably developed by James Winter. In 1811, the Burlingham family, prominent glovers in Worcester, were compelled to pay royalties to Winter in the form of a lump sum of £162 and £2 for each machine in use in their workshops.[15] The indenture describes 'a certain new machine for sewing and pointing leather gloves with neatness and strength much superior to that which is affected by manual labour'. It was not until the 1860s that specialist sewing machines were developed, however.[16] Initially used only for cloth gloves, then developed for use with fine leathers, these complex and expensive machines began to be mechanically powered in 1879, though the majority were still sited in outworkers' homes and operated manually. Machines were made by a wide range of manufacturers. In 1876, Dent Allcroft, for example, installed a range of machines manufactured by Thomas, Jelstrup, Necker, Leonard, Russell, Wilcox and Gibbs and Horstman, Vidal and Engler. These machines performed a variety of specialised functions – roundseams, prixseams, piquing and so on.[17] By 1899, the Dent Allcroft's factory housed a total of 849 machines, in addition to machines installed in outworkers' houses.[18] In Sturminster, near Yeovil, Dent Allcroft had installed over 120 machines including 35 chain stitch, 23 lock stitch and 59 prixseam machines.[19] It is unclear what the traditional arrangement was in terms of financing the machines installed in outworkers' houses. Stock books at Dent Allcroft in the late nineteenth century still have these entered, implying that they were regarded as a capital asset by the firm. Later oral evidence also suggests that machines were leased to workers by the firm.[20]

---

[13] Lyes, *Leather Glove Industry*, pp. 38–41.

[14] R. Burlingham, 'Once a Quaker: The Story of a Worcestershire Family Through Four Centuries', undated, p.12, WCRO.

[15] Indenture between John Burlingham, John Burlingham the younger, Thomas Burlingham and James Winter, 20th Feb. 1811, WCRO BA5021/1.

[16] Dent Allcroft, Stock Book, 1866, BRC.

[17] For full explanation of these styles, see Harper, *Sheep, Donkeys and the Pig*; also N.L. Leyland and J.E. Troughton, *Glove Making in West Oxfordshire: The Craft and its History* (Oxford City and County Museum Publication No. 4, 1974).

[18] Dent Allcroft, Stock Books, 1875, 1876, 1880, 1889, BRC.

[19] Dent Allcroft, Stock Book, 1899, BRC.

[20] Carole Anderson, Oxfordshire Museum, 'Gloving in West Oxfordshire' project.

Alongside Dent Allcroft, the other major firm in Worcester in the late nineteenth century was Fownes'. Fownes' employed the same factory/rural outworker dual labour configuration as Dent Allcroft. Evidence suggests that Fownes had a higher ratio of outworkers than their principal rival. This dual labour market continued well into the twentieth century. In 1923, for example, Dent Allcroft had over 200 outworking machines on their books, compared to 800 in the factory – though many more outworkers were employed in hand sewing, or may have owned their own machines. Outworkers were concentrated in certain villages, for example, Dent Allcroft employed outworkers in Evesham, Crowle, Inkberrow – sleepy rural settings redolent of market gardening and orchards.[21] There were still 72 machines with outworkers in Crowle in 1923 – a village of no more than a few hundred inhabitants. This village still had outworkers in the 1960s.[22]

These villages were known as 'stations' and work in them was coordinated by an appointed supervisor. The Fownes' factory of the 1920s has been remembered as 'very posh and very strict', in terms of the standard of conduct expected in the factory itself.[23] Evidence suggests that this regime was extended to the outworkers in the countryside. Workers in the rural stations were referred to as 'Fownes' Ladies' and certainly regarded themselves as a kind of elite among rural workers. This may be a reflection of the general acceptability of sewing as a respectable occupation, even pastime, for middle class women, which extended into the industrialised world of glove making in the nineteenth century. Moreover, gloves as a product, as noted above, were intrinsically linked to fashion, style and gentility – again reinforcing the notion of exclusivity among the workforce. (It is perhaps indicative that anecdotes abound in the oral evidence of pride in gloves made for the aristocracy or royalty.)[24]

This dual labour market, and its persistence into the twentieth century, provides one of the central paradoxes of the industry. The persistence of the employment of outworkers reflects the ability to install machinery for a key phase in the manufacture of gloves in remote and isolated areas. It also reflects the possibility of self-, or remote supervision of the workforce, against an increasing trend of centralised control in other industries. Yet the work done within the larger glove factories displayed an increasing trend towards mechanisation and control. (This mechanisation and concomitant economies of scale which became a feature of gloving firms in the later nineteenth century will be examined below.) Here we would re-emphasise the dual and parallel process of Fordist and pre-Fordist labour processes which typify the glove industry from the mid-nineteenth century. This reflected a combination of inertia, conservatism and tradition (itself a feature inherent in this most introspective of fashion sectors); skill configurations inherent in the portability

---

[21] Dent Allcroft, Stock Books 1899, 1923, BRC.

[22] Bob Ring, interviewed, 21 June 2000.

[23] M. Pryce, 'Glove Story', *Worcester Evening News*, 4 April 1997, p. 29.

[24] Oxfordshire Museum Project; Bob Ring, interview.

and nature of the product; and the continuing availability of a large rural labour force, compliant and controllable by informal means. To be a 'Fownes Lady', in effect, meant conforming to a self-regulating set of ideals and standards, imposed through ideas of status and local prestige.

Local and national networks and control

Networks operate in many forms, and with numerous functions. For example, they may transmit information, or enable concerted action to advance or protect trade, fix prices and supply, and so on. If we begin to trace the networks operating in the glove industry in Britain, we can gain an indication of the way in which networks took several forms and operated at a number of levels. These networks were multi-layered, existing at the level of individual families, religious groupings and formal institutional/organisational combinations of either workers or glove masters. We will return to the question of national networks below, but begin here with an analysis of local networks, focusing on Worcester.

Gloving in Worcester had been the subject of guild control since at least the fifteenth century. Guild ordinances issued in 1467 to prevent the casting of 'fylthe of beastys dongs or douste over Servern Brugge, ... beyond the said Brugge' mention glovers. Glovers often formed strategic alliances with proximate trades. The Glovers, Purcers, Pouchmakers and Poynters Guild was incorporated in 1497, reduced to Glovers, Pouchmakers and Purcers in 1651. Ten years later, the network of alliances was spread even further, as Tanners, Whittawers (saddlers), Pewterers, Braziers and Plumbers joined the guild.[25] The situation returned to an ostensibly more logical trade grouping in 1696, when the guild was reduced to Glovers, Tanners, Saddlers and Pewterers, though the continued inclusion of the latter shows that guild membership was partly trade and craft driven, and partly motivated by strategic economic and political concerns. The guild regulated trade in the normal way, setting and maintaining entry qualifications, overseeing quality issues, regulating monopoly, and so on. Seventeenth century rules, for example, forbade the manufacture of gloves from any material other than leather. Members were forbidden to employ 'strangers' if any local man was unemployed. They could also be fined for non-attendance at meetings (where they could, however, bring their wives.) Guilds still controlled the apprenticeship system, which remained at seven years into the nineteenth century.[26]

Another employers' collective emerged when the Society of Glovers was formed in 1786, to meet on a quarterly basis to regulate the general affairs of the trade and to provide legal provisions for any individual court action undertaken by any of the members. Informal groupings of glovers also coalesced in response to particular episodes which threatened a disruption of the *status quo*. In 1807,

---

[25] Amphlett, *History*, p. 3–4.
[26] Ibid.

for example, 56 glove masters met in Worcester and signed a petition 'To resist the combination of Grounders, Stoners and White Leather Parers to obtain an advance in wages'.[27] The influence of glove makers also extended beyond trade-specific organisations. In 1839, for example, on the formation of Worcester Chamber of Commerce four out of 14 members were glovers.[28]

To understand the networks operating in the glove industry, it is necessary to move beyond the activities of 'formal' organisations and institutions, however. One of the most striking features of the trade in Worcester is the prominence of Quaker families in gloving. Much has been written on the links between non-conformity and entrepreneurship, innovation or capital formation in industry, whether driven by dogma, education or alienation.[29] In the case of glove making, this may seem an odd association, since Quakerism is noted for its austerity and ultra-conservatism in terms of luxury, fashion and adornment. Nevertheless, Quaker families do figure prominently in the industry. In the seventeenth century, Quaker glover masters like Francis Fincher and Alex Beardsley can be found emigrating to Pennsylvania from Worcester. Thomas Burlingham, responsible for many of the innovatory techniques adopted in the industry in the eighteenth century, was also a Quaker. Prominent Quaker families in Worcester gloving from the eighteenth century onwards included the Bevingtons, Burlinghams and the Beesleys.

All glovers were not Quakers. Indeed, the big factory owners, Dent Allcroft and Fownes', who came to dominate the industry from the late nineteenth century, were not. Nevertheless, a significant proportion of Worcester Quakers were glovers. Leach has calculated that between 1730 and 1803, of the freemen of Worcester who were Quakers (where occupation is known) 69 per cent were glovers, and 81 per cent were in the gloving or allied trades (for example, tanner or currier).[30] Of the 29 merchants and manufacturers listed in Tunnicliffe's directory of 1788, 21 were glovers and 11 of these were Quakers.[31] In terms of activism and influence, however, this ratio was even higher. When the Society of Glovers was formed in Worcester in 1786, eight of the ten signatories to the Articles of Agreement were Quakers – Timothy Bevington, Thomas and Henry Beesley, Richard and John Burlingham, Seymour Whitehead, Thomas Foster and Thomas Newman.[32] The Quaker connections extended nationally into other gloving districts, and many of the glove sellers and merchants in London were also Quakers.

Control by workers in the dual labour market of gloving, a large part of which was atomised and rural, presents a complex picture. There is evidence that where

[27] Amphlett, *History*, p. 10.
[28] Burlingham, *Once a Quaker*, p. 8.
[29] See, for example, J. Walvin, *The Quakers: Money and Morals* (Murray, 1997).
[30] Data compiled by Annette Leach, from City of Worcester Freeman lists, WCRO.
[31] William Tunnicliffe, *Directory of the Principal Merchants and Manufacturers in Worcestershire*, 1788. WCRO.
[32] 'Articles of Agreement to be Observed by a Society of Glovers in the City of Worcester', 1786, p. 12, WCRO, C9/2.

workers were concentrated in the City, there could be militant collective action against mechanisation – even at a seemingly basic level. When the 'donkey' was introduced in 1807, for example, this 'was so much resisted by the females employed at Worcester that (John Burlingham) was obliged to employ others, first at Pershore, then at Evesham'.[33] There is also evidence that Yeovil was in advance of Worcester in introducing mechanisation, owing to the greater trade resistance in the latter. Early formal trade union organisation was effectively defeated in Worcester in the 1830s. Collective bargaining did re-emerge in 1884, as the Operative Glovers Society and the United Glovers Mutual Aid Society were both formed as part of new unionism movement, though the rural outworkers remained outside these organisations.

If we move beyond the power and influence of local groups and focus on the national-local interaction of influences, a complex interplay emerges. Glove manufacture appears to be a densely concentrated regional industry. It is clear, however, that the industry is more accurately identified as having dual regionality which is centred on Worcester and Yeovil, with minor clusters around Woodstock and Ludlow. These centres were in fact interconnected in many ways and are better described perhaps as a planetary industry with a central, bi-nodal cluster. Certainly, the correspondence of Timothy Bevington, a leading early nineteenth century Worcester glove master, reveals many links between Worcester and Yeovil. It is clear early on that technology transfer took place between these regions – as in the case of the 'donkey', for example, developed in the Yeovil region and rapidly diffused to Worcester. Later in the nineteenth century, Fownes' established work stations in the Yeovil region at Sturminster. Both Fownes' and Dent Allcroft were among the numerous Worcester firms which also expanded into the West Oxfordshire region around Woodstock, Whitney and Charlbury in the late nineteenth century, to take advantage of the rural labour market in that area.

A further strong connection within the network of the glove industry is that between the regional centres and London. Most glove production, though manufactured in the regions, was factored through London merchants and shops. London also formed the centre through which skins were imported. Indeed, there was an important trade in the re-exporting of skins through London and on to foreign markets. Many skins were re-exported to the American market in the eighteenth and nineteenth centuries, for example. The links between Worcester/Yeovil and the import-export hub of London went beyond simple trading functionality. They were part of a process whereby local or regional control could be extended to national or total market control.

Some sense of the way in which Worcester glovers sought to control trade and gain influence nationally can be gleaned from the correspondence of Timothy Bevington, a prominent Quaker and glover in Worcester in the eighteenth century and owner of Beckett and Co. Bevington corresponded continuously with merchants in London, such as Thomas Hodgson of Aldgate and Robert Price of

---

[33]   Burlingham, *Once a Quaker*, p. 12.

Milk Street, over prices and quality of skins. It is clear from the correspondence that he visited the capital regularly. Letters could deal with specific enquiries, or with the general prospects for trade. In 1778, for example, he solicited information from Robert Trick, in London, before committing himself to a large wholesale contract, as he did not wish to over-extend production or to 'disappoint anyone that may have dependence on me for supply'.[34] Beyond specific transactions and local trade factors, Bevington's correspondence reveals a broader attempt to control national conditions and trading environments. For example, Bevington was deeply involved in the selection process for local members of parliament – setting up conferences in London, orchestrating press campaigns, etc.[35]

Trade cycles and fluctuations in the market for gloves were a frequent occurrence. There was certainly a season for the production of gloves – either driven by the availability of raw materials, or by the seasonal nature of the consumer market. This is evident, for example, in Bevington's letter when referring to the difficulty of obtaining skins via Minehead or Bristol. As he noted, 'nevertheless as the season is so far advanced no time should be lost in sending them'.[36] Prices could also be unstable – even before the tariff-related collapse of the 1830s. In the late 1770s, for example, Timothy Bevington observed that there had been a 40 per cent drop in prices over the previous year.[37] There were also periodic disruptions to trade caused by rifts in the global trading system, as we shall see in the case of the loss of American markets in 1812.

One particular episode revealed in the Bevington letters is very enlightening, in terms of attempts to control the prices and output of the entire trade at a time when fluctuations were evident, partly due to the price of raw materials. Bevington called a 'meeting of the trade' after consulting with 'several principal manufacturers severally'. He proposed a two shilling rise generally in the price of gloves to cover rising prices, but more than this he proposed control over the one area beyond the grasp of local British manufacturers, the production of skins. As he noted, the:

> great object should be to keep down the price of leather, if the importers of skins would be more unanimous and agree that some few which might be fixed on should import all the skins and after have a fair division made on that we should agree to limit all our commisions [sic] positively and direct that none should be sent but under said limitation the evil would soon be cured and we might as well set a moderate price on skins as suffer the

---

[34] Timothy Bevington to B. Trick, 30 Jan. 1778, Timothy Bevington letter book, WCRO, BA8782/44 (hereafter Bevington letters).

[35] Bevington to Gabriel Bradley, 17 June 1780; Bevington to Edward Bearcroft 29 June 1780; 13 July 1780, Bevington letters.

[36] Bevington to Robert Grubb, 27 September 1778, Bevington letters.

[37] George Beckett and Co. to Robert Grubb, 2 June 1778; Bevington to Sam Hughes, 29 September 1778, Bevington letters.

Italians to put their hand in our pockets and take what they please[38]

At a later meeting, several glove masters resolved to go to London 'to call some of the principal glove sellers together and consult them in ye case that they might concur in such measures as may appear necessary for the present relief of the manufacturers'.[39]

Crisis and reaction: Testing the network

By far the greatest challenge to the glove trade in Britain came in the late 1820s, when tariff protection was withdrawn. This represented more than a passing exogenous shock, but rather set in train a series of phases of long-term rationalisation and restructuring which profoundly affected the industry. French gloves produced in centres such as Grenoble had for many years been produced more cheaply, due to reduced labour costs, proximate raw material supplies and a more amenable climate and water supply for the processes involved in tanning. However, it is probably also the case that British manufacturers were less effective in terms of productivity, and were reluctant to reduce their profit levels. The glove trade in Britain had been protected since the reign of Edward IV. There is stark evidence for the differential in prices between French and English gloves, in that there was a constant smuggling trade in operation throughout the seventeenth and eighteenth century. Duty varied between 20 per cent and 40 per cent. Manufacturers were unable effectively to control the level of smuggling and there is no evidence that the general population saw smuggling as a serious crime – clearly they were complicit in the process since they bought the gloves. Occasionally, when anti-French sentiments were running high, the wearing of French gloves could attract animosity. Southey, for example, relates the account of a person being attacked in the street for wearing French gloves.[40] If smugglers were caught, fines could be considerable – £200 and forfeiture of the gloves in the case of a Birmingham man caught smuggling in 1771, for example.[41]

In the decades after 1790, when French gloves had been banned altogether, Worcester industry had prospered, experiencing a growth rate of five per cent per annum between 1790 and 1816. International developments could also work against the industry – as in the case of the loss of the American market in 1812, which caused a short-term trade depression with as many as 50 per cent of workers thrown onto parish relief.[42] The major blow came in 1824, however, when President of the Board of Trade Huskisson introduced a free trade bill

---

[38] Bevington to Henry Penny, 30 January 1778, Bevington letters.

[39] Bevington to Penny, 9 February 1778, Bevington letters.

[40] Don Manuel Alvarez Espriella, *Letters From England* (1808), pp. 46–7. (The author is grateful to Dorothy Thompson for this reference.)

[41] *Berrows Worcester Journal*, 10 October 1771, p. 2.

[42] Lyes, *The Leather Glove Industry*, p. 11.

which included gloves, and which subsequently became operable in July 1826. Tariffs were progressively reduced until they were eliminated altogether in 1860.[43] As a result of these reductions, the number of imports rose dramatically. The price of gloves in Worcester in 1832 was eight shillings and eight pence per dozen pairs. While in Paris the price was similar at eight shillings, in Grenoble gloves could be bought for four shillings and seven pence per dozen pairs. French gloves were between 15 and 20 per cent cheaper in the American market in 1816.[44] Not surprisingly, once cleared of duty, imports into Britain rose to four million pairs by 1860. By 1875, the figure had reached 16 million pairs.

If clustering in an industry can produce inherent benefits, it can also promote vulnerability. The effect of cheap imports on the trade in Worcester was devastating and led to a fall in production and a consequent catastrophic increase in unemployment. Presaging the debates that were to emerge in the 1930s, we can see in the case of gloves the ways in which a densely concentrated industry was thrown into crisis so precipitously that local welfare provisions for disruptions of trade were inadequate. In 1832, it was calculated that only 113 out of every 1000 workers was in full-time employment.[45] 42 per cent were calculated to be totally unemployed. Responses to the crisis involved three processes – welfare support, political attempts to reverse the free trade policies, and systemic rationalisation of the industry.

There had long been a connection between parish relief and the glove trade. In 1746, for example, a St. Peter's workhouse had employed a person to instruct in the 'paring of leather and the sewing of gloves'.[46] The crisis of the 1830s was of an altogether different order, however. Worcester's poor rate increased from £3068 in 1824 to £5642 in 1832. In 1837, £1000 was raised by subscription and distributed to the distressed by a committee composed of master glovers.[47] There is evidence that a rift – or an emerging self-interest – began to build up between the city and the countryside. In the 1840s, in the midst of decline, the City Council set up a school to train City women as sewers. This was designed to offset the practice of sending gloves outside the city to rural workers, and reduce unemployment in the city at their expense. There is no evidence of resistance to this process from rural glove workers, perhaps unsurprisingly in view of their unorganised nature.

The second strategy to deal with depression was to oppose the tariff reforms politically. Concerted opposition to free trade in gloves began in the early 1830s. A series of petitions was presented to parliament in 1831 and 1832. In March 1832, for example, a petition containing 2200 signatures was presented to the House of Lords by the Bishop of Rochester, supported by the Earl of Coventry, and a motion was put forward supporting the creation of a committee of

---

[43]   Amphlett, *History*, pp. 11–12.

[44]   Lyes, *The Leather Glove Industry*, p. 19.

[45]   *Worcester Herald*, 3 March 1832, p. 3.

[46]   Amphlett, *History*, p. 6.

[47]   Amphlett, *History*, p. 12.

inquiry.[48] This petition prayed 'that the system falsely called Free Trade may be abandoned'.[49] An earlier petition to the Commons originated with a meeting of glove operatives, where the problems facing the industry were laid out:

> The existence of Corn Laws; the innovation of the foreigner in being permitted to supply our colonial and other possessions; the ineptitude of our own national skins for tawed leather; and the impracticability of facilitating or cheapening the process of manufacturing by machinery.[50]

The petition itself outlined the knock-on effect the slump on trade was having on the regional economy generally. It noted that: 'Glove manufacturing forms the chief resource of the City, that its various processes have furnished occupation and subsistence to some thousands of our fellow subjects in the town and adjoining country, that the produce of this trade has circulated wealth and activity through other branches of our local commerce', and that its present distress and decay are bearing heavily upon these collateral interests.[51] In Yeovil, there was great unrest in reaction to the lowering of tariffs. One commentator noted that the 'operation of the "free trade system" on the town of Yeovil will be well illustrated by the necessity of maintaining one or two troops of dragoons continually in town and neighbourhood, where a few years ago a horse rider would have been looked upon as a sort of centaur by the lower orders of people'.[52]

Despite efforts to curb the effects of free trade, the main outcome of heightened international competition was a rationalisation of the industry, the defining feature of which was a contraction in the number of firms, but also the emergence of the large-scale firm. The number of manufacturers declined from 108 in 1832 to 86 in 1836, 61 in 1840, 24 in 1851, 16 in 1869 and 11 in 1885. Fownes, which was to become the largest producer in the City, was originally founded in Worcester in 1777, but subsequently moved to Battersea. The firm returned to Worcester in 1884, however, when a large purpose-built factory was constructed. The other major firm which came to dominate the industry was Dent Allcroft. This firm had its origins in the eighteenth century too, but expanded rapidly in the nineteenth century, constructing a large factory in Worcester in 1853.

In addition to rationalising production and introducing a new range of mechanised processes, as we saw earlier, both Fownes and Dent Allcroft expanded horizontally and vertically. Fownes operated factories in Worcester, Torrington, Wandsworth and Paris. They also integrated forward into retailing,

---

[48]   *Worcester Herald*, March 3, 1832, p. 3.

[49]   T.C. Turberville, *Worcester in the Nineteenth Century* (Longman, Brown and Green, 1852), p. 42.

[50]   Lyes, *The Leather Glove Industry*, p. 25.

[51]   Ibid.

[52]   Hull, *History of the Glove Trade*, p. 41.

opening shops in London, New York, Sydney and Hamburg.[53] Dent Allcroft established factories in Worcester, London and Martock, near Yeovil, in addition to factories in the traditional rival glove-producing area of Grenoble, Brussels, Prague and Naples. The firms also owned tanneries and leather dressing factories, for example at Ottignies in Belgium. By 1884, Dent Allcroft alone were producing nearly 50 per cent of total British glove production. We can thus see the emergence by the end of the nineteenth century of a Chandlerian-style firm in the glove industry – large scale with professionalised management structures and exercising internalised control over market conditions. This form typified the industry into the post-war period, when two major changes destroyed the viability of British glove making. The first of these was represented by a new round of international competition, notably from producers based in Hong Kong. Imports rose from 15,000 dozen pairs in 1952 to over 39,000 dozen pairs in 1955.[54] The second major change came with a major exogenous shock – a global fashion change – which took place roughly from the 1960s onwards. Gloves, along with hats, no longer held their place in the popular styles of dress, as arguably the social hierarchies depicted by fashion became more democratised. This fashion market change meant the demise of the industry in its traditional form. Producers were left to fight over a dwindling market, or seek specialist niche sectors. Mergers and diversification formed part of the industry response – Dent Allcroft and Fownes eventually merging, for example – though neither strategy could reverse the inevitable eclipse of glove making in Britain.

Conclusions: Regions and networks; cycles and control

Glove manufacturing has been shown to be a fundamentally regional industry since at least the eighteenth century, concentrated in Worcester and Yeovil, with significant smaller clusters. There were no apparent natural advantages to either centre in terms of manufacturing gloves. Indeed, raw materials were largely imported from distant sources, and the labour processes involved had no particular regional characteristics or geographic determinants. The labour market and its divisions straddled both gender and space, with a notable fusion or co-existence of urban and rural workforces. Initially, this configuration of the industry was generated and presided over by a group of glove makers with strong family, and especially religious, ties – notably, Quakerism. These ties underpinned the control of local industry, through normal trade cycles and in times of crisis, and linked the centres of production with each other and with the capital where much of the factoring of raw materials and finished goods took place.

To what extent is the British glove industry between 1750 and 1950 best described as an industrial district, cluster, region or a network? How useful are

---

[53] Fownes' Catalogue, 1898, BRC.
[54] Hansard, 15 November 1955.

any of these concepts in understanding the growth trajectories, strengths or vulnerability of this sector? In terms of district or region, the industry developed a noticeable profile. In terms of regionality, Worcester became the epicentre of production, followed by Yeovil, with several much smaller, localised pockets of production in the predominantly rural towns, notably Woodstock and Ludlow. The dominant position of the Worcester-Yeovil axis suggests a bi-regional definition. This might be tempered to a certain degree by recognising the local specialisation which existed in each town – Yeovil's concentration on the important military market, for example, re-defining it as a separate, or sub-region.

One factor defining the industry as a district or region must be the level to which it constituted the dominant activity within the area. Certainly, in the case of the Worcester area the gloving industry took over from the broadcloth industry as the single most important employer by far. As noted above, for the city and surrounding rural areas gloving, and its closely related supply sectors, eclipsed all other industrial activity for most of the eighteenth and nineteenth centuries. Ancillary industries, notably tanning and leather preparation, existed purely as an adjunct to glove making. This is indicated by the lack of development of an independent general leather goods industry in Worcester, as in the case of Walsall, for example.

If we turn from geographic determinism to networks and connectivity, then perhaps we can delineate a slightly different, or stronger regionality. Certainly, the bi-nodal relationship between Worcester and Yeovil becomes somewhat more pronounced. Robust personal and business relationships between these two centres were not unusual, and innovative technology transfers between them were common. This connectivity was underpinned by the familial or, more importantly, religious affinities which were a feature of the industry for most of the eighteenth, and the first half of the nineteenth, centuries. In this respect, Quakers comprised by far the most important group of employers in gloving during this period. However, we can also detect a strong network connection between the industrial region and the central importing/factoring nexus which existed in London. Worcester manufacturers relied on their connections with London merchants for the supply of imported raw materials and as a conduit for city and world markets for gloves.

A further dimension in terms of networks within this sector is represented by the urban-rural dual labour market, which forms such a pronounced feature of the glove industry throughout its lifetime, persisting well into the twentieth century, despite concentration of manufacture into large-scale, purpose-built factories. This urban-rural network is overlaid by a closely matching gender divide which saw the persistence of a rural labour market comprised of women sewers. Groups such as 'Fownes' ladies' regulated and controlled their labour market in a self-selecting and self-perpetuating fashion which was driven both by economic considerations and by the symbolic admixture of status and social inclusion in a rural working elite. These workers, a network in their own right, were only umbilically connected to the firms in the centre.

The glove industry is then a clearly defined regional/networked sector - though this configuration is nuanced by a complex and layered set of connections of an economic, geographic, social and religious nature. If we do accept that it was a strongly regional or networked industry, we can then turn to questions pertaining to the forces which led the industry to emerge and sustain itself in this form. We can also consider the question of strengths and weaknesses inherent in this particular configuration.

There were undoubted advantages to be gained from the structures and connections that characterise the glove industry. The Quaker relationships undoubtedly had an impact, whether at the level of a common ideology and business ethos, internalised capital markets and reduced information asymmetries, or through self-regulation and positive or negative sanctions exerted via the Friends' Meeting House. At another level, the local long-term labour markets perpetuated and enhanced the formation of a critical mass of skill and knowledge, and formed a self-selecting series of stable and reliable rural and urban workforces. Local-national networks also provided the means whereby attempts to control national and international trading relations and markets could be orchestrated.

The concentration of the industry could also lead to a degree of vulnerability, however. The negative effects of regional dominance can clearly be seen in the major crisis of the 1830s, which saw the influx of cheap imports following the lowering of tariff protection. Extreme stresses were placed on local welfare provision as local unemployment rates soared – with little alternative industrial or rural employment available. In addition, tensions began to emerge, threatening to unravel the links between rural and urban interests. In fact, this episode revealed the potential fragility of the dual labour networks that characterised the industry. Though local power was adequate to deal with the periodic problems that faced the industry, it was unable to respond effectively to a national, politically-determined change in the world market environment. This was in spite of the careful and prolonged attempts, led by Worcester manufacturers, to control world markets. The weakness of the local-regional was clearly revealed in the inability of Worcester manufacturers and their allies in Parliament to effect a change in policies of free trade, which ultimately opened up the market to French competition.

Ultimately, the response of local manufacturers was to rationalise the industry internally, concentrating ownership and modernising parts of the labour processes. The shocks of the mid-nineteenth century did not see the end of regional concentration. This formation was strong enough to see itself re-forged in the form of a newly concentrated industry – though still characterised by strong urban-rural labour market networks which actually expanded into some rural areas – for example, as Worcester employers set up in the small towns and countryside of West Oxfordshire. As noted above, this new formation persisted into the twentieth century, in a fairly steady state, though at its heart was a growing conservatism and inertia, based on the confidence of established markets and traditional manufacturing methods. When the world market changed abruptly, ultimately in terms of a seismic shift in fashion, glove manufacturing firms in Britain could do little to respond – their expertise, competences and the legacy of regionalisation and networking was of little or no value in a world where the fashion glove market had all but evaporated.

Chapter 10

'Malefactors and Honourable Men': The making of commercial honesty in nineteenth-century industrial Birmingham

Francesca Carnevali

Introduction

As John Wilson and Andrew Popp point out in the introduction to this volume the industrial history of England can be written as a history of regions and industrial districts, a variegated narrative, rich in empirical detail and theoretical challenges. The purpose of this paper is to confront the literature on embeddedness and trust, presented in Chapter 1, with the complex pattern of relations that made up the jewellery industry in Birmingham in the late nineteenth-century.

The origins of jewellery-making in Birmingham

The origins of jewellery-making in Birmingham are to be found in the work of the buckle and button-makers that gave the city its reputation as the 'Toyshop of Europe' in the second half of the eighteenth-century and the manufacture of jewellery on any noticeable scale dates probably to about 1770. Swinney's *Birmingham Directory* of 1774 lists the names of 47 people making ornaments of gold and silver, 24 of whom made plated goods. However, it was only after about 1790 that the trade began to separate itself and develop that specialisation which by the mid-nineteenth century resulted in the sub-division of the trade into its numerous sections. By the end of the eighteenth century, as the buckle trade began its decline, the engravers, die-sinkers, solderers, platers, polishers, dealers in precious metals and makers of tools adapted their skills to the manufacture of small gold and silver accessories, including jewellery.

Birmingham's unincorporated political status and reputation for religious tolerance attracted artisans from other towns who could easily set up on their own as small masters. The lack of a charter meant that there were no guilds with regulations, which could hinder industry and trade.[1] The low capital outlay involved in setting up as a small master made jewellery an ideal outlet for craftsmen leaving the declining buckle trade. A leather apron, a few tools, a blow pipe and a bench set up at the top of the house where the light was stronger, together with a few gold sovereigns, allowed a skilled metal worker to make small gold goods, such as cravat pins and lockets. The goods would be given to a factor on the Saturday and the same factor would tell the craftsman what he required for the following week.[2] The establishment in 1773 of the Assay Office thanks to the efforts of Matthew Boulton and other local manufacturers gave Birmingham jewellery its own 'trademark', an anchor, and its story was set to begin.[3]

Wrightson's *Birmingham Directory* for 1839 lists 120 goldsmiths and jewellers, 20 lapidaries, nine refiners of gold and silver, 39 chasers and embossers, 26 stampers and piercers, 33 silversmiths, 18 makers of gold and silver chain and a number of tool-makers.[4] This list paints an early picture of specialisation where pieces of metal would travel across the city, carried by errand boys, to be stamped, pierced, engraved, assembled and have stones mounted, all in different workshops. The larger jewellers would often act as factors, rather than expand by integrating processes under one roof, organising the movement of pieces between workshops. The largest firms in the trade were those that specialised in goods used by jewellers, such as rolled sheets of gold and silver, wire, dies and stamps, chain and alloys. By 1845 the trade employed about 3500 but it was thanks to the gold discoveries in California (1849) and Australia (1851) that the trade experienced its period of most rapid growth, and by 1863 it employed more than 5000 people.[5]

Jewellery production was given impetus to grow over the course of the nineteenth century by the combination of discovery, invention and consumption. The gold and silver rushes, the commercial adaptation of electroplating and Queen Victoria's taste for personal ornaments were the elements that made jewellery acceptable, and affordable, to the expanding English middle-classes. The passing in 1854 of the Lower Standards Act legalised the manufacture of 9, 12 and 15 carat gold opening the way for the production on a large scale of cheaper novelty jewellery for a market that was

---

[1] E. Hopkins, *The Rise of the Manufacturing Town. Birmingham and the Industrial Revolution* (Sutton, 1998), p. 5 and M. Berg, *The Age of Manufactures 1700–1820*, (Routledge, 1994), pp. 265–6.

[2] Apart from the presence of skilled workers, another element that gave Birmingham an advantage over other towns was that gas, for the jeweller's blowpipe, was supplied (on credit) as early as 1817.

[3] In 1773 the Assay office was granted permission by the Crown to hallmark silver. Birmingham gold jewellery was given the anchor hallmark in 1824.

[4] These numbers are probably an underestimate of the total population as advertising was something only the larger concerns would budget for. In 1800 a single entry, with no engraved plates, in Pye's *Birmingham Directory* would have cost sixpence.

[5] J.C. Roche, *The History, Development and Organisation of the Birmingham Jewellery and Allied Trades*, (Birmingham, 1927), pp. 21-2.

expanding to include the better-off sections of the working class. Coloured and pink gold met the Victorians' taste for sentimental jewellery and Birmingham competed with Pforzheim, Gablonz and Providence, Rhode Island, to produce as much jewellery as possible. The death of Prince Albert in 1861 opened the way for the design of mourning jewellery in suitably sombre materials, such as onyx, jet and petrified bog oak. If the public wanted it, Birmingham jewellers could make it, and if necessary make it cheaply. The varying degree of combinations of craft skills and machinery allowed both the production of high quality jewellery and of large quantities of affordable pieces. Mechanisation, especially the use of the stamping press, helped greatly in the search for novelty as designs could be changed endlessly as jewellery was consumed more as an item of fashion than as something with an intrinsic value. By the mid-nineteenth century jewellery production in England had concentrated in London and Birmingham, with London depending on Birmingham for the supply of articles suitable for the middle classes.[6]

One of the city's trade directories for 1881 lists 386 manufacturing jewellers and goldsmiths, 167 gilt jewellery manufacturers, 111 plated jewellers, 37 jewellers's setters, 17 diamond mounters, 23 jewellers' stampers, 31 jewellers' materials manufacturers and dealers, together with jewellers' blowpipe makers, box and case makers, alloy makers, draw and gauge plate makers and enamel makers. The Census returns for 1881 show that the jewellery trade, including watchmakers, employed almost 20,000 people, making it the biggest employer in the region alongside the brass and copper trade.[7] By that date the industry had become concentrated in an area of only about 100 acres, north of the city centre, probably because of the absence of restrictions regarding the building of workshops in the gardens of the houses. The area developed as an industrial village within the city, where masters, employees and their families lived and worked and the name Jewellery Quarter gave the industry its spatial identity.

By the early 1900s, despite increasing levels of mechanisation and the adoption of mass production methods, for example for imitation jewellery and electro-plate, the average size of firms remained small. The most capital and energy intensive firms were the large firms of stampers (150 employed, on average), using heavy power presses, lathes and planning machines. Roller and wire-drawers came next, followed by silver and electro-platers who needed power to drive stamps and small polishing bobs. At the other end of the production chain even one of the largest of the high-class jewellery firms, Payton Pepper, did not employ more than 40 people and used little or no power driven machinery. The imitation jewellery makers and cheap silver or 9 carat gold jewellery makers used mainly women to operate fly presses and polishing

---

[6]   S. Timmins (ed), *The Resources, Products and Industrial History of Birmingham and the Midland Hardware District*, (Robert Hardwicke, 1866), p. 452.
[7]   G. C. Allen, *The Industrial History of Birmingham and the Black Country, 1860–1927* (London, 1929) Table 5, p. 459.

bobs while three or four men would assemble the pieces at the jeweller's bench.[8]

From out-workers to sew charms on cards to rolling mills selling gold sheets the Jewellery Quarter offered the full range of skills, processes and products needed to be defined as an industrial district as conceived by Alfred Marshall. The concentration of many small businesses of a similar character allowed these firms to benefit from external economies of scale and scope in the supply of inputs and labour.[9] Concentration in a very small area meant that transaction costs in the productive cycle must have been low, with contractual arrangements kept to the minimum.[10] Dishonest behaviour would have been weeded out quickly while trustworthiness was rewarded by a constant flow of work. Hence, in terms of the exchange of pieces between workshops, the Quarter can be said to have been a high-trust community. Malfeasance, however, was high in commercial relations, for reasons that will become clear in the following pages.

The Great Depression and the problems of the jewellery trade

The years 1885–6 witnessed a collapse in the price of jewellery. However while the fall in the consumption of jewellery might have been due also to exogenous factors, other problems tended to aggravate the evil, such as the sale of bankrupt stock without proper supervision. This led to the market being flooded with goods being sold at very low prices, with disastrous consequences for those manufacturers who were still solvent. This problem, however, was connected with one that could be defined as endemic to the trade, and that was speculation and the existence alongside reputable and honest firms of unscrupulous traders. Firms left with large stock continued to put goods on the market, giving them to anybody whom promised a return, often third rate shippers, dealers and retailers. Extended credit and the absence of a system of status enquiry meant that this type of venture often ended in bankruptcy. Reckless trading was coupled with illegitimate trading as insolvent traders resorted to buying goods on credit only to pawn them to pay off their debts to somebody else. Creditors rarely associated together and in many bankruptcy cases nothing was left for them after the stock was sold by auction and all the legal expenses paid.[11]

As the depression shrank the demand for jewellery, Birmingham jewellery makers also had to face the problem created by the low reputation of their wares. Birmingham jewellery suffered from a 'brand-name' problem tainted as

---

[8]   Roche, *The History*, pp. 66–7.
[9]   A. Marshall, *Principles of Economics* (Macmillan, 1952), p. 221.
[10]   Interviews with present day jewellery manufacturers have confirmed the informality governing the movement of pieces through the productive cycle within the Quarter.
[11]   Roche, *The History*, p. 31.

it was with the label 'Brummagen'.[12] The ability of Birmingham makers to imitate high-class jewellery and produce it for the lower classes had given its goods a reputation for shoddiness, cheapness and vulgarity. By the late nineteenth century the label Brummagen had stuck despite the presence of many producers of high-class work. A contemporary source reveals, 'It is only necessary to walk from the Bank to Hyde Park to enable any person to form an idea of the ingenuity, skill and taste of the Birmingham artisans. The shopkeeper will not voluntarily admit that his articles are Birmingham manufacture, yet we believe we speak within bounds if we say at least one-half of all the gold and silver work seen in the shops of the London jewellers is the production of this town'.[13] Low prices did not suggest quality to the consumer and the drop in prices due to dishonest commercial practices aggravated the problem. Matters were made worse by another endemic problem in the Quarter: a reputation for fraud and high levels of theft among workers. The following pages show how, apart from temptation, the incentive to steal was given by the presence in the Quarter of unscrupulous traders who acted as receivers, including bullion dealers.

The solution: The Birmingham Jewellers and Silversmiths Association

Attempts at association had been made by Birmingham jewellers earlier in the century. In 1851 a group of jewellers formed the Birmingham Jewellers, Silversmith and Dealers in Jewellery Protection Association. Its members agreed to prosecute at their joint expense in cases involving burglary, receiving and embezzlement. Records of this association are minimal and it appears to have been short-lived. A second attempt at co-operation took place in 1875 with the Master Jewellers' and Silversmiths' Association. The objects of this association were similar to those of its predecessor but there are no records of its existence except for a mention in the *Jeweller and Metalworker* issue of 1 August of that year.[14] These earlier attempts at association show the awareness of some of the manufacturers of the problems of the trade. However, it is likely that the positive economic climate reduced the incentive to associate: thanks to the gold rushes 1851 witnessed rapid growth while 1875 was another boom year, the height of market expansion. Little more than ten years later the depression that struck the trade spurred its members into action.

---

[12] Originally referring to the counterfeit coins made there in the late seventeenth century.

[13] Timmins, *Resources, Products and Industrial History*, p. 455. See also S. Wilson, 'Art and industry: Birmingham Jewellery or "Brummagen"?', in K. Quickend and N.A. Quikend (eds), *Silver and Jewellery: Production and Consumption since 1750*, (The University of Central England, The Article Press, 1995), pp. 41–8.

[14] S. Mason, *Jewellery Making in Birmingham 1750-1995* (Chichester, Phillimore, 1998) p. 58 and p. 70.

3 August 1887, witnessed the biggest meeting ever held in connection with the Birmingham jewellery trade, in St. Paul's schoolroom on Warstock Lane, in the heart of the Jewellery Quarter. More than 200 manufacturers attended, representing almost the whole of the employers in the trade. The aim of the meeting was to discuss the 'present wide-spread depression'. In opening the meeting its chairman, Mr. Jacob Jacobs, explained that the two factors most seriously affecting the trade were the decline in the custom of wearing jewellery and the fall in the price of jewellery. In May of that year Jacobs and another well-known jeweller, Charles Green, had taken action by lobbying the Princess of Wales to 'aid the trade in bringing about a revival of the fashion of wearing jewellery' and had taken some articles of jewellery to Malborough House. Subsequently the Princess bought some Birmingham jewellery and this was given a lot of prominence in the national press. Jacobs told the meeting how the depression had led to a general fall in demand and the reaction had been to flood the market with goods with a consequent fall in prices, 'Only the other day he himself [Jacobs] went on a journey of 250 miles and found jewellery pieces priced at a figure he could not make them for'. To keep their place in the market manufacturers were selling at a loss and retailers were selling at prices lower than wholesale. Retailers and wholesalers would order goods from manufacturers on credit only to undersell them and as a consequence could not repay their debts. The implications of this for the Birmingham jewellery trade were disastrous as 'there was not a shopkeeper in the whole country who had not an account with a Birmingham firm'. As the market shrunk 'the enormous credit that was given to small factors who failed, and thousand of pounds of stock had to be sold at an alarming sacrifice', as Mr. Nathan (another prominent jeweller) pointed out to the meeting. At the meeting Councillor Payton, representative of one of the leading jewellery firms, said, 'To come to the root of the matter, they had all been too easy in trusting their goods to people who wanted to buy them. Let them, as men with a desire to act honourably to each other, before they put new customers on their books make inquiry as to whether there was a reasonable chance of getting their money'.

The men of the jewellery trade in Birmingham were forced together by the depression to find a way to codify honour in their profession. The depression had revealed the absence of 'rules of the game' that could safeguard the interests of the trade. However, the depression had also shown the weakness of trusting on price alone as a competitive advantage. Birmingham jewellery needed to shed its 'Brummagen' label and develop a more 'tasteful' reputation. Though some jewellers at the meeting moaned that women did not wear jewellery any more, Nathan's intervention reveals that they were aware of the truth: that women wore less jewellery because of the depression but because of Birmingham's reputation ladies concentrated on good pieces, with the London hallmark. The meeting concluded that:

> Their disaster had thrown them a little closer together, and now was
> especially the moment when some trade association would be of lasting

benefit to their business. The association would assist materially in detecting fraud by investigating thoroughly a bankrupt's affairs. Then as to art education he thought a great deal might be done in this direction for the benefit of the trade. Let them found a technical school of art in their midst and have in it the best specimen of art metal work that could be got together. Their apprentices could be educated in the school and the result would be a vast lifting up of the trade.[15]

As a result of the public meeting a committee was created to set up the articles of association and canvass for members. This initial committee consisted of Councillors Jacob Jacobs and Charles Green, the same men who had shown Birmingham jewellery to the Princess of Wales, and of Councillor Payton and Messers. J.M. Banks, J.W. Tonks, W. Ginder, C.T. Shaw, J. Adie and B.H. Joseph, representatives of the most prominent jewellery firms of the time. The committee met over the summer to agree on the articles of association and report on the canvassing activity. The first AGM of the Birmingham Jewellers and Silversmiths Association (BJA) was held on the 27 November and by the then more than 80 people had pledged their support. At that meeting a fundamental disagreement between Jacobs and Green emerged and the latter gained the chair of the association. Jacobs' plan had been to organise a manufacturers' association with the intention of setting prices while Green's vision was wider, including wholesalers.[16] The two were inextricably linked as manufacturers often acted as wholesalers and any attempt to establish a code of conduct for the trade would fail without the co-operation of both.[17] It is also plausible to assume that Jacobs' notion of setting prices would not have encountered much favour with most of the people attending the meeting.

At the AGM the Rules of the Association were approved and its object listed:

1) The advancement of taste in the manufacture of jewellery and personal ornaments by developing the art education of employers and employed; by instructing apprentices and young persons in the true principles of decorative and constructive art.
2) To watch all measures brought forward in Parliament in any way affecting the trade; whether for the establishment of technical schools, in relations between debtor and creditor, working and trading regulations; the recovery or disposal of stolen property; the working of the Acts relating to pawnbrokers; the detection or punishment of fraud or crime; and to use its

---

[15] All the above quotes are taken from *Birmingham Daily Gazette*, 4 August 1887.

[16] *Birmingham Daily Gazette*, 'The Jewellery Trade in 1887', January 18, 1888. Jacobs however did not leave the Association, remaining one of its most active members until his death in 1896.

[17] Birmingham City Archives, Papers of the Birmingham Jewellers Association, MS 1646/1, 29 November 1887. (Hereafter referred to as BJA.)

best endeavours to have such Acts passed in a form calculated to place the trade on a sound commercial basis.

3) To ensure united action in all cases of the failure of persons engaged in the trade to meet liabilities in full; to initiate a distinct line of policy in reference to commercial fraud or reckless trading, and to bring to bear the full weight of its membership to promote a sound and healthy system of trading.

4) To ensure the detection and punishment of all dishonest and nefarious dealing on the part of workmen and employees.

5) The development of Colonial and Foreign trade in jewellery and personal ornaments.

6) To seek the removal through Parliament of prohibitive restrictions upon home, colonial or foreign trade; to secure the equal incidence of customs relations.[18]

It is worth listing these points in full because they show how all encompassing the plan of the founders of the Association was. Up to that moment the trade had been a cohesive whole only in a Marshallian sense: spatially concentrated in its own quarter of the city and connected by production and commercial links. In truly Marshallian fashion though these links had been 'effected without conscious effort'.[19] However these market-based mechanisms had not been sufficient to guarantee honesty and to generate trust, at least in the commercial sphere. Extreme contingency brought the jewellers together and the men who created the Association intended not just to regulate the trade and improve the quality of its products but also, as the rules show, to turn the trade into a visible whole, with lobbying weight and political power. This plan however could only work if the Association had the trade behind it and a large number of firms joined. At the same time the Association had to ensure its own reputation: a large club, but an exclusive one nonetheless. Entry had to be encouraged while being selective at the same time. Hence, the Association was open to all manufacturers and wholesalers and the subscription was not expensive, one guinea per year.[20] However members were elected by the Committee that run the Association,[21] only after nomination by another member of the same committee, ensuring the creation of a peer group. The Association signalled the quality of its membership by expelling any of its

---

[18] BJA, The Birmingham Jewellers and Silversmiths Association, Rules, Booklet, MS 1646/1.

[19] A. Marshall, *Industry and Trade*, (Macmillan, 1919), pp. 284–7.

[20] In addition members were asked to subscribe discretionary sums to the Association's individual activities, such as the Vigilance committee, the School committee etc.

[21] The Association was run by a Committee made of the Chairman, a Vice-Chair, Treasurer, Honorary Secretary, Auditor and Secretary plus ten other members on a one-year term (General Committee). The Committee elects the Emergency Committee (five members) and appoints sub-committees (Vigilance, Art and Technical School, Insolvency).

members who became bankrupt[22] and it also ensured the quality of the people who worked for the members' firms by stipulating that members would not engage workpeople previously employed by other members without first obtaining a character, either written or oral, from such last employer.[23] The rules were stringent and the Association could expel any member if the Committee was not satisfied with his conduct. Membership of the Association could be interpreted as possessing a 'visible badge' of honesty whose quality was guaranteed by the self-appointed leaders of the trade, men who were its most respected members.

In the context of a volume in which empirical evidence and theoretical models are brought together it is important to look at the personalities behind the creation of the BJA. The following pages provide the evidence to show that the invisible hand of the market had not created high trust links at a commercial level within the Birmingham jewellery industrial district. Honest behaviour had to be codified and trust created through the observance of clear rules. As Mark Casson writes, 'People need to be brought together before trust between them can be engineered. Creating a web of contacts from scratch is an entrepreneurial activity'.[24] Who were the men who created these rules, who brought the jewellers together?

The establishment of the BJA had been preceded by two other attempts at association that had sunk without trace. Certainly the adverse economic contingency experienced by the trade in 1887 focused the jewellers' minds and provided a strong incentive for collective action. The Association, however, grew and prospered beyond the contingent moment. The two entrepreneurs who initiated and carried on this process through the first difficult years were Jacob Jacobs and Charles Green. Great personalities, with high profile reputations, a Jew and an Anglican, representatives of the main religious communities in the Quarter, both city councillors and prominent businessmen. Jacobs was born in Sheffield in 1839 and his father, a wholesale jeweller, moved to Birmingham in 1852 where the trade was booming. Jacobs after working for his father as a traveller joined him as a partner and the business prospered and by 1871 he and his family had moved to a large house in Handsworth.[25] Zoë Joseph, the chronicler of Birmingham Jews defines him as, 'the outstanding entrepreneur in the jewellery trade'.[26] It was Jacobs who, in the spring of 1887, called a private meeting of the leading jewellery manufacturers to put forward the suggestion that they should, 'invite the aid of the Princess of Wales to bring about a revival of the fashion of wearing

---

[22] Or who had settled with his creditors payments of less than 20 shillings to the pound.

[23] BJA, Booklet, Rules, MS 1646/1.

[24] Chapter 2 in this volume.

[25] A leafy, residential area north of the Quarter.

[26] Zoë Joseph, 'Jewellers, Watchmakers and Silversmiths', typescript, Birmingham Central Library, c.a. 1965, p. 12.

jewellery'.[27] Subsequently Jacobs and Green travelled to London and were successful in gaining the Princess' support. Again it was Jacobs who called the meeting of 200 jewellers in August 1887 that led to the creation of the BJA. Jacobs' standing in the community owed to more than his success as a jeweller. In 1887 he had been successful in local politics being returned as a Conservative for All Saints' ward and had become well known for his severity as a magistrate.[28] Jacobs however showed himself to be a man of vision through another venture as one of the originators and founders of the Great Western Arcade built in 1875. This was the first shopping arcade to be built in Birmingham and Jacobs was chairman of the company that owned it. In the words of a contemporary source, '[The Great Western Arcade] is said to be the finest in the world, the arcade at Milan being the only one to compare with it ... Those tradespeople who were fortunate enough to secure shops in it when it was opened have for the most part found it profitable to remain. The rents are low and the traffic enormous'.[29]

Jacobs was the man who brought the jewellers together, however the first chairman of the BJA was Charles Green, his companion on the visit to the Princess of Wales. Born in 1844, to a well-established family of jewellers, Green was slightly younger than Jacobs but just as well known. In 1884 he had taken his seat in the Council Chamber as Liberal representative of St. Paul's ward (in the heart of the Jewellery Quarter), a seat he kept until his death in 1906.[30] If Jacobs was the visionary who realised the need for the Association, it was Green whose reputation validated its activities during the first difficult years. Green's reputation was not just that of a successful business man but, more importantly in this case, of a man of high standards and honesty, symbolised by his appointment by the Assay office as Guardian of the Standard of Wrought Plate in 1882.[31] His reputation led him to the appointment in 1890 as examiner for Great Britain and the Colonies in goldsmith's work to the City and Guilds of London Institute.[32] He too served as a magistrate and he also served as a member of the council of the Midland Institute and of the Central Library Association.[33]

The rules of the game

Initial interest in the Association was high and by the end of September 1887 at least 70 people had joined. However, the BJA's plans for the reform of

---

[27] Ibid.

[28] *Handsworth*, Obituary, Vol.2, 1895–1896.

[29] *Birmingham Faces and Places*, Vol. 4, 1891–2, p. 150

[30] Jacobs and Green's paths had crossed already in 1884 when Jacobs run, unsuccessfully, for the St. Paul's ward seat. *Birmingham Faces and Places*, Vol. 4, 1891–2, p. 150.

[31] *Birmingham Evening Dispatcher*, Obituary, 4 January 1906.

[32] *Birmingham Daily Post*, Obituary, 4 January 1906.

[33] *Birmingham Daily Gazette*, Obituary, 5 January 1906.

commercial behaviour could work only if a large number of people joined and conformed to the rules. Hence, the Association's strategy was to attract members by offering services that would protect their interests while at the same time enforcing a specific code of conduct that would enhance the trade's reputation. The most pressing problem that needed solving was that of bankruptcies and their effect on the trade. For this reason the first meeting of the Emergency Committee, held on 6 January 1888 at 14, Bennetts Hill[34] resolved that its initial purpose would be to deal with those traders who defaulted on their payments and to call meetings of those members who were creditors and represent them in negotiations.[35]

The absence of rules of the game to codify standards of honest behaviour and trustworthiness increased transaction costs, to the extent of taking debtors to court in the hope to extracting some money from a bankrupt dealer. However, when factors or retailers went bankrupt the legal costs would eat into the estate, the size of the estate being determined by the sale at auction of what stock was left, often without a proper evaluation of this stock. The Association's role was to call a meeting of creditors,[36] investigate the debtor's finances using the services of a chartered accountant and evaluate the stock with the aim of reaching a settlement (usually the repayment, in instalments of a percentage of the debt) between creditors and debtors that would avoid court action and bankruptcy.[37] A settlement, monitored by the Association, would ensure that its members recouped a part of their losses, would eliminate the cost of a court case, ensure that no jewellery was sold below cost (hence protecting prices) and protect the reputation of the dealers.[38] This last point is a very important one. In making its investigations the Executive Committee's main duty was to ascertain whether traders were unable to pay their suppliers because of adverse trading conditions, incompetence or dishonesty. In the first two instances the Committee would recommend that a settlement be reached while dishonest behaviour was punished by seeking prosecution and bankruptcy. The fraudulent, bankrupt jeweller Alfred Bishton, who had escaped to Argentina in 1889 was pursued there by the Association, through pressure on the police and the Foreign Office. He was finally extradited two years later and the Association could close his case.[39]

---

[34]   In the offices of the Associations' secretary, a chartered accountant.

[35]   BJA, Emergency Committee, Minutes, MS 1646/1, 6 January 1888.

[36]   In the case of traders in other towns the Association would represent the Birmingham firms who were owed money.

[37]   BJA, Case of Samuel Basnett, Emergency Committee, Minutes, MS 1645/1, 25 October 1888. This case also shows that the Association did not always get it right. The composition scheme devised for Basnett's creditors could not be carried through and the estate went into liquidation after less than one year. Emergency Committee Minutes, MS 1645/1, 14 March 1889.

[38]   BJA, Case of William Brown, of Evans and Brown, General Committee, Minutes, MS 1645/1, 1 May 1891.

[39]   BJA, Case of Alfred Bishton, General Committee and Emergency Committee Minutes, MS 1645/1, multiple entries.

The services of the Association would reduce transaction costs for members as all matters were organised by the Executive Committee and its expertise and mediation could increase the chances of recovering debts. Moreover the Association acted as a watchdog, by assessing the honesty of traders. Those found lacking would be prosecuted and, if members, expelled from the Association. However, the assessment procedure could save a man's probity if the Association judged him to have failed due to circumstances outside his control, or incompetence. In the case of John Ashwin, to convince creditors to accept a settlement Charles Green, the Chairman of the Association, city councillor and owner of one of the oldest and most reputable firms in the Quarter, personally went through the debtor's stock, to ascertain its value. Green staked his reputation in a case in which the Association had verified that there was nothing culpable in Ashwin's trading but that failure had been due to bad debt. At the creditor's meeting the Association's spokesman testified to the reputation of the trader and put together a statement of his affairs guaranteeing for its veracity.[40] In this case, by imposing mediation between creditors and debtor, the Association avoided an honest man's name being called out the in bankrupts' court and appearing in the papers.[41] Even in those cases when a member had to become bankrupt the Association would be involved and deal with the sale of the estate (jewellery) to make sure that as much as possible was realised.[42]

The Association did not just concern itself with commercial relations but also with the quality of the goods sold by its members. In October 1890 the Birmingham firm of Blanckensee and Sons took another local firm, Evans and Sons to court. Evans had supplied Blanckensee with bracelets with a lower gold content than the 9 carat Assay office stamp imprinted on them.[43] The court was to establish whether Evans had committed an innocent mistake or had acted fraudulently. The firm was a member of the Association but the BJA declined to represent them in court, or to send a witness to speak to the quality of the jeweller's goods. In the event Evans were found guilty of fraud under the Merchandise Marks Act and fined ten pounds, plus costs. Shortly after the conclusion of the court case the slur on the firm's character induced the BJA to ask for the resignation of their membership.[44] The Association could be quite ruthless when it came to protecting the name of the trade by punishing those who compromised the quality of its goods. A Mr. A.E. Dudley had fled to

---

[40] BJA, Case of John Ashwin, Emergency Committee Minutes, MS 1645/1, 14 January 1889.

[41] BJA, Case of Louis Davis, General Committee Minutes, MS 1646/1, 13 April 1891.

[42] BJA, Case of William Lister, Emergency Committee Minutes, MS 1646/1, 14 December 1888.

[43] Fraudulent manufacturers could easily do this as gold from which bracelets were made was sent to the Assay Office in strips, to be tested and marked before being sent back to the manufacturer to be shaped up.

[44] *Birmingham Daily Gazette*, 20 October 1890; *Birmingham Daily Gazette*, 5 November 1890; BJA, General Committee Minutes, MS 1646/1, 19 January 1891.

America to avoid being prosecuted for removing the hallmark and transposing it on fake gold jewellery. In 1895 he was extradited back to Birmingham, brought to trial and sentenced to 18 months hard labour. The BJA had provided the case for the prosecution and acted as the principal witness.[45]

The determination of the BJA to protect its members and keep the Jewellery Quarter free of tricksters was considerable as were the resources it could command to absolve this task. In April 1897 the Emergency Committee received information from one of its members, Mr. Griffin of Hylton Street, on the activities of a Mr. Rose, claiming to represent the Brussels firm of A. Baum. Rose was obtaining goods from the trade and allegedly selling them in Brussels. Griffin 'had trusted' the firm to the extent of £18 but could not get his money. Another BJA member, Mr. E.A. Marsh of Northampton Street, had also sent goods to Rose for £34, but could not get paid. On 27 April the Committee resolved to send Chief Detective Inspector Van Helden of the Birmingham Police to Brussels. On his return, three days later, he reported that there was no firm in Brussels with an office in the Jewellery Quarter and that Rose's real name was Rosenbaum. A visit to the firm showed that Rosembaum had fled taking jewellery belonging to four firms worth £101.[46] Episodes such as these were instrumental in the decision taken by the Association the following year to start a Trade Enquiry and Debt collection scheme.[47] This decision was taken after agreeing to exchange information with the London Wholesale Jewellers' and Allied Trades Association who had information on about 4500 jewellers. In addition to the London list the Association was to use an enquiry agency and build its own file by using information generated within the trade.[48] These sources, however, were not thought to be sufficient and the Association also resorted to make enquiries directly to members. The language used by the Association to ensure the success of this scheme is revealing and deserves to be related in full, 'Your Committee earnestly asks members, for their mutual benefit, to be perfectly loyal to each other when answering enquiries. Mutual trust is the basis of our system, and a member who answers an enquiry today may himself require a similar benefit tomorrow. The Committee trusts that no member will refuse to give information when requested'.[49] The debt collection scheme also shows the importance placed by the Association in peer pressure as it thought that 'demand for payment made from an Association containing the majority of the best known firms, comes with greater force and is more successful in obtaining the money [than] if the

---

[45]   BJA, Vigilance Committee report, Annual Report, 1895, MS 1646/262.

[46]   Rosenbaum had fled after receiving a letter from Marsh, dated 27 April threatening to put the matter in the hands of the police if R. didn't pay. BJA, Emergency Committee Minutes, MS 1646/3, 3 June, 1897.

[47] BJA, General Committee Minutes, MS 1646/3, 28 December 1898.

[48]   At the AGM in October 1899 the chairman of the Association urged members to provide information on any firm that had suspended payments.

[49]   BJA, Text of the letter sent to members advertising the scheme, Annual Report, 1899, MS 1646/263.

same demand is made by an outside agent'.[50] The trade enquiry and debt collection service cost members an additional guinea per year,[51] and how successful the Association's activities were can be judged by the following figures. By the end of 1899 more than 700 enquiries had been made, 182 debts had been sent for collection for a total of £1642, of which £1285 had been collected.[52]

The evidence from the Birmingham Jewellery Quarter shows that the embeddedness of social relations might have been effective at weeding out malfeasance only to some degree, such as the exchange of goods through the productive chain. In December 1888 the Emergency Committee presented the General committee with a report on theft and receiving stolen goods in the Quarter with a view to establishing a Vigilance committee. The Association had obtained evidence through interviews with the thirty leading firms in the trade that showed the scale of the problem. Theft in workshops by workers was systematic and it went mostly undetected as employers were reluctant to exercise constant vigilance. The BJA estimated that about £30,000 worth of gold and jewellery was lost every year because of theft.[53] Of the thefts detected a very small number were punished because it took time and money to get a prosecution and employers found it easier to discharge workers, who could just find a job elsewhere. Judges were very lenient and in the Association's view allowed 'flabby sentimentalism' to get in the way of their judgement and such leniency in fact encouraged theft. The real scourge of the trade, however, were receivers of stolen property. These were well known in the Quarter, jewellers, bullion dealers, even publicans providing temptation and 'corrupting apprentices and journeymen'.[54] Lack of proof made the conviction of receivers very difficult and in the seven years between 1883 and 1890 only two receivers were prosecuted successfully.[55] This evidence shows the failure of any invisible, social mechanism in eliminating dishonest behaviour, despite the existence of all those factors that should have encouraged embeddeddness, such as proximity and the regular repetition of transactions.

The Association understood that individual firm owners were not resourceful and powerful enough to fight this problem and that collective action was needed. After lengthy discussions, the General Committee decided in the spring of 1890 to require all its members to provide it with immediate information of any theft or suspicion of theft so that the person suspected could be traced back to the receivers if possible. In this the Association would be aided by two police officers, Detective Black and Inspector Monk, assisted by

---

[50]   BJA, General Committee Minutes, MS 1646/3, 28 December 1898.
[51]   For one guinea members could make twenty-fve enquiries, additional ones had to be paid extra. BJA, General Committee Minutes, MS 1646/3, 10 July 1899.
[52]   BJA, Annual Report, 1899, MS 1646/263.
[53]   In the report it was estimated that over the course of the year about fifty tons of precious metals were used by the trade, for total value of about £350,000 and the amount stolen represented about ten per cent of the total value of jewellery produced in the Quarter.
[54]   BJA, General Committee Minutes, MS 1646/1, 14 December 1888.
[55]   BJA, General Committee Minutes, MS 1646/1, 18 May 1890.

a boy employed by the Association at eight shillings a week.[56] Where prosecution was thought desirable this was to be undertaken by the Association and its officers, thus reducing the loss of time and money (as half of the legal costs were paid by the BJA) by individual members. Furthermore 'the moral effect of having a powerful association as a prosecutor [will] correspondingly dishearten and deter offenders'.[57] The pages of the minutes of the Vigilance Committee show the determination and ruthlessness of the Association in prosecuting thieves and its first case sets the tone of what was to follow. Three days before Christmas, in 1890, Mr. Allday, a BJA member, reported that one of his work-girls had been taken in charge for stealing a ring. He declared himself quite willing to prosecute the girl in the name of his firm but the Association decided to take the case up and make an example of her. The following February the girl, Annie Hemming, received two months hard labour for the theft of the ring. The solicitor's bill was £2 and 2 shillings, more than the cost of the ring, to which Allday contributed half.[58] The activities of the BJA from the management of insolvency, to credit checks and policing, established it firmly as the main body representing the Birmingham jewellery trade. By 1900 its membership had risen to 226[59] and the Association prospered beyond the contingency of the Depression, into the twentieth century and the present one.[60]

Conclusion

These pages paint a picture of endemic dishonesty, of an industrial district rife with malfeasance and mistrust, rather different from the cosy relationships described by embeddedness theorists. The example of the Jewellery Quarter shows that the district (in the Marshallian sense) does not necessarily generate the social capital needed to control malfeasance and opportunism. Dishonesty and the absence of trust in commercial relations increased transaction costs for honest traders. The BJA created the conditions for the reduction of these costs through the assessment of the character of its members and of the value of the stock belonging to insolvent traders. The Association monitored the activity of traders in the Quarter through credit checks and active investigation and enforced the law in the case of dishonest behaviour.

---

[56] BJA, General Committee Minutes, entry on Vigilance Committee, MS 1646/1, 17 March 1890. By 1893 the Association had convinced enough members to subscribe to the cost of plain-clothes Officers to patrol the Quarter at night. Their beats overlapped those of ordinary policemen and as a consequence night-time theft disappeared from the district. See Mason, *Jewellery-making in Birmingham*, p. 90.
[57] BJA, General Committee Minutes, MS 1646/1, 18 May 1890.
[58] BJA, General Committee Minutes, MS 1646/1, 22 December 1890 and 9 February 1891.
[59] BJA, Annual Report, 1900, MS 1646/263.
[60] A very summary history of the BJA can be found in: S.N. Nott, *The British Jewellers Association, 1887–1987, 100 Years of Service* (BJA, 1987).

The BJA was the expression of the will to co-operate to establish mechanisms to control the business community and codify norms of behaviour. *Conscious co-ordination* was needed. The embeddedness of social relations was not sufficient. It is probable that embeddedness did not work for at least two reasons. The ease of entry into the trade meant that social networks were constantly changing their configuration without the existing members being able to place any check on the size of the population. Certainly the BJA was not able to enforce honesty across the whole of the trade, but by restricting access to its membership it ensured standards of behaviour within its own community. The second reason for the failure of embeddedness within the Quarter was the strong incentive to behave in an opportunistic fashion created by the district's own productive structure. The production of jewellery relied on the existence of different workshops, bullion dealers, wholesalers/factors and the availability of skilled and semi-skilled workers. As long as production ran smoothly then the Quarter flourished and everybody prospered. However around this healthy body parasitic activities could flourish in the absence of standards of practice and of law enforcement, such as receivership, fraud and theft. Jewellery-makers, for example, might have strongly disapproved of bullion dealers acting as receivers of stolen property but as long as the precious metals provided were of the correct standard the manufacturer had no incentive to change supplier. At the same time moral sanctions were clearly not working as a disincentive with respect to the illegal activities of the bullion dealers.

The governance structures set up by the BJA were extremely successful in solving the problems that beset the district and might go a long way towards explaining the success of the Jewellery Quarter well into the twentieth century.[61]

---

[61] In 1991 48 per cent of the gold, silver and platinum pieces made in Britain were assayed in Birmingham. This figure can be used as a proxy for the precious goods manufactured in the Midlands. The other three assay offices, London, Sheffield and Edinburgh followed with 33, 16 and three per cent respectively. British Hall-marking Council, *Report 1990–1991*, Appendix 5, p. 10.

Chapter 11

Networks and industrial restructuring: The Widnes district and the formation of the United Alkali Company, 1890

Andrew Popp

Introduction

In the summer of 1871 Ludwig Mond wrote from Widnes to his parents in Germany, full of excitement at the potential offered by the rapidly growing Lancashire chemical town:

> here where we have fifty factories in a few square miles, are many factories, some of which have started in a very small way and which deal with only a very small part of soda manufacturing. They buy the by-products from the other factories, or sell their products to other factories for working up ... We have many examples of small factories which have hit on the right branch.

A year later, his enthusiasm undimmed, he noted how:

> there is nowhere in the world where a factory could be set up with such ease and small capital, and where such working power can be found.[1]

In these letters Mond provided a near-text book description of the industrial district; the clustered matrix of small, interdependent partial process firms, the ferment provided by the spur such an environment gave to entrepreneurship. And yet, less than twenty years later, this vibrant business structure was apparently swept away by the formation in 1890 of the United Alkali Company. The UAC, combining virtually all of that part of the British soda industry committed to the old Leblanc process, was a behemoth, for a time perhaps the largest industrial concern in the world, the very antithesis of that which it had supplanted.

---

[1]   Letters from Ludwig Mond to his parents, 17 September 1871 and 1872 (date unspecified), quoted in D.W.F. Hardie *A History of the Chemical Industry in Widnes* (ICI General Chemicals Division, 1950), p. 64.

Judgements on the UAC have been unvaryingly harsh. Reader, in his official history of Imperial Chemical Industries, into which the UAC was absorbed in 1926, condemned the firm as 'the supreme example of that decadence in late Victorian British industry which alarmed some contemporaries and has since fascinated economic historians'. He went on to detail how the firm was:

> dedicated to the preservation of a dying industry ... The management displayed nepotism, amateurism, lack of technical knowledge and scientific training, and it's policy was based on all the things right-minded people abhor: restrictions of output, price-fixing, market-sharing, instead of good, clean, ruthless competition.[2]

In other words, despite emerging directly from the environment viewed so positively by Mond twenty years earlier, the UAC was thoroughly rotten in intent and effect.[3] Our aim here is not a rehabilitation of the UAC but instead to revisit the formation of the company in the light of advances in network theory. In particular, we will argue that the formation of the UAC was more a continuation of rather than a break with the evolving networking behaviour displayed in the Widnes district prior to 1890. Existing networks, which had played a central role in successfully building the industry from the mid-nineteenth century onwards, facilitated and survived the formation of the company. It is hoped, first, that by studying this important case of restructuring insight will be gained into the relationship between networks, clusters and restructuring, hitherto a neglected dimension in many studies of districts and clusters.[4] Second, tracing the form and impact of networks before, during and after the restructuring process may allow us to discern more clearly their essential characteristics.

The important continuities between the networks of a vibrant Widnes c.1870 and the structure and governance of the UAC also points to reflection on choices made in Britain in this period with regard to corporate structures and in particular the emergence of the holding company structure as a characteristic organizational form. We may ask a simple question: if networks are almost always good then why is the similarly loosely structured holding company almost wholly bad? As Fitzgerald has argued, '[i]f established links, personal

---

[2]   W.J. Reader, *Imperial Chemical Industries: A History. Volume 1, The Forerunners, 1870–1926* (Oxford University Press, 1970), p. 122.

[3]   Perhaps this is to some extent a case of to the victor the spoils, for Reader does not adopt a similar stance towards Brunner, Mond's own participation in extensive market-sharing agreements with other firms.

[4]   For a critique of static approaches to industrial district research see: U. Staber, 'An Ecological Perspective on Entrepreneurship in Industrial Districts', *Entrepreneurship and Regional Development*, 9 (1997), pp. 45–64. For an attempt to address restructuring see: A. Rinaldi 'The Emilian Model Revisited (and Revised): Twenty Years Later', paper presented at *Responses to Innovation: The 2001 Conference of the Association of Business Historians*, 29-30 July 2001, Portsmouth.

connections and customary practice can substitute for formal administrative hierarchy, they might operate effectively within federated organisational structures, groups and holding companies'.[5] However, this avenue of enquiry is beyond the scope of the present study.

Chapter structure

The chapter is in five main parts. In the first, we will briefly review business networks in theory. In particular, we will probe the links drawn between network formation and the socio-economic context generated by spatial clustering; the social embeddedness perspective. This is important because the particularities of the context in which networks were generated in Widnes meant that only to a limited degree did 'community-based networks ... [form] an ideal interface between the market and firms'.[6] Widnes provides the exception with which to test the rule. Broad processes of restructuring will also be briefly considered. Then, third, the nature of network formation and function in Widnes prior to 1890 will be explored and contextualized in terms of the conditions under which they emerged. It will be argued that the Widnes chemical industry displayed a highly networked structure but did not fully conform to that of the 'ideal-typical industrial district'. The radical restructuring of 1890 will be explored in a fourth section outlining the characteristics, behaviour and impact of network structures immediately prior to and after 1890. The final section will reflect on networks and restructuring.

Regional business networks in theory

Prior to the 1840s the space that Widnes was to occupy was open farmland; host to neither socio-economic nor socio-spatial structures bearing any meaningful or determining relationship to the industrial town that was to blossom there. Thus the formation and growth of the Widnes chemical industry district poses a challenge to what Granovetter has labelled the '"strong embeddedness"' perspective on industrial districts.[7] Certainly, it is possible to detect *over time* the emergence of various patterns of social structure (norms

[5] R. Fitzgerald 'The Competitive and Institutional Advantages of Holding Companies: British Business in the Inter-war Period', *Journal of Industrial History*, Vol. 3, No. 2 (2000), p. 19. See also, G. Boyce, *Information, Mediation and Institutional Development: The Rise of Large-Scale Enterprise in British Shipping, 1870–1919* (Manchester University Press, 1995).

[6] M.B. Rose, 'Networks and Leadership Succession in British Business in the 1950s', in W. Feldenkirchen and T. Gourvish (eds), *European Yearbook of Business History*, No. 1 (Ashgate, 1998), p. 60.

[7] M. Granovetter, 'Problems of Explanation in Economic Sociology' in N. Nohria and R.G. Eccles (eds), *Networks and Organizations: Structure, Form and Action* (Harvard Business School Press, 1992), p. 28.

and conventions embodied in both formal and informal institutions) supportive of the deepening clustering of the industry in the district. But the embeddedness perspective, taking as its explanatory starting point the social matrix in which industry is embedded, offers few insights into either the *processes* or the *causal relationships* involved. This is particularly so with regard to the nature and role of business networks in Widnes.

Instead, respectful of the highly dynamic nature of the story that unfolded in Widnes over the second-half of the nineteenth century, we are intrigued by Nohria's claim that, from a network analysis perspective, networks 'are as much process as they are structure, being continually shaped and reshaped by the action of actors'.[8] This, then, will be one concern; to illuminate the processes of network formation. Such an approach necessarily problematizes issues such as the identification of network membership, a problem sublimated in the embeddedness perspective by an emphasis on the possession of shared attributes (defined *a priori* as significant) as a marker of membership. We are, for example, sceptical of Piore's claim that networks are a 'canonical organizational form' analytically separable 'from markets and hierarchies'.[9] Stress on the dynamic, processural nature of network relations recasts them permeable rather than bounded and mutable rather than stable, penetrating economic life, in Granovetter's words, 'irregularly and in different degrees'.[10]

However, we are also struck by the degree of agency afforded to actors in analytical perspectives on networks. Here it is important to stress how Nohria goes on to note that whilst actors may through their own agency shape their position in networks of relationships they are also 'in turn constrained by the structural position in which they find themselves'.[11] Melding both agency and constraint, network relations may then function as loci for the creation and operation of power, power lying in structural position. As outlined in Chapter 1, whether exerted through 'formal authority, informal influence [or] overt domination', power may be derived from three 'resources'; legitimacy, information and force. Power accrues to positions in networks characterized by relative centrality or autonomy, positions through which 'valued information and resources are transferred' from actor to actor.[12] Such claims obviously bear some relationship to Casson's emphasis, in this volume, on 'leadership' in regional business networks. However, they are also germane to processes of

---

[8]   N. Nohria, 'Introduction: Is a Network Perspective a Useful Way of Studying Organizations?' in Nohria and Eccles (eds), *Networks and Organizations*, p. 7. Similarly, Granovetter argues that structures of relationships can 'rarely be understood except as accretions of ... processes ... over time'. M. Granovetter 'Problems of Explanation', p. 34.

[9]   M.J. Piore, 'Fragments of a Cognitive Theory of Technological Change and Organizational Structure' in Nohria and Eccles, *Networks and Organizations*, p. 430.

[10]   M. Granovetter, 'Economic Action, Social Structure and Embeddedness', *American Journal of Sociology*, 91 (1985), p. 491.

[11]   Nohria, 'Introduction', p. 7.

[12]   W.W. Powell and L. Smith-Doerr, 'Networks and Economic Life' in N.J. Smelser and R. Swedberg (eds), *The Handbook of Economic Sociology* (Princeton University Press, 1994), p. 376–7.

allocation, coordination and restructuring. It is to a brief examination of the latter process that we now turn.

Processes of restructuring

Industrial restructuring, sectoral or regional, occurs through two mechanisms; through the birth and death of firms and through the growth or evolution of incumbent firms.[13] Restructuring through change within firms results from interaction between the economic environment and the capabilities, internal and external, available to the firm. Business networks may often play an important role in allowing entrepreneurs access to the varied resources necessary to grow or reshape the firm in response to new opportunities, fresh 'conjectures', perceived in the environment.[14] The birth of new firms arises from signals that there exist opportunities that incumbent firms are unable or unwilling to exploit. Again networks may assist in this process by conveying such signals.

Effective restructuring is then dependent on timely and accurate signalling with regard to opportunities for and constraints upon the allocation and co-ordination of resources. As already noted, networks very often play an important role in this process. However, they may also perform this role poorly, conveying inaccurate signals or blocking accurate signals. Networks need to be able to respond to the changing issues of allocation and co-ordination facing an industry.

Both processes of restructuring were at work in Widnes in the nineteenth century, with business networks playing a central role in both. However, across time, the two processes did not carry the burden of restructuring equally. Instead, as the environment altered and business networks evolved, there was a shift in the restructuring mechanisms prevalent in the Widnes district from the formation of new firms to the (radical) reshaping of incumbent firms.

Networks in Widnes before 1890

Reader traced the creation of the UAC to the formation in 1883 of the *Lancashire Bleaching Powder Manufacturer's Association* (LBPMA). For Reader:

> The main positive result of the Association seems to have been to force the leading men of the Lanchashire Leblanc industry to meet much more

---

[13] M.T. Hannan and G.R. Carroll, *Dynamics of Organizational Populations: Density, Legitimation and Competition* (Oxford University Press, 1992).

[14] J.S. Metcalfe, 'Institutions and Progress', *Industrial and Corporate Change*, Vol. 10, No. 3 (2001), pp. 561–86.

frequently. They seem thereby to have developed a liking for each other's company, at least in a business sense.[15]

The LBPMA was certainly an important institution in the evolution of the UAC, however the leading men of the Lancashire Leblanc industry had been 'forced' to develop a 'liking for each other's company' at a much earlier date.

What then was the context in which Widnes chemical district emerged and evolved? Contextualizing factors can be identified at meta, macro and micro-levels.

Important at a meta-level were the state of knowledge and modes of enquiry in chemistry as a science. Both were relatively unsophisticated in the first half of the nineteenth century. Much basic chemistry remained poorly or partially understood and knowledge imperfectly formalized and codified. Methods and equipment of process control, both in the laboratory and in manufacture, were characterized by rule-of-thumb. These conditions impacted on the nature of the knowledge and information both available to and required by potential entrepreneurs.

At the same time, at a macro-level, few countries hosted any significant chemical industries and amongst these Britain was dominant. However, despite rising demand consequent upon industrialization and urbanization, the range of products manufactured was limited. Chemical manufacture thus offered many opportunities. Moreover, the Widnes chemical industry was to develop in the context of powerful trading nation possessed of a highly sophisticated mercantile system and dedicated to a political economy of free trade. These conditions allowed British manufacturers of heavy chemicals to establish first mover advantage in the early nineteenth century even though several key innovations, including the Leblanc process, were made abroad. Narrowing the focus somewhat the North-west region, in which the Widnes district was located, was home to several important and growing industries for which chemicals formed key inputs, including glass, soap and paper making and, most obviously, cotton. This pattern of industrialization generated vital commercial and transport infrastructure and ancillary industries, including coal mining and engineering, on all of which the nascent chemical industry of the region drew.

The material flows and process linkages typical of the alkali industry at the mid-nineteenth century, embedded in a distinct spatial system, offered considerable potential for generating complex cross-sectoral, cross-regional, multi-institutional linkages. Key inputs, salt and coal, were sourced locally, from the vicinity of Northwich in Cheshire and St Helens respectively, but others, including pyrites and limestone came from further afield, Spain and Derbyshire respectively. In simple terms, the manufacture of alkali encompassed two basic stages, the manufacture of saltcake and, from that, the production of alkali. As Mond's letters implied, these two central processes

---

[15]   Reader, *Imperial Chemical Industries*, p. 102.

might or might not be performed by the same firm. Engineering, another important input, also rapidly became highly localized whilst there also grew up a secondary sector devoted to the extraction of copper from waste. Outputs were consumed in glass and soap manufacture, both highly localized in nearby St Helens and Warrington respectively, and in the Lancashire cotton textile industry. Considerable quantities were also exported through the brokers and docks at Liverpool. At the same time chemical manufacturers also reached both backward and forward through a variety of linkages. Thus, whilst rival manufacturers at the central stages might co-operate in securing supplies of Spanish pyrites, through the formation of the Tharsis Sulphur and Copper Co., individual alkali manufacturers might also act as partners in downstream industries, such as soap manufacture.[16]

However, a close reading of the network literature suggests that it is at the micro-level of the specific locale that we will find the most significant environmental influences on network formation and that these will be primarily located within community and other social structures. However, when John Hutchinson first leased land there in 1848, laying the foundations of its chemical industry, Widnes, to all intents and purposes, did not exist. There was no spatially and temporally rooted social structure in which business networks could be readily embedded or emerge from, only the very small farming communities of Appleton and Farnworth. Indeed, if the pioneers of the Widnes chemical industry shared anything it was their status as outsiders – many having pursued highly peripatetic careers prior to settling on the banks of the Mersey. If there was any tissue of culture linking entrepreneurs it was pan-European and scientific, with Professor Bunsen at the University of Heidelberg, for example, providing a node that linked several actors.

However, this situation did not prevent the rapid growth of the industry in Widnes so that it soon eclipsed older, more established centres in the region, most notably at St Helens but also at Runcorn and at Flint in North Wales. Equally rapidly there emerged a number of important complementarities; in labour supplies and in functionally associated areas, including engineering (supplying plant) and in copper extraction and in the manufacture of lime, fertiliser and soap (utilising waste and by-products). However, we reiterate, social embeddedness *cannot* provide a meaningful explanation of any role played by networks in these processes.

Nonetheless, networks of relationships did play a central role in this process. What was their basis? We can attempt to identify and classify the range of network-like linkages operating in the Widnes district chemical industry in the period 1850–90. It should be noted that here the nodes of the network are people and that the relative linearity of process linkages was replaced by a welter of criss-crossing interconnections. Linkage types included those based

---

[16] Founded in 1866 by Sir Charles Tennant but with important Widnesian Leblanc manufacturers, including Henry Deacon, on the Board. Reader, *Imperial Chemical Industries*, p. 105

in friendship, education, employment, partnership and contracting, often in combination.

Despite Mond's claim that nowhere could the chemical industry be so easily entered as at Widnes, aspirant entrepreneurs still needed to assemble large and complex sets of resources, not least some understanding of both the science of chemistry and experience of operationalising such knowledge on an industrial scale. These were complementary and overlapping but not identical requirements. At this stage in the development of the cluster, the varied resources to which they had access defined both actors' interests and their positions within nascent structures of relationships. Networks emerged in response to the need to assemble complementary sets of resources. The Leblanc process, though relatively old, was far from fully developed, particularly in terms of its industrial applications. Thus the situation was relatively fluid. Given the state of knowledge and modes of enquiry in chemistry, firm capabilities and routines were necessarily nascent. The primary requirement was for knowledge relating to processes rather than market information. At the same time, the potential for an array of interdependencies encouraged cross-fertilization and spin-offs.

The ramifications of this situation for both industry structure and networking behaviour are readily apparent if we examine a figure such as John Hutchinson. Hutchinson laid the foundations of the industry in Widnes in 1848 by establishing his own works and by leasing the land and installing the infrastructure that came in time to support many other firms. However, he also did much more. Hutchinson came to Widnes via employment at the St Helens works of A. Kurtz. At Widnes, Hutchinson soon employed Henry Deacon, then in his late twenties, as works manager. Deacon had roots in London mercantile society but had been apprenticed to the engineering firms of first Galloway and Sons and then, in Manchester, Naysmyth and Gaskell (who, in another link, installed the first steam hammer at Muspratt's Widnes works). This latter position was to be the foundation on which Gaskell, Deacon and Co. was built in 1855. However, in the meantime Deacon moved in to alkali, first at Pilkington's in St. Helens in 1846 and then at Hutchinson's. Having now gained considerable experience in both engineering and chemicals, Deacon, with the support of Pilkington's, his former employers, began on his own account in Widnes in 1853. Pilkington's soon withdrew but Deacon could again draw on contacts forged with earlier employers, Naysmyth and Gaskell. In time Deacon gave employment to Eustace Carey and Dr Ferdinand Hurter, respectively first Secretary and first Chief Chemist of the UAC.

Hurter gained his PhD at Heidelberg, where Ludwig Mond too studied. However, it was at Hutchinson's No. 1 works that Mond first established his career in England. From 1861, acting in a consulting role, Mond blended his own formal scientific training and inventiveness with Hutchinson's experience in producing alkali on an industrial scale to perfect Mond's sulphur recovery process, both men understanding the importance of fully utilizing all waste and by-products. Employed as clerks at Hutchinson's at this time were two young men of Swiss extraction, Henry and John Tomlinson Brunner. The initial link between Mond and the Brunners was one of friendship, and together they and others, including Eustace Carey, James Muspratt and other young managers of local works, formed a small, informal philosophical club.

Hutchinson's influence extended yet further. Ex-employees R. Powell and Thomas Snape were others to leave Hutchinson as part of a second wave of firm foundings in the 1860s and 1870s. Through Kurtz, Hutchinson also met St. Helens engineer Thomas Robinson, who helped construct much of the plant for his original No. 1 works. In turn, in 1860, Robinson left St. Helens for Widnes to establish a foundry on Lugsdale Road, reinforcing the town's growing array of complementary trades.[17]

In this period then the necessarily fluid business networks of the Widnes district expressed themselves in a pattern of structural growth and development shaped by the birth of new firms. Drawing on the range of network linkages available to them entrepreneurs assembled the resources and, in particular, accumulated the knowledge they needed to enter into business on their own account. As Metcalfe observes, '[t]he network relationships that provide conduits for … relevant information do not occur naturally; they too have to be constructed'.[18] These were networks of opportunity. In the process, patterns of learning and innovation were enscribed into the routines and capabilities of firms. At the same time relatively benign market conditions ensured that the challenge of fashioning a sectoral level governance system was relatively simple.

Mention of governance directs attention to the issue of power. Given the fluidity of the situation and the 'inherently situational … dynamic and potentially unstable' nature of power, this attribute remained relatively widely distributed. However, whilst not able to completely sever all ties of dependence on the resources possessed by others, a figure such as Hutchinson was clearly beginning to construct a position of some centrality or autonomy in the district. In part he played an important role as a broker controlling access to flows of important resources, such as information and, perhaps most crucially, experience. At the same time, as the founding father of the industry in the town, Hutchinson possessed both legitimacy (informal influence) and, through both control of land and transport infrastructure and the establishment of patron-client relationships with ex-employees, the potential for overt domination. Legitimacy and the potential for overt domination may have acted in mutually reinforcing ways.

---

[17] Information in the three preceding paragraphs derived from Hardie, *History of the Chemical Industry*. There are interesting parallels between Hutchinson and some of the Coventry firms described by Lloyd-Jones and Lewis (see Chapter 12 in this volume).

[18] Metcalfe, 'Institutions and Progress', p. 579.

Networks and the formation of the UAC

The proximate spurs to the formation of the UAC were, first, Brunner, Mond's successful innovation of the much cheaper Solvay process for the manufacture of alkali and, second, the formation of the Salt Union, which held an effective monopoly in the supply of salt. But networks in the Widnes district had begun to change from the 1870s onwards. In particular there was a shift towards more formal methods of co-operation that may be associated with both the growing maturity of the industry and with change in the interests of key actors. Associational activity now came to the fore. Reader dates the 'forcing' together of the Leblanc manufacturers to the formation of the LBPMA in 1883. However, they had much earlier embarked on formal association with the formation of the *Widnes Traders Association* in 1874. In Scranton's typography of regionally-centred associational forms, an 'area cross-sectoral organization', the WTA was in fact dominated by the town's leading chemical manufacturers and provided an effectively conducted forum through which the industry could meet and forge coherent policies with regard to shared issues.[19]

To an extent the WTA and LBPMA, active at the dawn of a major revolution with regard to processes, represented an attempt to stabilize the environment and to institutionalize the more loosely coupled networks that had characterized the district from the late 1840s through to the mid-1870s. As Scranton notes, such institutions often served to 'establish rules of business conduct ... regulating competition through governance practice'. Thus, the changing nature of network behaviour in the district was indicative of a shift in 'governance practice' that would help to prepare the ground for amalgamation.[20]

However, at first, the links between these initiatives and the formation of the UAC appear unclear. Indeed, in early 1890, the conditions for closer co-operation appeared inauspicious at best; the LBPMA had just failed under the pressure of re-negotiation, whilst the WTA appeared to be all but moribund. At the beginning of the year *The Weekly News* carried a review of the chemical trade during the previous year written by Liverpool chemical brokers Messrs John Haddock and Co. The author had no doubt that:

> [t]he most striking, and in effect the most important event was the failure of the BPA to make arrangements to continue the combination for a restriction in the manufacture of bleaching powder. A strong effort was made to reconstitute the combination on the 'salt basis', but without success. Ineffectual efforts were also made in the early part of the year to

---

[19] P. Scranton, 'Webs of Productive Association in American Industrialization: Patterns of Institution Formation and their Limits: Philadelphia, 1880–1930', *Journal of Industrial History*, Vol. 1, No. 1 (1998), p. 15.

[20] Ibid., p. 9.

form arrangements for the reduction of the output of caustic soda and chlorate of potash.[21]

A month later *The Weekly News* carried a report of the annual general meeting of the WTA, just four members attended, all of them current or past officers of the Permanent Executive Committee. Founding member T. Sutton Timmis unconvincingly averred that 'he thought the non-attendance of the members of the Association at that meeting showed that they were very busy and were satisfied with the way in which the association was conducted'.[22]

By May of the same year the local press was carrying reports of another joint response offered by the Widnes alkali manufacturers to the increasingly threatening situation they faced, the Widnes Brine Supply Bill, heard before a Committee of the House of Commons. The Bill proposed to raise a capital of £100,000 to lay a pipeline from the Cheshire salt fields direct to Widnes. In introducing their case, Counsel for the Widnes manufacturers noted the effect of both Brunner, Mond's innovation and the formation of the Salt Union, explaining how:

> [a]lkali was formerly made by a costly process known as the Le Blanc process; but recently a much cheaper process had been discovered, the ammonia soda process, by which alkali was made, especially by Messrs. Brunner, Mond and Co., and unless Widnes was enabled to obtain the brine direct her manufacturers would be most seriously handicapped.[23]

However, this was not simply a matter of self-interest, for:

> owing to the ingenious formation of the Salt Union the prices had much increased ... This increase in prices had reduced the export trade ... [and] prevented the development of the home trade. The Bill would, therefore, emancipate Widnes from an outrageous monopoly ... The opposition [to the bill] was not really that of the local boards nor of the occupiers but of the limited companies [i.e. Brunner, Mond and Co. and the Salt Union], who were very much alarmed lest their monopoly should come to an end.[24]

Several prominent members of the trade in Widnes appeared before the Committee, but their evidence was worryingly contradictory. Thus, WTA member C.K. Cross, of John Hutchinson and Sons, was 'of the opinion that unless they got the brine to work the new process [i.e. the Solvay process] the

---

[21] 'The Chemical Trade in 1890: Failure of the Bleaching Powder Association', John Haddock and Co., *The Weekly News*, 4 January 1890. The BPA had not been completely ineffectual for the review also noted that 'On it becoming generally known that BPA would terminate at the end of the year a steady fall in price took place'.

[22] *The Weekly News*, 8 February 1890.

[23] *The Weekly News*, 10 May 1890.

[24] Ibid.

Widnes works would have to close because they could not compete', but Thomas Snape, of T. Snape and Co., also a constituent firm of the UAC, when pressed on the alternative of moving closer to the supply of brine, admitted that '[t]hey would have to incur great expenses in altering their works to use the ammonia soda process. He wanted the salt cheaper so as to continue the Le Blanc process'.[25] The second day of the hearing exposed serious flaws in the engineering of the proposed pipeline and on the third and final day counsel for the opposition were able to successfully argue that the 'bill was really for the purpose of breaking up the Salt Union. The scheme was that of certain speculative gentlemen in Widnes and could not serve any public purpose'.[26] The bill was summarily rejected.

The events of early 1890 suggest that Widnes businessmen were receiving confused and ambiguous signals about the need to restructure, about the form any restructuring should take and how it might be achieved. The demise of the LBPMA and some of the evidence presented in support of the Brine Supply Bill suggests a failure to agree on how to respond to the threats posed by Brunner, Mond and the Salt Union, whilst poor attendance at the WTA suggests a simple lack of will to find grounds for agreement. In this light the very rapid formation of the UAC before the close of the year appears hard to explain. We need to dig deeper and explore the foundations that were to underpin amalgamation. These were much sounder than the trials of early 1890 suggested.

Certainly, the Brine Supply Bill was poorly thought out, a stopgap measure that was 'hastily considered and ill-matured' in the words on one opponent, but this was not the whole picture.[27] In contrast, the story of the WTA shows manufacturers working together successfully and provides an insight into the conditions under which such success might be achieved.

The WTA was long-lived, from 1874 until 1891, and its demise was due not to waning interest on the half of members but because its functions had been absorbed into the UAC. This relative permanency was matched by occasional employment of staff.[28] It was also an inclusive organization, attracting by far the greater part of its potential constituency. The reach of the organization's membership is demonstrated in an analysis of large local ratepayers in 1879 carried out by the WTA in relation to lobbying of the Local Board. Thus the 24 members of the WTA owned or occupied premises with a total rateable value (RV) of £30,739; the seven eligible non-members' total RV was £5726.

---

[25] Ibid. Hutchinsons and Snapes were both constituent firms of the UAC.

[26] *The Weekly News*, 17 May, 1890. Other arguments against the Bill sought to downplay the threat to Widnes of the Solvay process and Brunner, Mond. Indeed, G.E. Davies, former Government Inspector of alkali works, felt that 'there had been no substantial diminution of manufacture under the Le Blanc process. The new process would simply add to the trade of the place'.

[27] Ibid.

[28] DIC/UA17/30 WTA Committee Minute Book, CRO. Minutes of Permanent Executive Committee meeting, 8 January 1875, record that Wm. Perkins was 'temporarily employed ... to index papers'.

Members' total RV equalled 30 per cent of the annual rateable value of all properties in the town (including domestic properties) and 84 per cent of the rateable value of industrial and commercial properties. The equivalent figures for non-members are six and 16 per cent. Members were also typically larger than non-members, as measured by RV. The average RV of members was £1097 and of non-members £818. The only large chemical firms that were not members in 1879 were T. Snape and Co., the Atlas Chemical Co. and Mathieson and Co.[29]

Moreover, the *Association* seems to have had some authority with those firms that did not join. Thus in a circular issued by the WTA in 1878 to raise support for opposition to the Sheffield and Midland Railway Company bill the Association estimated its costs would be £400 and noted that:

> as the benefits of the clause, if obtained, will be enjoyed by all the Trades who have, or may have access to the S and M Committee's lines, the Executive Committee of the Trader's Association confidently appeals for support to those traders who are not members of the Association.[30]

This appeal was not in vain and the Committee was subsequently 'glad to be able to report that several firms, not members of the Association, paid the share of the levy that would have been theirs had they been members'. This easy relationship with non-members was underpinned by a sense of reciprocity, with the WTA promising that non-members would have first claim on any surplus funds.[31] Clearly the WTA had both formal and informal influence, derived from a perceived legitimacy founded on the scope of the organization's membership.

Moreover, the Association interacted vigorously with a wide range of other local, regional and national associations with both sectoral and cross-sectoral memberships; including, the Liverpool Branch of the *Alkali Manufacturers Association, St. Helens Chamber of Commerce*, the *St. Helens and Widnes and Rates Association*, the *Owners and Occupiers Association*, the *St. Helens Coal Owners' Association*, the *Railway and Canal Traffic Association*, the *Garston Traffic Association* and the Chemical Committee of the *Manchester Chamber of Commerce*.

Indeed, the WTA not only communicated with these bodies but also displayed a high degree of co-ordination and interlock with them, sharing campaigns, members, committee members and, on occasion, bank accounts. An excellent example is the *Garston Traffic Association*, a body formed in 1873 to represent the interests of all manufacturers and merchants using the Garston Docks at Liverpool, through which Widnes' exports were routed. WTA member firms represented at the general meeting of the *Traffic Association* held in Liverpool in 1889 included Gamble and Sons, Gaskell,

---

[29] DIC/UA17/31 WTA Scrapbook. CRO.
[30] Ibid.
[31] Ibid.

Deacon and Co., Golding, Davies and Co. Ltd., Mort, Liddell and Co., Muspratt and Sons, Pilkington Bros., and the Widnes Alkali Co. Ltd. Indeed both Gamble and Gaskell, Deacon thought it worthwhile to be represented by three senior partners whilst E.K. Muspratt was both a member of the Permanent Executive Committee of the WTA throughout its life and chairman of the *Traffic Association* at the 1889 meeting.[32] Here we stress the centrality of a figure such as Muspratt, who had purposively positioned himself so as to be able to act as a broker in the transmission of information to and from numerous different constituencies.

Also interesting are contacts between the WTA and the St. Helens *Chamber of Commerce* in the mid-1870s, which led in early 1875 to the resolution that the St. Helens body 'should appoint a Committee to meet the WTA Committee for the purpose of taking steps to carry out the proposed opposition and that each party lodge £400 to the credit of a joint account to be called the "St. Helens and Widnes Upper Mersey Account"'.[33] Meeting almost weekly, normally in the offices of Gaskell, Deacon and Co. the WTA drew on the business skills and resources of its members to ensure that its work was conducted efficiently, for example in the circulation of petitions against various bills or of forms to ensure that members claimed their various rights, such as those of Electors under the Upper Mersey Navigation Act of 1876.[34]

This considerable expenditure of energy was directed at well-defined ends. In particular the WTA was preoccupied with issues relating to transport. Whereas in the period from 1848 to the mid-1870s the networks active in the Widnes district were directed toward the facilitation of the birth of new firms, and, through that process, the elaboration of the mature, interdependent Leblanc industry, from the 1870s onwards the overriding concern became the defence and maintenance of those locational advantages analysed by Warren.[35] This was a task that could only be met through joint action, hence the shift from the loosely-coupled and informal networking that had characterized the earlier period to a growing emphasis on formal institution building.

To these ends the WTA constantly monitored, and employed legal advice in scrutinizing, all railway and canal company bills going before Parliament. They were concerned to ameliorate or block any negative impact arising from

---

[32] Ibid., Minutes of the General Meeting of the *Garston Traffic Association*, Law Association Rooms, Liverpool, 25 March 1889.

[33] DIC/UA17/30. Minutes of Permanent Executive Committee meeting, 4 February 1876. Trust was obviously not absolute for although the new account was to be in the names of WTA members Col. Gamble and Henry Deacon no 'large expenditure' was to be sanctioned until both parties had lodged the £400.

[34] DIC/UA17/31. Circular, issued 24 July 1876. The Association seems to have been well funded, for example in 1875 Honorary Secretary Henry Wades Deacon reported a balance to the credit of the Association's account of £732-6-8. In addition levies were frequently made with regard to specific actions, payments normally being calculated in relation to the rateable value of each firm's premises.

[35] K. Warren, *Chemical Foundations: The Alkali Industry in Britain to 1926* (Oxford University Press, 1983).

proposed new lines or cuts or from changes in powers to vary rates and were very often successful in forcing railway companies to include in bills clauses drafted by the WTA. They also met frequently with representatives of dock authorities to complain of poor service and lobbied the Board of Trade for changes in the classification of chemical products in relation to rail freights. The WTA never sought to control prices of output but did on at least one occasion jointly negotiate freight rates for the transportation of salt from Cheshire to Widnes.[36]

Turning inwards, the WTA's other central concern was with local rates and with the conduct of the Local Board, again this was an issue with an impact on all local firms – and on which they could co-operate without affecting the terms on which they competed with one another, demonstrating how the network relations embodied in the WTA were an alternative to neither hierarchy nor the market. Here the WTA co-operated in calling meetings of large Widnes ratepayers (indeed these and the WTA membership were virtually synonymous) and in 1875 went so far as to resolve that 'it is desirable concerted action be taken to ensure the choice of suitable candidates for Local Board Election'.[37] As a body the Leblanc manufacturers well understood the common ground that they shared in the period from the mid-1870s to 1890, small but incremental successes reinforcing their willingness to work together to solve dilemmas faced by all and building up a store of that 'warranted mutual trust' identified by Casson as central to effective networks.[38] Both the effectiveness of the WTA and the widespread support it commanded amongst its constituency must be ascribed to its clear and relatively tight focus on a series of well-defined and achievable ends, to its legitimacy as an organization and to the centrality and influence of its officers.

Of course, from 1883, the WTA was also operating parallel to the more significant LBPMA, which did seek with some success to control the output and price of bleaching powder.[39] Our intention in concentrating on the WTA has been to explore the form, extent and outcome of regional business networks operating from day-to-day at the micro-level. Within their remits both the WTA and the LBPMA were successful organizations. Their stories paint the chemical industrialists of Widnes as effective and enthusiastic, even inveterate, co-operators. The termination of the WTA and LBPMA in 1891 and 1889 respectively cannot be ascribed to a failure to develop effective channels of communication or realistic, common aims but instead to a realization that

---

[36] DIC/UA17/31. Circular, containing the text of letter from a Mr Findlay which read 'Without admitting the correctness of your contention, and reserving to ourselves the right to alter the rate at any time, I have given instruction for the rate 1s 7 1/2d per ton to be charged for the Salt in owner's wagons from Winsford to Widnes'.

[37] Ibid. Minutes of the meeting of Large Widnes Ratepayers, January 1875.

[38] Chapter 2 in this volume.

[39] Reader is again damning, asserting that while [I]t appears that prices for bleaching powder did rule somewhat higher while the Association was in existence ... nevertheless its life was ignominious and short'. *Imperial Chemical Industries*, p. 103.

both Associations were to be imminently superseded by the emergence of new and far larger issues of allocation and co-ordination, demanding a new response and an era of radical restructuring.

The configuration of dilemmas facing Widnes Leblanc manufacturers changed dramatically in the 1880s with, first, the growing success of Brunner, Mond with the Solvay process at Winnington and, second, the formation of the Salt Union in 1888. In particular the cost advantages of the Solvay process were becoming increasingly apparent. As the evidence presented in support of the Widnes Brine Supply Bill in 1890 demonstrated, the Leblanc manufacturers were under no illusions in this regard. The challenge they now faced was not to grow and develop the mature Leblanc system, nor to stabilize and reinforce the district's locational advantages, but instead to co-ordinate an orderly retreat from an obsolete production process to which all had considerable financial commitments. This would require a further tightening of the district's governance system.

In order to explore further the transition from independence to amalgamation it is necessary to re-emphasise how the district's networks had always been hierarchical, entrepreneur-led and structured according to issues of power. It was these characteristics that were continued and heightened through the process of restructuring in 1890. Obviously the leadership of the UAC overlapped considerably with that of the firms it absorbed, however, in addition, and more importantly, the relationships of power that had characterized the district prior to 1890 were also replicated and embodied in the governance structure of the new firm.

In the first instance, the first chairman of the UAC was John Brock, of Widnes firm Sullivan and Co. Ltd. Brock had also been chair of the LBPMA throughout its existence and an important member of the WTA. Perhaps more significant yet was the structure, membership, and, in particular, chairmanship, of the UAC's various functional committees. Though claiming a wide membership amongst the district's alkali manufacturers, the WTA had always been markedly hierarchical, with strong leadership provided by a relatively small cohort of entrepreneurs drawn from the district's largest firms. Especially prominent were Brock but also E.K. Muspratt, Henry Deacon and Henry Wade Deacon of Gaskell, Deacon and Co. and Major Cross, of Hutchinson and Company.[40] The significance of the repeated centrality of Muspratt is unmistakeable, but so too may be that of Major Cross for, as Powell and Smith-Doerr argue, 'though individuals come and go, the distribution of power among positions frequently remains stable'. Cross was the heir to the authority and influence amassed by Hutchinson.

This cohort was to secure many important positions throughout the structure of the UAC. In particular, immediately after the very first meeting of the Board of Directors on 31 November 1890, at which a series of committees were

---

[40] In 1884, Gaskell, Deacon and Hutchinsons were the largest and second largest alkali firms in Widnes. DIC/UA17/31. Tabulation of Large Widnes Ratepayers, 1884.

established, the important and influential Selling and General Purpose Committee (thereafter the General Management Committee) sat to elect E.K. Muspratt to the chair.[41] Under Muspratt's chairmanship this Committee quickly moved to assert control over strategy in areas such as not only buying and sales but also divestment of obsolete works, development of new processes and negotiation with competitors, including Brunner, Mond and Co.[42] Brock was appointed to the chair of the Debenture Deed Committee whilst Widnes men H. Gaskell and Wm. Pilkington took key positions on the Finance Committee and Eustace Carey, also of Gaskell, Deacon and Co. was appointed company Secretary.[43] The fact that a separate East Coast Committee was set up to oversee the industry on Tyneside only emphasized that region's marginal status, particularly as it continued to be the GMC that took all important decisions over investment and divestment.[44] The firm was also quick to appoint staff to headquarters in Liverpool, centralising sales under H. Banister (formerly of Muspratts), buying under T.H. Edwards (formerly of Pilkingtons) and accounting under T.Clarkson (of Golding, Davies, another Widnes firm). A Central Laboratory was also established under the leadership of Dr Ferdinand Hurter, previously of Gaskell, Deacon and Co.[45]

Simultaneously, senior directors attempted to consolidate and bequeath power in line with long-lived connections. Significant in this respect was the early resignation of Sir Edward Sullivan, an early champion of the LBPMA and again associated with Widnes, from the position of Vice-President, announced in a letter to the Meeting of Directors on the 7 July 1891. The letter read:

> I am sorry to sever my connexion with the Alkali Alliance [sic], but I think it so important that Col. Gamble should be in a position to take a leading part in the affairs of the Company that I have not the slightest hesitation in resigning my Vice-Presidency in his favour. I have already told him but understand that you require formal notice.

---

[41] DIC/UA6/2, CRO. The United Alkali Company Ltd. Minute Book. Meeting of the Directors, 31 October 1890 and Meeting of the Selling and General Purpose Committee, 31 October 1890.

[42] For example, the GMC was successful in resolving that 'District Managers to have power to expend not exceeding £100 and to report in each case'. Ibid. Meeting of Directors, 20 March 1891. However such attempts at aggrandisement did not always succeed. At the Meeting of Directors on the 23 January 1891 an amendment that 'The general question of the appointment of Managing Directors be ... remitted to the GMC for consideration' was lost.

[43] Ibid. Meeting of the Directors, 31 October 1890 and 19 December 1890.

[44] Thus, the first plant closed by the Company was the Wallsend works, the GMC introducing a resolution that the East Coast Committee (ECC) be instructed to 'take steps to dismantle the plant and realize the works'. Shortly after the Jarrow works met a similar fate, the GMC again resolving that 'these works be stopped as early as possible', though this time the process was to be handled by the GMC itself and not the ECC. Ibid. Meeting of Directors, 17 April 1891 and 19 June 1891.

[45] Ibid. Meeting of the Directors, 19 December 1890 and 9 January 1891.

Sullivan's hopes and intentions were fully met, Gamble being immediately promoted to Vice-President, leaving room on the Board for the appointment of J.C. Gamble as a Director.[46]

Moreover, the Board of Directors was stratified in other ways. In particular, in the summer of 1891 four directors, A. Allhusen, C.E. Barlow, J.E. Davidson and J. Tennant, were appointed Managing Directors on salaries of £1500 p.a. Attached to these appointments however were a series of conditions, including:

> [w]hile they continue Managing Directors they shall not be entitled to the benefit of any of the provisions in the articles of association for the remuneration of other directors. It is understood that the Managing Directors respectively shall devote the whole of their time and attention to the duties of their office and not engage in any other occupation or accept any other appointment.[47]

Whilst not stripped of their voting rights, these four directors, two of them intimately associated with the long history of the alkali industry on Tyneside and in Scotland, suffered a diminution in status to that of little more than salaried employees.[48]

Nonetheless, it may not be assumed that this ordering of power within the governance of the UAC was always harmonious. In particular, Henry Gaskell consistently dissented from the views of the Board on substantive issues of strategy during the first two years of the company's life, leading to damaging clashes with the GMC, chaired by fellow Widnesian, E.K. Muspratt. Thus at a meeting of the Directors in late 1891 the GMC presented and explained a draft agreement it had negotiated with Brunner, Mond and Co. Discussion was however immediately terminated and the meeting adjourned for a period of one week. The minutes of the adjourned meeting appear twice in the minute book, the first entry crossed through, suggesting dissatisfaction with the way in which they had been recorded. Both versions however open with the intervention of Gaskell, who 'called attention to the fact that the arrangement with Brunner, Mond and Co. was practically concluded without consultation with the Board and [he] recommended that in the future all committees shall refrain from concluding any important arrangements with previous consultation with the board'.[49] Clearly, Gaskell felt that real power lay not with the Board but with the GMC. Five directors, including Gaskell, Henry Gaskell jnr and Col. Gaskell, then voted against the carrying of the minutes of the GMC and at the next scheduled meeting of directors 'Mr Gaskell and Col. Gamble repeated

---

[46]   Ibid. Meeting of the Directors, 7 July 1891.

[47]   Ibid.

[48]   For exploration of contemporary understandings of the duties, responsibilities and commitments of directors see, J. Quail, 'The Proprietorial Theory of the Firm and its Consequences', *Journal of Industrial History*, Vol. 3, No. 1 (2000), pp. 1–28.

[49]   DIC/UA6/2. Meeting of Directors, 16 October 1891 and 23 October 1891.

their protest against the arrangement with Brunner, Mond' and attempted to vote down the GMC minutes'.[50] Ultimately, whilst again discussing the minutes of the GMC, Gaskell 'in consequence of some remarks withdrew *announcing his intention of retiring* from the Board'. Only after a hurried resolution that the Board '*beg Mr Gaskell to reconsider*' and assurances that 'no member even in the warmth of debate entertained any feeling but that of highest respect for his honourable intentions' did Gaskell consent to return.[51] The UAC had inherited from its antecedents multiple, cross-generational networks amongst which accommodation was not always possible.

Conclusion

This chapter would argue for a relational perspective on business networks, even where those networks are closely associated with the spatial clustering of an industry. In contrast to the embeddedness perspective on regional business networks we would view such networks not as determined primarily by their rootedness in community structures but as coalitions of imperfectly overlapping interests assembled by actors to meet the issues of allocation and co-ordination facing them. This view does not preclude consideration of issues such as trust and reciprocity but would simply argue that issues of power are equally salient. These coalitions are temporary and mutable, changing in response to both the changing positions of participants, determined by a combination of agency and constraint, and changes in the challenges of allocation and co-ordination faced. In turn this mutability impacts on the process of restructuring, the extent to which actors are able to accumulate knowledge through networks and to identify and align their (shifting) interests playing a part in shaping the speed and direction of restructuring. Inevitably, restructuring will in turn impact on the further evolution of the structure of relations.

Inevitably, perhaps, many of the important, fine-grain aspects of the processes we have sought to explore remain obscure. How did network members search for and assess potential linkages? How did entrepreneurs and firms 'articulate[d] and manage[d]' their 'external organization'? What implications were there in the organization of firms' external relations for patterns of knowledge accumulation and of those patterns for the framing of 'fresh conjectures' concerning possible business structures, strategies and processes?[52]

Nonetheless, it has been our aim to use this understanding of regional business networks to track in a coherent manner some (certainly not all) of the

---

[50]   Ibid. Meeting of Directors, 20 November 1891. Gaskell and Gamble again dissented at the Meeting of the Directors on 22 April 1892, against the adoption of agreement with French company Societé d'ElectroChimie.

[51]   Ibid. Meeting of Directors, 17 June 1892 (emphasis in the original).

[52]   Metcalfe, *Institutions and Progress*, p. 579.

dynamic processes central to the socio-economic transformations seen in Widnes. Applying this perspective to the Widnes district alkali industry in the nineteenth century results in a schematic story of the interdependent evolution of networks and industry structure divided into three stages. At each stage people and firms, not religion, nationality or community, formed the nodes or central organizing poles of networks. Thus, from 1848 to the 1870s, Widnes presented a blank slate in socio-economic terms, a context in which 'social embeddedness' has little meaning. A disparate group of actors, united by their immigrant status, brought to this scene a wide array of different capabilities and interests shaped by the stage reached in and previous paths of their careers. John Hutchinson and Ludwig Mond represent excellent examples of this. The challenge they faced individually and as a group was the elaboration of a chemical process that was far from fully developed in its industrial application. This encouraged the growth of the interdependencies identified by Mond in the letter with which this chapter starts. In this situation networking was loose and fluid and displayed a range of linkage types. In structural terms, this networking gave rise to the birth of many new firms and to the maturation over time of a distinct cluster. At the same time, repeated interactions laid down deep connections within and between firms that were to run like threads through the remainder of the period under study.

In the second period, from the 1870s to 1890, growing maturity and nascent external challenges created new issues of co-ordination. While continuing both to interact and to compete with one another, local manufacturers were able to identify a set of shared interests. These related primarily to the defence of the cluster's competitive advantages, particularly those arising from location and transport infrastructure. This required sustained and occasionally antagonistic interaction with a wide range of other institutions at both the regional and the national level. In response, networks became more formalized in structure and behaviour. Previously inherent structures of power and hierarchy became more concrete. Structurally, the growth of the industry through the birth of new firms slowed and, by the end of this period, halted.

From the early 1880s the industry faced increasingly severe external challenges, including the diffusion of the Solvay process and restructuring in the supply of important inputs. By the late 1880s these challenges were so severe that the only realistic response was to abandon the Leblanc process. The interests of all Leblanc manufacturers converged powerfully on this single point. For better or for worse, local industrialists, building on regional and extra-regional networks established over the preceding thirty years, sought to do this through radical industrial restructuring, forming the United Alkali Company in 1890. Entrepreneurs were able 'to update networking structures created to earlier market conditions', but continuities of interests, interdependence and of power are unmistakable across this apparent watershed in governance practice.[53]

---

[53] F. Munro and T. Slaven, 'Networks and Markets in Clyde Shipping: The Donaldsons and the Hogarths, 1870–1939', *Business History*, Vol. 43, No. 2 (2001), p. 22.

Chapter 12

Business networks, social habits and the evolution of a regional industrial cluster: Coventry, 1880s–1930s

Roger Lloyd-Jones and M.J. Lewis

Introduction

This chapter explores the emergence and evolution of business networks among an industrial cluster of firms in the manufacturing centre of Coventry. From the late nineteenth century, Coventry's industrial structure was rapidly transformed, as traditional industries such as ribbon weaving, sewing machines, and watchmaking were eclipsed by 'the new engineering products of cycles, motor vehicles and machine tools'. The Coventry district evolved into a cluster of interconnected industries, locked together by common products and technologies, and by markets.[1] We show that clustering was related to the emergence of the key industry of bicycles, which drew on engineering skills, technologies and entrepreneurial talent that had evolved in older forms of industrial activity. Of importance was the development of business networks which we define using Veblen's concept of institutionalised social habits. Such networks are difficult to detect from empirical investigation, because they are often informal in character and transcend simple economic transactions between firms. Nevertheless, to understand the evolution of networks requires an examination of how social habits were mediated both within and amongst firms at the local and regional level. The evolution of seed-corn firms such as the Coventry Machinist informally created a school of entrepreneurship. This led to the establishment of a cluster of bicycle and component supply companies which pursued a strategy of profusion and nurtured the flow of tacit knowledge amongst firms. The early development of bicycles in the city stimulated activity in related sectors of industry, machine tools and motor vehicles, creating a system of interrelated firms which played an important role in the expansion of a regional pattern of industry. Of particular interest is the firm of Alfred Herbert, the largest machine tool maker in Europe by the 1920s.

---

[1] See D. Thoms and T. Donnelly, 'Coventry's Industrial Economy, 1880–1980', in B. Lancaster and T. Mason (eds), *Life and Labour in a Twentieth Century City: The Experience of Coventry* (Cryfield Press, n.d.).

Association with the bicycle industry shaped its early product development, and Herbert's became a leader in the machine tool trade. Through its personal style of governance, the firm established business relations based on reputation and trust, and acted as a hub for a regional business network.

Social habits and regional business networks

Regional business networks are an institutional form that is embedded in history. As Staber claims: 'Business has always practised some form of networking ... They have done so to collect information, diffuse new ideas, or exercise political influence'.[2] An historical feature of the Coventry networks was personal capitalism, a form of managerial organisation which shaped the governance of business enterprise. Personal capitalism focuses on personal ownership and a style of management governed by a small, but clearly defined, governance structure, and this predominated at the local and regional level. The decentralised control structure of personal capitalism facilitated the utilisation of networks of local sources of capital. Through family ties, partnership links, and the legal use of private limited liability, firms sought to mobilise financial resources, link finance to technical expertise, and to maintain control over the firm.[3]

The notion of a regional business network provides a conceptual device for exploring business change, but the exact working of the networks is difficult to analyse.[4] As Casson cautions, 'theoretical speculation has [tended] to run ahead of systematic empirical research'.[5] Recognising these concerns, we suggest that a useful approach to the study of networks is that which identifies habit-forming modes of behaviour that may become embedded in social institutions. As they evolve, local business communities develop distinct cultural attributes, conventions and routines.[6] Social relations, whether firm-specific, inter-firm, or within the local environment in which firms evolve, are important to the analysis of regional networks.[7] As Veblen postulated, institutions constitute a basic unit of analysis, and they arise from more or less durable social habits. Defining institutions as 'settled habits of thought common to the generality of

---

[2] U. Staber, 'Networks and Regional Development: Perspectives and Unresolved Issues', in U. Staber, N.V. Schaefer and B. Sharma (eds), *Business Networks. Prospects for Regional Development* (de Gruyter, 1996), p. 1.
[3] See R. Lloyd-Jones and M.J. Lewis, 'British Industrial Capitalism During the Second Industrial Revolution: a Neo-Schumpeterian Approach', *Journal of Industrial History*, Vol. 1, No. 1 (1998), pp. 72–81.
[4] Staber, 'Networks', p. 3.
[5] M. Casson, 'Analysing Regional Business Networks: An Economic Perspective', Paper Presented at International Business History Conference, Glasgow, 1999, pp. 1–2.
[6] See A.J. Scott, *Regions and the World Economy: The Coming Shape of Global Production, Competition and Political Order* (Oxford University Press, 1998).
[7] W.W. Powell and L. Smith-Doerr, 'Networks and Economic Life', in N. J. Smelser and R. Swedberg', *The Handbook of Economic Sociology* (Princeton University Press, 1994), p. 368.

man', they are embodied in a 'cumulative causation' which have both cause and effect, and act in a sequence of reciprocity. Thus, Hodgson argues that habits and institutions may be seen 'as an outgrowth of the routinised thought processes that are shared by a number of persons in a given locality'.[8] Such institutions are not highly visible, but it is possible to identify a set of social habits which acted as key components of a regional business network in the Midlands (Table 12.1).

Table 12.1
Regional business networks: Social habits in the Midlands

Institutionalised Social Habit	Historical Origin	Operation of Network
School for Entrepreneurs	Structural change and firm mobility – the seed corn firm	Development of pool of business and technical know-how supported by inter-personal connections
Skilled and adaptable Human resources – labour with relevant knowledge	Established pool of flexible labour within region complemented by inward migration	Strategy of profusion and nurturing of tacit knowledge
Personal capitalist form of enterprise	Retention of personal governance and socio-legal form of control	Use of local/regional sources of financial capital, the creation of business trust and setting ethical standards of behaviour
Standard of quality production and business behaviour	Benchmark business relations that set norms for both product quality and ethical attributes of responsibility and obligation	Establishment of reputation based on commitment to socially agreed standards defining product quality and business relations

These played an important part in facilitating the growth of new industries, governed relations within and among firms, and could either promote or constrain the actions of individual actors.

---

[8]   G.M. Hodgson, *Economics and Evolution: Bringing Life Back to Economics* (Cambridge University Press, 1993), pp. 119 and 125–6; ibid., 'On the Evolution of Thorstein Veblen's Evolutionary Economics', *Cambridge Journal of Economics*, Vol. 22 (1998), pp. 463–77.

Also important in the context of networks was the action of leading business firms and personalities, and the notions of trust and power in business networks.[9] To examine these issues, we adopt the concept of the seed-corn firm, a concept related to structural diversity, in that it facilitates the propagation of an industry, not in the form of simple replication, but by the diffusion of human and information resources. Tacit knowledge is accumulated by the actions of seed-corn firms, and this encourages the development of entrepreneurial capabilities and leads to the formation of new firms. As firms perpetuate, the industrial district becomes more diversified and competitive, but reciprocal relations of personal commitment, loyalty and trust remain and enable collaboration between firms to co-exist with competitive behaviour. This view is based on the premise that the objectives of firms are 'culturally and institutionally specific'. According to Penrose, what is central about firms is their 'heterogeneity'.[10] As we show, enterprises such as Coventry Machinist and Alfred Herbert accumulated specific knowledge that they not only evolved internally, but also transmitted to other firms. The institutional means of transmission took the form of regional business networks that helped facilitate the clustering of related industries and promoted the co-existence of competition and collaboration.[11]

Industrial clustering and the Coventry bicycle industry

Coventry's traditional staple industries in the nineteenth century were craft-based, and as late as 1891 ribbon weaving still employed 3000 workers. However, from the 1880s bicycles emerged as a dynamic new sector. During the bicycle boom of the mid-1890s, Coventry makers employed over 6000 workers.[12] During the late nineteenth century, employment grew rapidly, as did the number of cycle firms (Table 12.2). In 1891, Coventry was the largest centre of the British cycle trade, employing 35 per cent of the labour force, compared to 22 per cent in its nearest rival, Birmingham. The example of bicycles in Coventry shows a development of business networks, premised upon both economic transactions between firms, and the evolution of social habits related to entrepreneurship and the transference of tacit knowledge.

---

[9]   See Chapter 1 in this volume.
[10]   G.M. Hodgson, *Economics and Utopia: Why the Learning Economy is not the End of History* (Routledge, 1999), pp. 138–9.
[11]   See M.J. Enright, 'Regional Clusters and Firm Strategy', in A. D. Chandler, P. Hagstrom and O. Solvell (eds), *The Dynamic Firm: The Role of Technology, Organisation and Regions* (Oxford University Press 1998), pp. 316–7.
[12]   R. Lloyd-Jones and M.J. Lewis, *Raleigh and the British Bicycle Industry. An Economic and Business History* (Ashgate, 2000), pp. 24–31.

Table 12.2
The Coventry cycle trade

	Employment	Firms[a]
Year		
1874/5	n.a	2
1881	593	17
1891	4059	30[b]
1897	n.a	75
1901	6101	n.a

Notes: [a] Includes makers of components and complete cycles.
       [b] 1890/1.

Sources: A.E. Harrison, 'The Competitiveness of the British Cycle Industry, 1890-1914', *Economic History Review*, Vol. 22, No. 3 (1969), p. 302; ibid., 'Origins', p. 43.

The growth of the bicycle industry was enhanced by tapping into an existing pool of entrepreneurial talent and technical knowledge in the staple trades.[13] Firm clustering in the Midlands created an environment where: 'Ideas and information flowed freely via personal contacts, both business and social, raising the possibility of new product developments through diversification or the creation of spin-off firms'.[14] A pioneering entrepreneur of the early cycle industry was James Starley, whose business ventures provided the seed-corn for the future development of the industry. In 1862, Starley founded the Coventry Sewing Machine Co., re-named the Coventry Machinist in 1869, and this acted as 'a nursery' for the fledgling bicycle industry. Through the enterprise of existing employees of Coventry Machinist, such as William Hillman and George Singer, spin-off bicycle firms emerged. Starley himself formed a partnership in 1874 with William Herbert to form the Automachinery Company, and with Borthwick Smith to produce cycles, sewing machines, and roller skates. By the end of the 1870s, Starley joined his two sons to form Starley Bros., a specialist producer of cycles.[15]

---

[13] Thoms and Donnelley, 'Coventry's Industrial Economy', pp. 13–14 and 20.
[14] W.R. Garside, 'Regional vs National Perspectives on Economic "Decline" in Late Victorian and Edwardian Britain', in Jean-Pierre Dormois and M. Dintenfass (eds), *The British Industrial Decline* (Routledge, 1999), p. 148.
[15] F. Alderson, *Bicycling: A History* (David and Charles, 1972), pp. 39 and 62; D. Thoms and T. Donnelly, *The Motor Car Industry in Coventry Since the 1890s* (Croom Helm, 1985), p. 14; Lloyd-Jones and Lewis, *Raleigh*, pp. 16–7; ibid., 'Regional Business Networks in Historical Perspective: The British Bicycle Industry, 1870–1914', in T. Slaven (ed), *Business History, Theory and Practice.* (Centre for Business History in Scotland, 2000), p. 147; *Coventry Trade and Commercial Directory* (Anslow and Roden, 1874–5), p. 102.

Entrepreneurial linkages were also enhanced by mergers within the industry.[16] The most notable, Rudge-Whitworth, created Coventry's largest cycle maker, producing 75,000 of the 310,000 bicycles made in the city in 1906. In 1874, George Woodcock founded the Watch Manufacturing Co. of Coventry, and in 1879 he formed Tangent and Coventry Cycle. Tangent merged with Daniel Rudge of Wolverhampton in 1880, becoming D. Rudge Ltd. in 1885, and in 1894 joined forces with Whitworth's of Birmingham. The merger brought fresh capital and enhanced the technical capabilities of the firm through patent rights on long-standing and original innovations. Rudge brought the advantage of being an integrated firm, manufacturing the complete cycle, and making a variety of patterns. It also had an 'old reputation for turning out first class ... machines', and this was aided by a fluent market for managerial talent. In 1893, Rudge appointed as General Manager R.L. Philpot, a former employee at Humber. He had 'made a large circle of friends and a very wide business connection', and pioneered new designs that were later transferred to Rudge-Whitworth. The company also expanded its reputation and networks abroad, employing agents with 'friends [who] are legion throughout the United States'.[17]

Two important inferences may be drawn from these cases. First, there emerged a network of business experience and learning that was crucial to the growth and evolution of firms within Coventry's cycle industry. As Staber observes: 'The crucial ingredient of successful networks is that the actors involved are embedded in supportive social structures which provide the meaning and motivation for co-operation and innovation'.[18] Second, the diffusion of good practice and technological innovation in the bicycle trade was not simply confined to lead firms such as the Starleys. The technical capabilities of entrepreneurs were facilitated by inter-firm networks, which created a fertile ground for technological change. For example, a habitual practice of early cycle firms in Coventry was the introduction of revised models for the new season. This 'ensured that changes relating to technical specifications and designs occurred with great frequency'. Flexibility was crucial to firms producing for markets that were both seasonal and conditioned by changes in fashion. Thus, in 1892 Rudge were faced with a sudden change of fashion in safety bicycles in the spring that necessitated a switch to 'diamond frames', and Wright & Son of Coventry boasted that they could build machines 'to any design'.[19] This tended to focus the industry on batch production systems, and in this context firms were required to meet specific

---

[16] See A.E. Harrison, 'The Origins and Growth of the UK Cycle Industry to 1900', *Transport History*, Vol. 6, No. 1 (1985), p. 45.

[17] Lloyd-Jones and Lewis, *Raleigh*, pp. 11–2; Nottingham Record Office, Raleigh Papers, Records of Rudge-Whitworth, DDRN 5/6/1, Cuttings, *Bicycling News*, 26 April 1892; *Wheeling*, 26 Oct. 1892, *Referee*, 25 November 1892; *Irish Athlete*, 16 November 1893.

[18] Staber, 'Networks', p. 7.

[19] Thoms and Donnelly, *Motor Car*, p. 20; Rudge Whitworth, Report of AGM of Rudge in *Cyclist*, 21 December 1892; *Coventry Complete Directory* (Robertson and Grey, 1894).

and 'time centre needs' based on 'institutional flexibility rather than routinization'.[20]

Batch production systems 'relied on general purpose machinery and tools that could be adapted to multiple tasks rather than seeking dedicated mechanisms devoted to accelerating the flow of standard items'.[21] Consequently, 'the choice between variety and volume had strong technical correlations built into the structure of production', and a high premium was placed upon the adaptability of the workforce. In the industrial centres of the Midlands, 'existing forms of industry ... were relatively unspecialised in plant and tools, permitting the non-specificity of investment, together with the existing pool of skilled labour to assist the generation of new products and market opportunities'.[22] As Staber argues, there are important business advantages associated with a spatial clustering of firms which allow the 'sharing of access to local pools of resources, such as labour, capital and business services', and the capture of agglomeration economies 'that facilitate speedy and accurate exchange of information'.[23] Weaving and watchmaking in Coventry provided bicycle firms with a flexible labour supply and allowed them to combine the buying-in of components with the design and fabrication of in-house tools. Bicycle construction 'called for mechanical skills similar to those required in the construction of lace and hosiery machinery', and this facilitated the transfer of skilled toolmakers.[24] During the bicycle boom of the mid-1890s,[25] pressures were exerted on Coventry's skilled labour resources, despite rising population. But Coventry manufacturers could tap into a pool of skilled labour concentrated in the West Midlands. As a result: 'New faces were to be encountered daily, some of the men from Birmingham full to the brim with energy'.[26]

Inward migration was important in equating labour supply with demand, but the advantages it brought transcended that of market processes. A fluid labour supply facilitated the growth of tacit knowledge in the cycle trade. Hodgson defines tacit knowledge as 'knowing how rather than knowing what'. It is a principle 'both prior to, and beyond the reach of explicit articulation'. Workers 'know more than they can tell', and traditional skilled workers helped to facilitate the transmission of knowledge between the boundaries of the tacit and the explicit.[27] This form of applied skill networking was of particular significance for Coventry cycle firms, and was given added impetus by the fact

[20] P. Scranton, 'Diversity in Diversity: Flexible Production and American Industrialisation, 1880–1930', *Business History Review*, Vol. 65 (Spring 1991), pp. 29 and 36.

[21] Ibid., p. 38.

[22] Garside, 'Regional', p. 144.

[23] Staber, 'Networks', p. 8.

[24] Harrison, 'Origins', p. 54; Thoms and Donnelly, *Motor Car*, p. 16.

[25] See Lloyd-Jones and Lewis, *Raleigh*, pp. 24–31.

[26] Thoms and Donnelly, *Motor Car*, p. 17; B. Lancaster, 'Whose a Real Coventry Kid? Migration Into Twentieth Century Coventry', in Lancaster and Mason (eds), *Life and Labour*, pp. 59–60.

[27] Hodgson, *Economics and Utopia*, pp. 46–7.

that the principles of cycle manufacture could be relatively easily acquired by artisans. These accumulated engineering skills gave cycle firms, in their early stage of development, a flexibility based on 'the traditional, empirically-based aptitudes of British engineering craftsmen'. The diffusion of tacit knowledge was given further impetus by the use of formal apprenticeship systems in the industry.[28] This was important because of the 'unorganised' and 'uncoordinated' provision of technical education in Britain.[29] As the bicycle industry expanded, it became closely linked to the development of machine tool technology and motor vehicle manufacture, both of which clustered in the Midlands, and in Coventry. This reinforced the cluster, creating a dynamic regional environment for economic and business change.

Coventry: The evolving industrial cluster

Bicycle output grew rapidly in the last two decades of the nineteenth century, inducing investments by both bicycle and component makers in 'expensive mass production machinery'. Demand was met initially by importing American machine tools, but British makers responded by switching their activities to meet the needs of the cycle trade, while new firms were attracted into the industry.[30] Table 12.3 shows the growth of the machine tool industry to 1913. The vast majority of these firms were small-scale and they were located in four regional clusters: Manchester, Halifax and Leeds, Glasgow, and the fastest growing area, the Midlands. In 1914, there were 64 firms in the West Midlands and Coventry, 'generally of somewhat greater size than firms in other areas and specialising in support for the local cycle, motor and small arms trades'.[31]

---

[28] A.E. Harrison, 'Growth, Entrepreneurship and Capital Formation in the United Kingdom's Cycle and Related Industries, 1882–1914', PhD (University of York, 1977), pp. 88–9; Garside, 'Regional', p. 144.
[29] *American Machinist* (hereafter AM), Vol. 23, 21 April 1900, p. 293E.
[30] S.B. Saul, 'The Engineering Industry', in D.H. Aldcroft (ed), *The Development of British Industry and Foreign Competition, 1815–1914, Studies in Industrial Enterprise* (Allen and Unwin, 1968), p. 213; R. Lloyd-Jones and M.J. Lewis, 'Technological Pathways, Modes of Development, and the British National Innovation System: Examples from British Industry, 1880–1914', in L. Tissot and B. Veyrassat (eds), *Technological Trajectories, Markets, Institutions* (Peter Lang, 2001), p. 150.
[31] R. Floud, *The British Machine Tool Industry, 1850–1914* (Cambridge, CUP, 1976), p. 38; A.J. Arnold, 'Innovation, Deskilling and Profitability in the British Machine Tool Industry: Alfred Herbert, 1887–1927', *Journal of Industrial History*, Vol. 1, No. 2 (1999), p. 53.

Table 12.3
The machine tool industry, 1870–1913

Year	No. of Firms in Industry	No. of Firms (Industrial Midlands)	Output of Leading Firms (£)	Output Excluding Herbert's (£)	% Herbert's
1870	131	12	32,238	–	–
1890	228	22	227,481	219,532	3.5
1900	315	53	497,648	379,994	25.7
1913	250	64	1,219,878	693,925	42.1

Source: Floud, *Machine Tool Industry*, pp. 33, 36–7 and 41.

This created an environment for technological developments in machine tools, as demonstrated by the origins of Herbert's, Britain's largest maker in 1914. Founded in 1887, the company began by producing a range of components and machine tools for the Coventry bicycle trade, as well as machinery for the ribbon trade.[32] Bicycle production stimulated machine tools in Coventry, and Herbert's 'among others, took its share in the designing and building of machines particularly suitable for the cycle trade'.[33] This early association with the bicycle industry set a technological pathway for future product development, as well as its strategy of diversification into general engineering. As Alfred Herbert recalled:

> Although our first machine tool efforts were directed mainly towards the requirements of the bicycle business, we soon began to supply machines to the much wider field of general engineering ... It has often been suggested to me that we should have done better if we had specialised more intensively on a limited range of machines ... but in the early days I doubt very much whether there was scope for a growing business, which confined itself to the production of only one or two machines. Rightly, or wrongly, I was more attracted to the idea of covering a fairly wide field. The cycle business, which was our principal customer, required in those days a variety of machines and not many of them of one kind.[34]

Herbert's was not uncommon among early machine tool makers in Coventry. Webster & Bennett, founded in 1887, manufactured boring and

---

[32] J. Lane, 'Herbert, Sir Alfred Edward', in D.J. Jeremy (ed), *Dictionary of Business Biography* (Butterworths, 1984), pp. 174–5.
[33] *The Machine Tool Review*, Vol. 18 (Alfred Herbert Ltd., 1930), p. 58.
[34] Cited in Floud, *Machine Tool Industry*, p. 53.

turning mills for 'the cycle trade'. Its original premises were located in the West Orchard district, the location of the main cluster of bicycle firms, and similar to Herbert's, its mutual dependence on bicycles diminished. By the late 1890s, Webster & Bennett supplied diverse machine tools for the engineering trades and had made design innovations to their duplex vertical-boring mill. By 1911, its new Northley Works integrated flow production technology with the best practices of quality control. As machine tools expanded, inter-firm transactions evolved and the company's workshops included 'several Herbert machine tools ... in the production of component parts'. The firm also utilised the factoring services of Herbert's to sell its milling machines abroad, to Japan, Italy and France.[35]

While these examples demonstrate a high degree of inter-firm trading, the aggregate growth of the machine tool industry and its product diversification were linked to the emerging motor vehicle industry in Coventry, which also owed its origins to the bicycle trades. Motor vehicle production grew rapidly. James Archdale & Co., of Birmingham, a major producer of machine tools for the motor trade, could claim in 1902 that they 'had more orders awaiting execution than can be got together in the ordinary working hours'. Motor production eclipsed that of bicycle manufacture, so that by 1913 Alfred Herbert could note that: 'We in Coventry are largely concerned with motors'. By this date, the city employed 30 per cent of the West Midland workforce engaged in motor vehicle production, and was the home of nationally known manufacturers such as Rover, Singer, Humber, Daimler, Riley and Swift. A number of these manufacturers originated as bicycle makers, 'absorbed' into the automobile industry during the early stages of its development. In this respect, Coventry was a 'unique' industrial centre, and many firms continued to combine both products before 1914. Following the lead of the bicycle industry, motor producers evolved technologies to manufacture 'small batches' of high quality. In addition, a number of component makers for the car industry owed their origins to bicycle manufacturers. Of the 61 motor component firms in Coventry in 1912, 17 had been involved in cycle manufacture. The decision to produce car components in Coventry was often premised upon the vagaries of the trade cycle. For example, the downturn in the bicycle market in 1897 led the Smith Stamping Co. to switch to automobile component manufacture. Its 'early success was largely due to the fact that many of the "new" customers were former cycle manufacturers and were familiar with the Company's working arrangements'. The West Midlands displayed a pattern of development which involved a set of inter-firm linkages: bicycles and components to motor vehicles and components. All these sectors demanded

[35] *Machine Tool Review*, Vol. 17 (1929), pp. 102–3, 105; Coventry Record Office, (CRO), Webster and Bennett, 1050/105/3, History, 1050/9/1, Sales Register.

new and modified machine tools to operate 'new processes and to make old processes more efficient'.[36]

Industrial clustering was reinforced by entrepreneurial linkages between firms, which built upon the social habits developed in the early bicycle industry. Herbert's again provides an example. The pioneers of the machine tool industry had one common characteristic: they had served formal apprenticeships at a small range of firms as mechanical engineers. This enabled 'a stream of new ideas, new machine tools, or modifications to old tools'. In-house training in engineering was a prerequisite to success, and in 1880 Alfred Herbert was apprenticed to Jessop's of Leicester. This enabled him to secure the post of works manager at the engineers Cole & Matthews in 1887, and in partnership with William Hubbard they purchased the firm, having been provided with £2000 each from their fathers. It also transpired that his brother, William, was influential in securing the purchase, providing F.S. Matthews, the owner, with an 'alternative source of income' as a sales manager for his Premiere Cycle Co. in Germany. The new firm acquired its initial reputation by manufacturing weldless bicycle tubes, using a French patent secured by William Herbert. The profits earned 'from the tube agency business were ploughed back into machine tool manufacture', but 'also laid the foundations of the agency side of the business'. Pursuing a strategy of profusion, manufacturing a wide range of specialist machine tools for the expanding cycle trade, success was ensured by guaranteed orders from the Premiere Cycle Co.[37]

Early success provided a financial platform for diversification from 1894, when Alfred became sole owner. Converted to a private limited in 1908, Alfred became 'Governing Director', ably supported on the board by his brother William, who was a major shareholder. As the firm expanded, the share base was marginally widened, but Alfred retained the direct controlling interest. Under his control, Herbert's diversified by supplying machine tools for general engineering and the evolving motor industry of Coventry. Employing 12 men in 1887, this rose to 500 by the end of the bicycle boom in 1897, 1500 in 1910, and 2000 by 1914. The company also gained a reputation as the most progressive British machine tool firm, following American production methods and producing equipment of the highest quality.[38]

---

[36] *AM*, Vol. 25, 8 February 1902, p. 60E, Vol. 32, 24 Oct. 1909, p. 845; Thoms and Donnelly, 'Coventry's Industrial Economy', pp. 12–3; ibid., *The Coventry Motor Car Industry: Birth to Renaissance?'* (Ashgate, 2000), pp. 37–8; Floud, *Machine Tool Industry*, pp. 39 and 54; B. Beavan, 'Growth and Significance of the Coventry Car Components Industry, 1895–1914', *Midland History*, Vol. 18 (1993), pp. 108 and 110–1; R. Church, *The Rise and Decline of the British Motor Industry* (Cambridge University Press, 1995), pp. 8–10.

[37] Floud, *Machine Tool Industry*, pp. 43 and 46–8; J. Mc G. Davies, 'A Twentieth Century Paternalist. Alfred Herbert and the Skilled Coventry Workmen', in Lancaster and Mason (eds), *Life and Labour*, pp. 102–3; Lane, 'Herbert', p. 174; Lloyd-Jones and Lewis, *Raleigh*, p. 22; Thoms and Donnelley, *Motor Car*, p. 22.

[38] Floud, *Machine Tool Industry*, p. 74; Saul, 'Engineering', p. 213; Mc G. Davies, 'Paternalist', p. 103; Lane, 'Herbert', pp. 174–5; Arnold, 'Innovation', pp. 53, 56; S. Pollard, 'Entrepreneurship', in R. Floud and D.N. McCloskey (eds), *The Economic History of Britain Since 1700*, Vol. 2 (Cambridge University Press, 1994), pp. 81–2; CRO, Records of Alfred

Crucially important to the development of interrelated firms and industries was the transfer of tacit knowledge. For example, pioneer firms in the cycle industry, such as Rudge-Whitworth and Starley, developed interchangeable parts, a practice which was carried over into the motor car industry.[39] This rebounded on the practices of machine tool makers. Thus, Herbert's in 1901 were producing a wide range of standardised machines for the motor trade, taking advantage of the use of jigs, gauges and 'special appliances' to reduce production costs and secure a reliable interchange of work.[40] Such developments enhanced the level of specialisation within the district, raising the importance of well-designed tools and equipment for the efficient use of machine tools. Consequently, Coventry firms paid considerable attention to the design and manufacture of small tools. Herbert's symbolised this by making the renowned 'Coventry chuck' and 'Coventry dieheads', and also sub-contracted to other local producers. Overall, Coventry firms produced large quantities of diversified tools that could be 'interchanged without bringing the machine to rest'.[41]

This level of specialisation meant that there was a high degree of inter-firm transactions and many smaller manufacturers, engaged in interchangeable manufacturing, found it more economic to have their jigs and fixtures made by specialists. Herbert's acted as a seed-corn firm, and a number of firms in Coventry were established to provide such equipment. For example, Morton & Weaver, founded in 1900, produced quality machine tools and also 'various labour-saving tools and jigs for engineers'. More specialised was the Coventry Gauge & Tool Co., which later became TI Matrix. Established in 1913 by Harry Harley, a former apprentice at Herbert's, the company supplied ready-made jigs and fixtures to firms devoid of 'tool rooms and design staffs of their own'. There was a ready market for such products, so they could 'supply ... machinery and tools at short notice'. Another firm, Monk Engineering, undertook 'all kinds of [experimental] work for manufacturers and designers', as well as supplying jigs, tools and fixtures.[42] It would be a mistake to assume that such firms were normally specialist makers. Rather, they followed a strategy of 'profusion' by concentrating on batches 'of goods skilfully made'.[43] There was a strong emphasis on product quality, and of the reputation of the product linked to the company name. Relations with suppliers and customers went beyond the instrumental, and customer needs were paramount: '[it] is the opinion of the user that is wanted. It's he who is able to compute the numerous changes and costs to which a tool is liable, and in a position to estimate its

Herbert, 926/1/4/1-3, Minute Books of the Departmental Board of Directors, 1911–41, 586/11, General Minute Book, 1894–1950, EGM, 24 Aug. 1911.

[39] Thoms and Donnelley, *Motor Car*, p. 26.
[40] *AM*, Vol. 24, 2 November 1901, p. 1155E.
[41] Herbert's Departmental, 17 October, 28 November 1922; 'The Versatile Coventry Chuck', in *Machine Tool Review*, Vol. 14 (1926), p. 19; *City of Coventry Official Handbook, 1927* (Cheltenham, Edward Burrows), p. 58.
[42] *Coventry Handbook, 1927*, pp. A 12, A23, A30; Lane, 'Herbert', p. 176.
[43] Scranton, 'Diversity', p. 38.

value as a money maker'.[44] In this context, the company becomes more than a supplier of commodities and takes on a social dimension, 'inserting itself in a network of relations with ... customers which is reliable, ethical, and not bounded purely by self interest'.[45] Coventry built a reputation, while: 'Visits are often paid ... by engineering associations and individuals, the main objective of which is to gather information ... The great majority of local firms favour the policy of the open door'.[46]

Early pioneers of motor cars in Coventry, such as Daimler, also acted as a seedbed for the transfer of tacit knowledge. Founded in 1896 by Harry Lawson and merged with BSA in 1910, Daimler built its reputation on high quality standards. The company held a distinctive role in the history of the industry, providing local car producers with experienced design and production workers. Daimler also supplied the trade with components, providing externalities in the transfer of technical knowledge. Relations with component suppliers took on more formal dimensions when in 1907 Daimler invested £30,000 in the Coventry Chain Co., a major supplier to the cycle trade, which enabled it to move to a purpose-built factory. Daimler personnel joined the management board. This arrangement formalised past business transactions, but was premised on the close personal relationship between the two general managers, Percy Martin of Daimler and Alick Hills of Coventry Chain. These social and business connections meant that 'the links between some manufacturers and component firms became very close'. In 1907, Daimler invested in the expansion of Albion Drop Forgings, the latter becoming sole suppliers to Daimler in return for a further loan of £6000 in 1912. The links between component suppliers and car producers 'was more complex than a conventional buyer and seller relationship'.[47] They were embedded in a set of supportive institutional arrangements that regulated the form of collaboration and competition.[48]

Large firms developed in the interconnected sectors of engineering in Coventry by 1913, and it had become one of the leading component manufacturing centres in Britain.[49] But in their early stages of development the majority of firms were predominately small-scale, often owing their existence to capital injected by family, friends and business contacts of the original founders. This reflects the personal capitalist form of organisation in the regional business economy;[50] the majority of investors in early motor companies had 'links with the local or regional economy'. The Herbert family

---

[44] *AM*, Vol. 23, 21 April 1900, p. 307E.

[45] Lloyd-Jones and Lewis, 'Regional Business Networks', p. 150.

[46] *Coventry Handbook*, 1927, p. 58.

[47] Thoms and Donnelley, *Motor Car*, pp. 35–6; ibid., *Birth to Renaissance*, p. 41; Beavan, 'Growth and Significance', pp. 116–7.

[48] Staber, 'Networks', p. 4.

[49] Thoms and Donnelly, *Birth to Renaissance*, p. 45; Beavan, 'Growth and Significance', p. 104.

[50] For a general discussion see G. Jones and M.B. Rose, 'Family capitalism', *Business History*, Vol. 35, No. 4 (1993), pp. 8–9.

played its role in these early developments. William Herbert, through a long personal friendship, provided the capital to enable the Calcott brothers to acquire new factory accommodation for the production of motor cars. His brother, Alfred, was a major shareholder in the Standard Motor Co. by 1913. This was facilitated through a long friendship with Standard's founder, Reginald Maudsley, in addition to the contractual relations between machine tool makers and users. These personal networks mobilised local investment funds and were nurtured by Coventry's many clubs and societies.[51] To explore these networks further, the next section examines the evolution of Herbert's in the Coventry machine tool industry and its emergence as a lead firm.

Building a business reputation: Alfred Herbert Ltd.

Central to the Herbert organisation was the building of networks of trust. Trust, both warranted (behaving in a trustworthy way) and mutual (reciprocal), is linked by Casson to the notion of 'reputation'.[52] In turn, 'trust' and 'reputation', as historically specific notions, are linked in the first half of the twentieth century to those of personal capitalism and product quality. These are two of the institutionalised social habits identified in Table 1. Alfred Herbert saw his company as a lead firm and the 'ideals of the tool maker [were] to lead – to make others follow – to make a reputation'. He added that: 'This may mean more money or perhaps not, but in any case leading is better than following, if more difficult'.[53] In this respect, it gave itself a key role because the British machine tool industry in the 1890s and early 1900s came under heavy criticism, not least from observers in the USA. For example, Charles Churchill, an American who had established a successful business in London importing machine tools, described British makers as 'conservative and careful', stating that they 'showed very little disposition or inclination to copy American machine design'.[54]

Such a criticism is misplaced in the case of Herbert's and the emerging machine tool industry clustering around Coventry and Birmingham.[55] Herbert's quickly established a reputation for using American machine tools. The firm were well aware of 'the value' of developing a 'factored business ... and maintaining an effective selling organisation'.[56] Technological developments followed 'American lines', but Herbert's were no mere imitators; rather, they

[51]   Thoms and Donnelly, *Birth to Renaissance*, p. 45; J.R. Davey, *The Standard Car 1903-1963* (Shelbourne, 1964), p. 18.

[52]   Casson, 'Regional Business Networks', p. 146.

[53]   *Machine Tool Review*, Vol. 14, No. 90 (1926), p. 1.

[54]   *AM*, Vol. 19, 3 October 1896, p. 987E.

[55]   For example, *AM*, Vol. 23, 18 January 1900, p. 69E: leading makers in Manchester 'pooh-poohed the introduction of American tools as not in anyway affecting the high class British engineering and machine tool trades'.

[56]   *Alfred Herbert News*, Vol. 1, No. 6 (1927), p. 126.

used their own skilled engineers 'to better adapt them to the British market'.[57] This process was facilitated by Oscar Harmer, who joined Herbert's in 1897 and was well connected with American machine makers, as well as with the Coventry trade. Harmer's knowledge of American methods enabled Herbert's to perfect new designs, allowing the company to diversify when the bicycle boom collapsed in 1897. Harmer also persuaded Alfred to establish a network of UK sales branches as well as agencies 'in practically every country in the world'. Herbert's foreign agencies were used extensively by local firms, such as Webster & Bennet, who could gain external economies by association with the Herbert organisation and the accumulated knowledge of foreign markets and technological requirements. Technological information was also provided *gratis* to firms world-wide via the *Machine Tool Review*, a Herbert publication.[58] This pattern of trading, connecting the region to the international market, is an example of strategic networking by a market-led firm.[59] Herbert's were market creators and acted as intermediaries between producers and consumers in inter-regional as well as intra-regional networks. This role fitted the 'Herbert philosophy', which was to supply a wide range of products both to machine tool firms through inter-firm purchasing, a common feature of the industry, and to the general engineering trades.[60] One of many examples was Coventry Gauge & Tool, which installed in its factory extension in 1920 a number of Herbert lathes, and also American machines imported by Herbert's factored division.[61]

Herbert's was also interconnected to the trade through its practice of sub-contracting, which facilitated flexible production by easing the pressure on production capacity. For example, in 1913 the company sub-contracted their designs for standard lathes to Brown and Ward of Birmingham, allowing Herbert's to fully utilise its own plant for the increased output of turret lathes. In 1917, Herbert's sub-contracted the production of drilling machines to the Coventry Acme Motor Co., and contracted with Tangey of Birmingham for that company to build Herbert's-designed medium and heavy machine tools to the value of £75,000. In return, Herbert's agreed to sell Tangey machines by advertising them in their own sales catalogue. There was also technological collaboration between both firms. Tangey produced machines under Herbert designs, but also used its experienced designers to make 'special' machines for Herbert's. This added further to Herbert's production flexibility, but the company was equally keen to ensure that its 'reputation was not damaged by too cosy a relationship with a particular firm'. Herbert's network was extensive, and when in 1920 Herbert's management reported that Tangey's were not meeting delivery targets they quickly sub-contracted heavy machine

[57] *AM.*, Vol. 23, 16 January 1900, p. 514E.
[58] Herbert Records, PA 1270/4/1, Oscar Harmer for the Alfred Herbert Testimonial, 23 July 1917.
[59] Casson, 'Regional Business Networks', p. 19.
[60] See report of John Millman at Herbert's Departmental, 23 September 1918.
[61] *AM*, Vol. 52, 11 January 1920, p. 165E.

tool work out to other producers. Indeed, in 1918 Herbert's had exclusive sub-contracts with six firms for vertical and horizontal milling machines.[62]

Coupled with the firm's technical enterprise was the reputation of Herbert's, and its role as a lead firm had much to do with the dominant personality of Alfred himself. The firm's advance was consolidated by Alfred's reputation, both among his own workers and managers and with other firms, regionally, nationally and internationally. Alfred cultivated the 'Herbert spirit',[63] believing that his business was 'considerably more than a mere machine for earning profit'. Herbert's had 'won a reputation in every corner of the world where machine tools are used, for sound design, good workmanship and honest dealing'.[64] Under Alfred's personal leadership, the firm did develop a high reputation for the technical quality of its products and its innovative marketing. Experimentation in machine tool design, according to the General Manager John Millburn, was the key to competitive success. Learning-by-doing led to 'an accumulation of knowledge to enable us to build really good machines for the purposes involved'. However, their strategy was not insular and management was aware of the need to disseminate good practice through promoting national and international exhibitions for its own and its factored tools. At the Olympia Exhibition of 1920, Herbert's displayed more machine tools than any other exhibitor, launching their 'outstanding' new auto lathe. Herbert's marketing strategy led it quickly to develop international linkages through its overseas branch agencies, as well as extending its role as an agent for American, Continental and British firms. As a means of cementing its reputation as a lead firm, the management recognised the importance of after-sales service, and inspected their machines under operating conditions. The aim was to 'educate' the user to the advantages of 'labour saving machines and methods'. By the late 1920s, Herbert's was 'educating' users to convert from turret lathes to auto lathes, 'as in the past we converted them from the engine lathe to the turret lathe'. Furthermore, they provided users with technical specifications on production times and 'layouts' to bring out the 'valuable features of our ... machines ... backed up with all available information'. As it was also vitally important that senior managers were aware of technological trends, they were sent out on fact-finding missions both at home and abroad. On a fact-finding tour across the USA in 1926, it was noted that in the USA Herbert's 'have a big reputation'.[65]

The evidence presented suggests that Coventry provides an example of an industrial district with a strong clustering of interrelated firms, and that seed-corn firms acted to provide leadership in their respective industries. Indeed, the

---

[62] Herbert's Departmental, 9 January 1913; 30 April, 26 November 1917, 25 February, 11 March, 22 July 1918, 22 January 1920.

[63] Mc G. Davies, 'Twentieth Century Paternalist', pp. 100, 112 and 114.

[64] *Alfred Herbert News*, Vol. 1, No. 5 (1926), pp. 1–2.

[65] Herbert's Departmental, 9 September 1918, 7 December 1926, 1 February 1927, 12 November 1929, 9 July 1930; *AM*, Vol. 52, 11 December 1920, p. 164E; Lane, 'Herbert', p. 174; *Alfred Herbert News*, Vol. 1, No. 2 (1927), p. 23.

evolution of new industrial types before the War endowed the Midlands 'with a degree of resilience in the turbulent interwar period'.[66] The robustness of business networks is, of course, often put to the test during periods of economic downturn and crisis. As Staber claims, 'networks are not purposeful entities in their own right and have no identifiable intentions'. This is compounded by the fact that if we reject a neo-classical approach, it follows that even firms which compete in the same industry, and are located in the same region, will differ significantly in 'functions, organisational maturity, business strategy ... etc'. Therefore, local conditions for industrial development 'are heavily infused with historical ... idiosyncrasies'.[67] Consequently, the next section will examine the reaction of the machine tool industry through the actions of its core firm, Herbert's, as it faced adversity during the interwar years. In particular, we will emphasis the loose and informal nature of the Coventry business networks and the problems of industry-wide collaboration in a business environment conditioned by a competitive spirit.

Herbert's as a lead firm in the inter-war years

A successful regional business network would have been seriously compromised without Herbert's acting as a hub. As Casson argues: 'Networks tend to be built by individual leaders'.[68] In 1914, Herbert's produced twice the output of its 'nearest' European 'rivals', and by 1925 employed 2600.[69] Its dominant role at the local and national level was severely tested during the interwar years, as the machine tool industry faced severe economic problems. The external shocks of the early 1920s and 1929 rebounded hard on an industry whose fortunes were tied to both export markets and to the cyclical rhythm of Britain's engineering trades, the main domestic users of machine tools. By the mid-1920s, the volume of machine tool output was 37 per cent lower than in 1913, and values were down by 20 per cent. While recovery set in during the second half of the 1920s, between 1929 and 1933 the value of output fell by 42 per cent. Exports also followed a similar trend, falling sharply from 1921. As Alfred observed, machine tools were a 'barometric' industry, 'the basis on which all manufacturing industry ultimately depend'.[70] How did Herbert's respond to the crisis which hit the industry from 1921? Did Alfred take a dominant role at the local and national level?

A predictable response by employers to the economic crisis was to cut wage costs. As the crisis deepened by December 1920, with 25,000 unemployed in

---

[66] Garside, 'Regional', p. 144.
[67] Staber, 'Networks', pp. 6 and 13–4.
[68] Casson, 'Regional Business Networks', p. 15.
[69] Arnold, 'Innovation', pp. 58–61.
[70] D.H. Aldcroft, 'The Performance of the British Machine-Tool Industry in the Interwar Years', *Business History Review*, Vol. 40 (Autumn 1966), p. 282; A. Herbert, 'The Machine Tool Industry', in *AM*, Vol. 69, 22 December 1928, p. 96E.

Birmingham and Coventry, questions were raised about the costs and efficiency of machine tool makers. By 1921, the depression in the Midland district was described as 'all-pervading'. While it was suggested that there was a 'need for improvement in [the] organisation of machine tool shops', it was also acknowledged that for 'many firms it is not the time for the play of new ideas'. The immediate issue facing makers was negative profits.[71] This was not confined to less progressive firms, Herbert's recording an average net loss of £34,000 between 1920 and 1922.[72] Machine tool makers had to navigate a passage through the harsh business terrain that confronted them, and in particular to confront the problems of wages and the hours of work in the industry. Wage rates, on a 47-hour basis, were 'held to be incompatible with labour conditions abroad unless substantial countervailing advantages can be devised'. Many employers thus believed that labour should 'bear its share in pulling the situation round – if prices are to be stabilised the wage bill must decline along with ... production costs'.[73]

The management at Herbert's strongly endorsed these views and led a move to impose 'wage cuts locally and nationally during the trade depression of the early 1920s'.[74] In December 1920, John Millburn for Herbert's 'proposed to the Coventry and District Engineering Employer's Association [CDEEA] a reduction in wages'. Despite an earlier declaration to consider a counter-proposal by the engineering unions for a reduction in overtime and a two-shift system, a number of Coventry firms, including Humber, Lea & Francis, Swift, Triumph, Rover and Rudge-Whitworth, endorsed the lead taken by Herbert's. Continuing its aggressive policy towards trade unions, Herbert's drove home the message during the engineering lock-out of March 1922, reminding the CDEEA that it was imperative to force 'the question of a wage reduction'. The outcome was a victory for Herbert's, earnings in Coventry falling by 25 per cent. Representatives from Coventry on the National Negotiating Committee of the Employer's Federation, including Millburn of Herbert's and Colonel Cole of Humber, were accordingly thanked by the CDEEA for devoting their 'time and energy for the benefit of all members of this organisation'.[75]

Herbert's took a lead role at the local level, acting as the hub in implementing wage cuts and maintaining the trust of local firms who supported its robust strategy towards organised labour. At the same time, Herbert's secured the 'best of both worlds': it was trusted by its fellow employers over its industrial relations stance, while at the same time sustaining its reputation as a model employer with a loyal workforce. Alfred prided himself in providing good working conditions, and his workers felt that it was as a mark of status to work 'for the firm which produced the best machine tools in the world'. The

---

[71]   *AM*, Vol. 52, 11, 25 December 1920, pp. 165E, 177E, Vol. 53, 15 January 1921, p. 198E.

[72]   Arnold, 'Innovation', pp. 60–1.

[73]   *AM*, Vol. 53, 15, 22 January 1921, pp. 195E, 205E.

[74]   Mc G. Davies, 'Twentieth Century Paternalist', pp. 108 and 114.

[75]   Ibid., pp. 108–9.

management carefully cultivated the 'Herbert Spirit', emphasising long service, loyalty, and a reputation based upon skilled work.[76] These are examples of social habits that institutionalised worker behaviour at Herbert's and allowed the firm to retain its workforce, while at the same time leading the attack on wage costs. Collaboration and competition co-existed in a fragile business environment. At the local and regional level, employers followed Herbert's lead, and institutionalised habits sustained more or less workable business networks. At the national level, however, Herbert's role was less decisive, suggesting some limitations to the network approach.

At a national level, Alfred was instrumental in founding the Machine Tool Trades Association (MTTA) in 1919, of which he was President until 1934. The MTTA was primarily an institution for promoting the marketing of machine tools and the dissemination of technical knowledge through national and international exhibitions.[77] This objective constituted a practical form of networking at a national level through social habits that became embedded in supportive institutional arrangements for regulating co-operation and competition among member firms.[78] An examination of the activities of the MTTA, however, suggests that its role was minimalist, as was that of Alfred himself. On the important issue of common pricing for machine tools, it stood aloof, despite the call for collaboration from individual members.[79] During 1919, uniform price clauses in contracts, based on movements in wages and material costs, were introduced on a voluntary basis by member firms, but these were abandoned in 1920 as the onset of depression led to falling prices and a squeeze on profits. Consequently, firms began to question the operational value of a common price policy and the MTTA abandoned any attempt at common action. Alfred summed up their stance: 'It was impossible to adopt a uniform policy with regard to prices', because of the varying circumstances of different firms within the industry. This remained a consistent policy throughout the interwar years. In 1939, the President, W.B. Lang, on rejecting calls for uniform price increases, claimed that they 'had never interfered with freedom ... it was not a price controlling Association'.[80]

On the public stage, Alfred reflected this competitive spirit. In 1928, he claimed that business should not be sheltered from competition, but should look closely at its own production practices. Machine tool prices were determined by the interdependent actions of demand and supply, and by competition amongst employers. His solution to depressed prices was not collusion, but rather innovative management to 'improve designs and thus

---

[76] Ibid., p. 108.
[77] Private Records of MTTA, London, Minute Books of the Council 1919–25, 15, 30 April 1919, and of the Directors 1933–39, 22 March 1934. Our Thanks to Simon Brown for his kind permission to use and cite information from the archive.
[78] Staber, 'Networks', pp. 1, 4.
[79] Letters from firms to MTTA, Council, 14 April 1920.
[80] MTTA, Council, 23 July 1919, 14 April 1920; Directors, 13 September 1939.

stimulate the market'.[81] The issue, however, did not go away, and in 1934 the management of BSA Tools urged 'a strong effort ... to bring together the principal Tool Manufacturers' to fix prices and output quotas. Percy Martin, the Managing Director of the parent company, was, however, far from optimistic about success, because 'Sir Alfred Herbert will not move' on this matter, a factor that significantly reduced the probability of a general agreement. Instead, BSA sought a bilateral arrangement with the Churchill Machine Tool Co. of Manchester to co-ordinate prices on the two company's lathes.[82] Herbert's, the lead firm, gave no support to collaborative price policies, weakening attempts to build successful business networks at the national level.

No discussion of the business response to the depression can ignore the issue of rationalisation and technological collaboration.[83] The machine tool trade took considerable interest in the strategies of German and Swiss tool makers to provide central co-ordination on design and research through the combination of firms with similar patterns of production. In 1924, the MTTA 'noted with interest' the working arrangements between Swiss Machine Tool Makers and the Magdeburg Machine Tool Works of Germany to co-ordinate standardised output.[84] A.B. Winters, a production engineer, pushed the merits of standardised production via amalgamation in 1929. He argued that British makers should recognise that they were facing competition on a world-scale, something that necessitated a 'co-operative attitude' by the industry. Such co-operation was detectable in Germany, where 'fusions' among firms were allegedly inducing 'revolutionary changes in the theory and practice of business'. Winters concluded that given the competitive climate facing British makers there was 'no other alternative' but to adopt rationalisation and pursue a strategy of closer technical collaboration. He also noted that the spatial clustering of the machine tool industry in the Midlands was favourable to 'more concerted action'.[85] Local networks could thus be used to build national networks, facilitating the co-existence of co-operation and competition.

Winter's remarks sparked off a heated debate, but the general tone was negative and sought to undermine a rationalisation strategy. For example, F.E.S. Johnson, a Glasgow maker, evoked a competitive market argument, asserting that amalgamation 'stifled' competition and 'stultified' design innovation.[86] Here was a clear reference to the virtues of personal capitalism, with its institutional social habits of reputation through quality production, the respect for user-needs and for providing a variety of up-to-date designs.

---

[81] Sir Alfred Herbert, 'Machine Tool Prices', in *AM*, Vol. 69, 8 December 1928, p. 242E.

[82] CRO, Records of BSA, 594/2/1/2/4, Correspondence file of A.P.F. Rogers, copy of BSA Tools Monthly Report, 31 January 1934, and Martin to Rogers, 26 January 1934.

[83] See L. Hannah, *The Rise of the Corporate Economy* (Methuen, 1983), Chapter 3.

[84] MTTA, Council, 9 July 1924.

[85] A.B. Winter, 'Are Amalgamations Possible in the Machine Tool Industry', *AM*, Vol. 71, 23 November 1929, pp. 167–8E.

[86] F.E.S. Johnson, Letter in *AM*, Vol. 71, 7 December 1929, p. 195E.

Johnson was also aware of the possibilities of amalgamations to open up personally-managed firms to control by the 'powerful non-engineering financiers' whose motives were driven simply by profit.[87] Johnson was supported by other makers, including W.B. Lang, who informed the MTTA in 1930 that 'the individual factor in industry' prevailed, and 'that rationalisation in engineering could not succeed unless individualism played its full part'.[88] Such views were evident at Herbert's, when in 1918 the formation of a research association for machine tools was raised and found support from John Millman. He believed that an association would promote greater standardisation, but Alfred thought it impracticable because 'jealousy and secrecy do of necessity exist and ... most companies would prefer to solve their own problems themselves, rather than to submit same to an institution'.[89] Twenty years later the Department of Scientific and Industrial Research wrote to the MTTA inquiring if it would again consider supporting a research association. The answer was negative, the MTTA affirming that it existed 'primarily for the promotion of exhibitions'.[90] Both Herbert's and the MTTA adhered to the social habits of personal capitalism, while the leading firm in the industry eschewed closer formal collaboration and the formation of national business networks.

Conclusion

A basic premise of this study is that business networks are habit-forming modes of behaviour that become embedded in history. Informed by Veblen, the empirical investigation has suggested the existence of regional business networks in the evolving industrial cluster of Coventry. There was a close interconnection between bicycles, machine tools, motor vehicles and components in the pre-war period. The networks that were formed operated at two levels. On the first level, entrepreneurial linkages were associated with the predominance of personal forms of governance, and these persisted into the interwar years. Family connections were important and there were seed-bed firms which stimulated business development. At the second level, the cluster of interrelated firms stimulated the evolution of a variegated industrial structure in Coventry.

By the interwar years, Coventry's industrial district was characterised by flexible production, the high quality of its products, the meeting of customer needs and by a set of inter-firm relations that were complex and diverse. An important player in this game was Herbert's. The firm was the hub of a set of networks associated with factoring and sub-contracting, building regional,

[87]   Ibid.
[88]   Reported in *AM*, Vol. 72, 3, 10 May 1930, pp. 192E, 199E.
[89]   Herbert's Departmental, 28 October 1918.
[90]   MTTA, Directors, 21 September 1938.

national and international marketing networks. At Herbert's, personal capitalism related to social habits of trust and reputation, facilitating the building of business relations at the inter- and intra-regional level. Locally, Herbert's led the way in labour issues in the 1920s, because it was trusted by local firms to do so. This raised the question as to whether local business networks could be used to build national networks, particularly in terms of a response to the harsh economic environment of the interwar period. Our evidence shows that the response was minimalist. The MTTA, with Alfred as its President, gave little support to collaboration on pricing, rationalisation and technology. Instead, they remained committed to individual solutions to the competitive process facing firms and rejected national schemes of collaboration. As Staber claims, 'networks are not purposeful entities in their own right'.[91] Consequently, the role of prominent business leaders such as Alfred Herbert is of key importance in the formation of successful networks. Further, our approach has demonstrated that a set of institutionalised social habits which help foster the formation of successful regional business networks may act to constrain such networks nationally.

---

[91]   Staber, 'Networks', p. 13.

Chapter 13

A false dawn?
Military procurement and Manchester industrial district, 1935–1960[1]

Till Geiger

Introduction

Increasing defence expenditure is often a means by which governments attempt to generate employment in depressed areas, promote regional economic development and advance technological progress. This chapter examines the extent to which increased defence expenditure can contribute to the economic revival of declining industrial districts.

In his *Principles of Economics*, Alfred Marshall suggests that industrial districts offer considerable external economies to the small firms located in their midst, on the grounds that the heavy concentration of small producers in the same industry will lead to the emergence of auxiliary industries, development of specialised labour markets, and exchange of ideas. At the same time, he argues that industrial districts are particularly vulnerable to depression, because a downturn in demand for their primary products may trigger a profound economic crisis in those regions grouped around one industry. Marshall concludes that, therefore, large industrial districts or towns with several different industrial clusters may better withstand the drop in demand in one of its industries. The other industries would then alleviate the crisis by sustaining the demand for services and allowing shopkeepers to support local communities. However, Marshall failed to examine the impact of a continued production crisis on the future development of an industrial district.[2]

While several of the studies in this volume have focussed on the development of industrial districts and the underlying business networks over time, they too largely ignore the issue of the decline of an industrial district after its development has reached saturation. Given the potential problems

[1] I am grateful to Igor Filatotchev, Roger Lloyd-Jones, Lucy Newton, Hilary Owen and the participants at the Preston workshop conference for their helpful comments and suggestions, and to the Controller of Her Majesty's Stationery Office for the permission to cite Crown Copyright material.
[2] Alfred Marshall, *Principles of Economics* (Macmillan, 1949 reprint), pp. 221–7.

arising from a monolithic industrial structure, Wilson and Singleton argue, following Peter Swann's work, that when an industrial district reaches the saturation stage, the regional business networks should seek to diversify the industrial base of the district in order to assure the continued economic stability of the regional economy. At the same time, any attempts to diversify the industrial structure may be hampered by the fact that other localities often offer a more favourable environment for new clusters to emerge around new technology. Moreover, the question remains regarding the extent to which local business networks can successfully attract new firms to an existing industrial district, particularly as the emergence of new enterprises will potentially undermine the local labour market and redirect finance away from established producers. For example, the Manchester industrial district entered into its saturation phase during the inter-War period and continued to decline until the late 1970s. It was consequently a prime candidate for diversification of its industrial structure. Wilson and Singleton note in their chapter that despite the considerable efforts of certain local business leaders, the attempts to diversify the industrial base during the inter-War period failed to rejuvenate the regional economy. While a number of electrical engineering and aircraft firms managed to gain a foothold in the Manchester industrial district, their establishment did not lead to the formation of new industrial clusters.[3]

Besides their own initiatives, local business networks in depressed regions may choose to lobby government for financial assistance, in order to attract new industries to the area. Some firms experiencing financial difficulties may approach the government for subsidies or large public procurement contracts to bolster production. However, Mark Casson has suggested that such rent-seeking lobbying may have detrimental effects on regional economic development.[4] For example, winning a large production contract for military hardware may put a defence contractor in an advantageous position over other firms. Clearly, the economic success of defence contractors depends to a significant degree on its relationship with the government supply departments. In order to gain lucrative government contracts, defence firms will exploit their own contacts to lobby not just central government, but also local politicians and officials in an attempt to influence the procurement process. However, such economic behaviour (or rent-seeking lobbying) may undermine existing

---

[3]   Chapter 3, in this volume. This chapter adopts the same definition of the Manchester industrial district as Wilson and Singleton. This definition equates the Manchester industrial district with the two main Lancashire cotton districts of the weaving area around Blackburn, Burnley and the Rossendale Valley and the spinning area around Rochdale, Oldham, Bolton, and Preston, as well as the Manchester conurbation including the adjoining industrial fringes of Cheshire and Derbyshire. The Manchester industrial district constituted a part of the North-Western region used by government regional statistics, which includes Merseyside, other parts of Lancashire, Cumbria as well as adjoining parts of Northern Cheshire. On the definition of the sub-regions, see Michael F. Fogarty, *Prospects of the Industrial Areas of Great Britain* (Methuen, 1945), p. 207.

[4]   See Chapter 2, in this volume.

business networks, particularly if other industries are depressed or lack a similarly strong voice in the corridors of power. As a consequence, a locality may well become overly dependent on defence-related employment. In contrast to good networking, there is a real danger that government-defence industry relations will become closed and opaque due to the involvement of politicians and anti-entrepreneurial social elites.[5] This observation raises intriguing questions as to whether business networks in the defence industries are just a case of bad networking with a detrimental impact on regional development.

This chapter analyses the impact of increased defence expenditure on the declining Manchester industrial district from the 1930s. The analysis examines whether Wartime mobilisation during the Second World War and the Korean War rearmament programme disrupted regional economic development during a crucial period of adjustment to decline when the business networks should have sought to diversify the industrial structure of the regional economy. The next section discusses the interrelationship between business lobbying, local business networks, government defence procurement and regional economic development. Building on this discussion, the following sections examine the changing position of the aircraft industry within the Manchester industrial district since its inception.

Defence expenditure and regional economic development

In addition to physical advantages, in his analysis of industrial districts Marshall highlighted government decisions (or 'the patronage of a court') as a major cause for the location of industry in a particular place. Indeed, he attributes the emergence of some industrial districts to the deliberate settlement of immigrants by governments in certain areas.[6] Writing at the same time, the German economist, Werner Sombart, suggested that government demand for increasingly sophisticated armaments spurred on the development of technology. According to Sombart, military procurement agents encouraged the formation of large arms factories capable of supplying standardised weapons of high quality and at short notice to armed forces. Relying on large suppliers made it easier for governments to ensure proper control over the procurement process.[7] However, these large producers of military goods depended on constant government orders in order to justify the investment in large amounts of machinery to mass produce the weapons to meet government

---

[5]   Mark Casson, *Enterprise and Leadership: Studies on Firms, Markets and Networks* (Edward Elgar, 2000), pp. 161 and 180.

[6]   Marshall, *Principles*, pp. 223–4.

[7]   On this point, see Werner Sombart, *Der Moderne Kapitalismus: Historische-Systematische Darstellung des Gesamteuropäischen Wirtschaftsleben von Seinen Anfängen bis zur GegenWart. Band 2: Das Europäischen Wirtschaftsleben im Zeitalter des Frühkapitalismus Vornehmlich des 16., 17. und 18. Jahrhunderts*, 5th ed. (Duncker und Humbolt, 1922), pp. 894–5.

demand in a crisis. In the early nineteenth century, the industrial districts of small arms manufacturers in Birmingham clung to their traditional workshop-based production methods, because government demand for rifles was too erratic to sustain a large modern rifle factory such as the Springfield Arsenal in the United States. When the artisanal Birmingham gunmakers could not expand their production to meet the increased demand during the Crimean War, the British government decided to build its own government factory, the Enfield Arsenal, using imported American machinery, in order to mass-produce rifles for the Army. This development forced the small gun manufacturers in the Birmingham area to merge their undertakings in the Birmingham Small Arms Company in order to finance the purchase of machinery in 1861. Arguably in the British case, this development hampered the emergence of new industries, such as the machine tool industry around the Springfield arsenal.[8] In areas of high concentration of defence-related industry, defence contractors will enlist local politicians and officials to lobby for military contracts to ensure continued employment in the local economy.[9] Despite the drawbacks of making a region dependent on continued government contracts, local business networks in areas of high unemployment may regard attracting military contracts as beneficial to the local economy. While military production contracts may only alleviate the local unemployment problem temporarily, the award of a research and development contract might lead to the creation of a cluster of high technology firms. Indeed, studies by economic geographers and economists show that defence procurement proved instrumental 'in the development of high-technology, and particularly electronics industries, both nationally and locally'.[10] At the same time, governments may have their own reasons such as military security or employment creation for siting a new defence factory in a certain area.

For example, during Korean War rearmament, the centre of American military aircraft production relocated from the New England seaboard to Southern California. Around these newly-created or relocated firms, a growing number of small sub-contractors sprang up, particularly in the electronics field. The emerging networks between the large prime defence contractors and sub-contractors benefited tremendously from the close proximity to and regular contact with scientists at Stanford and the California Institute of Technology who were engaged in fundamental research funded by the American Department of Defence. Peter Hall notes in his study of the creation of the American aerospace complex that this move from the East to the West Coast involved a process of Schumpeterian 'creative destruction'. In the aftermath of

---

[8]   Edward Ames and Nathan Rosenberg, 'The Enfield Arsenal in Theory and History', *Economic Journal*, 78 (December, 1968), pp. 827–42; William H. McNeill, *The Pursuit of Power: Technology, Armed Force, and Society since A.D. 1000* (Basil Blackwell, 1982), pp. 232–6.

[9]   Casson, *Enterprise*, p. 180.

[10]   Michael J. Breheny, 'Introduction,' in Michael J. Breheny (ed), *Defence Expenditure and Regional Development* (Mansell, 1988), p. 2.

the Second World War, the changes in aircraft technology forced the established industry to adapt to the new developments in the field of jet-propulsion, supersonic flight, missiles and electronics. In order to adapt to this challenge, established aircraft manufacturers invested in the emerging new microelectronics industry in California. Military procurement fostered the strong links between established aircraft firms and their subcontractors in this new location, which lead to the emergence of a new industrial cluster of aerospace and electronics firms. Hall argues that the aerospace industrial complex grew and solidified during the decade after the end of the Korean War, just as in the case of other industrial clusters around military production centres since the mid-nineteenth century. In this sense, the preference of defence procurement agents for purchasing weapon systems from established defence contractors 'effectively helps maintain inertia in a location pattern already established as long ago as the 1920s and 1930s'.[11] This bias towards inertia in the regional distribution of defence production raises the question of the extent to which military procurement can induce the creation of new industrial districts.

Returning to the British case, the regional distribution of the British aircraft industry has remained fairly static since the late 1930s and has changed very little since 1945. The industry has largely been located in the South East, in Lancashire, and around Bristol, for primarily historical reasons. Given this regional distribution, David Edgerton has suggested that development and production became an almost entirely English (love) affair.[12] In contrast to the Californian aerospace industry, the British aircraft industry failed to develop similar close networks between rival firms and allied industries. Even where there existed regional concentrations of aircraft firms, John Lovering notes that design teams had little contact with their rivals, leading to the duplication of research and development efforts. As a consequence, staff from one factory rarely used the facilities such as wind tunnels of neighbouring plants, even after the merger of aircraft firms in the 1960s. Lovering attributes the relative autonomy of individual factories to the British system of defence procurement in this period. Rather than empowering individual defence contractors to build up a chain of local suppliers and sub-contractors, the Ministry of Supply centralised many of these procurement decisions. By the time the British government adopted the American prime contractor system in the early 1960s, the regional distribution of the industry had solidified further, partly due to the low levels of labour mobility among engineers, drawing room staff and skilled workers. As a consequence, it proved difficult for the two newly formed

---

[11] Peter Hall, 'The Creation of the American Aerospace Complex: A Study in Industrial Inertia', in Breheny (ed), *Defence Expenditure*, pp. 102–21 (quote p. 118). On this point, see also Edward J. Malecki and Lois M. Stark, 'Regional and Industrial Variation in Defence Spending: Some American evidence', in ibid., pp. 76–98.

[12] David Edgerton, *England and the Aeroplane: An Essay on a Militant and Technological Nation* (Macmillan, 1991), p. xviii.

aircraft firms (British Aircraft Corporation and Hawker-Siddeley) to amalgamate plants even within a small region like the North West.[13]

Only the Wartime imperative to expand production led to the establishment of some aircraft production facilities in Northern Ireland, Scotland and Wales. However, aircraft firms tended to operate these production facilities as branch plants from their main development and production centres in England. As a consequence, many of these shadow factories, such as the Rolls-Royce aero-engine factory on the Hillington industrial estate in Glasgow, were sold off by the Ministry of Aircraft production at the end of the Second World War. Rolls-Royce reorganised its Hillington plant to service and repair Merlin engines. As a government report noted,

> [i]n this way the large organisation and the engineering skills built up at Hillington during the War were in considerable measure retained ready for rapid expansion if and when the need arose.[14]

This statement reflected the government's intention to maintain the war potential of the British economy by preserving a significant proportion of defence production facilities in the immediate post-War period. At the same time, the government decided to concentrate on the development of new military technology, rather than spend its limited financial resources on new weaponry. Without major production orders, defence contractors lacked the incentive to modernise the defence production facilities in line with new weapons technology in this period. When the outbreak of the Korean War forced the British government to rearm again, the shortcomings of the government's war potential policy became obvious. While the British aircraft industry remained at the forefront of aircraft technology in the late 1940s, the production facilities of most firms failed keep up with rapid technological change. For example, British aero-engine firms, such as Rolls-Royce, led the world in the development of jet engines, but lacked the production lines to mass-produce them. Despite the war potential policy, the British government found in late 1950 that it would have to build new factories for jet engines production in order to meet the sudden increase in demand due to its defence programme. However, the over-full employment of the British economy hampered the conversion to a Cold War economy. Therefore, government initially aimed to restrict the expansion of defence production to a minimum.[15]

---

[13] John Lovering, 'Islands of Prosperity: The Spatial Impact of High-technology Defence Industry in Britain', in Breheny (ed), *Defence Expenditure*, pp. 29–48.

[14] Scottish Record Office (hereafter SRO) SRO SEP 4/14: note 'Rolls-Royce Limited: East Kilbride Factory Opening', 3 November 1953.

[15] Till Geiger, *Britain and the Economic Problem of the Cold War: The Political Economy and the Economic Impact of the British Defence Effort, 1945–1955* (Ashgate, forthcoming), Chapter 5.; ibid., '"The Next War is Bound to Come": Defence Production Policy, Supply Departments and Defence Contractors in Britain, 1945–57', in Anthony Gorst,

If military requirements necessitated any new investment, then economic planners argued that new defence factories should be established in areas of relatively high unemployment, such as Scotland.[16]

The needs of the rearmament programme led to a conflict of interests between on the one hand the supply departments and defence contractors, and on the other hand the Board of Trade and the regional business network. Eager to expand jet production, the Ministry of Supply tried to persuade Rolls-Royce to convert its existing factory in Glasgow to the production of Avon jet engines. However, Rolls-Royce argued that the Hillington site would be too small to accommodate such a production line. The firm insisted that the government make available one of the advance factories the Board of Trade had built in East Kilbride, near Glasgow, in order to attract American firms to the area. While the Board of Trade accepted the need to expand jet engine production capacity in Scotland, officials argued that Rolls-Royce should be encouraged to establish its new jet engine factory in an unemployment hotspot of Greenock.[17] The Scottish Council (Industry and Development) similarly protested against the East Kilbride site being allocated to Rolls-Royce.[18] After months of wrangling, the Ministry of Supply managed to secure the East Kilbride site for Rolls-Royce, despite the fact that this move required the construction of new factory buildings and ignored the serious shortage of skilled labour and adequate housing in the area.[19] Within a year of its opening in 1953, the future of Rolls-Royce's jet engine factory in East Kilbride was called into doubt by cuts in the defence procurement budget following the end of the Korean War. The firm contemplated shifting the production of a new type of jet engine to Derby and winding down its Scottish operations. In the end, an American offshore procurement contract for Hunter jet fighters secured continued production at the East Kilbride factory.[20] The government blocked

---

Lewis Johnman, and W. Scott Lucas (eds), *Contemporary British History, 1931–61: Politics and the Limits of Policy* (Pinter, 1991), pp. 95–118.

[16] The following analysis of impact of Korean War economy on Scotland is drawn from Geiger, *Britain and the Economic Problem*, Chapter 9.

[17] Public Record Office (hereafter: PRO) PRO BT 177/325: letter Oakley - Raffan, 1 December 1950.; PRO BT 177/325: letter Miller - Oakley, 22 December 1950.; PRO BT 177/325: letter Raffan - Oakley, 28 November 1950.

[18] Scottish Council (Development and Industry), Edinburgh (hereafter SCDI) SCDI SC 2/3/1/1: EC (50) 5th, Minutes of the 5th meeting of Executive Committee, 11 September 1950.; SCDI SC 2/3/1/2: EC (51) 3rd, Minutes of the 3rd meeting of Executive Committee, 13 April 1951.

[19] BT 177/325: letter Raffan - Oakley, ; PRO BT 177/325: minute Monier-Williams - Calder, 7 December 1950.; BT 177/325: letter Oakley - Raffan, ; BT 177/325: letter Miller - Oakley, ; PRO BT 177/325: letter Oakley - Reading, 9 March 1951.

[20] Scottish Record Office (hereafter SRO) SRO SEP 10/16: brief for Estimates Debate, 14th-15th July, 1953; 'Industry, Employment and Economic Well-Being', 14 July 1953. On offshore procurement contracts, see Till Geiger and Lorenza Sebesta, 'A Self-Defeating Policy: American Offshore Procurement and Integration of Western European Defence Production, 1952–56', *Journal of European Integration History*, 4 (1998), pp. 55–73.

the company's attempt to move some of its production from Scotland to Ashford in Kent.[21]

The example of the Rolls-Royce factories in Scotland demonstrates the ambivalent relationship between defence contractors, defence procurement agencies and other government departments. Creating additional aero-engine capacity in Scotland disrupted the efforts of the Board of Trade to attract American inward investment to Scotland. Rearmament empowered defence contractors to lobby for preferential access to economic resources and the location of new factories. The danger of such private bargaining between government departments and defence firms is that it might prevent regional business networks from emerging, therefore hampering local economic development in the longer-term.[22] Without the co-operation of Rolls-Royce, the Ministry of Supply would not have been able to meet the production targets for jet engines. Therefore, Rolls-Royce effectively chose the location of their new factory against the opposition of a number of government departments.

At the same time, the Scottish Council (Industry and Development) lobbied hard to ensure Scotland would receive its share of rearmament contracts. For example, the chairman of the Scottish Council (Development and Industry) met with the Minister of Supply, Duncan Sandys, in spring 1952 in order to press the Council's case for the creation of a new defence factory in North East Scotland. He extracted a promise from the Minister that Scotland would receive a fair share of all new defence-related capacity.[23] However, he offered no assurance that any new defence factory would be located in North East Scotland. In contrast to the half-hearted support of the Ministry of Supply, the Board of Trade supported the Council's endeavour to attract a defence contractor to the Aberdeen area.[24] However, the Board of Trade lacked the financial resources to build advance factory units, as suggested by a working party of the Scottish Council (Development and Industry).[25] As a consequence, Aberdeen and the fishing ports in North East Scotland remained areas with high structural unemployment. However, some defence procurement contracts were awarded to the local textile factories and fish canneries in order to reduce unemployment in the area.[26]

---

[21] SRO SEP 4/14: note of a conversation between the Minister of State and Mr Craig Mitchell, Mr Crow on 28 October 1953, 31 October 1953.; SRO SEP 4/14: excerpt from minutes EPC (55) 9, 12 October 1955.

[22] Casson, *Enterprise*, pp. 161 and 180.

[23] SCDI SC 2/3/1/2: EC (52) 3rd, Minutes of the 3rd meeting of Executive Committee, 18 April 1952.

[24] A large electronics firm, which had shown an interest in establishing a factory in Aberdeen, decided to locate in the Midlands due to the high transport cost; see SCDI SC 2/3/1/2: EC (51) 7th, Minutes of the 7th meeting of Executive Committee, 5 November 1951.

[25] SCDI SC 2/7/4/1: Miscellaneous Publications: copy of *Report of the Committee on Unemployment in Aberdeen and District*, 1952.

[26] SEP 10/16: brief for Estimates Debate, 14th-15th July, 1953; 'Industry, Employment and Economic Well-Being',; SCDI SC 2/3/1/2: EC (53) 4th, Minutes of the 4th meeting of Executive Committee, 15 June 1953.

The Scottish Council (Development and Industry) was more successful in persuading the government to fund its electronics programme under the defence programme. Based on a suggestion by Jack Toothill of Ferranti, this project proposed the establishment of a joint laboratory for collaborative research among local electronics firms, in order to create an electronics industrial cluster in Scotland. The Ministry of Supply responded favourably to this proposal.[27] With the prospect of defence-related development contracts in the offing, several Scottish electronics and engineering firms created their own research and design teams in order to undertake such work.[28] Under the scheme, the government financed the building of a new laboratory opposite Ferranti's Crewe Toll site. Besides its important role facilitating collaborative research, the Council hoped that the new laboratory would become a training centre for skilled workers for the nascent Scottish electronics industry.[29] In order to achieve this objective, Ferranti managers applied to the government for their apprentice school to become the local examination centre for basic engineering qualifications.[30] After some doubts over continued government backing for the scheme, the new laboratory was opened by the Duke of Edinburgh in 1954.[31] With the end of the defence programme, the Scottish electronics programme withered, possibly because of its close links to Ferranti and its dependence on military research and development work. The need for secrecy severely limited the potential for both technological spin-off and the emergence of an effective business network in the local electronics industry. Benefiting from further defence-related development contracts, the Scottish divisions of Ferranti remained an important defence contractor. As Wilson highlights, incoming American electronics firms benefited hugely from the presence of a skilled labour force as a result of Toothill's electronics scheme.[32]

Despite the visionary electronics scheme and the lobbying of the Scottish Council (Development and Industry), the Scottish economy benefited only temporarily from the increased defence spending of the Korean War rearmament programme. On balance, the increased military expenditure disrupted the government's regional development strategy, exacerbating local housing and skill shortages, which were only partly offset by positive initiatives like the Scottish Council's electronics scheme. Indeed, a report

---

[27] SCDI SC 2/3/1/1: EC (50) 7th, Minutes of the 7th meeting of Executive Committee, 23 November 1950.

[28] SC 2/3/1/2: EC (51) 7th, Minutes of the 7th meeting of Executive Committee.

[29] SCDI SC 2/3/1/2: EC (51) 6th, Minutes of the 6th meeting of Executive Committee, 5 October 1951.

[30] John F. Wilson, Ferranti: A History, Building a Family Business, 1882–1975 (Carnegie, 2000), p. 333.

[31] SCDI SC 2/3/1/2: EC (51) 8th, Minutes of the 8th meeting of Executive Committee, 14 December 1951.; SC 2/3/1/2: EC (52) 3rd, Minutes of the 3rd meeting of Executive Committee, ; SCDI SC 2/3/1/2: EC (52) 4th, Minutes of the 4th meeting of Executive Committee, 27 May 1952.; SCDI SC 2/3/1/2: EC (54) 1st, Minutes of the 1st meeting of Executive Committee, 30 March 1954.

[32] Wilson, Ferranti, pp. 322–4.

compiled by the Local Development Committee of the Scottish Council (Development and Industry) in 1952 criticised the government for refusing to support new industrial investment outside the development areas near the main industrial centres which were more attractive to inward investment. At the same time, the report urged the government to locate a defence factory in Aberdeen or along the North East coast, which could be converted to peace production when the defence demand subsided. However, the committee saw only limited scope for the rearmament programme to contribute to the longer-term development of the Scottish economy.[33]

The present analysis only partly supports Casson's suggestion that government-defence industry relations are inimical to the creation of successful business networks within regions or an industrial district, due to their closed nature. The example of the Californian aerospace complex, in particular, shows that under certain circumstances government procurement can foster the creation of successful business networking and defence-led regional development around newly emerging industries. In order to examine this issue further, the remainder of this chapter will examine the impact of military procurement on the Manchester industrial district in the 1940s and 1950s. The cluster of aircraft firms which had existed in the North West since before the First World War formed the basis for the massive expansion of aircraft production in the area during the Second World War. After 1945, the government sought to preserve a significant proportion of this production capacity under its War potential policy as a nucleus for future wartime expansion. At the same time, the government thought about encouraging defence firms to move from the South-East and Midlands to regions less vulnerable to air or missile attack.[34] While this policy might have benefited the aircraft industry in the Manchester industrial area, the Board of Trade and the Ministry of Supply asked defence firms to relocate to unemployment hot spots in line with the government's full employment policy. However, defence firms were rather reluctant to move from their traditional sites as relocation would disrupt existing industrial clusters in these regions. The other reason for the overt reluctance of defence firms was the reduced prospects of substantial defence contracts in the immediate post-war period. As a consequence, most defence contractors started scaling down the production at outlying shadow factories and concentrating their main factories close to their design and development departments. Nevertheless, the continued government support for the aircraft industry provided the opportunity for a new industrial cluster to emerge around the region's aircraft manufacturers, which could replace the

---

[33] Scottish Council (Development and Industry), *Report of the Committee on Local Development in Scotland* (Edinburgh: Scottish Council Development and Industry, 1952), p. 34–5.
[34] Michael P. Fogarty, 'The Location of Industry', in G.D.N. Worswick and P.H. Ady (eds), *The British Economy, 1945–1950* (Oxford University Press, 1952), p. 255.

declining cotton industry as the driving force of the Manchester industrial district. This proposition will be examined in the following section.

The Lancashire aircraft industry and the Manchester industrial district

The factors leading to the emergence of the Lancashire aircraft industry conform closely to the Marshallian model. On the one hand, location decisions were largely motivated by the proximity of supplies and finance; on the other hand, they resulted from government decisions. For example, the pioneering aircraft builder, Alliott Verdon Roe, decided to move his small aircraft workshop from Hackney to the basement of the surgical webbing factory, Everard & Co., managed by his brother Humphrey, at Broomsfield Mill in Manchester in 1910. Even before his move to Manchester, Humphrey's firm had supplied Alliott's workshop with materials such as braces and webbing straps. With financial assistance from Humphrey, Alliott established A.V. Roe & Company in 1910.[35] During the First World War, A.V. Roe & Co. expanded its production facilities by taking over an extension of the Parks Works in Salford.[36] The increased demand prompted several firms such as Dick Kerr's in Preston to enter aircraft production. This firm converted its electric railway and tramway factory on Strand Road to the construction of Felixstowe F3 and F5 flying boats.[37] Towards the end of the War, observers raised concerns about whether the supply of aircraft should be left to private suppliers.[38] Therefore, the government decided to build three large national aircraft factories, rather than rely on small sub-contractors with limited financial resources. In order to meet the urgent demand for a long-range bombing fleet, the second of these national aircraft factories was erected in Heaton Chapel, Stockport, in autumn 1917. This factory, the National Aircraft Factory No. 2, managed by Crossley Motors, built 326 de Havilland DH9 day bombers by the end of the War.[39] At first sight, this record compared rather poorly with the output of 5446 Avro planes during the War.[40] Since the contribution to aircraft production failed to live up to the expectations of the Wartime planners, some observers attributed the factories' poor performance to state ownership, arguing that private firms

---

[35] Peter King, *Knights of the Air: The Life and Times of the Extraordinary Pioneers Who First Built British Aeroplanes* (Constable, 1989), pp. 81–2; A.D. George, 'A.V. Roe and the Beginnings of the Aircraft Industry', *Manchester Memoirs* 122 (1981–82), pp. 70–1.

[36] A.D. George, 'Aircraft Factories: Origins, Development and Archaeology', *Occasional Paper* (Manchester Polytechnic, 1986), p. 3.

[37] George, 'Aircraft factories', p. 5–6.; Geoffrey Timmins, *Made in Lancashire: A History of Regional Industrialisation* (Manchester University Press, 1998), p. 306.

[38] Alfred Marshall, *Industry and Trade*, 3rd ed. (Macmillan and Co., 1920), p. 228, fn. 1.

[39] King, *Knights of the Air*, pp. 190–2.; A.D. George, 'The National Aircraft Factories in the First World War', *Research Papers* (Manchester Polytechnic 1989), pp. 1–2.

[40] A.D. George, 'New Reflections on A.V. Roe and the Birth of the Aircraft Industry', *Manchester Memoirs*, 125 (1985–86), p. 91.

would have built the new factories more quickly.[41] However, an example of the relative efficiency of the public sector was the construction of the Oldham aircraft factories by 3000 American personnel in a six-month period just before the end of the War.[42]

After the end of the War, many wartime British aircraft producers ceased aircraft production. In 1918, Dick Kerr's merged with other firms to form English Electric and decided to stop building aircraft.[43] Crossley Motors converted National Aircraft Factory No. 2 to the manufacture of cars, extending its production facilities into a neighbouring industrial estate.[44] However, the firm did not leave the sector totally, but acquired the majority shareholding in A.V. Roe & Co. in 1920 after Alliott Roe fell out with his brother.[45] This acquisition led to the company's new aircraft factory in Newton Heath, Manchester, being used by their new owners for the production of car bodies in the early 1920s. At the same time, the firm moved its testing ground from the Alexandra Park Aerodrome after its closure to Woodford in Cheshire in 1923. Even though A.V. Roe was making a slight profit, Crossley Motors was forced to sell its stake in the aircraft business to Armstrong-Siddeley.[46] While Crossleys continued to produce cars, it sold its premises in Heaton Chapel to another aircraft firm, Fairey Aviation, which had been induced to move North by government pressure in 1935. After its move to Manchester, Fairey's established a development section, paint shops and hangars at Ringway airport in 1937.[47] In the lean years of the 1920s, aircraft firms were forced to diversify in order to generate enough revenue.[48] For example, A.V. Roe organised joy rides from local aerodromes and established regular air services from Manchester to Blackpool and Southport.[49] Until the early 1930s, the production of wooden and fabric-covered planes predominated, allowing firms to continue building aircraft along traditional workshop lines. The availability of large numbers of skilled workers led aircraft firms to reject large-scale mechanisation of production, as suggested by American aircraft builders during the War years.[50] By adhering to their flexible production methods, aircraft firms proved capable of weathering the downturn in demand

---

[41]   Edgerton, *England and the Aeroplane*, p. 75.
[42]   George, 'Aircraft Factories', p. 12.
[43]   Timmins, *Made in Lancashire*, pp. 301–2 and 307.
[44]   George, 'Aircraft Factories', p. 10.
[45]   King, *Knights of the Air*, p. 214.
[46]   King, *Knights of the Air*, p. 238; George, 'Aircraft Factories', p. 15.
[47]   George, 'Aircraft Factories', pp. 10 and 19; ibid., 'Fairey Aviation in the North-West', *Manchester Memoirs* 127 (1987–88), pp. 117–9.; Timmins, *Made in Lancashire*, p. 305.
[48]   On the British aircraft industry during the inter-war period, see Keith Hayward, *The British Aircraft Industry* (Manchester University Press, 1989), Chapter 1.
[49]   King, *Knights of the Air*, p. 270; Timmins, *Made in Lancashire*, p. 306.
[50]   Marshall, *Industry and Trade*, p. 228, fn. 1.

in the 1920s.[51] Until the start of rearmament, the employment in the aircraft sector remained largely concentrated in the Manchester metropolitan region. While expanding in terms of employment between 1923 and 1937, the increase was largely due to increased demand for military aircraft from the mid-1930s onwards. Therefore, the industry never assumed the role of a new leading sector in the inter-war period, particularly when compared with the growth of the electrical engineering, electric cable and appliances, and clothing industry in Manchester and Salford in the same period.[52]

Rearmament in the late 1930s heralded better times for local aircraft firms like A.V. Roe. Given the increased orders, A.V. Roe started to expand its facilities at Woodford under the shadow factory scheme in 1938. Other shadow factories built by the government in this period included two *Lancaster* assembly plants, one managed by A.V. Roe in Chadderton situated in a depressed area north of Manchester and the other the Manchester Bomber Factory in Trafford Park. Besides the *Lancaster* production line, the Ministry of Aircraft Production also constructed a factory for the production of *Merlin* aircraft engines in Trafford Park. These aircraft and engine assembly plants relied on smaller surrounding firms to supply them with components and parts. While the Manchester Bomber Factory alone employed 8411 workers at the height of the War, a total of over 26,000 workers were engaged in aircraft production in Trafford Park and the surrounding industrial estates. Most of the additional workers for the Wartime aircraft industry came from outside the immediate area served by the Stretford Employment Exchange. As a consequence, the percentage of total insured population working in Trafford Park and the surrounding estates increased from 6.8 per cent in 1939 to 12.8 per cent in 1944.[53] In the area around Oldham, the opening of the A.V. Roe aircraft factory had a similar effect, leading to the employment of over 18,000 men and women in the aircraft sector. As in Trafford Park, a number of engineering firms benefited from subcontracts to supply the aircraft factory by converting disused textile mills to produce components and aircraft parts. The increase in employment in the aircraft industry absorbed most of the workers released by the cotton spinning mills.[54] Indeed, the textile industry in Oldham developed problems recruiting workers at the height of the War. This development led to conflicts between the Cotton Controller and the Ministry of

---

[51] Peter Fearon, 'Aircraft Manufacturing', in Neil K. Buxton and Derek H. Aldcroft (eds), *British Industry Between the Wars: Instability and Industrial Development, 1919–1939*, (Scolar Press, 1979), pp. 22–9.

[52] Fogarty, *Prospects*, 231, Table 53. The available figures strongly suggest that the development of the Manchester-based aircraft industry conformed to the national trend in this period; see Fearon, 'Aircraft Manufacturing', pp. 216–7.

[53] George, 'Aircraft Factories', pp. 20–1; Lancashire Industrial Development Association, *The South East Lancashire Area and Parts of Cheshire and Derbyshire*, Industrial Report No. 4 (Lancashire Industrial Development Association, 1949), p. 34, Table 18.

[54] Lancashire Industrial Development Association, *The Spinning Area*, Industrial Report No. 5 (Lancashire Industrial Development Association, 1950), pp. 28–30.

Aircraft Production over the release of former textile workers from aircraft production.[55] However, this problem reflected the general trend that young entrants to the job market did not see a job in the cotton industry as desirable, because of the low earnings and poor conditions in the sector. At the same time, the Nuffield Social Reconstruction Survey voiced concerns as to whether the aircraft factories in Chadderton would continue to provide sufficient jobs in the area after the War.[56]

Rearmament also brought jobs to another nearby town in the Spinning Area of the Manchester industrial district. Even though Bolton had been less affected by unemployment than neighbouring Oldham, the opening of the De Havilland propeller works reduced the unemployment in the town. Similarly, the construction of a Royal Ordnance Factory (ROF) in Chorley and expansion of the Leyland motor works and English Electric Company, as part of the rearmament effort, generated new employment in the Preston and Chorley area on the north-western edge of the Manchester industrial district. In 1950, a report of the Lancashire Industrial Development Association noted that Wartime mobilisation deepened the changes in the industrial structure of this district. The resulting diversification of employment had reduced the chances of high structural unemployment reoccurring after the War.[57] As part of its post-war planning for the defence industry, the government intended to keep the aircraft factories in Chadderton and Bolton, as well as the ROF Chorley, open after the War. With the reduction of military expenditure after the end of the War, the key question was whether or not the diversification of the industrial structure in parts of the Manchester industrial district would prevent the re-emergence of the high structural unemployment of the inter-war period. While employment in the aircraft industry fell by 70 per cent to 3291 in the Bolton area and by 58 per cent to 7618 in the Oldham area in 1947, the stimulus of new employment created by wartime mobilisation led to the diversification of the local industrial structure away from cotton textiles.[58] While the resulting reduction in unemployment levels was in line with the national trend, the Board of Trade survey area of South Lancashire had the lowest unemployment rate of all development areas in the immediate post-war period.[59]

As far as individual firms were concerned, employment figures for the wartime and post-war period are only available for the two major airframe firms in the Manchester industrial districts, A.V. Roe and English Electric.[60]

---

[55] J. Hurstfield, *The Control of Raw Materials* (Her Majesty's Stationery Office, 1953), pp. 32–5.
[56] Fogarty, *Prospects*, pp. 221–4.
[57] Lancashire Industrial Development Association, *Spinning Area*, pp. 19–21.
[58] Lancashire Industrial Development Association, *Spinning Area*, pp. 19–30.
[59] Fogarty, 'Location', pp. 266–7 and 276, Table 7.
[60] Unfortunately, the paper did not assess the prospects of aircraft engine and component firms; see PRO T 225/369: minute Humphrey-Davies - France and Pitblado, 29

A.V. Roe had employed 23,600 workers in its own and associated shadow factories at the height of the War. This figure had dropped to 8000 in 1950. Employment in the aircraft division of English Electric fell from a wartime peak of 12,700 to 3000 workers on the eve of the Korean War. Both firms' superb wartime record meant that Ministry of Supply officials singled out both companies as essential to the future procurement of military aircraft. When government departments reconsidered the future size and shape of the British aircraft industry in April 1950, both firms were engaged in vital development projects. As part of this government review, a Ministry of Supply's paper assessed the importance of A.V. Roe in the following terms:

> Designers and producers of the best bomber of the last War, the Lancaster. Have large production resources and are able to draw on ample labour in South Lancashire. Their new bomber (B.35/46 [Vulcan]) is to meet a requirement designated as of 'Supreme' importance. The design side is being steadily strengthened.

However, the same document warned that 'the new jet bomber will not provide production work for some years'. At the time, the only production work undertaken by the firm was the construction of twenty-one *Shackleton* early-warning aircraft. However, the paper noted that English Electric had managed to become a fully-fledged aircraft firm from assembling Hampden and Halifax bombers during the War.

> The latest recruit to the aircraft industry. Exceptionally fine production record during the War. Have since acquired first-class research and development resources, including a design team, who already have the first British jet bomber, the Canberra, to their credit. Because of the wide range of their products, have a much larger peacetime production force than aircraft production would warrant, and this makes them particularly valuable as War potential.

While A.V. Roe were still busy developing a medium bomber for Britain's strategic bomber force, English Electric was about to start producing a highly successful light bomber. Therefore, the prospects of its aircraft division were markedly better than those of A.V. Roe for the immediate future.[61] To a large extent, English Electric owed its success to William Petter persuading the Air Ministry to order the *Canberra*, based on his original idea in early 1945. The *Canberra* was frequently cited as the outstanding example of a successful aircraft development, with the project having taken just six years from its

---

March 1950. As a consequence, there are no employment figures available for the De Havilland factory in Bolton.

    [61] PRO T 225/369: letter Musgrave - Humphrey-Davies with attached draft paper on 'Size and Shape of the Aircraft Industry: Need for planning to Preserve War Potential', 10 February 1950.

inception to the first aircraft entering service. Indeed, the American Department of Defence bought a large numbers of *Canberra* bombers for the Air Force built under license in the United States.[62]

The Ministry of Supply review highlighted the real problems faced by aircraft firms in the immediate post-war period. Without sufficient production orders for military aircraft, firms potentially struggled financially. At the same time, the government could no longer afford to maintain all the aircraft firms eligible to tender for development contracts. Moreover, the production of civilian aircraft did not offer a real alternative to obtaining a substantial military procurement contract.[63] This dilemma was noted by the Chairman of the Cotton Board, Sir Raymond Streat, after visiting the Chadderton factory just before the end of the War. Reflecting on the visit in his diary, he worried that the potential demand for passenger aircraft would not be sufficient to justify the massive development cost of building a new generation of jet aircraft as proposed by the Brabazon Committee. Moreover, he wondered how these costs would be shared between the government and the aircraft industry and what role university departments of aeronautical engineering would play in this effort.[64] His private observations were rather poignant, given the relative failure of the Brabazon programme. As Streat predicted, demand for civilian aircraft proved insufficient for the government to recover its financial contribution to the development of civilian aircraft between 1945 and 1959. In the local context, the massive government subsidies to the aircraft industry allowed the region's firms to absorb a disproportionate share of engineers, scientists, and skilled workers.[65] By the mid-1950s, it had become obvious that other NATO governments remained reluctant to buy British military aircraft over domestic or American planes. The limited market for aircraft increased the dependence of aircraft companies on government contracts and subsidies.[66]

At the same time, government policy on aircraft procurement arguably undermined regional economic development in Lancashire. As the present analysis shows, the expansion of aircraft production during the War led to the

---

[62] Ely Devons, 'The Aircraft Industry', in D. Burn (ed), *The Structure of British Industry: A Symposium* (Cambridge University Press, 1958), pp. 48, 56 and 82, footnote 1.

[63] Devons, 'Aircraft industry', pp. 45–7; Geiger, *Britain and the Economic Problem*, Chapter 5.

[64] Diary entry, 30 April 1945; reprinted in: Marguerite Dupree (ed) *Lancashire and Whitehall: The Diary of Sir E. Raymond Streat; Volume 2: 1939–57* (Manchester University Press, 1987), p. 7. On the Brabazon committee recommendations, see Devons, 'Aircraft industry', pp. 9–70.

[65] The British government spent £35 million on civilian aircraft projects between 1945 and 1959 recovering only £11.5 million from the aircraft sales. In addition, the government supported six aero-engine projects to the tune of £53 million of which it recouped £13 million. Only on the Viscount did the government get back its initially outlay; see Ministry of Aviation, *Report of the Committee of Inquiry into the Aircraft Industry*, Cmnd. 2853 (Her Majesty's Stationery Office, 1965), p. 125, Appendix G.

[66] Economist Intelligence Unit, *Britain and Europe: A Study of the Effects on British Manufacturing Industry of a Free Trade Area and the Common Market* (Economist Intelligence Unit, 1957), pp. 149–53.

formation of small clusters of sub-contractors around the large aircraft factories. To some extent, wartime production brought the aircraft industry into close contact with the region's electrical engineering and electronics industry. However, Metropolitan-Vickers took over the Manchester Bomber Factory at the end of the War, leading to the disappearance of the small cluster of aircraft component manufacturers in Trafford Park.[67] The government's decision to purchase aircraft components in bulk wiped out the other small component producers in the Oldham area.[68] Through this emphasis on central co-ordination of aircraft projects, the Ministry of Supply hoped to reduce the overall costs of projects by avoiding the duplication of development efforts for electronic components common to aircraft. This policy caused problems in integrating components developed without reference to a particular aircraft project. Moreover, the government reduced its total expenditure on the further development of defence electronics. For example, the further development of military communications equipment was cut by 30 per cent in 1948 and some of the scientists were transferred to other more important development programmes (e.g. atomic energy, and guided weapons).[69] Given the limited nature of government support, most electronics firms shunned government development contracts, preferring to produce radio and television sets to satisfy the growing consumer demand after 1945. However, Korean War rearmament led to a five-fold expansion of defence electronics, imposing a considerable strain on the industry. By 1955, government contracts accounted for 20 to 25 per cent of the industry's output. Despite its achievements in the development of radar, Britain started falling behind the United States in the development of the transistor and electronic components, which became increasingly important in the next generation of military aircraft and guided weapons. Arguably, the emphasis on developing airframe and aero-engine technology in the late 1940s led to the drop in government demand for advanced electronic components in the late 1940s, breaking up local networks of aircraft and electronics firms which had emerged during the Second World War. Whereas by the mid-1950s, aircraft firms started entering the electronics field in response to the declining government demand for military aircraft, by concentrating on the development of missiles and guided weapons.[70]

Advances in aircraft technology presented a massive challenge to the industry. The shift to all-metal aircraft in the 1930s forced the industry to adopt more mechanised production methods. The increased need for capital

---

[67] Lancashire Industrial Development Association, *South East Lancashire*, pp. 34–5.

[68] On the decision to centrally purchase aircraft components, see Devons, 'Aircraft Industry', pp. 64–5. On Oldham, see Lancashire Industrial Development Association, *Spinning area*, p. 30. The report is unclear on the impact on the Bolton and Preston area.

[69] PRO AIR 20/6937: letter Croyton – Robb, 19 March 1948. On the development of the British electronics industry in immediate post-war period, see Thomas Wilson, 'The Electronics Industry', in Burn (ed), *The Structure of British Industry*, p. 145.

[70] Wilson, 'Electronics industry', pp. 136–58.

equipment meant that the industry could no longer absorb the drop in government demand for military aircraft. Under the war potential policy, the government aimed to sustain the core capacity of the industry through development and repair contracts. Therefore, a firm's ability to compete for government contracts depended on maintaining a design and development team, as well as a limited production capacity.[71] For example, English Electric decided to add a development section to its Strand Road works in order to compete for rearmament aircraft production contracts in 1938. As the example of the *Canberra* shows, an innovative design team proved the key to English Electric's success as an airframe firm after the War.[72] While the government provided some financial assistance to the industry, it expected firms to shoulder some of the financial burden by covering any capital expenditure even at the development stage. This stipulation meant that firms remained reluctant to modernise their factories before receiving a substantial production order for an aircraft. Another aspect of government policy caused additional complications for aircraft firms. In their attempt to maintain as many aircraft firms as possible, the Ministry of Supply tended to divide production orders for an aircraft between several firms. For example, the Ministry of Supply placed production contracts for the *Canberra* with A.V. Roe, Shorts and Handley Page. Given the uncertainty surrounding government orders, most British aircraft firms diversified in the immediate post-war period in order to reduce the economic risks associated with aircraft production. As part of the Hawker-Siddeley group, A.V. Roe was well placed to sustain a number of development projects in the immediate post-war period. Within a larger aircraft concern consisting of several firms, other aircraft divisions generated the income which allowed the group to subsidise firms engaging primarily in development work, such as A.V. Roe did in the late 1940s. At the other extreme, English Electric regarded its aircraft division as one activity among many, including some involvement in consumer electronics and aero-engine production, besides its more traditional activities producing electric trams and generators. In contrast to other aircraft firms, the aircraft division of English Electric concentrated on a single aircraft project at a time. As part of its diversification strategy, English Electric became engaged in tank development after 1945, when Leyland rejected the government's advances to become one of the four core tank contractors in 1945. However, the lack of government orders forced English Electric in 1949 to transfer its work to Vickers.[73]

Both Lancashire airframe firms expanded their facilities during the Korean War rearmament in order to produce the *Canberra*. A.V. Roe invested £160,000 in machinery, while the Treasury financed the £720,000 expansion of

---

[71]   Geiger, 'Defence Production Policy', pp. 97–8.
[72]   George, 'Aircraft Factories', pp. 5–6; Devons, 'Aircraft Industry', pp. 56 and 82, footnote 1.
[73]   Devons, 'Aircraft Industry', pp. 47–58; Geiger, 'Defence Production Policy', pp. 98–100.

English Electric's facilities in Preston.[74] These additional investments secured the firms during the 1950s before they were absorbed into two newly-formed large aircraft companies: the aircraft division of English Electric becoming a part of the British Aircraft Corporation and A.V. Roe part of the enlarged Hawker Siddeley Aviation in 1960. Both firms seemed to thrive on the back of military aircraft orders for the English Electric *Lightning* P.1 fighter and Avro *Vulcan* bomber.[75] In June 1965, the former English Electric aircraft factories employed 7950 workers. At the same time, 16,541 employees worked for Hawker Siddeley Aviation, of which 9614 were engaged in aircraft production and 6927 in guided weapons and missile work.[76] Employment in the aerospace sector remained fairly static until the mid-1980s, when nearly 23,000 people still worked in the industry. While the industry employed 16 per cent of the region's workforce, the aerospace sector generated 36 per cent of its net output.[77]

As this analysis shows, the aircraft industry remained an important employer in the Manchester industrial district throughout the post-war period. Due to the changes in aircraft technology, production increasingly centred on large production facilities, thereby limiting the emergence of a new industrial district. However, the contraction in government defence procurement in the 1940s disrupted the local supply networks that had emerged during the War. To some extent, the aircraft industry provided employment in depressed textile districts. The resulting diversification of the industrial structure softened the impact of the declining textile industry in the Manchester industrial district, but failed to provide a locus for industrial rejuvenation.

Conclusions

This analysis underlines the rather ambiguous impact of defence expenditure on regional economic development. The Lancashire aircraft industry neither hastened nor reversed the economic decline of the Manchester industrial district. However, the large degree of central control exercised by the Ministry of Supply over the defence procurement process meant that aircraft firms primarily cultivated their relationship with the supply departments in London and to a lesser extent networked with other airframe firms. The predominance of a 'star model' network in the defence procurement process prevented the

---

[74] Devons, 'Aircraft Industry', pp. 47–65.; PRO T 225/655: Capital Scheme, Progress Report No. 5, 1951. On English Electric's involvement in tank production, see Cambridge University Library (hereafter: CUL) Vickers J99: letter Nelson – Micklem, 5 December 1949.; letter Micklem – Nelson, 7 December 1949.

[75] Lancashire and Merseyside Industrial Development Association, *Industrial Lancashire and Merseyside 1961* (Lancashire and Merseyside Industrial Development Association, 1961), pp. 19–22.

[76] Ministry of Aviation, *Report into the Aircraft Industry*, pp. 115–7, Table iv.

[77] Timmins, *Made in Lancashire*, p. 308.

continuation of the Wartime regional supplier networks in the immediate post-war period. This over-arching policy network arguably undermined the efforts of the local business community to develop links between industry and universities through the Manchester Joint Research Council.[78] Given this initiative, it is tempting to speculate whether or not an aircraft-electronics cluster, not unlike the one in Southern California, might have emerged in the Manchester industrial district if the British aircraft firms as main contractors had been free to obtain components from local firms. At the same time, this analysis has revealed the rather limited role that regional business networks such as the Scottish Council (Development and Industry) and the Lancashire Industrial Development Association were able to play in determining the direction and location of defence-related investment. On balance, this study suggests that while networking is of vital importance for the success or failure of a defence firm, such networking may not be effective or indeed desirable from the perspectives of both regional economic development and social welfare.

---

[78] On the Manchester Joint Research Council, see diary entry, 20 January 1945; reprinted in: Dupree (ed), *Lancashire and Whitehall*, Vol. 2, pp. 240–3.

Chapter 14

Conclusion

John F. Wilson and Andrew Popp

Introduction

In bringing together this collection of essays on English industrial districts we
are well aware that over a century ago Alfred Marshall was providing powerful
insights into very similar issues. In this respect we are merely standing on the
shoulders of giants. At the same time, by offering original empirical evidence
on a variety of different scenarios, from micro-studies, such as those of
Darlington, Gomersal, Worcester and the Birmingham jewellery quarter,
through to more expansive cases, including Lancashire and West Yorkshire, we
have extended our understanding of what was an essential feature of English
industrial evolution.

Certainly, these chapters have also provided fresh insights into the questions
posed in the introductory chapter, especially in relation to the emergence and
performance of the patchwork of individual industrial districts, clusters and
regional systems that characterized England from the mid-eighteenth century
through to the mid-twentieth century. Thus, it has also been possible to begin
to assess the extent to which the theoretical insights provided by social
scientists can be used to improve our historical understanding. This allows for
emergence of a firm link between the work of those historians and social
scientists who have written so extensively on these subjects over the last
twenty years. In this concluding note then, we shall be especially concerned
with two issues: the long-term picture revealed by the empirical chapters and
the historiographical challenges facing scholars in the future. While we will be
careful not to seek to impose a research agenda on future generations,
significant issues do arise from this collection which others may wish to
address.

Our introductory chapter finished by highlighting three inter-related sets of
questions derived from a review of relevant literature across a number of social
science disciplines. There we identified as key issues: the forces that either
drive or impede processes of change in districts and clusters; the impact of the
wider context or environment within which regional developments unfold and,
finally, the mechanisms through which the forces driving or impeding change
are mediated and accommodated. At the same time, these issues were set
within a focus on change, continuity and the potential for path dependencies,

inspired largely by life-cycle models of district or cluster dynamics. In consequence, drawing on Swann and Preverzer's assertion that 'a cluster has in effect a life cycle, conceptually distinct from but related to the life cycle of the technologies produced at the cluster', we wish to explore further the possibility of developing a coherent dynamic perspective on the cluster development in England from the mid-eighteenth century to the mid-twentieth century.[1] This emphasis on the dynamic properties of clusters, though necessarily couched here at a relatively high level of generalization, should provide a natural habitat for the historian. Indeed, the historian may be able to suggest significant refinements to the concepts offered by social scientists. These several themes will then provide our organizing framework here.

Districts and clusters

However, it is important to first briefly survey the key characteristics of the districts and regions studied here. The reader will be struck immediately by the highly heterogeneous nature of English clusters. They have varied in terms of the markets they served, from heavy producer goods, through consumer goods to financial services. They have therefore also varied enormously in terms of the technologies that they employed. They have also varied in terms of their degree of sectoral focus, from mono-industrial Worcester through to multifaceted Coventry, itself set in the heart of the variegated East-midlands region. They have also displayed different internal business structures; in terms of the number and sizes of firms and of their patterns of vertical and horizontal integration; from the hundreds of small, specialized shops that populated the Birmingham jewellery quarter to the less than thirty firms that constituted the Widnes chemical cluster in its heyday.

Most strikingly perhaps, they have suffered very different fates. The Lancashire cotton textile industry underwent a prolonged and painful decline across the great part of the twentieth-century and has now essentially gone. Widnes is still a chemical town, but, from the formation of Imperial Chemical Industries in 1926, has largely existed as part of a branch plant economy directed from London; the Birmingham jewellery quarter, on the other hand, remains surprisingly unchanged and vibrant; whilst the East-midlands continues to attract significant inward investment on the basis of strengths 'inherited from past conditions'.[2] What commonalities can be we identify then and how do they relate to the theoretical literature?

[1]   Swann and Prevezer, 'Introduction', in G.M. Peter Swann, M. Prevezer, and D. Stout (eds), *Dynamics of Industrial Clustering: International Comparisons in Computing and Biotechnology* (Oxford University Press, 1998), p. 2.
[2]   The phrase is Marshall's. Witness the renewed investment made by Toyota in their Derby plant in 2001, won by the city on the basis of strengths across the local labour force derived from a long history of involvement in a number of metal-forming industries, light engineering and machine tools.

Drivers

As the work of Swann and Prevezer argues, any cluster dynamic must be closely related to technological change. This observation is not original; indeed, Marshall gave considerable prominence to the role of technological change as a driver of institutional change at the level of both the firm and the district. However, our examples do provide us with fresh insights into the way in which technology impinged on cluster dynamics. In effect then a major force shaping all major English industrial clusters was the progressive elaboration of their technological bases and capabilities. However, this was a complex process in which causality could run in different directions. In part it was a function of simple technological imperatives, but it was also in part a function of the ability of clusters either to act as innovation systems or to absorb and profit from innovations made elsewhere. Thus, for example, the failure of Widnes' Leblanc manufacturers to achieve either of these goals, though not examined in detail in this volume, had a critical impact on the future growth and development of the district.

The key for districts seeking to disrupt or escape from seemingly ineluctable technological trajectories was the ability to foster diversity and to build on fresh opportunities suggested by complementarities in existing technologies, products and practices. In this respect the exemplar in English industrial history is perhaps the East-midlands, which, from the mid-nineteenth century onwards, progressively built on capabilities in the manufacture of textile machinery to move, in turn, into bicycles, motorcars and motorcycles and machine tools. Lloyd-Jones and Lewis contend that it was, above all else, regional business networks, founded on the growth of 'social habits' and expressed through personal capitalism, that allowed the region to follow this strategy of technological and product flexibility and profusion.[3] However, as Wilson and Singleton demonstrate, for some districts this was no easy task and the Manchester region, despite the example offered by the establishment of Trafford Park and its complement of American manufacturing firms, signally failed to exploit the technologies and products associated with the Second Industrial Revolution at the very moment that the product life-cycle in cotton textiles was reaching maturity.[4] However, as Geiger's work on the growth and development of the aerospace industry in the Manchester industrial district demonstrates, this was an area where policy intervention could be fraught with

---

[3]   R. Lloyd-Jones and M.J. Lewis, 'Business Networks, Social Habits and the Evolution of a Regional Industrial Cluster: Coventry, 1880s–1930s', Chapter 12 in this volume. See also, ibid., *Raleigh and the British Bicycle Industry: A Business and Economic History* (Ashgate, 2000).

[4]   J.F. Wilson and J. Singleton, 'The Manchester Industrial District, 1750–1939: Clustering, Networking and Performance', Chapter 3 in this volume.

difficulties or even harmful, possibly undermining the existing strengths of the district.[5]

Technology impacted on district development as both an exogenous and an endogenous force. The significance for the Leblanc soda manufacturers of Brunner, Mond's diffusion of the Solvay process is an excellent example of almost pure technological exogeneity, but is also probably exceptional in that the Leblanc manufacturers were effectively excluded from adopting the new process. Worcester glovers were perhaps more typical in their ability both to make innovations of their own and to absorb those made elsewhere.[6] The Worcester case is also instructive with regard to the linkages between technological change, its impact and structural factors. In particular, the relationship between the process of technological elaboration and its concomitant institutional context, defined here as business structure and associated governance structures, was far from straightforward. In Coventry, a proto-typical industrial district in structural terms, a disintegrated business structure, allied to a reliance on personal capitalism, proved a fertile environment for technological innovation, not least through the actions of what Lloyd-Jones and Lewis label 'seed-corn' firms.[7] In Worcester, however, whilst the nineteenth century may have seen the emergence of a new, larger type of firm associated with 'heightened technological innovation and changes in the labour process', these were also, as Coopey observes, contradictory and paradoxical in nature'.[8] Thus, it is not possible to accept uncritically Piore's contention that in relation to technology 'organization is a derivative concept'. Nor, though all the studies included here have highlighted the importance of networks, does it follow that the 'organizational form associated with flexible specialization is the *network*'.[9] Piore essentially contends that innovation breeds organization and does so with particular results in districts, but the histories detailed here suggest that patterns of innovation are also shaped by organizational structures and that any association between particular regimes of production and innovation (such as 'flexible specialization') and particular organizational 'architectures' (such as 'networks') is, at best, weak.

However, beyond its complex association with technological change, business structure is in itself an important driver of district development. Districts displayed then a clear, progressive structural dynamic that was nonetheless, as both Caunce and Cookson argue here, contingent and systemic

---

[5]   T. Geiger, 'A False Dawn?: Military procurement and Manchester Industrial District, 1935–1960', Chapter 13 in this volume.

[6]   R. Coopey, 'The British Glove Industry, 1750–1970: The Advantages and Vulnerability of Regional Industry', Chapter 9 in this volume.

[7]   Lloyd-Jones and Lewis, 'Business Networks, Social Habits'.

[8]   Coopey, 'The British Glove Industry'.

[9]   M. Piore, 'Fragments of a Cognitive Theory of Technological Change and Organization Structure', in N. Nohria and R.G. Eccles, *Networks and Organizations: Structure, Form and Action* (Harvard University Press, 1992), p. 431 (emphasis in the original).

rather than strategic.[10] Moreover, it is of course clustering and its associated structural dynamics that are the source of the externalized agglomeration economies, central to the competitive advantages of districts, such as those explored by both Wilson and Singleton and Toms and Filatotchev.[11] In this context, many of the studies in this collection, but especially those by Wilson and Singleton and Popp, not only attest to the significance of 'Marshallian' external economies but also provide important historical evidence for the utility of Swann's life cycle model beyond contemporary high-technology clusters.[12] However, it cannot be assumed that these structural dynamics, often taking the form of lower barriers to entry, are at all times positive, for lower barriers to entry have often been accompanied by raised barriers to exit. We see this clearly in cotton textiles in Lancashire, in chemicals and in other districts and clusters. This structural feature of clustering could, potentially, conflict with unfolding technological trajectories, whether generated internally or externally. Thus, we argue that whilst highlighting the links between clustering and barriers to entry Swann is wrong to neglect conditions affecting exit rates. Moreover, with regard to both entry and exit the life cycle model as it currently stands assumes a high degree of rationality on the part of both potential entrants and exits in response to relevant signals. This collection would strongly suggest that such rationality cannot be assumed. Instead, adjusting to or finding solutions for challenges to existing practices and structures was never simply a technical issues subject to the dictates of rationality, even where those challenges appeared to be 'purely' technological. At the same time, there were also always complex, often socially mediated, issues of governance to be resolved in such situations. However, we here begin to stray into the issue of accommodation mechanisms, to which we will return shortly.

However, if technology and structural dynamics have proved to have been important drivers of cluster development then we cannot ignore the importance of competition and markets. Again, this was a theme that assumed a central role in the pioneering work of Marshall and others on districts. At a basic level then, as Hobson argued, 'as human life continues, the art of living must continually change, and each change alters the value attached to the several forms of consumption, and so to the industrial processes engaged in the supply of different utilities'.[13] For the proponents of flexible specialization this

---

[10] S. Caunce, 'Banks, Community and Manufacturing in West Yorkshire Textiles, c. 1800–1830', Chapter 6 in this volume; G. Cookson, 'Quaker Networks and the Industrial Development of Darlington, 1780–1870', Chapter 8 in this volume. This dynamic is explored in detail in A. Popp, *Business Structure, Business Culture and the Industrial District: The Potteries, c. 1850–1914* (Ashgate, 2001).

[11] Wilson and Singleton, 'The Manchester Industrial District'; S. Toms and I. Filatotchev, 'Networks, Corporate Governance and the Decline of the Lancashire Textile Industry, 1860–1980', Chapter 4 in this volume.

[12] A. Popp, 'Networks and Industrial Restructuring: The Widnes District and the Formation of the United Alkali Company, 1890', Chapter 11 in this volume.

[13] J.A. Hobson, *The Evolution of Modern Capitalism: A Study of Machine Production* (Walter Scott, 1906), p. 159.

constant evolution in the art of living and consumption favours the capabilities of districts and clusters. However, this evolution in markets interacts with a constant expansion in the geographical scope of competition, itself driven by improvements in transport and communication technologies, to ensure that 'this world competition, however free it may become, can lead to no finality, no settled appointment of industrial activity to the several parts of the world'.[14] As Marshall himself observed 'the opening out of new sources of supply or new markets for sale may quickly overbear the strengths which old districts have inherited from past conditions'.[15] Thus the historically situated, path dependent nature of clusters could as easily plant the seeds of decay as it could the spark of vitality. All of the industries studied in this collection were driven to change by changing market conditions, though perhaps none experienced so brutal a threat as Worcester, trapped between new, lost-cost competitors and radical and exogenous, fashion driven changes in demand.[16] To a large degree, of course, markets are not only drivers of change but also important elements in the context within which districts and clusters develop. It is to this second theme that we now turn.

Contexts and environments

First, the wide span of time covered by this collection allows us to observe that, due to the influence of a range of environmental factors, the date of cluster formation is important. These environmental factors include physical and socio-economic infrastructure, from transport and communication technologies to education systems, through the evolution of political and legislative frameworks, most obviously important in relation to the evolution of company law, to the development, already noted, of international markets of supply and demand. Indeed, it is probable that we can speak of a shortening or speeding up of cluster life cycles over time. Thus, in Lancashire, West Yorkshire and Worcester the take-off, critical mass and maturity phases were extremely prolonged and the decline phase relatively so. Moreover, many firms formed early in the evolution of these clusters have demonstrated remarkable longevity, examples abounded in Lancashire and Coventry and, to an even greater extent, the Sheffield and the North Staffordshire Potteries (the latter district not studied here).[17] In contrast, in Widnes, from take-off to maturity took less than quarter of a century and from take-off to cessation of existence as a distinct, relatively autonomous district less than fifty years.

[14] Ibid., p. 159.
[15] Marshall, *Industry and Trade*, p. 287.
[16] Coopey, 'The British Glove Industry'.
[17] Popp, *Business Structure, Business Culture and the Industrial District*; G. Tweedale, *Steel City: Entrpreneurship, Strategy and Technology in Sheffield, 1745–1993* (Clarendon Press, 1995).

Reference to specific studies allows us to flesh out this broad picture of the relationship between the development of clusters and their environment. Both Caunce and Cookson, studying fairly early examples of cluster formation, argue for the appropriateness of network organizational forms in the context of relative regional under-development and poorly articulated legislative frameworks. Thus, another feature highlighted by the historical record is the essentially contingent nature of cluster formation, the degree of uncertainty attached to risk and opportunity alike during the early phases and the importance then of supportive social structures to the creating of effective business structures. At these stages, at least, regional business networks, often-based on pre-existing links, such as those derived from family, religion or community, could form viable governance structures. Interestingly, Newton finds that networks were also important to the adaptation of Sheffield, a relatively mature industrial district, to the changed environmental conditions and heightened risk and uncertainty associated with the reform of company law from the mid-nineteenth century.[18] We have already noted the influence of secular market change but both Bowden and Higgins and Coopey also highlight the importance of business cycles as well. Most suggestive is Bowden and Higgin's speculation that supposedly central features of districts and networks, and trust in particular, are actually highly dependent on the environment rather than being inherent and immutable attributes.[19] Bowden and Higgins raise a further interesting question. Why was the woollen textile industry of West Yorkshire able to mount an effective response to changing environmental conditions when, as Wilson and Singleton also demonstrate, Lancashire and the Manchester industrial district proved themselves singularly unable to? This question directs our attention to that of how pressure for change was accommodated in English industrial districts.

Accommodating change

All of the studies in this collection attest to the importance of networks to the growth and development of clusters and districts. Networks are key institutions of governance. However, we wish to address in more detail three particular aspects of regional business networks; their attributes, their efficacy and their spatiality. In doing so we can make several important connections to insights from other social sciences, including the work of economist Mark Casson.[20]

---

[18] L. Newton, 'Capital Networks in the Sheffield Region, 1850–1885', Chapter 7 in this volume.

[19] S. Bowden and D.M. Higgins, 'Much Ado About Nothing?: Regional Business Networks and the Performance of the Cotton and Woollen Textile Industries, c.1919–1939', Chapter 5 in this volume. See also A. Popp, 'Trust in and Industrial District: The Potteries, c. 1850–1900', *Journal of Industrial History*, Vol. 3 No. 1 (2000).

[20] M. Casson, 'An Economic Approach to Regional Business Networks', Chapter 2 in this volume.

First, though a number of the studies presented here, from those of Caunce and Cookson to Lloyd-Jones and Lewis, highlight a role for community in buttressing networking, there is a striking absence of evidence for what Mark Granovetter has labelled the 'strong embeddedness perspective' on regional business networks. Indeed, Popp suggests that embeddedness is a largely meaningless concept in the context of Widnes while Carnevali argues persuasively that embeddedness was signally incapable of combating malfeasance and opportunism. As a result the Birmingham jewellery quarter was plagued by 'endemic dishonesty'. Trust had to be consciously engineered to overcome systemic and structural characteristics of the trade that were intimately associated with the fact of clustering.[21]

It is significant that trust in Birmingham owed much to a few key figures for just as all of these studies are, at best, ambiguous about embeddedness all find a central role for leadership in regional business networks, echoing the model developed by Casson in Chapter 2. In Worcester, Birmingham, Coventry, Widnes and Sheffield network formation and functioning was driven on by small cohorts of key actors. Networking is, as Casson claims, a highly entrepreneurial function. It is not network structure *per se* which is the key determinant of regional performance but instead the quality of the entrepreneurship for which networking serves as a vehicle. This leads us to the issue of the efficacy of regional business networks.

The evidence of these studies may then appear uncertain in relation to the efficacy of networks. Only Newton unambiguously claims the networks studied to have been successful. Lloyd-Jones and Lewis do note the effectiveness of networks at the local level in Coventry, but contrast this with their relative ineffectiveness at the national level, an experience repeated in Worcester and an issue to which we will return. Networks in Widnes may also be said to have been successful, but only in the limited sense of managing decline relatively smoothly. Others, in particular Wilson and Singleton, Toms and Filatotchev and Bowden and Higgins are far stronger in their condemnation of the potentially sclerotic impact of networks. Elsewhere, Cookson notes that once effective networks in Darlington contained the seeds of their own decay and showed a tendency to become slowly more exclusive and autonomous. Thus, this ambiguity may be clarified by situating the evidence on networking in the context of the life cycle model, for there is a strong suggestion that the efficacy of networks alters and declines across the cluster life cycle. As already suggested with reference to the Darlington case, one aspect of the decline of networks across time may be related to their tendency to become increasingly opaque, an element of 'bad' networking highlighted by Casson. Toms and Filatotchev provide particularly compelling evidence in this direction, arguing that in Lancashire the growing self-

---

[21] F. Carnevali, '"Malefactors and Honourable Men": The Making of Commercial Honesty in Nineteenth Century Industrial Birmingham', Chapter 10 in this volume.

sufficiency and secrecy of networks undermined accountability and blocked desperately necessary restructuring.

Widening these arguments, we would also wish to situate this discussion of the efficacy of networks in relation to the question of district level governance. In particular, though responses may have been very different, we can identify in all the cases studied clear changes in the challenges of governance across the cluster life cycle. Indeed, contra to the model of the 'ideal-typical industrial district', we find that the greatest governance challenges have not been those of achieving a (static) balance between co-operation and competition, but those of handling transformative moments, however induced.

In Lancashire history had by the early twentieth century generated powerful collusive forces within both capital and labour which ensured that governance structures remained regionally controlled but which also acted to forestall adjustment, organizational and technological. In this situation the inherited strengths of the industry could only ensure survival for so long. In Birmingham, Widnes and Worcester at different points in the nineteenth century firms faced increasing cost-based competition. At the same time in Birmingham, as in the Potteries,[22] internal tensions were rising as the practices of some were deemed to threaten the stability and reputation of the trade as a whole. Outcomes were different in each case. In Widnes, manufacturers managed to move very rapidly under the direction of leading local industrialists to a thorough and lasting restructuring through merger. In Birmingham, in contrast to Stoke, entrepreneurially led institution building proved successful, ameliorating tensions within a regionally centred governance structure that obviated the need for radical industrial restructuring.[23] In Lancashire, on the other hand, the principal 'change agents' clearly refused to tackle external challenges head-on, resulting in inexorable decline.[24]

Structural factors may be central to explaining these different outcomes. In Widnes firms could vary in size but not to the degree found elsewhere, including Worcester. Moreover, they were relatively few in number. In Birmingham firms were very numerous but size disparities relatively small. In this context, jewellers found it relatively easy to forge common goals and the institutions to put them into effect. Clearly though more needs to be done in terms of exploring the nexus between network efficacy, business structure, cluster life cycles and governance challenges.

However, the differing degrees to which clusters were able to meet governance challenges also held important implications for their interactions with and linkages to wider systems, or for what we may terms the spatiality of clusters and networks. First, and perhaps most importantly, these studies confirm the importance of extra-local, especially metropolitan, linkages posited by Casson in Chapter 2. This was clearly true in Darlington, in Sheffield, in

---

[22] Popp, 'Trust in an Industrial District'.

[23] Carnevali, '"Malefactors and Honourable Men"'.

[24] Wilson and Singleton, 'The Manchester Industrial District'.

Coventry and in Worcester. However, more generally, we also find that there was a broad change in the spatiality of all districts over time, not least because the historical evolution of English districts has been set in the context of the concurrent evolution of national and international markets and economies. At the same time the spatiality of each individual cluster also seems to have changed over time. In the earliest stages of cluster formation then, particularly those emerging furthest back in time, network linkages were densest and strongest at a highly localized level, this is a central message of both Cookson and Caunce's studies. We should be wary of overstating this argument, for all clustering necessarily implies an increasingly specialized division of labour that is spatial as much as it is socio-economic. Intuitively, the tendency is for deepening specialization at the regional level to be accompanied by a progressive extension of the geographical scope of numerous linkages between the cluster and other spheres and systems. Nonetheless, this process may well be attended by powerful centripetal forces, specifically with regard to issues such as the generation of competitive advantage, the evolution of industry structure and cluster level governance. The histories of all English clusters, particularly in their take-off, critical mass and maturity phases, attest to this powerful truth.

However, during those periods when governance challenges were most intense and networks severely tested, often a natural corollary of maturity and decline phases in the life cycle, these spatial forces could easily be thrown into reverse, becoming centrifugal and potentially hastening the waning attractiveness and competitiveness of a cluster. In Lancashire, powerful corporate interlocks seemed able to sustain local control and to exclude the City, but ultimately it was the refusal or failure to countenance adjustment that ushered in intervention by the Bank of England and the formation of the Lancashire Cotton Corporation. Paradoxically, in Widnes the formation of the UAC was in large measure a locally determined outcome but was in itself an important step towards the formation of ICI and the transfer of power to metropolitan headquarters. Only in Birmingham did adjustment successfully strengthen local distinctiveness and advantages, staving off the loss of control to higher level forces.

In summary, the nature of governance in clusters and the efficacy of networks remains a considerable challenge, theoretically and empirically. We would claim that the studies presented here are suggestive of the utility of the perspective outline in Chapter 1; namely that networks are best viewed not as distinct alternatives to either markets or hierarchies but instead as interpenetrating both. Markets, hierarchies and networks do seem to exist along a continuum of governance forms, which firms and clusters employ in a constantly altering blend. We would also again stress the role of networks as both providing structure, that is as institutional arrangements that both constrain and facilitate actors, and as structured by purposive actors seeking to construct or alter the network positions they occupy. In other words, networks can function as important vehicles for agency. This perspective clearly accords with Casson's emphasis on the relationship between networks and entrepreneurship.[25] Above all governance and networking are intensely iterative processes, a perspective to which the historian can bring vital skills.

Historiographical challenges

The study of industrial clusters and districts as historical phenomenon presents the historian with a series of challenges. First, it is obvious that many of the most important advances in cluster studies have been made in other social sciences, not only in economics but also, in particular, in the economic branches of sociology and geography. The historian must then judge how to accommodate the model-building urges of these other social sciences with the empirical methodologies that historians have traditionally drawn upon. The aim of a dialogue with other disciplines is conceptual enrichment, but this must not be at the expense of the historical record. An example may be helpful. In so far as we accept the conceptualization of clusters as complex sets of overlapping systems then one of our most important challenges as historians is to find a persuasive balance between the explanatory claims of factors such as structure and agency. Firm entry is a useful issue here. Patterns of firm entry into a clustered industry are not only themselves shaped by clustering, through effects on barriers to entry for example, but also themselves have important systemic effects. They may, for example, impinge on governance issues by impacting on district-wide levels of trust, as they did in Birmingham. But each separate case of firm entry is the result of an individual act of purposeful agency. Thus it is important to recognise that in this example our explanatory factors exist at two distinct levels that are not easy to reconcile.

Second, what implications do these studies have for the dominant theme in the historiography of English industry and business since the late nineteenth century; decline? In particular, how do they relate to the theses of Chandler and Elbaum and Lazonick?[26] The position with respect to Chandler is complex, not least because he failed to accommodate the extensive nature of English industrial clustering into his analysis. As Chandler argued that the evolution of industrial capitalism was principally dependent on securing *internal* economies of scale, any notion that performance was determined by the availability and exploitation of *agglomeration externalities* was largely ignored. At the same time, one might ask whether the networks associated with clusters were effective hierarchy-substituting organizational arrangements or barriers to the implementation of Chandler's three-pronged investment in technology, management and marketing? The answer may depend on the industry

---

[25] Casson, 'An Economic Approach'.
[26] A.D. Chandler, *Scale and Scope: The Dynamics of Industrial Capitalism* (Harvard University Press, 1990); B. Elbaum and W. Lazonick (eds), *The Decline of the British Economy* (Oxford University Press, 1987).

examined and perhaps also on the stage of the cluster life cycle, with networks most effective at the earlier stages of development and further back in history. Also germane here is the resurgence of interest in other networked organizational forms, not only in relation to small business but also in big business, including multinational enterprise.

With regard to Elbaum and Lazonick's thesis of institutional rigidity it is sufficient to raise two issues. First, did clustering in English industrial history induce a locational inertia that compounded any institutional rigidity. Second, while networks are commonly portrayed as highly flexible arrangements, might they also have functioned at times and under certain conditions as highly defensive and *exclusionary* mechanisms that acted to block restructuring. Toms and Filatotchev argue that this was the case in Lancashire cotton textiles, but the evidence from Widnes, particularly with regard to the formation of the UAC, is much less clear cut. In this context, it is also interesting to note that Wilson and Singleton provide clear evidence of networking shading into defensive collusion in the Manchester industrial district, thereby undermining the region's chances of withstanding the competitive onslaught from more efficient producers. This indicates how clusters must continually adapt to exogenous pressures; 'sticking to the knitting' cannot provide the basis for long-term survival.

The highly variegated nature of English industrial districts' experiences consequently provides an empirical challenge to those social scientists who have attempted to create universal generalisations aimed at explaining and contextualising the creation, impact and long-term performance of industrial clusters. While our case-studies provide the basis for a series of generalisations on such issues as life-cycles, network operation and leadership, it is clear that combining theoretical and empirical approaches remains problematical. But this should never deter others from trying to create greater synergy, especially if this means delving further into the histories of case-studies that this collection has been unable to include.

Author index

General index